DATE DUE			

Pricing in the Electrical Oligopoly, Vol. II

Pricing in the Electrical Oligopoly, Vol. II

Business Strategy

Ralph G. M. Sultan
Formerly Associate Professor of Business Administration
Harvard University

Division of Research
Graduate School of Business Administration
Harvard University
Boston · 1975

Distributed by
Harvard University Press
Cambridge, Massachusetts
and
London, England

338.43621

Su5p

100048

Feb. 1977

Library of Congress Catalog Card No. 73-93777
ISBN 0-87584-110-4

Printed in the United States of America

Foreword

At the annual meetings of the American Economic Association, at least one spot on the program (occasionally several) is customarily reserved for scholarly papers purporting to update the theory of oligopoly—that very special, popular, and somewhat mystifying branch of microeconomics concerned with equilibrium solutions in industries limited to a few competing companies. Deferential to tradition, the program for the most recent of such annual gatherings, convened in San Francisco in December 1974, included a session on "The Behavior of Firms in Oligopolistic Markets: In Theory and Practice." If such sessions are to be assessed in terms of the quantum of new knowledge contributed on the subject under review, this endeavor, by virtually unanimous agreement among the participants and attendants alike, was not notably successful. Nevertheless, it served the very useful purpose of confirming the increasingly widely held view that contemporary microeconomic theory falls considerably short of providing a satisfactory explanatory hypothesis for the behavior of oligopolistic firms, and that empirical studies have barely begun to remedy this deficiency.

This gap in our knowledge, concerning the operative mechanics by which industries comprised of a few large companies are governed, is all the more grievous because (1) a large portion of the gross national product of most nonsocialistic industrialized economies is accounted for by industries more or less oligopolistic in character, and (2) public policy as embodied in our antitrust laws, lacking a more firmly established basis, often proceeds on the rule that since oligopoly is *different* from atomistic competition it is inherently *anti*competitive.

Mr. Sultan succinctly captures this state of affairs with his opening observation: "Through an unfortunate accident of semantics, economic theory denies that an industry structure which is highly concentrated or 'oligopolistic' can also be 'competitive.'" He then offers a carefully documented analysis of how competition works in the turbine generator industry—an oligopoly consisting of only three competitors—as a refutation of this proposition.

Sultan contends that the shortcomings of oligopoly theory—and indeed of most empirical studies of oligopolistic industries—are largely attributable to their complete neglect of the variety of strategies a company may employ and the decision-making processes by which they are implemented. Turbine generator manufacturing has been characterized by rapid and persistent technological change, and costs are very much reflective of the "experience" curve —unit costs decline with cumulative output. The critical strategies available to each of the triopolists in this setting involve the interactions among rivals in respect to product technology, manufacturing capacity, and market share/ relative price.

Since price is the critical variable in conventional oligopoly models, Sultan focuses heavily on how prices may logically be determined in a market environment where companies must constantly assess these strategic interactions. General Electric is the largest of the three companies, with the largest market share, has generally set the pace in product technology, and has the lowest production cost by virtue of having progressed further along the experience curve. Hence, Sultan hypothesizes, General Electric should have a wider range of discretion than its smaller rival, Westinghouse, and its much smaller rival, Allis-Chalmers. In short, one would expect General Electric to be the price leader. What then should be its guiding price rule?

A price must obviously relate to a product. In the turbine generator industry the product is unusually complex—it is not a shelf item nestling among a host of competing products to be selected on the basis of appeal to taste. Utilities, the purchasers of the product, weigh carefully the technologically advanced product's cost effects on electrical power generation—its technical specifications that can be translated into capital and operation costs per kilowatt-hour. The seller, therefore, confronts essentially three possible pricing strategies:

(1) recoup all the value added through technological change, thereby keeping the utilities' real costs constant;

(2) pass along all technological gains to the utilities; or

(3) share the technological change with the utilities—employ a "fair" or conscionable price policy that induces the buyer to invest in the more advanced turbine generators (electrical power generation is a growth industry) thus enhancing the earnings of the technological leaders.

These options establish the "discretionary zone" of pricing: "direct costs" as a lower bound and "full value" as an upper bound. Where the price will actually be set depends on competitive zeal, and this in turn will logically be conditioned by the relationships among such factors as (1) the rate of incoming orders; (2) the utilization of plant capacity; (3) order backlogs; and (4) such "special events" as collusion among competitors, government price controls, and the threat of entry.

By use of regression analysis, Sultan then subjected his model to empirical tests. The requisite data abounded. The court records generated in the highly publicized electrical equipment cases of the 1960s and the many damage suits that followed therefrom produced extraordinarily rich data, in both quantity and detail. Sultan developed his remaining factual requirements through extensive field research covering the three turbine manufacturers.

The resulting statistical analyses confirmed the operability of his model. Quarterly price movements over the period 1948–1963 fluctuated within the indicated bounds. Price increases stayed below the maximum value limit and far below their monopoly limit while, during the 1955 White Sale and 1959–1961, Westinghouse and Allis-Chalmers were forced to sell at prices approaching their direct costs, and General Electric's earnings margin was substantially diminished. Between these limits, prices fluctuated systematically with (1) the de facto upper bound established by inflation in factor prices, (2) the average industry percentage utilization of capacity, and (3) the minimum backlog, measured in years of production capacity across all three competitors. Significantly, prices were not statistically related to the rate of incoming orders, foreign competition, OPS price controls, or conspiracy.

This study is unquestionably a significant piece of research holding important implications for public policy, economic theorists, and business managers. In the 1960s the electrical equipment manufacturers were found guilty of price-fixing conspiracies in violation of the Sherman Act, resulting in jail sentences and heavy fines for the management involved. In the years that followed, the defendant companies paid a total of upwards of $1 billion in settlements and litigated damage suits. One can only speculate on how these events may have been affected had Sultan's analysis been available when the initial antitrust case was litigated.

Further, Sultan has contributed greatly to our understanding of how oligopolists in high-technology industries function and, as a not insignificant by-product, called into serious question the indiscriminate application of conventional conjectural interdependence models to such industries. When decreases in order backlogs for any one of the competitors harbinger a pending loss of market share, independent price actions follow. Further, competition through technological progress in turbine manufacturing has resulted in spectacular gains to society by increased efficiency in electrical power generation. This, as those familiar with the writings of Joseph A. Schumpeter will readily recognize, is the kind of competition that he contended had the highest payoff to society. (See especially his *Capitalism, Socialism and Democracy.*[1]) Not surprisingly, Sultan offers his results as an unabashed confirmation of the Schumpeterian hypothesis.

Finally, Sultan's assessment, through computer simulations of the many alternative strategies turbine generator manufacturers might have pursued, is of special interest to business managers as well as economic theorists. Sultan appropriately points out that such results should be viewed with healthy skepticism, but they tend to confirm his essential hypothesis that the strategy

---

[1] New York: Harper & Bros., 2d Ed., 1947, pp. 88–106.

actually employed by the industry leader not only had the highest payoff to society but also to the industry leader.

In an earlier companion volume *Pricing in the Electrical Oligopoly, Vol. I: Competition or Collusion* (Harvard Business School, Division of Research, 1974), Sultan had relied on the emerging analytical results contained in the present volume in interpreting the industry's price behavior and its import for public policy. The detailed analysis presented here makes available for the first time the full documentation of his earlier conclusions. He is to be commended for having produced an eminently useful, thorough, and interesting two-volume work on one of the economy's more vital oligopolistic industries and one that has heen given so much attention, often unflattering, in the public media for over fifteen years.

While on the Faculty of the Harvard Business School, Sultan included himself among those of us who have urged that economic models of oligopoly can be made more pertinent to the real world of business by upgrading them to incorporate the relevant strategies that establish the boundaries of the decision-making processes in which company managers are engaged. His study of the turbine generator industry is persuasive testimony to the merits of this approach.

The bulk of the research was funded by gifts to the Harvard Business School from The Associates of the School under the auspices of the Division of Research. The project was administered at various stages by Professors Bertrand Fox, Lawrence E. Fouraker, and Richard E. Walton, Directors, and James P. Baughman, Associate Director. Special time-sharing computer analysis and simulation work on the computer was conducted through the generosity of the IBM Corporation, Project CP-67, and also through the support and assistance of Dr. Charles Warden of Data Resources, Inc., Lexington, Massachusetts. On behalf of the School and the author, I should like to thank these contributors for their valued support of this project.

JESSE W. MARKHAM
Charles E. Wilson Professor
of Business Administration

Soldiers Field
Boston, Massachusetts
February 1975

Preface

IT IS REASONABLE TO ANTICIPATE that sometime during the remainder of the 1970s, the American public will wonder what happened to its electricity supply. The industry's amazing record of success in supplying cheap and abundant electrical energy is now jeopardized. This study may offer some insights as to why we have arrived at this unhappy threshold.

This book addresses one important segment of our energy supply industry: the turbine generator oligopoly and its utility customers. My first book on this industry pays particular attention to the "antitrust period" of the early 1960s, a period which racked the manufacturers, diverted the energies of utility executives, and titillated the public, as a consequence of blatantly criminal violations of the Sherman Act. I concluded that, as outrageous as the conspiracy may have been, it was ineffectual. This second book supports that first study by presenting a more detailed analysis of the oligopolistic rivalry which motivated the three American turbine generator manufacturers both during and after that famous conspiracy. Both volumes of the study deal with the determination of prices in a high-technology, high-growth oligopoly. These prices originated from the fairly predictable interplay of rival electrical manufacturers, their electrical utility customers, and utility load growth, utility load forecasting and ordering behavior, manufacturers' backlogs and delivery delays, and manufacturers' strategies as epitomized by their relative pricing, costs, manufacturing capacities, and—in particular—discretionary management judgments and goals.

This present Volume II eschews the conspiracy theory of pricing in the oligopoly. It concentrates instead on the building of a formal economic model which attempts to capture the competitive interplay which actually exists. This model emphasizes such key factors as product technology, pricing, and market share. The model was then used to simulate the results of alternative strategy decisions made by management.

The history of my involvement in these issues is documented in the preface to Volume I and need not be repeated here. However, it may be helpful to note that this research builds upon personal experience as a professional engineer, as a price negotiator and industrial salesman in oligopoly, as a student and teacher of industrial marketing at the Harvard Business School, as a seminar leader and consultant to electrical equipment manufacturers, and as an economist.

Oligopoly is a subject long on economic theory and short on solid empirical analysis. This unfortunate state of affairs works to the disadvantage of oligopoly, which is all the more unfortunate since oligopoly is our most common form of business enterprise. Many economists truly abhor this situation. They regard the oligopolists' power of discretion in such areas as price, market share, product quality, technology, and manufacturing capacity, with deep suspicion. My own biases are in the opposite direction. I view their skepticism with skepticism. In my view, oligopoly is an inevitable industry form. Economists, therefore, have an obligation to understand it better, from the inside, before recommending fundamental structural reform.

The Methodology of this Study

This study commenced in 1968 and originally evolved in the case study tradition of the Harvard Business School. There was a heavy schedule of interviews with the managers involved in the various utilities and manufacturing organizations. In addition, voluminous litigation testimony from both utility and manufacturer managers was analyzed. This initial work demonstrated that the industry could best be analyzed as a closely interlocked "system"; one could not study any single element of pricing or of technology or of demand in isolation. I have therefore attempted to take into account, via a model, the principal industry interactions which have an impact upon price, technology, and other variables. Field interviews demonstrated the particular importance of discretionary management strategy which, it seemed to me, had been inadequately developed in much of contemporary microeconomics.

Research then proceeded along three parallel paths. First, there was the synthesizing of rules of managerial and market behavior as extracted from the interview process and recorded deposition testimony. Second, there was statistical model building. The approach here was to employ how the managers *said* they operated the industry as the material for behavioral hypotheses which were then verified or rejected using techniques of statistical analysis.

The third path of analysis involved a review of prior economic investigations of this industry. Of major importance in this analysis were those studies, frequently prepared by economic consultants, which were developed during the electrical litigation of the 1960s. The lawsuit of Ohio Valley Electric v. General Electric provided a major storehouse of analytical studies which aided this present study immeasurably.

The statistical model in the present volume defines the major interdependencies in the electrical supply oligopoly with particular emphasis upon decision-making behavior in the 1950–1964 period in the United States. The statistical analysis is eclectic. Quantitative results which "made sense" when referenced against other management testimony, were accepted, even if the statistical properties of a particular equation were less than elegant. Similarly, I did not hesitate to fit alternative models to the data and to choose the one which looked the most promising, according to my own a priori judgment. Modeling techniques more commonly applied to the economy as a whole, or to total industries, are here applied to interacting firms in the oligopoly. To my knowledge, this is the first attempt to build an empirically based model of cost and strategies of three interacting competitors in oligopoly.

What evolved is a simultaneous economic system. One pervasive question during the litigation of the 1960s was: "What does determine prices in the oligopoly?" One can rephrase this question as: "Are any particular relationships superfluous in the total system?" The answer is "no." All elements of both strategy and behavior, when entwined in a mutually determined system, have a role to play. Therefore, ripples in electric power demand determine prices—and everything else—just as surely as do manufacturing costs or discretionary management behavior or anything else in the system. It is the system as a whole which matters.

The reader should note that this research was substantially completed in the autumn of 1973, based upon data from the decades of the 1950s and 1960s. But little in the more recent industry history suggests that the behavior of the principal actors has changed in more recent years.

It may also be noted that the findings of this research have been "market tested" upon the audience perhaps most capable of criticizing the results: the executives of the industry itself. This was accomplished via private seminars and I am indebted to those anonymous managers for substantially improving the final research product.

Acknowledgments

This research exploits the rich vein of data embodied in three electrical lawsuits: Ohio Valley Electric v. General Electric (S.D.N.Y. 1965) and City of San Antonio v. Westinghouse (W.D. Texas 1964), the major turbine generator actions; and Philadelphia Electric v. Westinghouse (E.D. Pa. 1964), the major power transformer case in the electrical equipment antitrust actions. I am indebted to the officers of the U.S. Courts in New York and in Philadelphia, for permission to have access to the court files in these actions.

The funds for this research were administered by the Division of Research, Harvard Business School. In this present Volume II, the advice and suggestions of several colleagues at Harvard University, namely, Professors Jesse W. Markham, John Lintner, E. Raymond Corey, and Richard Caves, were particularly helpful. Professor Tom Wilson of the University of Toronto, Professor Paul Sultan of Southern Illinois University, and Frederic Scherer of the Federal Trade Commission, were also helpful.

Other persons heavily involved in the model building of Volume II were

Larry Samet of the University of Michigan and Ms. Wing Hing Tsang of The Royal Bank of Canada. My secretary, Joy Corti, was indispensable. Shirley Nestor and Joan Toohey typed the several versions of this manuscript with unflagging care and patience. Mr. William Minty and Mrs. Elsa Susta prepared the drawings. Finally, Ms. Hilma Holton, Associate Editor of the Harvard Business School, Division of Research, managed the final production with good judgment and humor. To these persons, thank you.

RALPH G. M. SULTAN

Montreal, Canada
April 1975

Table of Contents

Foreword v
Preface ix

Chapter One   Overview   1

Chapter Two   A Theory of the Oligopolistic Firm 7

The Setting for the Model 8
The Long-Run Model 19
Duopoly Assumed 20
The Short-Run Model: Conjectural Interdependence . . 36

Chapter Three   Demand   40

Orders: The Statistical Record 40
Factors Which Influence Turbine Generator Demand:
The Manufacturer View 42
Factors Which Influence Turbine Generator Demand:
The Utility View 47
Planning Models Employed by the Industry 54
Summary 66

Chapter Four   The Forecasting of Peak Loads 68

The Uncertainty of Growth in the Long Run 68
How Utilities Forecast Short-Term Peak Loads 72
Forecasting Methodology: Some Case Histories 74
How Utilities Forecast Peak Loads: Statistical Evidence 78
How Utilities Update Their Load Forecasts: Statistical
Results 79

Chapter Five   Manufacturers' Backlogs and Throughput 81

Manufacturing Delay 81
Installation Delay 90
Summary 92

Chapter Six   Utility Generating Capacity and Reserves 94

The Targeting of Utility Generating Reserves 94
Changes in Generating Capability 101
Summary 103

Chapter Seven   Order prices 105

The "Value" Philosophy of Pricing 105
The Data 107
Results: A Model of Turbine Generator Prices 109
The Sensitivity of Pricing Response 113
Strategic Implications 113

Chapter Eight   Escalation 117

Types of Escalation 117
History of Escalation 118
Limits on Escalation 119
Impact of Escalation on Prices 123
Variations in Escalation Practice Among Manufacturers 124

Chapter Nine   Long-Term Trends in Value 130

The Trend in Prices of Other Electrical Equipment ... 131
Empirical Results: Long-Term Trends in "Value" 131
Comparing the Rates of Progress: Three Products 134
Adjusting Long-Term Values for Product Mix 135

Chapter Ten   Direct and Overhead Costs 139

Direct Costs 139
Overhead Costs 153

Chapter Eleven The Strategy of Manufacturing Capacity . . 163

Manufacturing Capacities: The Historical Record 164
Individual Competitors' Manufacturing Capacities 166
Explaining the Capacity Expansion Decision 180
Benefits from Scale in Manufacturing: Backlogs and Throughput Smoothing, and Capacity Utilization 185

Chapter Twelve Technological Strategy 190

Technological Change in Turbine Generators 191
The Demand for New Technology: Utility Cost Structures 198
Leadership-Followership Roles in Technology 204
The Tactics of Introducing New Technology: The Price-Size Relationship 206
Technological Risk 213
The Strategy of Follower Firms 223

Chapter Thirteen Market Share Strategy 226

The Key: Market Share of Orders 226
Consumer Preference 228
Manufacturer Strategy 231
Statistical Analysis of Market Share Determinants 231
The Integration of Strategy with Corporate Goals 235
Statistical Analysis of General Electric Strategy 240

Chapter Fourteen The Simulation of Alternative Strategies in Oligopoly . . . 246

Goals, Operating Decisions, and Results 247
The Judgmental Simulations 249
Optimizing Simulations 258
Criteria 262
Welfare Effects 262
Other Key Assumptions 263
Results 264

Conflict and Cooperation in Oligopoly 281
The Cause of Variations in Profit Results 282

Chapter Fifteen   Conclusions for Public
Policy 291

Appendix 1   Utilities' Turbine Generator Orders 301

Appendix 2   The Long-Range Load Forecasting Bias 302

Appendix 3   How Utilities Forecast Peak Loads 306

Appendix 4   How Utilities Adjust Their Forecasts of Peak Loads ... 307

Appendix 5   Utilities' Increase in Generating Capability 308

Appendix 6   Utilities' Generating Reserves 309

Appendix 7   Utilities' Forecasts of Generating Capability 310

Appendix 8   Utility Retirements of Generating Capacity 311

Appendix 9   The Average Order Price 312

Appendix 10   Long-Term Trend in Average Value Per Kilowatt of
              Steam Turbine Generators Shipped 315

Appendix 11   Long-Term Trend in Value Per Unit of Output, Power
              Capacitors and Power Transformers 317

Appendix 12   Direct Costs Per Kilowatt of Steam Turbine Generators
              Shipped 319

Appendix 13   Models of Overhead Costs 320

Appendix 14   Manufacturing Capacity 322

Appendix 15   Market Share Determinants 324

Appendix 16   General Electric's Strategy: Share v. Earnings 327

Appendix 17   A Note on Cost Accounting Practices and Pricing
              Strategy 329

Appendix 18   The Integrated Model 332

Index 351

ABSTRACT

Pricing in the Electrical Oligopoly, Vol. II

Business Strategy

RALPH G. M. SULTAN

This second volume on pricing in the electrical oligopoly is in three parts. First, the author presents a theory of competitive interaction and equilibrium in oligopoly. Second, there is an intensive empirical analysis of the workings of the United States turbine generator oligopoly over the 1950–1970 period, including an analysis of utility buying behavior. And, third, a computer model of the industry is constructed and used to test alternative manufacturer strategies, with simulations of industry behavior up through the 1970s.

Ralph G. M. Sultan was formerly Associate Professor of Business Administration, Harvard University, Graduate School of Business Administration. He is currently Chief Economist of the Royal Bank of Canada.

This is a study of a major link in our energy supply system: the handful of firms—the oligopoly—which makes the machines which generate our electricity, and the electric utility firms which use those machines. A handful of suppliers, a few purchasers, it makes for an interesting marketplace. Surprisingly, there is little public knowledge of the workings of this marketplace so vital to our energy supply, but that may be attributed to the highly technical nature of the product, and the secrecy which has traditionally surrounded transactions in this industry. The present volume, second of the author's two-volume study, deals with the manufacturers' business strategies and the utility firms' purchasing behavior. It develops a theory and empirical analysis of how management's discretionary judgments with respect to technological strategy, capacity strategy, and market share strategy, largely determine price and product performance in the marketplace.

The Industry Setting

In the United States, the turbine generator oligopoly largely consists of General Electric, Westinghouse, and Allis-Chalmers, and it is the rivalry among these three firms which is the focal point of this study.

The findings of this study call into serious question the indiscriminate application of conventional conjectural interdependence models to oligopolistic industries. And they call into serious question legislative endeavors to "deconcentrate" the oligopolistic industries today.

The Theory

The first portion of Volume II presents the theory of oligopolistic rivalry which has both long-range and shorter-range aspects. The longer-term model has similarities to that developed by Sylos-Labini, but it is extended to encompass the critical variable of technological *funding*. In this respect it unabashedly embraces the views of Joseph Schumpeter. The important conclusion is that there is an equilibrium set of market shares among competing firms in an oligopoly, under which the funding rate for new technology is consistent with the demand for new technology and a certain rate of decline in the effective price level in the industry. If market shares change, then the equilibrium funding rate and the rate of technological progress in the long run will also change. Maximum "progress" is achieved under conditions of maximum disparity in the market shares of the oligopolists, or approximately when there is a maximum degree of concentration in the industry.

In its shorter-term aspects, the theory developed in this volume suggests that price levels are subject to five- to ten-year cycles throughout which prices may depart significantly from the equilibrium level, leading to periodic "price war" phenomena. These cycles in market price are attributable to the inexorable decline in costs due to "learning," and the workings of discretionary management strategies, both interacting with customer buying behavior. At any point in time, average price levels in the marketplace are determined by what the customers can be persuaded are "fair," and by competitive pressures acting upon marketing decision makers through such operating statistics as the orders backlog and the average utilization rate of the factories. The ambient rate of inflation, rather than direct or total costs, is viewed as having a key role in determining the "fair" or "equitable" market price in the short run. This in turn builds the foundation for truly sharp and sudden market price corrections, or price wars, from time to time.

The Empirical Analysis

In the second portion of this book, the author analyzes the behavior of rival manufacturers in terms of direct and overhead costs, manufacturing capacity, technology, and pricing, over the 1950s–1960s time period. In order to develop fully the rationale for managerial decisions in these aforementioned areas, the author also describes and interprets the behavior of the customer electrical utilities: their load forecasting and load growth experience, their ordering behavior, and their management of the reserve margin between the electrical energy which utilities could produce and what they do produce.

Several findings with respect to pricing in the oligopoly are significant. The author demonstrates that it is the *minimum* backlog, expressed in terms of capacity, among the three competitors, which has a major role in determining the average industry price level. Relative prices, among the three rivals, are largely influential in inducing shifts in market share. The leader firm in market share is demonstrated to be the laggard firm in changing the average level of its own bids; thus, the leader is a follower in matters of price, and the conventional wisdom of price leadership is called into question.

Manufacturing capacity is seen as analogous to weapons system capacity in an arms race. Each oligopolist seeks to maintain, or expand, its share of total industry manufacturing capacity. The motivation is to increase one's market share, for share of orders is highly determined by share of manufacturing capacity. Thus, the stage is set for oligopolistic blackmail in terms of additions to manufacturing capacity.

The most potent strategic weapon is new technology, and the study demonstrates how the leader firm in technology, General Electric, systematically priced the various models in its market basket of goods for sale, or its product line, so as to give the larger and more sophisticated customers maximum incentive to be loyal to General Electric and maximum incentive to adopt new technologies, while at the same time giving follower firms a minimum incentive to strike to overtake the leader firm in new techonology. The profit-cost tactics of product line pricing are described, including the favored "tilting the curve clockwise," which refers to the periodic adjustment of the relative price of technologically advanced versus technologically obsolescent models in the product line.

The Computer Simulations

In the third portion of Volume II, various empirical findings concerning the behavior of the turbine generator suppliers and their utility customers, are woven together into an econometric model of the industry. This model has one sector which explains utility ordering behavior, capacity addition decisions, and generating reserves management; it has another sector which explains the manufacturers' market shares, their factory backlogs and throughput, market shares, and their factory expansion decisions; and it has a third sector which explains the direct and overhead cost performance of the turbine builders, their profits, and their market share strategies.

The econometric model attempts to capture the competitive interaction of the three supplier firms along the key strategic dimensions of pricing, manufacturing capacity, and market share. Modeling techniques more commonly applied to the economy as a whole, or to total industries, are here applied to interacting firms. This may be one of the first attempts to build an empirically based model which explains the simultaneous strategies of three firms in an oligopoly.

The model is subjected to a validity check by being used to forecast actual performance of the industry in terms of price, orders, and utility reserves through to the 1970s—far beyond the time period used in construction of the model. The model finds support in these results.

As a final element of analysis, the model is used to test alternative strategies, to determine the impact of alternative modes of oligopolistic conduct on price levels, demand, supply availability, and so on. In a series of simulation experiments, the leader firm, General Electric, is alternatively hypothesized to adapt more aggressive and less aggressive market tactics. Special focus is laid upon the price variable, and the related market share objectives of follower versus leader firms in the oligopoly.

From these simulation experiments, two main conclusions stand out. First, the actual decision rules which, according to the analysis of history, seemed to govern General Electric pricing behavior during the 1950s–1960s period, were "optimal" in the sense that it was not possible to devise alternative managerial decision rules which produced even higher returns to General Electric over the simulated 1950s–1970s period. Second, for all three competitors combined, there was a consistent and predictable relationship between profits, market share, and change in market share, regardless of strategy employed. There was only one exception: so-called "blitzkrieg" strategies. Thus, successful blitzkriegs aside, profit performance was largely determined by the fundamental attributes of competitive standing in the marketplace, and the market maneuver, if any, being implemented. It was influenced but little by the specific tactics or specific decision rules being employed by management. In other words, "what" was much more important than "how," in determining profit results for each firm in the oligopoly.

(Published by Division of Research, Harvard Business School, Soldiers Field, Boston, Mass. 02163. LC 73-93777; ISBN 0-87584-110-4. xxii + 356 pp.; $17.50; 1975). Distributed by Harvard University Press, Cambridge, Mass. and London, England.

List of Tables

3.1 Composite Balance Sheet: Privately Owned Electric Utilities in the United States, December 31, 1969 61

3.2 Composite Income Account: Privately Owned Electric Utilities in the United States, December 31, 1969 62

3.3 Details of Operation and Maintenance Expenses, Privately Owned Electric Utilities in the United States, 1969 63

4.1 Average Revenues per Kilowatt-Hour Sold to All Classes of Customers, Total Electric Utility Industry 70

4.2 Energy Output and Peak Loads of the U.S. Electric Utility Industry, 1946–1970 73

4.3 Delivery Data: Northern States Power Company 75

5.1 Manufacturing Lead Times: Turbine Generators (Allis-Chalmers, Westinghouse, and General Electric Combined) 86

5.2 Average Manufacturing Delay and Average Years of Backlog 87

5.3 Regression Results: Average Manufacturing Delay 89

8.1 Relationship Between Order Price Escalation and the Concurrent Change in Market Price Level: Individual Unit Orders 124

8.2 Regression Results: Finding Best-Fitting Escalation Period ... 126

9.1 Long-Term Trend in Values per Unit of Electric Equipment Shipments, Based Upon Learning Curve Analysis 135

10.1 Elasticities Bearing Upon Direct Costs of Steam Generators ... 151

10.2 The Overhead Expenditures Model 158

10.3 Statistical Results: Overhead Spending Behavior By Three Firms, 1948–1963 159

11.1 Mean and Standard Deviation of Backlogs of Unfilled Orders, 1951–1963 185

11.2 Average Kilowatts Backlog Divided by Average Kilowatts Shipments per Quarter, 1951–1963 186

11.3 Quarterly Shipments of Turbine Generators, 1951–1963 188

12.1 Average Pressures and Temperatures for Shipment Years 1947–1962 193

12.2 National Average Heat Rates for Fossil-Fueled Steam-Electric Plants—Total Electric Power Industries—1938 to 1969, Inclusive 195

12.3   Steam Electric Plant Construction Cost and Annual Production
         Expense in the Commonwealth Edison Company System, 1969   201
12.4   Estimated Power Production Costs   202
12.5   Distribution of 1948–1962 Orders by Turbine Generator Size   204
12.6   Distribution of Orders by Steam Temperature and Pressure of
         Turbine Generators, 1948–1962   205
12.7   Distribution of Orders, 1948–1962   206
12.8   Westinghouse Expenditures on Research and Development ...   216
12.9   Allis-Chalmers Expenditures on Research and Development ...   218
12.10   General Electric Expenditures on Research and Development   219
13.1   Market Share: Steam Turbine Generators Ordered by U.S. Util-
         ity and Industrial Organizations, 1948–1962   227
13.2   Percent Share of Turbine Generator Orders by U.S. Utility and
         Industrial Organizations   228
13.3   Size of Turbine Generator Purchases, 1948–1962, According to
         Size of Utility Organization   230
13.4   Initial Steam Temperature of Turbine Generators Ordered,
         1948–1962, According to Size of Utility Organization   230
14.1   Summary of Alternative Goals, Antecedent Theorists, and Oper-
         ating Decision Rules   250
14.2   Average Market Shares, 1956–1972   264
14.3   Average Sales Revenue, 1956–1972   265
14.4   Average Operating Profits, 1956–1972   265
14.5   Average Operating Profit Rate, 1956–1972   266
14.6   Present Value: Millions of Dollars, 1956   266
14.7   Average Rate of Overhead Spending   267
14.8   Average Industry Order Price Index, 1956–1972   267
14.9   Average Industry Manufacturing Capacity Utilization, 1956–
         1972   268
14.10   Utility Reserves of Generating Capacity   268
14.11   "Best" Strategy According to Various Criteria   283
14.12   Analysis of Profit Results   284
14.13   Welfare Implications of Strategies   289
14.14   Welfare Consequences: Summary   290

List of Charts

2.1 Product Engineering Expenditures as a Percentage of Sales Revenues, and as a Percentage of Direct Costs, and Selling Price Index, 1919–1969 18

2.2 Direct Costs, Overhead Costs, and Profits of Duopolists in Period t 24

2.3 Cumulative Industry Overhead Spending—A Function of Industry Concentration and Cumulative Throughput 24

2.4 Percentage Change in Overhead Fund Determined by Concentration Ratio and Annual Throughput 25

2.5 Trend in Direct Costs at Various Time Periods t_1, t_2, t_3 26

2.6 Feasible Annual Rate of Price Change Under Varying Rates of Technological Change 27

2.7 Relation of Price to the Annual Rate of Industry Shipments ... 28

2.8 Relation Between the Rate of Growth in Stocks and the Rate of Change in Prices 28

2.9 Percentage Increase in Stock of Overhead Knowledge v. Rate of Change in Average Unit Rating or Average Unit Size 29

2.10 Relationships Between Demand, Price Change, Technology, Overhead Funding, and Throughput 30

2.11 Equilibrium Path of Required Funds, and the Path of Available Funds for a High or Low Concentration Situation 31

2.12 Equilibrium Between Available and Required Funds 32

2.13 Slow Market Growth and Atomistic Structure 32

2.14 Impact of Industry Maturity and Incipient Decline in Growth 34

2.15 Feasible Pricing in Alternative Environments of Inflation and Technological Change 38

3.1 Annual Orders for Turbine Generators by U.S. Utility Organizations 41

3.2 Quarterly Orders for Turbine Generators by U.S. Utility Organizations, 1948–1970 43

3.3 Turbine Generator Monthly Orders by 170 Investor-Owned Utilities, 1952–1959 53

3.4 Total Kilowatts Orders, Steam Turbine Generators 58

4.1   Capability and Peak Load Kilowatts, Total Electric Utility Industry 69

4.2   Growth of Base Interconnected System Peak Loads, 1910–1963 (Northern States Power Company) 74

4.3   Generating Capabilities and Forecast of Peak Loads Based on Guaranteed Ratings (Northern States Power Company) 76

4.4   Perceived Forecasting Error and Updating of Three-Year Forecast 79

5.1   Total U.S. Utility Turbine Generator Orders, Shipments, and Ratio of Backlog to Shipments 82

5.2   Total Industry Orders, Shipments, and Backlogs 83

5.3   Comparison of Manufacturers' Shipments and Additions to Utility Generating Capacity: Steam Turbine Generators for U.S. Utilities 92

6.1   Utilities' Track Record in Forecasting Their Generating Capability Three Years into the Future 98

6.2   Current and Forecasted Percentage Margins of Reserve: Electric Utility Industry 101

6.3   Retirements of Steam Turbine Generating Capacity from U.S. Utility Service 102

6.4   Utilities' Forecasted Loads and Generating Capability v. Actual Loads and Capability for Year T 103

7.1   Test of Conspiratorial Impact: Results of Fitting Regression Model to Data for Nonconspiratorial Period Only, and Then Using the Resulting Model to Estimate Prices for the Conspiracy Period 107

8.1   General Electric Annual Dollar Sales: Turbine Generators 127

8.2   Westinghouse Annual Dollar Sales: Turbine Generators 127

8.3   Allis-Chalmers Annual Dollar Sales: Turbine Generators 128

9.1   Dollar Value Per Kilowatt: Turbine Generators 132

9.2   Price Per Kilovar: Power Capacitors 133

9.3   Dollar Value Per MVA: Power Transformers 134

10.1 Direct Costs Per Kilowatt v. Cumulative Kilowatt Shipments for General Electric, Westinghouse, and Allis-Chalmers 147

10.2 Overhead Costs Per Kilowatt v. Cumulative Kilowatt Shipments for General Electric, Westinghouse, and Allis-Chalmers 157

10.3 Annual Change in General Electric Turbine Generator Overhead: 1948–1963 159

10.4 Annual Change in Westinghouse Turbine Generator Overhead: 1947–1961 159

10.5 Annual Change in Allis-Chalmers Turbine Generator Overhead: 1947–1962 160

11.1   Estimated Annual Manufacturing Capacity: Domestic Turbine
       Generator Manufacturers, 1946–1963   164
11.2   Percent of Manufacturing Capacity Scheduled: One Year, Two
       Years, and Three Years Out: Edison Electric Institute Reports,
       Steam Turbine Generators   167
11.3   Orders Received, General Electric Company Large Steam Tur-
       bine Generator Department   172
11.4   Average Share of Industry Manufacturing Capacity: General
       Electric, Westinghouse, and Allis-Chalmers   180
11.5   Quarterly Shipments of Steam Turbine Generators by General
       Electric, Westinghouse, and Allis-Chalmers   187
12.1   Maximum Steam Pressures, General Electric Turbine Genera-
       tors: 1903–1936   192
12.2   Maximum Initial Temperature, General Electric Turbine Gen-
       erators: 1905–1953   192
12.3   Maximum Size of General Electric Turbine Generators: 1902–
       1935   195
12.4   Growth Trends of Tandem Compound Steam Turbines   196
12.5   Effect of Fuel Price and Efficiency of Use Upon Cost of Fuel
       Per Kilowatt-Hour Generated   200
12.6   Performance and Cost Characteristics: Coal-Fired Steam-Electric
       Plants   202
12.7   Histogram, Showing Shift in Size Distribution of Turbine Gen-
       erators Marketed to Utility Organizations, Over Time   207
12.8   Typical Price-Size Relationship at One Point in Time   208
12.9   "Tipping the Curve" Clockwise   209
12.10 Altering the Competitive Lineup of Products Through Product-
       Line Extension   209
12.11 Maximizing the Price Increase for the Bulk of Current Orders:
       An "Unbending-Type" Rotation of the Price Curve   210
12.12 Simultaneous Clockwise Tilting of More-Sophisticated Product
       Line, and Counterclockwise Tilting of Less-Sophisticated Prod-
       uct Line   211
12.13 Ratio of Maximum to Average Kilowatts Rating of Turbine
       Generators Shipped to U.S. Utility Organizations, 1947–1971   215
13.1   Moving Average Market Share of Steam Turbine Generator
       Orders Received, 1951–1963   229
13.2   Actual Order Price of General Electric Relative to Industry
       Average Price, 1948–1963   232
13.3   Typical Profit Rate–Market Share Relationship for General Elec-
       tric Turbine Generator Division, 1948–1962   242
13.4   Typical Tradeoffs Which Can Be Achieved Between Reported
       Profit Rate on This Year's Business, v. Market Share of Orders,
       Under Varying Market Environments   243

13.5   Investing a Portion of an Expected Earnings Gain in Increased
        Market Share   243
13.6   Fully Constrained Zone of Preferred Operating Results Which
        Guide the Tactics of Operating Managers   244
14.1   Seventeen-Year Average Profit Rate and Variability of the An-
        nual Profit Rate   287

Pricing in the Electrical Oligopoly, Vol. II

CHAPTER One   Overview

THROUGH AN UNFORTUNATE ACCIDENT OF SEMANTICS, economic theory denies that an industry structure which is highly concentrated, or "oligopolistic" can also be "competitive." This study seeks to refute that proposition through analysis of the intense competition in one of our most important oligopolies: the turbine generator industry. This industry forms a critical link in the energy industry of the United States, for turbine generators are the machines which produce the bulk of our electrical energy. It is also an industry which is little known among the general public—except for the burst of lurid publicity which emanated from the electrical industry price-fixing scandal of the early 1960s.

The industry is one of our most concentrated oligopolies. It was virtually a triopoly over the period of this study, and remains so today. General Electric is the dominant firm, with about 60 percent market share. Westinghouse has traditionally held about 30 percent market share, and Allis-Chalmers the remainder. In recent years foreign competitors have become a factor in the American market place, but they too are highly oligopolistic.

The inner workings of oligopoly are usually hidden from public view, and little understood. This is unfortunate. Competitive *interaction* among oligopolists is a basic characteristic of modern industrial economies. Yet our economic theory of oligopoly lags behind. Pure and perfect competition, and fewness in numbers, are assumed to be mutually contradictory and inconsistent. In this study, that view is rejected. The weapons with which oligopolists engage in intense competition are examined in detail. Oligopolists fight one another in varying degrees of intensity, using the cudgels of product technology, of manufacturing capability and ability to produce on a time schedule, and of relative price and shifts in market share. Often their struggle is conducted in silent unobtrusive ways, but it is real enough—a clandestine war covered up by surface diplomacy.

It is characteristic of oligopoly that managers have strategic options. Management must choose between leading or following in product technology, between operating with slack or tight manufacturing capacity, between investing in, or divesting, market share. The behavior of the triopolists along these three important dimensions of discretionary "strategy" (i.e., product technology, manufacturing capacity, and market share/relative price) is opened up for view in this study. It is the discretionary strategy of managers, as much as anything else, which determines the performance of the industry.

The study unfolds in three sections: a statement of theory, an empirical examination of the facts, and, then, a simulation study of alternative behavioral assumptions, using an empirically derived computer model of the industry.

First is presented a long-run theoretical model of the oligopoly, and of the process whereby the oligopoly attains competitive equilibrium (Chapter Two). This model is unabashedly Schumpeterian in its outlook (following the precepts of the economist Joseph Schumpeter). The dominant firm in the oligopoly (by definition, the firm with the largest market share) is assumed to have the lowest direct costs by virtue of "learning" and by virtue of economies of scale. Market prices, on the other hand, tend to be established by the rate of technological change. If technological change is rapid, the direct cost-selling price margin may be sufficient to permit several higher cost firms to co-exist with the dominant firm. The burden of spending for advanced research and development falls mainly on the leader firm, and this rate of funding of technology determines—in the long run—the feasible rate of technological change in the product. For any given set of market shares, and any given level of technological risk, there is an equilibrium rate of product innovation which can be sustained in the long run. These assumptions support the Schumpeterian hypothesis: large firms which possess market power are the mainspring of economic progress and efficiency.

The maximum rate of progress is achieved when there is a maximum degree of concentration, or market share disparity in the industry. This hypothesis is pure Schumpeter in origin, and not a surprising one to practicing business strategists, but it is sharply at variance with the commonly received theory of economic performance, as correlated with competitive industry structure. The remainder of the study is largely a testing of this theory.

The second or empirical portion of the work is itself in three parts, each drawing upon the historical experience of the electrical industry. First (Chapters Three through Six) we examine how the demand for electrical energy grows, how it is then forecasted to grow by utility managers, and how their views and expectations become translated into orders for turbine generators; and, finally, how this demand is fulfilled by the turbine generator builders. The industry is one which, since its origin, has sustained rapid growth. But it has also been a highly cyclical growth managed, to a degree, by the suppliers themselves, and this feedback of supplier decisions upon demand has had a pervasive impact on the workings of the oligopolistic system. For example, the electrical utilities are perennially in an "*underforecasted*" state, which generally makes for a generating capacity deficiency, in relation to electric power demand, and which also makes for a "taut" turbine generator market. The timing of the utilities' orders is conditional upon their growth expectations, their revisions to their load growth expectations, and upon perceived delivery times at the turbine factories. The utilities dart between extremes of panic and procrastination, propelled by rumor and emotion as much as by their intrinsic generating capacity needs. The oligopolists' marketing organizations feed and exploit these waves of emotion as an element of their respective strategies in the marketplace.

The next empirical portion of the work is an examination of the financial structure and behavior of the turbine generator oligopolists themselves (Chapters Seven through Ten). Here short-run *prices* in the marketplace are determined not by costs, but rather by the degree to which backlogs are balanced among the oligopolists, in proportion to their shares of total industry manufacturing capacity. Here also it is demonstrated that there is virtually no empirical support for the common belief that overt conspiracy in the 1950s actually did rig industry prices. The analysis in this study suggests that the conspiracy was impotent.

The cost structures of the triopolists are examined in detail, using the wealth of internal operating statements, and testimony, which poured forth from the electrical price-fixing litigation. From these cost data, it can be seen that direct costs per unit of output behave according to the learning hypothesis; in this respect General Electric has an almost uncatchable competitive edge. Allis-Chalmers, on the other hand, was often reduced to selling at close to prime cost. The leader firm used its advantage in gross margin to fund overhead spending on a grand scale by comparison with that of its two smaller rivals. From this cost and market share advantage was derived General Electric's leadership position in turbine generator technology.

In the short run, overhead spending—including spending on technology— was adjusted to a targeted percentage of each oligopolist's sales revenue. Targeted expenditures depend upon a management choice between reported profits today, and investments in people, marketing, and product technology for tomorrow, as hypothesized in the long-run general equilibrium model. The model finds support in these data.

The final portion of the empirical work is concerned with describing and interpreting the various elements of discretionary management action—what is termed "management strategy" (see Chapters Eleven to Thirteen). It is demonstrated that market shares are determined according to the relative technological prowess of each competitor, the competitors' relative capacities to deliver on time, and their relative prices in the marketplace.

The leader firm manages its own market share in order to present internally a "balanced" profit-market share result. In this respect, the various managers are responding to a perennial internal corporate struggle for resources. Managers in the leader firm also try to make life easier for the weaker, smaller rivals during any market downturn, because severe price competition will threaten their own profits—and the very existence of small rivals—when orders become scarce. On the other hand, the leader firm prices its products in an ultra-aggressive manner when the market and prices are rising. This form of cyclical "hard-and-then-soft" behavior on the part of the leader firm we term "buffering." Surprisingly, then, so-called price leadership is, in this dimension of pricing behavior, actually price followership.

Manufacturing capacity is another tool of oligopolistic warfare seen in the turbine generator oligopoly, a form of rivalry which has its counterpart in the international arms race; that is, a striving to maintain manufacturing capacities in some fixed ratio to the capacity of one's rivals. The two largest rivals, General Electric and Westinghouse, apparently followed such an outward-sensing "parity-race" decision rule in their capacity expansion. But the third rival, Allis-Chalmers, followed an essentially inward-looking program of capacity expansion, disregarding any oligopolistic counter-response. Through its disregard of any such parity rules, Allis-Chalmers helped to generate the large swings in capacity, market shares, and price levels, which characterized the industry.

The final element of strategy which was studied at length was the product variable itself, especially the new technology which was embodied in the product line of each competitor. Of particular interest was how this new technology was introduced gradually to market through careful product-line pricing. The basic strategic formula, which was imposed on its rivals by the leader firm, was the following: New technology offered dramatic unit cost savings, which were temporarily available only to the leader firm in technology. The leader firm wanted to dampen the ability of follower firms to fund from current profits the advanced technology which could threaten the leader's position in technology. At the same time, for very practical reasons of customer goodwill and antitrust, the leader wanted to keep the follower firms in the competitive race. Also, under the dual motivations of selfish gain and consumer welfare, the leader firm wanted to force the utility industry—at a controlled pace—into advanced new technology. The manner in which these several objectives were attained was relatively simple: the most recent technology was priced very low, so as to induce the desired shift in product mix, but not so low as direct costs would warrant.

Price-cost margins on the older, middle technology "bread and butter" machines were maintained at a slim but livable amount, giving follower firms an adequate but not threatening overhead spending capability. Periodically, the upward thrust of inflation in the economy, plus the downward thrust of cost-reducing technology, would be cause for a general realignment of product-line prices by the leader firm. These were occasions when the published price curves would be adjusted to maintain the desired price-cost margin across machines of all types. The net result, what has been called "clockwise price-curve tipping," seems to have been symbiotic: customers were force-fed the new technology at a controlled risk pace, the leader firm received compensation in terms of market control and increased earnings for its investment and risk-taking in new technology, and the follower firms were forced to innovate, but at a slower pace which threatened neither their financial capacity nor their ability to maintain market share.

With the empirical portion of the work completed, the third major section of this study then pulls together the various behavioral elements of demand, pricing, cost structures, and strategy, into an econometric model. This model is used to test alternative short-run pricing strategies through simulation on the computer. The suggested theoretical strategies of such economists as Baumol, Fellner, Cournot, and Irving Fisher were subjected to a 17-year experiment on the model. The simulation results were not always in accord with theoretical expectations. (See Chapter Fourteen.)

Alternative strategies to be followed by the leader firm were also tested. None of the dozen hypothetical strategies which were tested on the model was as profitable to the leader firm as was the historical *actual strategy* which the leader firm had pursued. General Electric's actual strategy was propelled by considerations of buffering, of maintaining a long-term 60 per-cent share, and of the internal "balanced" reporting of profit-share results. This was also a highly profitable—indeed the optimum—strategy from the point of view of maximizing General Electric's long-range profitability. This experimental findng was unexpected, and a measure of the shrewdness of General Electric's turbine generator strategists.

Another interesting result obtained from the simulation study was the relationship between profits, market share, and *change* in market share. For *all three* competitors, there was one common linear relationship between market share and the percentage profitability likely to be achieved (a positive relation); and another between *change* in share and change in profitability (a negative relation). This implied that the particular *tactics* of any short-run strategy were largely irrelevant; what really counts, in terms of profit result, is the starting investment, in terms of market share, and the degree to which that investment in market share is yielded or increased. In general, the con-clusion reached was that it would be highly profitable to invest in market share in this industry; the payout on the market-share investment was rather rapid. The fact that in this industry smaller rivals did not usually succeed in their endeavor to wrest market share from the leader must therefore be attrib-uted to the workings of oligopolistic strategy, and to competitive thrust and counterthrust, not to any lack of potential profit reward.

In summing up this study, I am particularly aware of the hostile public environment of the concentrated industries today—an unfriendly environ-ment which Schumpeter predicted with uncanny accuracy some 35 years ago. Big business and oligopoly do not present sympathetic images, and in-dividuals are increasingly disposed to lash out at the bigness, impersonality, and hidden power, which characterize much of modern industrial society. But our research highlights the Schumpeterian dilemma. The dilemma is that market power, oligopoly, fewness in numbers—call it what you will—constitute the engine of technological progress, and they are absolutely imperative to maintain, even increase further, for the productivity of the economic machine which underpins the modern world society. However, while the highly concentrated industries are most productive, they are also highly vulnerable to unfriendly social and political forces. This study casts light upon the concentrated industries' dilemma. If external realignment of such industry structures is to be the accepted intellectual or public judgment, at least we should be informed as to the probable cost of such "de-concentration" policy measures, through understanding how competition works in oligopoly. This task has been undertaken in the following chapters.

CHAPTER Two A Theory of the Oligopolistic Firm

MANY ECONOMISTS, IN SURVEYING THE THEORY of the oligopolistic firm, conclude that the theory needs further development, that there is but modest correlation between theory and the real world of business, and that, despite these deficiencies, this is one of the most important areas of economics. They claim we need better theories if we are to better understand the modern industrial system.

Martin Shubik is typical of the surveyors when he complains, "Oligopoly theory provides one of the clearest examples for the malaise in microeconomics. There is no oligopoly theory. There are bits and pieces of models."[1] Some attribute the failure to an underestimation of the power of the large corporation. Kenneth Galbraith, for example, argues convincingly of the supremacy of the corporation over the marketplace, and then observes: "The need to keep the modern corporation *subordinate* to the market causes grave problems for the otherwise estimable subject of economics. But nowhere are the contradictions so evident, and the problems of illogic so melancholy, as in the theory of price behavior that results."[2] Richard Cyert and Charles Hedrick apparently believe that the fundamental problem with the traditional theory of the firm is its neglect of the process of *internal* decision making by managers. They conclude, "The real world still escapes our models: our explanations remain at the aggregate level. The problem is clearly difficult, but we wonder whether economics can remain an empirical science and continue to ignore the actual decision-making processes of real firms."[3] Other economists would have us think harder about the complexities of rivalry external to the firm. Oskar Morgenstern, for one, presents the economics profession with a list of major unresolved theoretical problems,

---

[1] Martin Shubik, "A Curmudgeon's Guide to Microeconomics," *Journal of Economic Literature*, Vol. VIII, No. 2, June 1970, p. 415.

[2] John Kenneth Galbraith, *The New Industrial State* (Boston: Houghton Mifflin, 1967), p. 179.

[3] Richard M. Cyert and Charles L. Hedrick, "Theory of the Firm: Past, Present and Future; an Interpretation," *The Journal of Economic Literature*, Vol. X, No. 2, June 1972, p. 398.

laments its fixation with general equilibrium analysis, and argues for more attention to *games* among the few, since this would be of greater relevance to real-world economic activity. Morgenstern notes even our sins of nomenclature: "Competition means struggle, fight, maneuvering, bluff, hiding of information—and precisely *that* word is used to describe a situation in which no one has any influence on anything, where there is *ni gain, ni perte,* where everyone faces *fixed conditions, given prices,* and has only to adapt himself to them so as to attain an individual maximum which may even be zero as in the case of profits. Yet this is what most economic theorists and their textbooks are primarily concerned with!"[4]

The theory indeed requires further development. There is little need here for yet another review of the standard theories of the firm in oligopoly. Excellent summaries are available in Scherer,[5] Shepherd,[6] Machlup,[7] Vernon,[8] and Sylos-Labini,[9] to mention only some of the best. The sheer vastness of the literature on the subject is both dismaying to the reviewer and an encouraging tribute to the importance of the topic.

The model which follows borrows from existing theorizing on the subject. It is also a theory of oligopolistic competition which was inspired by the observed behavior of firms in the electrical equipment industry.

THE SETTING FOR THE MODEL

The setting for the model is very tight and high-technology oligopoly, an increasingly typical market structure. (In the case of turbine generators, for example, the domestic industry has fluctuated in recent times from duopoly to triopoly, with the active participation of Westinghouse, General Electric, and sometimes Allis-Chalmers.) In addition, there is assumed to be hovering nearby a group of firms which periodically estimates the rewards and penalties of entry. (In the turbine generator industry, North American Rockwell was such a calculating contender in recent years, and there have been others.) Because of the fewness of competitors, the actions of one will impinge directly upon the operating results of another, a fact which managers accept as being the natural order of things.

---

[4] Oskar Morgenstern, "Thirteen Critical Points in Contemporary Economic Theory: An Interpretation," *The Journal of Economic Literature,* Vol. X, No. 4, December 1972, p. 1,163.

[5] F. M. Scherer, *Industrial Market Structure and Economic Performance* (Chicago: Rand McNally, 1970), Chapters 5–8.

[6] William G. Shepherd, *Market Power and Economic Performance* (New York: Random House, 1970), Chapter 1.

[7] Fritz Machlup, "Theories of the Firm: Marginalist, Behavioral, Managerial," *The American Economic Review,* March 1967, pp. 1–33.

[8] John M. Vernon, *Market Structure and Industrial Performance* (Boston: Allyn and Bacon, Inc., 1972).

[9] Paolo Sylos-Labini, *Oligopoly and Technical Progress* (Cambridge, Mass.: Harvard University Press, 1969), Chapter 1.

While the set of assumptions which follows is based upon the electrical manufacturing industry, these assumptions should also be reasonable for other real-life oligopolies, including computers, aircraft, military hardware, and automobiles. In this setting, customers are influenced by considerations of loyalty, price, and technology. Products embody technological innovation, and innovation follows a programmed course laid down by the manufacturers.[10] Demand for these products grows at a rate which is determined by the rate of technological innovation. This is because innovation leads both to cost reduction and to product improvement, either of which permits secular price reductions per unit of "real" output, or to put it another way, a growth in product value which may outstrip any increase in selling prices. Competitors' products are differentiated chiefly by the degree to which advanced technology is embodied in them. A secondary distinguishing feature of each manufacturer's "marketing mix" is the size, innate wit, and degree of training and specialization of its sales and service organization.

Customers are differentiated or segmented in their buying behavior. Some customers purchase technology which is at the technological frontier. Other customers are more plodding in their engineering tastes, or inherently limited in their ability to digest advanced technology. In such a marketing setting, therefore, there tends to evolve a coupling of the individual suppliers and the respective market segments, according to their product technology and innovativeness.

My earlier research on pricing in the electrical industry demonstrated that prices shift in response to short-run fluctuations in supply and demand. Price flexibility is achieved in part through secret discounts (below the list price), and through granting concessions in the product itself. List prices may shift in disciplined stair-step fashion, giving the appearance of uniformity among competitors, but actual prices will be determined by bargaining between individual suppliers and individual customers, and transactions prices will therefore display, in the short run, a large variance around a fluctuating average level.[11]

Management Organization and Objectives

Management organization is critical to understanding the behavior of the competitors in the oligopoly. Each "firm" in the oligopoly is merely one component of some larger corporate enterprise, a conglomerate which is

---

[10] For an analysis of technological innovation under such a market structure, with particular reference to the electrical equipment industry, see Richard E. Caves, "Market Structure and Embodied Technological Change," a paper prepared for the Brookings Institute Workshop on Economic Regulation, Harvard University, February 1973.

[11] For an analysis of price behavior in the electrical equipment industry, see my companion study: Ralph G. M. Sultan, *Pricing in the Electrical Oligopoly*, Vol. I: *Competition or Collusion* (Boston, Mass.: Harvard Business School, Division of Research, 1974).

operating in many economic spheres. In Williamson's terminology, these are "multidivisional" firms, rather than "unitary" firms.[12] Furthermore, each separate business unit or "firm" within the corporation is subject to central corporate planning and budgeting.

Within the corporation, the managers of each operating unit hardly enjoy the quiet life. For them, life is a never-ending series of clashes and assaults upon vested positions—both in terms of management (jobs, power, authority), and in terms of the market (market share, leadership in new products, leadership in pricing). Rivalry *within* the corporation may be as potent a behavioral determinant as is rivalry *outside* the corporation. Each operating unit of the corporation is typically headed by a self-reliant general manager. One General Electric manager described the relationship between such operating managers, and the chief executive officer of the entire corporation, as an uneasy alliance akin to that which existed between a medieval king and his coterie of powerful and semi-autonomous dukes. Each year, the dukes compete for the king's favor, by pointing to past accomplishments and to the gold and territory which they expect to win for the realm in the future. The king dispenses resources (money and people) accordingly. This process forces each individual business unit of the corporation into an annual competition for resources, in an internal capital market.

The competition for corporate resources forces each operating (or "line") manager into a performance race, the goals of which are not necessarily clearly identified or quantified. There is generally considerable latitude here, so that a manager may choose to maximize some combination of his actual earnings, market share, and sales volume performance, combined with some set of future promises, depending upon what seems to be the best ammunition in the annual bargaining for corporate resources. In painting his portrait of accomplishments, facts can be adjusted by the line manager to suit many diverse objectives. That is, the operating results of the business can be managed or adjusted, through budget and market actions, to yield a portfolio of operating statistics in line with the preferences of top management—preferences which have been actually laid down as explicit targets, or which may be attributed by rumor and hearsay to the top management audience. As Baumol suggests, there will typically be some minimum profit bogy which must be met.[13] When this goal has been achieved, the manager may then give priority to the creation of an impregnable performance record in terms of market share. If line managers perceive themselves as having long tenure of the job, they may be inclined to invest heavily in the market,

---

[12] Oliver E. Williamson, "Managerial Discretion, Organization Form," in *The Corporate Economy: Growth, Competition, and Innovative Potential*, Robin Marris and Adrian Wood, eds. (Cambridge, Mass.: Harvard University Press, 1971).

[13] William J. Baumol, *Business Behavior, Value and Growth* (New York: Harcourt, Brace & World, 1967), Chapter 6.

or in modernizing the factory, or in R&D, for the long-run strength of the business. To further complicate the goals and objectives, many operating decisions are also influenced by the human vanities: self-aggrandizement and the wish to acquire large staffs and other accoutrements of office.[14] The final set of operating objectives may therefore be complex indeed, defying any simple formulation on paper.

The resources which the corporate center will invest in each operating unit of the corporation are the result of a bargain between the operating management of the individual businesses, and the centralized corporate officers. Each operating unit argues its case. The annual negotiating for resources tends to become highly politicized, and a major consumer of line management time. Understandably, the individual line managers would prefer to make their resource allocations autonomously, without passing through the annual appraisal mill of the central corporate staff. This feeling is a strong inducement for the line officers to manage their businesses at least neutrally, or preferably slightly positively, in their net cash flow, since it is the annual tussle for *new* capital dollars which places the operating units most directly under the thumb of the central president and his staff. If, beyond that, extra funds are generated by current operations, managers will tend to commit them immediately by initiating plant expansions, product development programs, overhead and staff expansions, and the like. This will minimize the possibility of cash being drained off in large amounts from that particular business for use elsewhere in the corporation.[15] This tendency toward fiscal autonomy through astute programming of expenses has important consequences for oligopolistic behavior. It arises from operating managers in each business unit having a strong incentive to achieve self-sufficiency in resources, thereby avoiding the internal capital market. Prices, overhead spending, and capital investment programs will therefore be shaped *according to the available dollars*. In Parkinsonian fashion, expenses—particularly the postponable, discretionary expenses—will tend to rise and fall according to the tide in available revenues.[16]

In this decision-making milieu, maximizing behavior of any sort may be difficult to discern. Maximizing decisions are further complicated by the uncertainty surrounding day-to-day decisions. Information is never perfect, neither information concerning competitors' prices, nor current market shares, not even of one's own costs. Long delays between decision input and result output further compound the confusion. It is, therefore, not surprising that many decisions lack the precision which economic theory is

---

[14] Oliver E. Williamson, *The Economics of Discretionary Behavior: Managerial Objectives in a Theory of the Firm* (Englewood Cliffs, N.J.: Prentice-Hall, 1964), Chapter 3.

[15] For a description and analysis of the corporate resource allocation process see: Joseph L. Bower, *Managing the Resource Allocation Process* (Boston, Mass.: Harvard Business School, Division of Research, 1970).

[16] C. Northcote Parkinson, *Parkinson's Law* (Boston, Mass., Houghton Mifflin, 1957), an underestimated masterpiece in the economic theory of the firm.

prone to prescribe for management. "Muddling through" one step at a time, in the manner postulated by behavioral theories of the firm, for example, may seem to be the best decision making feasible under the circumstances.[17] However, most managers do seem to strive to achieve a set of goals; the attempted maximization of some objective function has *not* been overplayed in the theory of the firm. What has been overplayed is the ability of managers to discern a logical path for attaining their objectives.

Costs, Learning, and Technology

The behavior of costs is also fundamental to the behavior of our hypothesized firm. In the context of tight, high-technology oligopoly, Sylos-Labini's model of oligopoly has great appeal because of its stress upon the differences in costs among competitors.[18] Sylos-Labini believed there were very pronounced discontinuities in the available technologies, as between large and small producers. Plants can only have sizes which are very specific and very far apart; the large plants in the industry operate with low costs and earn a high profit. A fringe of small plants, on the other hand, operates at a very high cost and low profit. An equilibrium prevails. The small firms do not have the capability to overtake the large firms, and the large firms have no incentive to take over the market share of the small.

Sylos-Labini's sharp dichotomy in the available technology seems to be an artificial and unnecessary assumption in the American industrial context; similar conclusions would be obtained if scale economies were continuous, although no less significant as between large and small firms. In any case, Sylos-Labini was correct when he asserted that the cost disadvantage of the smaller ("follower") firms is basic to the workings of the oligopolistic system.

The source of diseconomy for the smaller firms warrants close inspection, particularly since the resulting profit advantage of the dominant firms is often attributed to pure market power, in the context of a concentrated industry, and not to any comparative advantage in costs of the dominant firm.[19] Perhaps the source of cost advantage lies in large-firm, small-firm differ-

---

[17] Richard M. Cyert and J. G. March, *A Behavioral Theory of the Firm* (Englewood Cliffs, N.J.: Prentice-Hall, 1964).

[18] Sylos-Labini, *Oligopoly and Technical Progress*, Chapter 3; see also Franco Modigliani, "New Developments on the Oligopoly Front," *Journal of Political Economy*, Vol. LXVI, No. 3, June 1958, p. 215.

[19] See: H. Michael Mann, "Statement Concerning the Concentrated Industries Project of the Federal Trade Commission," before the Marketing Committee Meeting of the National Association of Manufacturers, Washington Hilton Hotel, Washington, D. C., November 11, 1971, referring to the studies by Normal R. Collins and Lee Preston, and by Leonard Weiss on the relationship of concentration, costs, and profitability. Also S. 3832, a bill to supplement the antitrust laws, submitted by Senator Philip A. Hart, which provides for the presumption of monopoly power by any corporation which averages a return on net worth exceeding 15 percent annually for five consecutive years out of the most recent seven. (U.S. Senate, *Congressional Record*, 92d Cong., 2d Sess., Vol. 118, No. 115, p. S11498.)

ences in the factory utilization rate. As Sylos-Labini and others point out, however, the results of statistical studies of actual costs do not encourage one to assume there is much variation in the short run in direct costs (marginal costs) as the throughput of the firm fluctuates. Instead, empirical evidence usually suggests that marginal costs are constant over the output range.[20] Fixed overhead costs are a more likely source of the cost differential. The larger firm may win the race to lower overall costs through spreading its overhead expense over a larger production volume. Further long-run cost advantages may be attributed to scale. The whole gamut of long-run costs seems to decline in many industries without limit. In Marshallian terms, this is the case of decreasing costs.[21]

To understand the source of decreasing long-run costs, it is helpful to refer to aggregate production function theory, particularly in its treatment of technical change. In early growth models of the economy which incorporated technical change, the new technology was assumed to appear exogenously. Productivity thereby increased, and costs were reduced, through spontaneous inventions, production line speedups, augmentation of labor and material inputs, and through better engineering. More recent aggregate growth models have required the expenditure of resources to create the new technology before it yields the benefit of lower direct costs. Because of its larger market share, and its lower costs, the large firm will have a scale advantage in funding the development of cost-reducing technologies. If intrafirm transfers of technology are minimized, this difference in funding capacity will inexorably perpetuate any differential in the *direct* costs (ex-overhead spending) of large versus small firms in a market.

Other cost advantages may accrue through sheer accumulated experience, wisdom, or institutional knowledge. Arrow, for example, analyzed the theory that much technological change may actually be "learning by doing"—where the extent of historical "doing" is measured by the accumulation of invested capital.[22] Alternative measures of such experience may also be proposed, such as the cumulative volume of production. Solow added that "it is the essence of this model that even the *Titanic* is still contributing to maritime productivity. Even if it can no longer carry passengers, the fact that it was once built makes all current (ships) a little bigger than they would other-

---

[20] For a summary of empirical evidence concerning constant marginal costs, see: A. A. Walters, "Production and Cost Functions, an Econometric Survey," *Econometrica*, January-April, 1963; also J. Johnston, *Statistical Cost Analysis* (New York: McGraw-Hill, 1960).

[21] Marshall attributed the phenomenon of decreasing costs to the availability of external economies (for example, the more specialized suppliers which are feasible in a larger market). In a tight oligopoly, with a high degree of vertical integration, and with marked differences in market shares of the rival firms, Marshall's decreasing costs may be captured by the very largest supplier first. See Kenneth E. Boulding, *Economic Analysis* (New York: Harper & Brothers, 1955), p. 180.

[22] Kenneth J. Arrow, "The Economic Implications of Learning by Doing," *Review of Economic Studies*, Vol. 29, June 1962, pp. 155–173.

wise be and therefore all current capital more productive."[23] It seems likely
that what is being observed, in the main, are interfirm differences in the
accumulation of human problem-solving ability and organizational skill and
the resulting impact of this on productivity.

Relating costs to experience is an old idea in project-type businesses.
Wright, in the 1930s, discussed the tendency for unit labor costs to decline
in the aircraft industry as output increased.[24] He estimated cumulative direct
labor to decrease by a constant percentage with each doubling of the number
of aircraft produced. If the first 100 aircraft parts averaged 2 hours of direct
labor each, then the first 200 should average 80 percent of that, or 1.6 hours
each. During World War II, this 80 percent learning curve was adopted as
a cost-estimating and control procedure by the United States aircraft industry, as reported by Harlan.[25] Subsequently, the application of learning curves
to military procurement contracts became widespread.[26] Years later, Bruce
Henderson of the Boston Consulting Group (and formerly a vice president
of Westinghouse) would argue that the learning curve (or "experience
curve") was *generally* applicable to *all* costs, for a wide range of products,
from aircraft passenger seat miles to electronic components.[27] In 1970 a
Du Pont analyst published similar conclusions concerning cost trends for 19
basic industrial chemicals.[28] Henderson states the argument for decreasing
costs as follows:

> There is a natural reluctance to accept the possibility that costs can

[23] Robert M. Solow, "Some Recent Developments in the Theory of Production," *The Theory
and Empirical Analysis of Production* (New York: National Bureau of Economic Research, 1967).
See also: William Fellner, "Specific Interpretations of Learning by Doing," *Journal of Economic
Theory*, Vol. I, 1969.

[24] T. P. Wright, "Factors Affecting the Cost of Airplanes," *Journal of Aeronautical Sciences*,
Volume 3, February 1936. Cited in Neil E. Harlan, *Management Control in Airframe Subcontracting* (Boston, Mass.: Harvard Business School, Division of Research, 1956), pp. 143–144.

[25] Harlan, ibid. See also: Eugene W. Pike, "A Note on 'Learning Curves,'" *Journal of the
American Statistical Association*, Volume 64, No. 328, December 1969, pp. 1,276–1,278. The
usual formulation was of the type: $y_i = ai^b$. Where y_i equals the cost of the ith unit and a and b
are parameters to be estimated. Better fitting relationships were suggested. Pike, for example,
advised that cumulative cost Y_i through ith aircraft $= A(i + C)^B$ provided a better statistical
"fit." In either formulation, however, the basic notion of a logarithmic dependence of unit costs
upon cumulative production prevailed.

[26] See A. R. Gallant, "A Note on the Measurement of Cost-Quantity Relationships in the
Aircraft Industry," *Journal of the American Statistical Association*, Volume 63, No. 324, December 1968; Armen Alchian has suggested that cost functions may have several dimensions, including
the production rate, the total elapsed time of production, and the total volume produced, with
apparent reference to aircraft-type production runs and projected businesses. See, for example,
A. A. Alchian, "Costs and Outputs," in M. Abramovitz, *The Allocation of Economic Resources:
Essays in Honor of Bernard F. Haley* (Stanford, Calif.: Stanford University Press, 1959).

[27] See: Bruce D. Henderson, Patrick Conley, Sandra Moose, and James Kunkemueller, *Perspectives on Experience* (Boston, Mass.: The Boston Consulting Group, Inc., 1968). BCG
estimates that 70 to 80 percent learning curves are common; that is, typically, costs in constant
monetary units go down between 20 and 30 percent when accumulated experience doubles.

[28] D. Robertson and A. Billon, "Pricing of Industrial Chemicals," talk before American Marketing Association, Annual Conference, Boston, Mass., August 31, 1970.

always be reduced, but costs must go down forever. Some of the improvement can be due to actual learning by operatives to perform their production tasks more effectively. Some of the improvement can be caused by the adoption of better methods, scheduling, and work organization. Some of the improvement may be ascribed to improved tools and their capital investments. A major cause of increases in productivity may be technological change which periodically provides a new basis to which the traditional improvements can be applied. Regardless of the complex reasons, it does happen consistently.[29]

In the industrial learning models of the Henderson-Du Pont type, unit costs are assumed to be a linear function of the cumulative production volume or "experience" of the business, measured from the day it commenced in business. In a world of stable market shares, this means unit costs will tend to be inversely proportional to each firm's market share.

Yet another reason for large-firm, small-firm cost differentials may exist: the large firm's earlier *adoption* of new, lower cost technologies. The technology is created, and eventually will be available to all. But the largest firm may exploit it first—often because it created the technology in the first place. In the dynamics of the situation, the continual ability of the dominant oligopolist to move into lower cost technologies one jump ahead of its rivals can insure the dominant firm's permanent cost advantage.

To sum up, in the cost model of this research, it is hypothesized that marginal costs (direct costs) are constant with respect to output; but that large firms enjoy the cost advantage of spreading their required *overhead* charges over a larger production base; and that this gives them a comparative advantage in financing new technology. It is also assumed that "learning by doing" is present, which gives the large firms an advantage in *direct* costs. Finally, the larger firms also benefit by being the early adopters of cost-reducing technological innovation, both in products and in manufacturing processes. For all of these reasons the dominant firm has a cost advantage.

The Production of Technology

The manner in which rival oligopolists first create, and then deploy, their technological innovation is another key to the working of the oligopolistic system. Technology is produced not as the "free" byproduct of inspiration, but rather through programmed effort. William Nordhaus observes that this fact is frequently overlooked in economic theory: "Although in most modern price and growth theory technological change is treated as exogenous, this must be interpreted as an analytical convenience rather than as a serious statement about the economic system."[30]

---

[29] Bruce Henderson, "Price Policy," in *Perspectives*, No. 76 (Boston, Mass.: The Boston Consulting Group, 1971).

[30] William D. Nordhaus, *Invention, Growth, and Welfare, a Theoretical Treatment of Technological Change* (Cambridge, Mass.: The M.I.T. Press, 1969), p. 9.

How is this production of technology financed? We assume an internal funding of the new technology, notwithstanding that in many sectors of industry the funding of technology has been permitted to fall into the lap of government. (The nuclear reactor industry is a good example.)[31] But we are interested in modeling a world of markets, not a world of socialism, so we assume that the current customers are exploited as the source of funds for R&D financing. (This is the case in the electrical equipment industry, with technology financed through purchases of equipment. This is also the situation in most of nondefense industry, despite the rise of government R&D spending in recent years.)[32] We therefore seek to understand the oligopolistic mechanism which permits the *internal* accumulation of funds for large-scale, long-range product-development programs.

This is a vital issue to society. It remains to be seen whether, in contrast, the *external* capital market can operate effectively to fund innovation in an increasingly complex technical world.[33] As technological innovation becomes a matter of high-risk, long-term payout, mammoth scale, and a high degree of externality of benefits, the continued private financing of new technology is placed in doubt if that financing must rely solely upon the raising of new investment funds in the capital markets; thus, the emphasis on internal cash flows.

It is difficult to predict the efficiency with which technological funds will be expended: that is, the degree to which individual cleverness may compensate for the sheer volume of effort. But it is only realistic to bet that the technological payoff will tend to be proportional to the technological effort; that is, proportional to the total dollars expended on technology by the individual firm. Neither significant economies of scale, nor significant *diseconomies* of scale, are readily apparent in research and engineering spending. This is consistent with empirical findings from other studies.[34] The view

---

[31] As an example of the analysis of external financing of nuclear reactor programs, see: Paul W. MacAvoy, *Economic Strategy for Developing Nuclear Breeder Reactors* (Cambridge, Mass.: The M.I.T. Press, 1969).

[32] Excluding military spending, research and development spending in the United States is divided roughly equally between private industry and the federal government. See Edwin Mansfield, *Industrial Research and Technological Innovation* (New York: W. W. Norton & Co., 1968), Chapter One.

[33] Such a model of R&D financing may have renewed relevance in an era of government cutbacks in research and development. But disquiet also reigns concerning the effectiveness of private sector financing of research and development in the electrical equipment industry. Some suggest there has been a breakdown of traditional incentives. For example, Andrew Schultz, dean of engineering of Cornell University, stated, "The time is now past when the electric utilities can rely on the well-developed techniques of an earlier day to promote the knowledge and skills that will be required to implement the future that Mr. Sporn projects for the power industry. Equipment and appliance oriented manufacturers are evidently increasingly reluctant to undertake open-ended investigations for the utilities industry unless they can foresee a relatively immediate market application." Andrew Schultz, Jr., from the Foreword to Philip Sporn, *Research in Electric Power* (London: Pergamon Press, 1966).

[34] For a counterestablishment interpretation of the empirical findings of William Comanor, Edwin Mansfield, Frederic Scherer, and others, on the subject of firm size, concentration, and

that small firms spend their development dollars more efficiently than do large firms is a romantic but undemonstrated notion.

If the hypothesis of constant technological returns to R&D spending is combined with the previous hypothesis concerning the direct cost advantage of the dominant firm in oligopoly, there is a very simple consequence: Dominant firms will have the capability to spend more on R&D, and if they actually *do*, they will normally become technological leaders. Furthermore, once technological leadership has been acquired, it can be used to perpetuate the leading firm's position of dominance in market share. And as soon as the follower firms become educated to the facts of their disadvantage, there will be a decline in the frequency of outright assaults upon vested market positions, and the hierarchy of existing market shares will tend to stabilize.

The Schumpeterian Hypothesis: An Empirical Test

The proposition that the highest technological competence tends to accrue to the largest and most powerful firms is unabashedly Schumpeterian. Economist Joseph Schumpeter argued that it was innovation, or the "creative destruction" of monopolistic firms which fueled economic progress. He observed:

> The theories of monopolistic and oligopolistic competition may be made to serve the view that capitalist reality is unfavorable to maximum performance in production—that all along, output has been expanding in spite of the secular sabotage perpetrated by the managing bourgeoisie. [But] if we economists were given less to wishful thinking and more to the observation of facts, doubts would immediately arise as to the realistic virtues of [this] theory. As soon as we inquire into the individual items in which progress was most conspicuous, the trail leads not to the doors of those firms that work under conditions of comparatively free competition but precisely to the doors of the large concerns, and a shocking suspicion dawns upon us that big business may have had more to do with creating that standard of life than with keeping it down.[35]

A major problem when one attempts to verify or refute any such Schumpeterian hypothesis is the long time delay between input and output in the normal research and development process. The analyst is forced to grapple with the "apples and oranges" problems of a study across industries, or else to seek very long time series. Fortunately, it was possible to subject the Schumpeterian hypothesis to a test at the very outset of the research: on a very long time series.

---

technological effort and results, see: John S. McGee, *In Defense of Industrial Concentration* (New York: Praeger Publishers, Inc., 1971), Chapter Seven.

[35] This quotation has been abstracted from opening paragraphs of Chapter VII, "The Process of Creative Destruction," in Joseph A. Schumpeter, *Capitalism, Socialism, and Democracy*, 3d Ed. (New York: Harper & Brothers, 1950).

The test is based on confidential data on engineering costs, direct and indirect costs, market shares, and profits, for one competitor in the electrical equipment industry in the United States. The product is a mass-produced, standardized item used in the distribution of electric power. There was a continuous history of technological innovation and cost reduction. From the manufacturer's archives it was possible to piece together one 50-year time series concerning technological inputs and outputs. The data plotted in Chart 2.1

CHART 2.1.   Product Engineering Expenditures as a Percentage of Sales Revenues, and as a Percentage of Direct Costs, and Selling Price Index (Dollars per Unit of Output), 1919–1969.

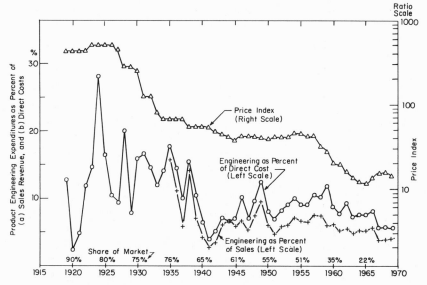

SOURCE: Confidential records of manufacturer.

show prices, engineering expenditures, and market share for this major item of electrical equipment sold in the utility market. The product was first produced commercially in 1919, and the data series commenced in that year. Over the 1920–1969 period, the business evolved from high-profit infancy to low-profit maturity. Simultaneously, three other things occurred: (1) prices declined (from an index of 500 in the 1920s to an index of approximately 15); (2) the market share of the leader declined (from a position of near-monopoly in the early 1920s, to less than 25 percent in the late 1960s); and (3) spending on research and development by this firm, whether measured as a percentage of sales or as a percentage of direct costs, declined (from a high of almost 30 percent of direct costs in 1924, to approximately 5 percent of direct costs in the late 1960s). These data hint at a possible relationship between price levels, price-cost margins, spending on research and development, and market shares.

More precisely, as the firm gained experience with this item of electrical apparatus, the following occurred: New competitors entered the market, forcing down the market share of the innovating, leader firm. Prices declined dramatically. Direct costs declined dramatically. The margin available for overhead spending was squeezed. The percentage of the sales dollar devoted to research and engineering declined. And, finally, the rate of progress in the industry, as measured by the rate of change in the selling price per unit of capacity to the customer, also declined.

This pattern is not uncommon: many industries, from chemicals to electronics, at their commercial origin experienced a high rate of technological change, only to slow down as the industry proceeded to an advanced state of maturity.

The data tend to support the Schumpeterian hypothesis. The rate of funding of technology, and the rate of change in technology, tend to be proportional to the degree of *monopoly* elements which are present in the market. The instant rebuttal, to be sure, is that these data reveal no such thing: they merely reveal the progressive drying up of technological opportunities as an industry matures. However, one should not be so ready to concede the inevitability of decline in technological opportunity. Instead, what we may be observing is a link between the degree of "excess" profits which are generated in an oligopoly, and the tightness of the oligopoly; and a further link between the ability of an oligopoly to generate "excess" profits, and its proclivity to invest those excess profits in new technology. Thus, as the tightness of the oligopoly declines, there is a decline in the rate of funding of new technology, and—inevitably—a decline in the rate of technological progress itself.

These data merely hint at the existence of such a long-run phenomenon in oligopoly. The model will now be defined formally.

THE LONG-RUN MODEL

In high-technology, highly concentrated industries a ubiquitous process of long-term adjustment establishes the rate of technological progress. In this process of long-term adjustment, there is an implied interrelationship between price levels, overhead spending, the investment in new technology, the price elasticity of market demand, and market shares, which may be approximated by a simplified model. The distinguishing feature of this model is the implication that an equilibrium growth path for an industry may be achieved either at a very slow or a very rapid rate of technological change. The rate of growth of technological innovation which is finally achieved in the long run will be a function of the market shares of the competing firms, and other factors which will be discussed at appropriate points.

This model describes a world in which autonomous suppliers finance their own research and development from current revenues. Government development contracts are unknown. Capital for physical assets and working capital may be raised external to the system, but the external financing of investments in product development is discouraged by the risks and uncertainties, and by the "nonbankable" character of assets which do not happen to appear on the balance sheet. Under certain circumstances, when existing suppliers reap very high profits or when they fail to satisfy market opportunities, entry by new competitors may be induced.

DUOPOLY ASSUMED

For simplicity of exposition it is assumed the industry is a duopoly, with two suppliers of high-technology capital equipment, such as turbine generators. Call them firm "A" and firm "B." Additional suppliers could be accommodated through an extension of the model. By some historical accident—the intervention of a Thomas Edison perhaps—one firm acquires an initial superiority in market share over the other. Thereafter, in any particular year t, firm A has a certain level of direct costs in the factory, D_{At}, which may be perceived, in the case of turbine generators for example, as the cost of labor, materials, and indirect factory costs, all measured in dollars per kilowatt.

It is assumed there is "learning" in the manufacturing of products, through improvement in work methods, employee training, and so on. For firm A, the relevant measure of production experience or learning is Q_{At}, the total physical units produced since beginning production at some previous period. In turbine generators, this would be measured in total kilowatts of cumulative output. The current rate of output for firm A is dQ_{At}/dt, measured in kilowatts per year.

Total industry shipments equal the sum of shipments from firm A and from firm B, measured in kilowatts per year. The following identity therefore applies:

$$\frac{dQ_T}{dt} \equiv \frac{dQ_{At}}{dt} + \frac{dQ_{Bt}}{dt} \tag{1}$$

In addition, firm A has accumulated a stock of general knowledge and experience outside the factory, a blend of technical judgment and management knowledge, which may be measured by O_{At}, the cumulative dollars of its overhead spending since firm A entered the business. The current rate of overhead spending is dO_{At}/dt, measured in dollars per year.

Overhead spending has two components. First, there is a mandatory portion dO_{AMt}/dt which is absolutely necessary to maintain the business at its current state (to pay, for example, for heat, light, rent, basic administration, marketing, and sufficient engineering expenditures to maintain—but not to advance—the state of the art in technology), and to fund the growth to which the business is already committed. Second, there is a discretionary portion dO_{ADt}/dt which largely consists of current spending on advanced technology and product development. Total overhead spending in any year for firm A or for firm B is the sum of the discretionary and mandatory amounts. The following identities apply:

$$\frac{dO_{At}}{dt} \equiv \frac{dO_{MAt}}{dt} + \frac{dO_{DAt}}{dt} \tag{2}$$

$$\frac{dO_{Bt}}{dt} \equiv \frac{dO_{MBt}}{dt} + \frac{dO_{DBt}}{dt} \tag{3}$$

Firm A experiences an accounting profit rate on sales of R_{At}, also measured in dollars per kilowatt. The profit rate will include both the normal charges to compensate the invested capital in the business, plus any "extra" profit or quasi-rent which may be acquired by virtue of the unique cost advantage of this firm. The profit which firm A reports is a managed result, depending upon how much of its available margin it chooses to devote to discretionary overhead spending, and dependent as well upon other factors in the situation, notably the industry price level. For the moment, consider prices as given; we will examine subsequently the market process of price adjustment. Because of the discretionary spending, the profit shown at "the bottom line" of the annual report is a figure which is subject to management discretion. We will examine other *short*-run aspects of the budget decision at appropriate points in later chapters.

Both A and B sell into a marketplace which has a prevailing price level of P_t. This is the average *revenue* per kilowatt, for the current average bundle of products which is marketed by both A and B together. It is not, strictly speaking, a price index, since the composition of the product bundle is constantly shifting. The prevailing price level is actually not an exogenous variable for the firm. The leader firm, in particular, has great discretionary power to determine the level of P_t which will prevail. However, if prices are held at a level inconsistent with the other elements of the system, then shifts must occur in the rate of spending, or in market shares, to bring the market into equilibrium once more.

The follower firm, B, has its own unique direct costs, overhead spending, annual throughput, cumulative production experience and knowledge, and profit rate on sales. Total revenue for each firm equals the sum of its direct costs, overhead costs, and profits, all measured in dollars per year, so the following identities apply:

$$P_t \frac{dQ_{At}}{dt} \equiv R_{At} \frac{dQ_{At}}{dt} + \frac{dO_{At}}{dt} + D_{At} \frac{dQ_{At}}{dt} \tag{4}$$

$$P_t \frac{dQ_{Bt}}{dt} \equiv R_{Bt} \frac{dQ_{Bt}}{dt} + \frac{dO_{Bt}}{dt} + D_{Bt} \frac{dQ_{Bt}}{dt} \tag{5}$$

A final important variable is a measure of the current state of technology, X_t. A convenient way to assess the state of technology is through the average industry product mix. In the turbine generator business, for example, X_t could be measured as the average size of turbine generators (kilowatts per unit) shipped in year t. As X_t increases in magnitude, the technology embodied in the current bundle of industry products climbs to a more advanced level.

Direct Costs

The first behavioral relationship in the system defines the level of direct costs of firm A in period t. Direct costs are assumed to be a function of accumulated production experience Q_{At} and accumulated overhead spending O_{At} of the firm. A unique level of productivity and acquired knowledge and entrepreneurial acumen produce a unique level of direct costs for the firm. (Direct costs could conceivably be influenced by the current rate of factory utilization, but this is a short-run cyclical phenomenon and, in any case, constant direct costs can be assumed in the short run.) The direct costs of firm B are similarly related to its production experience Q_{Bt} and its accumulated overhead spending O_{Bt}. To describe this function a general operator (f_1) is employed for this and subsequent relationships.

$$D_{At} = f_1 (Q_{At}, O_{At}) \tag{6}$$

$$D_{Bt} = f_2 (Q_{Bt}, O_{Bt}) \tag{7}$$

Mandatory Overhead Costs

Mandatory overhead costs for each firm are a function of the scale of operations of each firm. There are economies of scale, so that mandatory overhead dollars per kilowatt of output will be smaller, the bigger the kilowatts of annual output for the firm:

$$\frac{dO_{MAt}}{dt} = f_3 \frac{dQ_{At}}{dt} \tag{8}$$

$$\frac{dO_{MBt}}{dt} = f_4 \frac{dQ_{Bt}}{dt} \tag{9}$$

Profits and Discretionary Overhead

Firm B is assumed to have higher direct costs and a smaller current volume of throughput relative to firm A. Because of its direct cost and market share disadvantage, firm B may be termed the "follower," and firm A the "leader." Costs and market share tend to be inversely correlated.

The managers of firm B establish their budget so that a portion of their revenues will compensate the invested capital in the business at some competitive market rate, a rate which may be dictated by a corporate treasurer's office. It is convenient to assume that equilibrium capital-output ratios change but slowly, so that invested capital tends to be some unique ratio of the trend in sales revenues for this industry. Thus, budgeting to achieve an accounting profit rate which is competitive will be equivalent to budgeting profit dollars as a constant percentage of sales revenue dollars. This is equivalent to budgeting profits per kilowatt in proportion to p_t; that is, in proportion to revenue per kilowatt.

$$R_{Bt} = f_5 (P_t) \qquad (10)$$

Firm A must adopt some pricing policy, consciously or unconsciously. It is convenient but not essential to assume that market price levels are driven down by competitive behavior to the point where firm B has no margin available for discretionary overhead spending, after paying mandatory overhead and a competitive return on investment: (O_{DBt} = zero).

Firm A is in a privileged cost and earnings position. A market price which leaves its competitor with just a sufficient return on investment, and no discretionary spending power beyond that, may give firm A the capability to report an above-average return on investment, and to invest in discretionary overhead spending as well. These rewards are a form of economic rent received by firm A in compensation for its past accomplishments.

One simple assumption concerning firm A's budgeting rule is that A splits the available margin dollars equally between profit payout and discretionary overhead spending:

$$R_{At} \frac{dQ_{At}}{dt} = \frac{dO_{DAt}}{dt} \qquad (11)$$

This arbitrary breakdown may be altered by management at any time, as long as R_{At} exceeds the minimum required return on investment for firm A. It represents firm A's discretionary budget choice.

Chart 2.2 illustrates the cost and profit situation of the duopolists, as of some period t. The output of firm A is measured along the horizontal axis from the left; the output of firm B is measured from the right. The direct costs of firm A (OE) are lower than the direct costs of firm B (CD). Market price P_t is adequate to cover B's direct costs, mandatory overhead, and a competitive return on B's investment, but no more. Firm A has the margin $(P_t - A)$ either to pay out in profits, or to invest in discretionary overhead.

As market share (the ratio of OB to OC) changes, the market price which will keep firm B in the race will rise or fall. As B's market share declines, its

CHART 2.2.   Direct Costs, Overhead Costs, and Profits of Duopolists in Period t.

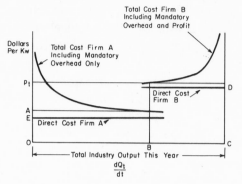

costs rise, A's costs decline, and there is a rise in A's margin available for discretionary overhead spending and profit. If there was a third competitor, a triopoly, the phenomenon would be even more pronounced. The equilibrium market price is determined by market share and the costs of the smallest producer.

The margin for discretionary overhead spending will be proportional to the disparity in market shares. Over time, cumulative industry spending on overhead of all types will tend to be proportional to cumulative industry throughput. However, if there is a high degree of disparity in market shares, the rate of overhead accumulation will be faster than if there is a low disparity in market shares, as shown in Chart 2.3. The annual percentage change

CHART 2.3.   Cumulative Industry Overhead Spending—a Function of Industry Concentration and Cumulative Throughput.

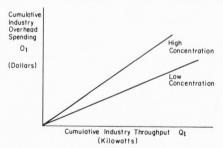

in O_t, the accumulated overhead "fund," will tend to be proportional to the annual percentage change in Q_t, the cumulative industry output, as shown in Chart 2.4.

It is convenient to refer to an industry structure where market shares are highly *unequal*, as one showing a high degree of *concentration*. The two statistics are, in general, not synonymous, although they are related.[36] It is

---

[36] The inequality index and concentration index can be related by a transform. See: I. M. Grossack, "Toward an Integration of Static and Dynamic Measures of Industry Concentration," *Review of Economics and Statistics*, August 1965.

CHART 2.4.   Percentage Change in Overhead Fund Determined by Concentration
Ratio and Annual Throughput.

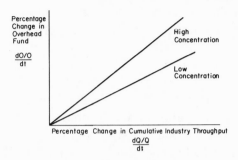

possible to have a high measure of concentration (for example, the share of industry output held by four firms together), *and* great equality of market shares. But in duopoly the two are indistinguishable from one another.

In the case of turbine generators, direct costs per kilowatt are a function of the average size of the units produced X_t. The feasible rate of price decline is directly related to the annual rate of advance in technology, which may be measured by the rate of change of the average size of unit produced; that is, by the rate of change in product mix dX_t/dt:

$$\frac{dP}{dt} = f_6 \left(\frac{dX_t}{dt} \right) \tag{12}$$

The Feasible Annual Price Change

The feasible annual change in the market price P_t is determined by the rate of technological innovation in the industry. This is a direct cost phenomenon. Prices trend downward as direct costs trend downward, through technological innovation. In the short run, technology may increase customer "values" and thus warrant, psychologically, a price *increase* with technological change. But this will be a transient phenomenon. In the long run, the cost savings from advanced technology will tend to be passed through to the customer, by virtue of competition, or else captured by factor suppliers.

The tendency to "pass through" the bulk of technology-based cost reductions is a key to the workings of the system. Five years of empirical observation of the electrical equipment industry have convinced me that this is the average long-run result, and the reason is simple: competition along the product dimension. The promulgation of new technology is a principal weapon in maintaining market position. Furthermore, suppliers are keenly aware that they must give their customers a strong motivation—lower effective cost—to adopt advanced technologies, because of the risks and uncertainties of new product performance. Thus, at a minimum, technological gains must be shared between customers and suppliers.

An alternative assumption, equally workable in the model, but less likely to occur, based upon empirical observation, is to assume that some constant fraction of the cost reductions is passed through to the customers—this fraction being determined by the degree of competition among the duopolists, along several dimensions.

The important point is that, in spite of the market power of the leader firm, technological advances are *not* converted into a *permanent* monopoly reward; rather, for strategic reasons, the leader firm, through pricing, aggressively promulgates its new and unique technology, and would only *temporarily* reap an increment of benefit—until the competitor had caught up to that particular level of technological art. But this is a short-run transitional gain at best, and we are here examining the long-run equilibrium tendencies.

Chart 2.5 depicts the trend in direct costs, measured in current dollars

CHART 2.5.   Trend in Direct Costs at Various Time Periods t_1, t_2, t_3.

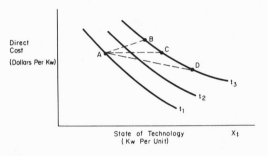

per kilowatt, at three successive time periods. Inflation drives costs up. Increasing the state of product technology drives costs down. A firm may follow several typical paths. If the rate of change of technology is low, direct costs will rise, and price increases will be necessary (path AB). If the rate of technological change is rapid, a direct cost reduction may be achieved and prices may decline (path AD). Or technological change may just offset the general inflation in the economy.

One possible resulting relationship between the feasible price change and the rate of change in product mix (average kilowatts per unit) is shown in Chart 2.6. In the absence of technological change, the rate of change of unit prices is positive, perhaps even exceeding one benchmark which the manufacturers, for reasons of customer goodwill, strive to beat: the rate of inflation in the economy. At rapid rates of technological change, costs decline faster than the upward push of labor and material inflation, and a price reduction is feasible, in current dollar terms.

This point should be explained further: When technology is stagnant or unchanging ($dX/dt = 0$), then the suppliers have no cost-reducing techniques to cushion the impact of general inflation in the economy, and the annual rate of price change is a high, positive number. Indeed, because of

CHART 2.6.   Feasible Annual Rate of Price Change Under Varying Rates of Technological Change.

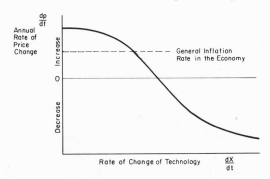

the monopoly elements in the system, factor suppliers (components producers, labor unions, etc.) may try to exploit the oligopoly and force costs upward in this sector of the economy at a faster rate than the general inflation in the economy; the manufacturers will then pass these costs along to their customers. However, as the rate of technological change accelerates, such tactics can be more than offset by—indeed, tend to stimulate—cost-reducing changes in manufacturing and product technology. The feasible rate of price change will therefore decrease, perhaps dropping below the psychological barrier of general inflation in the economy (so the manufacturers can tell their customers that they are "beating inflation"), and perhaps beyond that, dropping below the zero level (so the manufacturers can point to an effective *decrease* in their selling prices).

As the rate of technological innovation increases, it is inevitable that technological barriers will be met, thus retarding the feasible pace of technological advance in a single year. For example, new and untried metallurgical techniques must be developed, which will take time, and this process will retard the feasible technological change in a single year. As the rate of technological change accelerates, there will be a tendency to outrun the existing base of technological experience. At some point, diminishing returns to technological endeavor will set in, and this accounts for the inflection point in the curve of Chart 2.6.

Demand

Demand is responsive to price in the long run.[37] Chart 2.7 shows three possible expansion paths, over time, relating price to the annual rate of industry shipments. The economy is growing, which means there is a built-in annual expansion of demand. However, if prices are declining, the growth

---

[37] In the turbine generator industry, for example, demand is derived from the demand for electric power, and the price elasticity of demand for turbine generators is some fraction of the price elasticity of demand for electrical energy. See: Dale W. Jorgenson, "Econometric Studies of Investment Behavior: A Survey," *Journal of Economic Literature*, December 1971, pp. 1,111–1,147.

CHART 2.7.   Relation of Price to the Annual Rate of Industry Shipments.

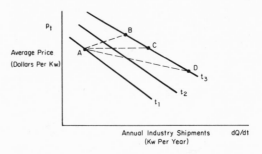

in annual shipments will be accelerated (path AD). If prices are rising, on the other hand, the growth in annual shipments will be retarded (path AB). In addition, there may be saturation effects. Demand may be less responsive to price as the existing stock of units in the hands of customers grows. Chart 2.8 shows one possible resulting relationship between the rate of growth in stocks Q_t in the hands of customers, and the rate of change in prices:[38]

$$\frac{dQ/Q}{dt} = f_7 \ (Q, dP/dt) \tag{13}$$

CHART 2.8.   Relation Between the Rate of Growth in Stocks and the Rate of Change in Prices.

Technology Production Function

Technology is produced by both kinds of overhead spending, endogenous to the system. It is not manna from heaven. This model assumes that technology derives from the pooled overhead spending efforts of both competitors. There is a full transfer or leakage of technology between competitors, after a time delay. It would require a slight modification of the model to unpool the technology, leaving it dependent upon each duopolist's own overhead

---

[38] See: Alfred Marshall, *Principles of Economics* (New York: Macmillan, 1948), Book III, for a discussion of stock saturation and its impact on demand. An important second-order phenomenon, the effect of new technology on the obsolescing of existing stocks, is not treated here.

spending over time. Under the latter assumption, price levels must permit a sufficient overhead funding rate for the follower firms, so that they do not fall farther and farther behind the leader firm.

The annual production of technology "endogenously" by this industry rests upon a core of basic research which is provided from outside the system, at an exogenously determined flow rate. It is probable that there are diminishing returns in the rate of creation of new *endogenous* technology as the industry matures, as the more obvious technological paths become explored, and as the flow of *exogenous* basic research is exploited. The functional relationship suggested in Chart 2.9 is based upon this assumption. If basic research is exploited rapidly, the cost of product development will be high.

$$\frac{dX}{dt} = f_8 \left(\frac{dO/O}{dt} \right) \tag{14}$$

CHART 2.9.   Percentage Increase in Stock of Overhead Knowledge v. Rate of Change in Average Unit Rating or Average Unit Size (Proxy for Technology).

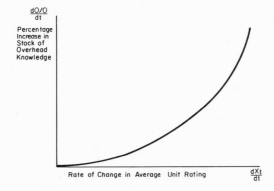

Reaching an Equilibrium Growth Path

Now consider the circumstances under which the market will be in equilibrium. Whatever price level prevails will generate gross margins which will be absorbed into, first, the profit required to sustain capital investment in the industry; and, second, some budgeted mix of spending on discretionary overhead and other "extra" profit payouts. The overhead funds create new technology. The new technology brings lower unit costs and price reductions. But it is not assured that the available funds will be compatible with the overhead funding rate required to balance the system. It is instructive to examine the circumstances under which the market may be "cleared" of funds.

It is necessary to bring the system into balance insofar as technology is

concerned. Any given rate of technological change requires a particular
funding level to sustain it. However, any given rate of technological change
also generates a certain growth rate in the market, a certain profit level,
and a certain sustainable flow of overhead spending. The firms may have
insufficient, just sufficient, or oversufficient funds to invest for this purpose.

Referring to Chart 2.10, at any point in time the equilibrium situation

CHART 2.10.   Relationships Between Demand, Price Change, Technology (Product
Mix), Overhead Funding, and Throughput.

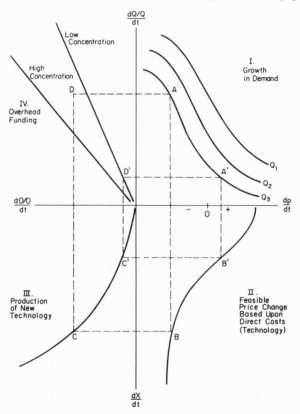

NOTE: (1) The upper right quadrant shows the relationship between price change and growth
in demand. (We will work with a given level of stocks, Q_3.)

(2) The lower right quadrant shows the relationship between product-mix change (change
in technology) and price change. This is due to direct cost reduction.

(3) The lower left quadrant indicates the relationship between overhead spending and
the change in product mix. This is the production function for new technology.

(4) The upper left quadrant depicts the link between industry throughput and the industry overhead funding rate. The slope of this relationship depends upon the disparity of market shares—crudely, the degree of concentration—in the industry.

It is necessary to bring the system into balance insofar as technology is concerned. Any given rate
of technological change requires a particular funding level to sustain it. However, any given rate of
technological change also generates a certain growth rate in the market, a certain profit level, and a
certain sustainable flow of overhead spending. The firms may have insufficient, just sufficient, or
oversufficient funds to invest for this purpose.

of the industry will be depicted by a set of points such as ABCD, or alternatively A′B′C′D′. It will be noted that the *required* overhead funding to support this degree of technological innovation, shown as points A′B′C′D′ happens to coincide with the *available* overhead funding generated by the business under an industry structure of "low" concentration (point D′). On the other hand, the required overhead funding to maintain the industry technologically at points ABCD is greater than the funds which are actually available from "low" concentration (point D). If the industry concentration was "high," an overabundance of funds would be generated; in contrast, if it was "low," insufficient funds would be generated internally.

The point is that for a given set of market shares, a given demand saturation, some given feasible rate of price decline, the equivalent required rate of technological change, a corresponding funding rate, and a corresponding rate of growth in shipments, it is not necessarily the case that the *available* overhead funds will match the *required* overhead funds. A succession of points such as D and D′ may be plotted from Chart 2.10 tracing the equilibrium path of required technological funding which will satisfy the rest of the system. The generated technological funding rate is independently determined by the industry concentration rate and the budget choices of the leader (the system is overidentified; it has 14 equations and 15 variables).

Chart 2.11 shows the equilibrium path of required funds (E), and the

CHART 2.11.   Equilibrium Path of Required Funds, and the Path of Available Funds for a High or Low Concentration Situation.

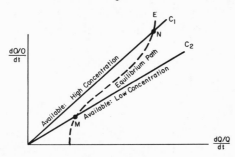

path of available funds for a high concentration situation (C_1) or a low concentration situation (C_2). Under high concentration, overall equilibrium will be attained at point N. This corresponds to conditions of high industry growth and a rapid increase of technological funding. Under low concentration, the available and required funds will be in balance only at point M. This corresponds to a much slower growth in shipments and in overhead spending.

If the industry is highly concentrated, but market growth is slow, it is possible for new technology to be "overfunded." However, the available pool of funds for advanced technologies need not be spent. It may instead be paid off in dividends or else stored as retained earnings. This is easily accomplished by altering the leader's budget decision (equation 11). Chart 2.12 shows an equilibrium between available and required funds at point P;

CHART 2.12.   Equilibrium Between Available and Required Funds.

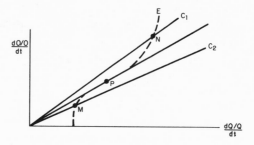

this has been achieved under circumstances of high industry concentration C_1 merely by a shift in the leader firm's allocation of the available gross margin dollars. The leader firm clears the market by deciding to spend a smaller proportion of its available margins on advanced technology, and to report a greater proportion of this margin as earnings in its accounting statements.

Alternatively, the leader firm may bring the system into equilibrium by spending on advanced technology, and by forcing up the industry growth rate.

It is conceivable that the competitive disparities in market share (and in costs) will be so slight that all "extra" margins are competed away, leaving no margin for the internal funding of advanced technologies. Such a situation is depicted in Chart 2.13. Industry concentration is now so low (C_3)

CHART 2.13.   Slow Market Growth and Atomistic Structure.

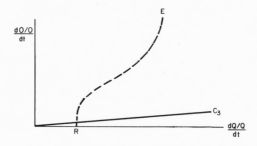

that the discretionary overhead fund is barely supplemented each year. The rate of growth of the market has stabilized at some steady state (R) consistent with existing technology. This is the equivalent of a highly competitive (atomistic) industry structure, and a stagnant technology.

If the existing concentration level is so *high* that "excess" funds are being generated, the leader firm may simply strip the extra earnings from the system. In the long run, this may encourage entry by new competitors (who look to the reported earnings of current producers for clues as to the business opportunity) or else the expansion of existing competitors. Either event will reduce the concentration of the industry, reduce the funding capability of the industry, and thence bring required and available funding into balance. This chain of events eliminates, of course, further opportunity to strip huge profits out of the system.

If industry concentration is *too low* to generate the technological funding which equilibrium requires, another set of adjustments may be set into motion. Perhaps there is no change in concentration levels, but outside funds are supplied temporarily to the system. This would then be the typical situation in a fledgling industry which is a net consumer of venture capital from the outside. Alternatively, the enhanced opportunity for gain through meeting the funding rate which the market is asking for, may be met by the entry of new competitors. However, this will not satisfy the requirement for long-term balance, because further deconcentration of the industry will also reduce the opportunities for self-financing. In the long run, this could mean equilibrium would be forced upon the industry at a lower growth rate, to accommodate the lower funding capability. A third possibility for achieving equilibrium is for the concentration ratio, or degree of market share disparity, to climb. This could occur if the market leader exploited the market opportunity to put overhead dollars to work, eliminating other "extra" profit payments, and leaving the smaller competitors behind.

A comparable situation, wherein the available funding of advanced technology is insufficient to meet market equilibrium demands, may arise if the leader firm is taking too much out of the business in the form of extra earnings, and investing too small a proportion of its available discretionary margin in advanced overhead items. The adjustments proposed in the previous paragraph would apply to this situation as well.

The impact of industry maturity and incipient decline in growth may be seen in Chart 2.14. As the market becomes saturated, stocks Q_t grow, and the overhead funding rate and growth rate which is compatible with a given concentration ratio (C_1) will decline (from S to T). But some of the decline in growth can be forestalled if industry concentration is simultaneously increased to the level (C_2) with a final equilibrium at point U. Increasing concentration may be a natural corollary of increased industry maturity, if growth in technology is to be preserved.

Finally, there is an interesting relationship between technological risk and concentration. Consider a strategy of forcing a faster rate of product development without increasing the rate of overhead funding. This is tantamount to increasing technological risk, since more technological product is demanded without any increase in the resources input. Graphically, this is equivalent to the counterclockwise twisting of the technological production

CHART 2.14.   Impact of Industry Maturity and Incipient Decline in Growth.

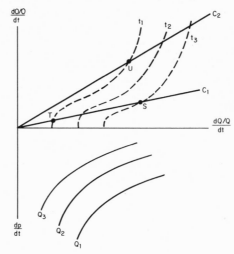

function to yield a greater rate of change in product mix for the same amount of money. (See Chart 2.10.) Risk of technological failure increases. If we now accelerate the market *introduction* of the new technology as well, at this higher risk level, this will necessitate a lower concentration ratio to clear the market, or alternatively a greater takeout of excess earnings by the leader firm. From a public policy perspective, these are dubious companion moves at a time when technological risk levels are increasing. At the higher risk level, since less technological funds are required, the funding rate of new technology will be diminished and long-run market equilibrium will be restored. But the incidence of product failures will surely rise, and this may not be in the consumer interest.

The Stability of the System

While the system, as defined, may have an "equilibrium," this is a non-conventional usage of the term. Would not the leader firm in this model seek to exploit his cost advantage and drive his rivals into bankruptcy? Thereafter, he could charge the monopoly price. It is a long-standing prediction. Karl Marx was impressed by the efficiency of large-scale enterprise, asserting that as a consequence, "One capitalist always kills many."[39] Alfred Marshall argued, with reference to the case of increasing returns, that the largest firm would soon drive his rivals from the field.[40] Patinkin discussed the instability of oligopoly even under the more moderate assumption of *constant* costs.[41]

---

[39] Karl Marx, *Capital, a Critical Analysis of Capitalist Production*, Vol. I (Moscow: Foreign Languages Publishing House, 1961), p. 763.

[40] Alfred Marshall, cited in Edward Hastings Chamberlin, *The Theory of Monopolistic Competition*, 7th Ed. (Cambridge, Mass.: Harvard University Press, 1960), p. 36.

[41] Don Patinkin, "Multiple Plant Firms, Cartels, and Imperfect Competition," *The Quarterly Journal of Economics*, February 1947.

Smithies analyzed the stability of competitive equilibrium in monopolistic competition for duopolists,[42] and for many firms, and observed, "if marginal costs are decreasing sufficiently for all competitors, there is no economic reason for saying that [the condition of stability] is necessarily satisfied, so that if marginal costs are decreasing sufficiently, the situation will be unstable."[43] Johnston pointed out that the statistical evidence of constant short-run marginal costs and L-shaped long-run costs is incompatible with the very existence of the equilibrium under perfect competition which is assumed in most textbooks.[44] (Other theoretical discomforts are presented by the model, not the least of which is the impossibility of imposing the welfare ideal of a Pareto optimum, without public subsidy.[45]) It is not therefore surprising, as Johnston notes, that such cost models are often greeted with hostility.[46]

As noted in my earlier analysis of the history of the electrical industry, initial market shares in this oligopoly were attained through accidents of history.[47] Once a hierarchy of market shares is established, the following factors will enforce an equilibrium upon the oligopolistic system: (1) The cost of increasing market share is considerable. For the leader firm to drive out its rivals would require a price war of prodigious duration and magnitude. A never-ending countervailing subsidy, from other profit centers of a rival multi-business corporation, may thwart any effort to "run them out of business." Even should this hurdle be overcome, it is not obvious that the incremental rewards at the end of the war would warrant the investment. (2) The Sherman Act discourages the dominant firm from exceeding some market share limit. (3) Customers insist upon having a choice, or alternative sources of supply, and will keep several rivals in the marketplace, even if this is a seemingly costly policy for the customers to pursue in the short run.[48] (4) Potential entry into the industry from other rivals makes it unrealistic for the dominant firm to contemplate a future peaceful situation, even if monopoly was attained. (5) Managers further recognize that competition is a useful bureaucratic device to control their own internal costs. Profitability in fact

---

[42] A. Smithies, "Equilibrium in Monopolistic Competition," *Quarterly Journal of Economics,* Vol. 55, November 1940, pp. 95–115.

[43] A. Smithies, "The Stability of Competitive Equilibrium," *Econometrica* (1942), pp. 258–274.

[44] J. Johnston, *Statistical Cost Analysis* (New York: McGraw-Hill, 1960), p. 193.

[45] See, for example, I. M. D. Little, *A Critique of Welfare Economics* (London: Oxford University Press, 1958), Chapter XI.

[46] Johnston, *Statistical Cost Analysis,* p. 193.

[47] Sultan, *Pricing in the Electrical Oligopoly, Vol. I.: Competition or Collusion,* Chapter One.

[48] The fostering of alternative sources of supply is a standard technique of procurement in industry. See: Wilbur B. England, *The Purchasing System* (Homewood, Ill.: Richard D. Irwin, 1967), Chapter 6. As a case example, Allis-Chalmers was favored by some utilities when it was in difficulty in the early 1960s. American Electric Power and others purchased foreign turbine generators in order to prevent a situation of duopoly in the American market, once Allis-Chalmers had withdrawn.

declines if market share becomes excessive. (6) Finally, market competition notwithstanding, there is an element of fraternity among the rivals, and a reluctance to deal a nonthreatening competitor the final mortal blow. For all of these reasons, equilibrium among rivals of unequal strength is common in industry—theoretical discomforts notwithstanding.

THE SHORT-RUN MODEL: CONJECTURAL INTERDEPENDENCE

The preceding model describes the central tendencies of oligopoly in the *long run*. However, in the *short run* there will be departures from those central tendencies, in response to cyclical variations in supply and demand. ("Short run" in this context refers to the four- or five-year cycles which are characteristic of the turbine generator industry.) It is here, in the short run, that theories of conjectural interdependence may have some application.

The distinguishing feature of oligopoly, in Chamberlin's terms, is "mutual dependence recognized."[49] Every oligopolist worth his salt is well aware that his own short-term profit and sales results will be in part determined by the price, output, and technological decisions of his few competitors. When the oligopolists' joint profits depend upon their mutual decisions, theory says they will tacitly join forces to harvest maximum gain from the market-place. There remains the second-order problem of dividing the spoils, and the final theoretical solution may incorporate bluff, threat and counter-threat, signaling, interdependent decision making, and tacit collusion. Game theorists such as Shubik,[50] Morgenstern,[51] and Coddington[52] apparently believe such models are realistic general depictions of market behavior in oligopoly.

A second group of theorists despairs of a large number of theoretical solutions which may be derived from the elaborate assumptions of mutual interdependence, and reject them as descriptions of oligopoly in real life. Baumol notes, "So long as the oligopolist's thought process is taken to be a compound of the form, 'I know that he knows that I know,' we may expect almost anything to emerge from the resulting confusion."[53] And he offers a more conventional model of the firm instead. Sylos-Labini similarly notes the "alarming proportions" to which the output of "reaction curves" and "conjectural variations" has arisen, and in lieu of them proposes a more traditional economic model of oligopolistic behavior.[54] A third group of theorists follows a middle road. Fellner, for example, concludes that limited joint-profit maxi-

---

49 Chamberlin, *Theory of Monopolistic Competition*, p. 46.
50 Martin Shubik, *Strategy and Market Structures* (New York: John Wiley and Sons, 1959).
51 Morgenstern, "Thirteen Critical Points."
52 Alan Coddington, *Theories of the Bargaining Process* (Chicago: Aldine Publishing Co., 1968).
53 Baumol, *Business Behavior, Value and Growth*, pp. 14–15.
54 Sylos-Labini, *Oligopoly and Technical Progress*, p. 19.

mization may best describe the oligopoly result. According to Fellner, the maximizing of the oligopolists' pooled profits, through conjectural interdependence, is qualified by such real-life considerations as the oligopolists' unwillingness to pool their resources and earnings; the incompleteness of coordination attributable to differences in their costs, advertising, product quality, and technological methods; and long-run considerations which motivate them to maximize instead the present value of the enterprise.[55]

Conjectural interdependence, signaling, deliberately parallel behavior, and the like, certainly play a role in oligopoly in real life. My own dispute with such theory is not that the convoluted reasoning of "if I do this, he will do that" does not occur; it is instead the game theorists' common insistence that competitors will by this route reach quasi-agreements which have stability and which will endure, even when the resulting price, capacity, or technological decisions are in defiance of the normal forces of supply and demand. The model of oligopoly which is adopted for this research assumes that decisions based upon conjectural interdependence are often attempted but that only sometimes do they endure. Parallel behavior to raise prices, for example, will succeed when manufacturing capacity is tight, when backlogs are high, and when the factories are busy. It will fail, on the other hand, when the order flow is low, backlogs are slim, and manufacturing capacity is greatly in excess of shipments. In operation, it will be "on" or "off" depending upon conditions of supply and demand. This periodic functioning of conjectural interdependence, rather than any behavior of marginal costs and marginal revenue, will produce the short-term, cyclical variations in price which may be observed in oligopoly.

If the effective functioning, or periodic collapse, of conjectural interdependence propels prices up and down cyclically, we are interested in the constraints which may limit (1) the upward movement, and (2) the downward movement. There are effective limits to the short-term price perturbations around the long-term trend. There will normally be a limit to the *upward* movement of prices, even when conjectural interdependence is operating with full force. Will this be the point of Fellner's limited joint-profit maximum? I think not. Other constraints will probably operate before that rate of upward price change is achieved, in particular, the leader firm's desire to maintain the customer goodwill which is a cornerstone of his market influence. In real life, therefore, the rate of increase in selling prices may not exceed a rate which can be justified by some reasonable criterion of "fairness" according to a "cover story," such as the increase which is seemingly justified by the rate of inflation of labor and materials prices; or else an increase which, in combination with an advancing product technology, results in zero effective price change to the customer.

---

55 William Fellner, *Competition Among the Few, Oligopoly and Other Similar Market Structures* (New York: Augustus M. Kelley, 1960), Chapter Seven.

Such constraints on upward price movement, in the short run, may better be conceived with reference to Chart 2.15, which shows once again the annual *feasible* rate of price change (dP/dt) as a function of the annual rate of change of product technology (dX/dt), based upon the long-run equilibrium model. It will be recalled that in the long run the feasible reduction in selling prices is determined by the amount of reduction in direct costs, which is in turn correlated with the rate of change in product mix, or technology. We now introduce a fluctuating external rate of inflation in wages and materials prices, indicated on Chart 2.15 by r_1, r_2, r_3, the low, medium, and high rates of inflation respectively.

CHART 2.15.   Feasible Pricing in Alternative Environments of Inflation and Technological Change.

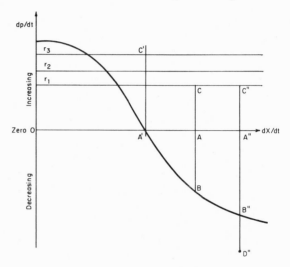

Consider first an environment of low inflation, r_1, combined with rapid technological change. At rate of product-mix change OA, the equilibrium rate of price *reduction* is AB, but the "reasonable" rate of selling price *increase* is AC. An alternative high-inflation environment (r_3) may be combined with a slower rate of technological innovation (OA'). Now there is an equilibrium rate of price change of zero, but a "reasonable" or "defensible" or seemingly "fair" rate of price increase equal to A'C'. But even with the higher rate of inflation, note that there is now less room to depart from the long-term equilibrium price change (A'C' is shorter than BC).

The general rule is the following: the amount of latitude for short-term departures of prices from costs will be determined by (1) the rate of change in technology, and (2) the rate of inflation in labor and materials prices, and these are controlling factors because they provide a reasonable sounding cover story, not because of any short-run optimization of marginal costs versus marginal prices in the oligopoly.

The combination of a high rate of inflation and rapid technological change imposes the least pricing constraint upon management in the short run. If supply and demand conditions are then ripe, the stage is set for conjectural interdependence to cause a large departure in the change in selling prices from the change in direct costs. Contrariwise, a low rate of inflation combined with a low rate of technological innovation will crowd upon management and discourage the forces of conjectural interdependence. Even when supply and demand conditions seem to be ripe, it will be difficult for managers to create a sharp disparity in the movement of selling prices away from the movement in direct costs, fervent signals to their fellow oligopolists notwithstanding.

What will limit the *downward* movement of prices, when conjectural interdependence collapses? The obvious limit is the level of direct costs itself. The relevant floor is the level of direct costs of the highest cost competitor, which in our previous notation was duopolist B. Now we deal with absolute prices (P_t) and absolute costs (D_t) per unit of output, and not with rates of change. We establish the following constraint upon the·downward movement in selling prices, even under price-war circumstances, since selling at an out-of-pocket loss is unlikely: $P_t \geqslant D_{Bt}$.

In Chart 2.15 the corresponding downward rate of change in selling prices may push *below* the curve which defines the feasible rate of change in prices. At rate of technological change OA″ and inflation rate r_1, therefore, the full scope of price changes attributable to the working (or nonworking) of conjectural interdependence, in the short run, may be the amount D″C″. This accounts for the periodic phenomenon of price wars, followed by an extreme upward movement in prices—common price behavior in oligopoly.

What remains to be defined are the elements of supply and demand which modulate the oligopolistic system in the short run, and which permit effective conjectural interdependence to be achieved, or which cause interdependence to collapse. Most of the remainder of this study is devoted to that task.

The following chapters present a short-run model of the interplay between supply and demand in an oligopoly. The turbine generator industry will be the vehicle for analyzing month-to-month movements in pricing—but these cyclical variations in price are ordained to follow a long-term trend which is determined according to the model of the preceding pages.

CHAPTER Three   Demand

THE ANALYSIS BEGINS BY CONSIDERING the nature of demand for turbine generators. In the long run this is virtually the same as the demand for generating capacity as a whole, since over 80 percent of electric power is produced by means of turbine generators. However, this study will concentrate upon the empirical evidence concerning turbine generator demand in the short run. The thrust of the analysis is to build a model which accounts for the cycles in orders for turbine generators placed by the electric utility industry. We are particularly interested in the degree to which the oligopolist suppliers could control or manage the utilities' demand.

ORDERS: THE STATISTICAL RECORD

Orders for turbine generators follow one of the most persistent and extreme cyclical patterns of any industry. Orders have fluctuated by a factor of ten from year to year. Sudden surges in demand cause manufacturer backlogs to fluctuate and this fluctuation ultimately has an impact upon price. Oscillations in the order rate are accentuated by feedback links from the manufacturers to the utilities.

The roller-coaster behavior of the annual order rate for turbine generators (measured in units and in aggregate kilowatts of generating capacity) is illustrated in Chart 3.1.[1]

---

[1] The information in Chart 3.1 was derived from *Manufacture of Heavy Electric Power Equipment in the United States, 1948–1966* (Edison Electric Institute, New York, Publication No. 67-63); from *Survey of Power Equipment Requirements of the U.S. Electric Utility Industry, 1968–1977* (survey sponsored by Power Equipment Division, National Electrical Manufacturers Association, New York, and National Industrial Conference Board, Inc., New York); from *EEI Semi-Annual Electric Power Survey*, Vols. 1–52 (reports of the electric power survey committee of the Edison Electric Institute, New York); and from various unpublished reports of the Association of Edison Illuminating Companies, New York. Supplementary information for this section has come from U.S. Congress, Joint Committee on Atomic Energy, *Nuclear Power Economics 1962 through 1967*, Report of Joint Committee on Atomic Energy (Washington, D.C., February 1968); Federal Power Commission, *National Power Survey, 1964*, Parts I and II (Washington, D.C., October 1964); Federal Power Commission, *National Power Survey, 1970* (Washington, D.C., 1970).

CHART 3.1.   Annual Orders for Turbine Generators by U.S. Utility Organizations.

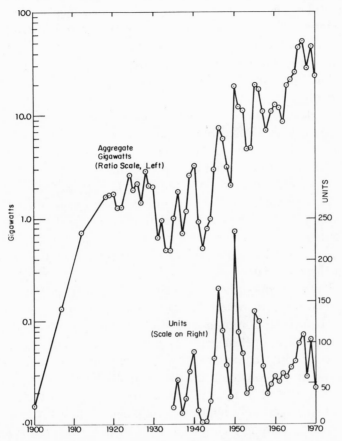

SOURCE: Edison Electric Institute, Association of Edison Illuminating Companies.

The cyclical order flow has been superimposed on a long-term trend which, over a 40-year period, approximates 6.8 percent annual compound growth. This is comparable to the long-term growth rate in demand for electric power itself.

Chart 3.1 also shows orders in units, as disseminated by the Association of Edison Illuminating Companies (AEIC) for the period 1935–1950 and by the Edison Electric Institute (EEI) for 1951–1970. Because of the continued increase in the average size of each unit, the total number of units ordered has not grown apace with total gigawatts.[2] (Note that in Chart 3.1 gigawatts are shown in ratio scale, whereas units are not.) In fact, the peak year in number of units ordered was 1950–51, when 234 turbine generators were reported by AEIC. In recent years, 50 to 100 units have been more typical of the annual industry order rate. The technological advance toward

---

[2] Along with the increase in unit ratings and total utility loads of this industry has come a parallel leap in terminology: a gigawatt is a million kilowatts.

bigger and bigger unit ratings has enforced a process of concentration upon the industry. The total available pool of business becomes divided into fewer, ever-larger increments. Simple extrapolation of the historical trend would suggest that in 25 years the single unit of order may be a 5- or 6-gigawatt power plant with associated turbines, and perhaps an annual 150 units of orders.[3] The "lumpiness" of order flows contributes to the difficulties of smaller oligopolists.

Quarterly orders for the 1948–1970 period are plotted in Chart 3.2. These are orders placed with United States manufacturers by United States public utility organizations.[4] Excluded are orders for small turbine generators placed by industrial organizations (such as paper companies and petroleum refiners, which frequently generate their own power). Export orders for turbine generators are also excluded, because such orders are probably influenced by considerations other than those which determine domestic demand. Export and industrial orders represent under 10 percent of total industry demand. Export and industrial shipments tend to exaggerate, rather than dampen, the volatility in the order rate.

Chart 3.2 also distinguishes between conventional and nuclear turbine generators. The surge in orders for nuclear units which occurred in 1966–1968 was probably due to promotional factors with no historical counterpart; namely, a decision by nuclear generating system manufacturers to accelerate the adoption of this technology through very low pricing, and through assuming some of the construction risks normally borne by utility customers. The consequence of this acceleration in the rate of introduction of new technology was not entirely happy, a result consistent with the suggestions of this research concerning technological strategy, pricing, and risk. However, the suppliers, through their ploy, did succeed in rebuilding their order backlogs and elevating industry prices.

FACTORS WHICH INFLUENCE TURBINE GENERATOR DEMAND: THE MANUFACTURER VIEW

During the electrical litigation, the marketing research and engineering specialists of the turbine generator manufacturers expounded upon the factors which, in their practical view, influenced turbine generator demand, and, therefore, determined the extreme volatility in the quarterly rate of new turbine generator orders. Charles Kilbourne of General Electric, for example,

---

[3] For a discussion of probable unit ratings in the year 2000 A.D., see C. E. Sutton, Jr., General Manager, Large Steam Turbine Generator Department, General Electric Company, "A Kilowatt Gap—Fact or Fancy?", talk presented at the 11th Annual Conference of the Electric Council of New England, Boston, Massachusetts, October 26–27, 1967.

[4] The data were obtained from Edison Electric Institute, *Manufacture of Heavy Electric Power Equipment in the United States, 1948–1966*, New York, 1967; from various *Year-End Summaries of the Electric Power Situation*, published by the Edison Electric Institute; and from other unpublished statistics supplied to the author by utility and manufacturer organizations.

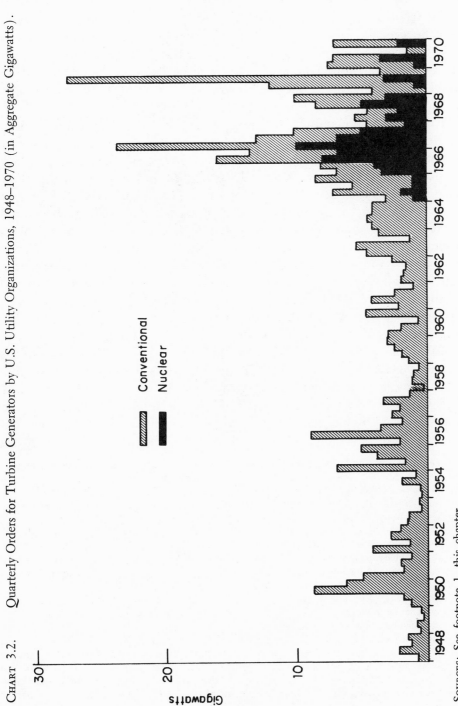

CHART 3.2.   Quarterly Orders for Turbine Generators by U.S. Utility Organizations, 1948–1970 (in Aggregate Gigawatts).

Conventional

Nuclear

Gigawatts

30

20

10

1948   1950   1952   1954   1956   1958   1960   1962   1964   1966   1968   1970

SOURCES: See footnote 1, this chapter.

former turbine department manager and an acknowledged expert in his field, asserted that "fundamental factors" shaped the turbine generator market as noted below.[5]

The fact that energy cannot easily be stored means that generating capacity must be available on demand. The utilities had no alternative but to order turbine generators to meet peak load growth—at least no alternative short of rationing and "load shedding," an unthinkable prospect during the simpler era of this study prior to the fuel supply and generating capacity shortages which now confront the utility industry.

According to Kilbourne, the specific rate of turbine generator orders, quarter by quarter, was influenced on the one hand by the need for power to generate continuity of service—which pushed the utilities in the direction of more frequent, smaller sized turbine generator orders—and on the other hand by the utilities' need to economize on fuel consumption—which pressed them toward purchasing very large units, less frequently, and which resulted in very "lumpy" ordering behavior. Furthermore, the extreme capital intensiveness of the utility industry, and the consequent need to plan expansion programs with an eye to capital costs, discouraged the utilities from investing very far in advance of need, a policy reinforced by demand uncertainties and by the rapid rate of obsolescence of current turbine generator technology.[6] This meant there was a high degree of responsiveness in order rates to the perceived rate of growth in loads for the immediate future.

Kilbourne also observed that the basic demand factor relevant to the turbine generator industry was kilowatts peak load, and not energy consumption (kilowatt-hours).[7] Manufacturer forecasting of utility kilowatts peak load was seen as a routine exponential extrapolation of historical growth rates, modified by judgment. This peak loads projection was then converted into a forecast of required utility capacity, and hence orders, by imposing a

---

[5] Testimony of Charles Kilbourne, manager of marketing research and product planning at the General Electric large steam turbine generator department, Schenectady, New York, in the civil action Ohio Valley Electric v. General Electric, 62 Civ. 695 (S.D.N.Y. 1963). This case was central to the antitrust litigation surrounding turbine generators. It served as a principal source of information in this research. Exhibits are on file at the U.S. District Court, New York.

[6] Many of the utility companies had experienced considerable changes in their load needs due to national events completely beyond their scope of control. They therefore were somewhat hesitant to project their needs. Secondly, in the power generation business, the technical characteristics of the machine which is purchased have a vital interest to the purchaser, and the utility companies felt quite strongly that we should give them some advice of what they should purchase, what size, and what efficiencies would be available, and therefore they could, considering this broader picture, give us a better identification of what they could forecast.
Testimony of Charles Kilbourne, stenographer's minutes, Ohio Valley Electric v. General Electric, 62 Civ. 695 (S.D.N.Y. 1963), pp. 1,840–1,841. Testimony from this court action will hereafter be referred to simply as "OVEC," with appropriate page number of stenographer's minutes.

[7] "We are interested in kilowatts of capacity that will be needed, not the kilowatt-hours generated, and peak loads only as a procedure from which the kilowatts of capacity to be needed can be estimated." (Kilbourne, OVEC, p. 2,023.)

target reserves margin on the utilities' peak load extrapolation.[8] Modifications of the peak load forecast, obviously, would modify the turbine generator orders forecast.[9] The sizes of individual units to be ordered, and therefore the pattern of investments year by year, were estimated as some percentage of total system load, according to the maximum capacity which the utility could risk losing in the event of an accident.[10] This means that the growth rate in the maximum size of turbine generator unit which the utilities would install was constrained by the size and growth rate in the total electrical demand of each utility system, a clear example of market structure shaping the path of technological development in the turbine industry.

The seasonality of utility orders for turbine generators was determined by the "mix" of winter-peak and summer-peak utilities within the group of utility customers.[11] As more utilities shifted from having a winter peak load, into the category of having a summer peak, their turbine generator buying would tend to shift from the late spring and summer, to the late fall and

---

[8] "It so happens that many of the utility growth characteristics, as plotted year by year, result in very close to a straight line plot on a logarithmic vertical scale. This is our estimate of the trend line of the growth of the American Electric Power System." (Kilbourne, OVEC, p. 1,864.)

Total generating capacity for each system was projected at some percentage margin above the extrapolated peak load, say 15 percent: "We have drawn in an arbitrary calibration reference, the dotted line, which is 15 percent above the actual peaks as shown on the solid line." This is purely an estimating line of reserve capacity characteristic of the actions of this individual utility. (Kilbourne, OVEC, p. 1,865.)

[9] "A decline in the forecast of the peak load for a particular year would indicate to us that the utilities would require less installed capacity . . . in a given year than we had thought they would have wished to install had the forecast been higher. And so as the forecasts decrease, the total installed capacity which is needed decreases; that is, one breaks down the other." (Kilbourne, OVEC, p. 1,880.)

[10] Utilities cannot buy units of such large capacity that the loss of this unit from service would jeopardize their continuity of service. As one studies the utilities, it is often possible to learn of a general pattern of size additions.

Typically, this pattern can be expressed as, let's say, 8 percent expansion. They will install a unit of 8 percent of their system capacity, [and] continue to add to their capacity until the size of this unit becomes 5 percent of the total system installed capacity. They may then very well step to a larger sized unit.

As one studies the utility companies, these patterns become obvious. Some are eight to five, others are nine to six, depending on the characteristics of that system in its relations with its neighbors in terms of interchange of power and other factors. (Kilbourne, OVEC, pp. 1,866–1,867.) See also: William R. Hughes, "Scale Frontiers in Electric Power," in W. M. Capron (ed.), *Technological Change in Regulated Industries* (Washington, D.C.: Brookings Institution, 1971).

[11] Winter peak companies will have encountered their maximum loads in December and in January, and they will at that time recognize what the peak loads of that particular season are, and plan ahead from this known reference point. . . . Their desires for quotations are usually heaviest in the months immediately following the winter peaks. . . . Summer peak companies recognize their peaks in the early fall, perhaps as early as September, but certainly in October, and therefore they take the time to appraise their loads, know what their futures will be, and their activity comes to us mostly in the winter months.

(Kilbourne, OVEC, pp. 1,838–1,839.)

winter months. This is because the utility wanted the latest evidence of its peak load before releasing its turbine generator commitments.

From the perspective of the manufacturers, turbine generator demand seemed virtually price inelastic.[12] However, some managers were equally convinced that they could "scare in" turbine generator orders merely by announcing a pending price increase.[13] The tactic here was to urge the utilities to "get in under the wire" of a price increase.

According to Westinghouse testimony, high backlogs at the factory caused utilities to order far in advance of need, whereas very low backlogs encouraged many utilities to postpone placing their orders, almost until it was too late.[14] Finally, according to manufacturer testimony, the replacement of obsolescent units could be stimulated through technological advances which made it all the more attractive to replace less efficient machines.[15]

---

[12] Prices and discounts have no effect whatsoever on the load growth in our calculations. The capital investment of a utility system to deliver a kilowatt of capacity is in the general range of $300 to $400 per kilowatt. The cost of kilowatt of turbine capacity lies in the general range of $25, $30, perhaps $35, depending on the size and type of turbine involved at the time. Consequently, a change in price in the turbine alone, say 10 percent considered as part of the power system's capital structure, would influence the capital cost structure by a very small amount, perhaps 1 percent, and would not determine what the utility company decided to do. It is even further of minor significance in that the total cost of power is about three times the capital investment; this is the cost for fuel and the cost for operating and the other things. Therefore, the impact of a change even of 10 percent in the turbine prices on the cost of generating power is a very small number. It is approximately a third of one percent. It is for these reasons that we do not take into account the prices of turbines at the time when we are looking at the future needs of utility industry, thinking that those needs will [not] be limited or influenced in any way by turbine price.

(Kilbourne, OVEC, pp. 1,860–1,861.) And also: "In the turbine business no one buys a turbine unless they need it, so the price has very little to do with volume." (Deposition of C. A. Lilly, Electrical Equipment Antitrust Actions, in all U.S. district courts, March 4, 1963.)

[13] We have contributed to early purchasing by announcing large price increases and then making it attractive for our customers to purchase at the price level in effect prior to the increase. More than 60 percent of all orders booked since early 1955 were received at a time when handbook prices were increased by a substantial amount. We feel confident that smaller and more frequent price increases (in the order of three or four percent twice a year) will not provide the same stimulant to early purchasing and are planning to implement such a practice.

(Internal General Electric memorandum of 1957, cited in cross-examination of Kilbourne, OVEC, pp. 1,847–1,848.)

[14] When we had a full shop our customers tended to place more orders and add to the backlog at a heavier rate than under more normal conditions. Conversely, when our shop was not loaded, the tendency of our customers was to wait almost too long before placing their orders. This waiting to place their orders tended to create spots in our schedule that we just were not able to fill. Even if we had the opportunity to sell a machine, we did not have the time to design it, get the materials and produce it early enough to fill those spots that had been missed.

(Eikner, OVEC, pp. 2,275–2,276. L. M. Eikner was general manager of the Westinghouse Large Turbine Division at Philadelphia.)

[15] The rate of change in technology influenced the total growth in demand. New, more efficient technologies could hasten the obsolescence of older, in-place machines. Joe Burrus, Man-

Factors Which Influence Turbine Generator Demand: The Utility View

There is parallel testimony from utility executives concerning the various factors which influence turbine generator demand. The testimony was largely centered upon *short-term* factors which affect the cyclicality of demand. It is helpful first to consider the decision *process* by which utilities order their new turbine generator capacity.

At the New England Electric System, for example, it was observed that the decision to add capacity was a "team job" involving design engineers who would study alternative plant configurations, the "power study group" which estimated loads up to five years into the future, and the chief executive officer himself.[16] Later, after the fundamental decision to add a certain amount of capacity and plant configuration had been made, purchasing managers would enter the picture to aid in source selection, and the board of directors would be asked to approve the capital expenditure. It is interesting to note that the very highest level managers were typically involved in turbine generator planning and in the final procurement decision. This was because the turbine generator decision was the pivot point of the entire capacity expansion program. This was not true of lesser categories of electrical equipment.[17] Also, the early stages of planning were dominated by engineering and load forecasting considerations, and questions of timing to take advantage of particularly low price levels do not seem to have entered

---

ager of Operations of the Electrical Transmission and Distribution Division of Allis-Chalmers testified that the utilities purchased heavily during the 1956–1957 period "for efficiency alone, to improve the performance of (their) system." (OVEC, p. 2,638.)

[16] William Webster, chairman and chief executive officer of New England Electric System, testified as follows:

> A decision as to the timing and need for additional generating capacity is a team job, as a rule. We have engineers that say what you can expect out of certain size plants and units, what they will cost. We have a power study group who are always revising their estimates of what our load will be three, four, five years out and who are weighing the merits of supplying that load by units of various sizes located in different situations, hydro or steam, atomic, whether you will purchase or not.
>
> I have been personally very much interested in this part of the work myself. [The authorization] would be jointly between our engineers and treasury people . . . . This would necessarily be approved by the directors of the New England Power Company. On any authorization we have a dollar figure. . . . It is somebody's or some group's best guess. We have styles in this. For a long while when prices were going up, all of them overrun, we had the very embarrassing situation of coming back to boards of directors. I have accused their engineers of guessing high after that happened. Either our estimates are better or they have put plenty in . . . .

(Deposition of William Webster, Electrical Equipment Antitrust Actions, in all U.S. district courts, New York, January 16, 1964, pp. 55–64.)

[17] Webster of NEES could relate the procedures and factors involved in turbine generator purchases, but confessed that he knew little about the purchases of even the large power transformers (Webster deposition).

the deliberations, according to this writer's review of a massive volume of litigation testimony on the subject.

At The Southern Company, the large multiutility group in southeastern United States, there was a similar team effort, with individual utilities in the group forwarding their individual load forecasts to a "power pool department" which consolidated them, and then through a series of discussions and meetings arriving at some consensus view as to future load demands and future generating capability requirements. A three-to-five-year planning horizon was typical.[18] Each year the forecasts were updated, and generating equipment requirements revised accordingly.[19]

These glimpses of the decision process at New England Electric System, The Southern Company, and other organizations, suggest that complex organizational relationships have an effect on the capacity expansion decision. Load forecasting itself is viewed as a technical exercise in which price considerations are not particularly germane. Through engineering studies, load forecasts become translated into a recommended plan for new generating facilities. Final authorization is a top management decision, after the analytical spadework has been performed jointly by engineering, purchasing, and financial managers within the utility, and outside consultants. The chief executive officer is typically involved in the bargaining for a turbine generator, and in the choice of supplier. The board of directors must finally approve, and, it is indicated, sometimes may not. The utility managements perceive, throughout, a rather large element of risk-taking on their part, or "sticking your neck out" in terms of the precise load growth to be expected, the financing of capital dollars involved, the size of the expansion, and the complex technological decisions to be made. Their concerns are to avoid premature investments, but also to avoid being caught with short supply. In technology, they want the most recent, but they tend to shun the prospect of debugging new technology and its attendant reliability problems. Given the complex organizational web of decision making, one should not be surprised at (1) rather long and variable delays, and (2) emotional "nonrational" inputs, as the decisions filter through the utility bureaucracy.

Against this background on the *process* by which generating capacity needs are recognized, and translated into orders, we now turn to utility management testimony concerning six factors which, they say, modify the order rate: (1) fluctuations in load growth; (2) interconnection; (3) the impos-

---

[18] The process of peak load forecasting, and conversion of this forecast in a capacity requirements forecast, was outlined both for The Southern Company and for New England Electric. A three-to-five-year planning horizon was mentioned. Presumably the three-to-five-year load forecast was the forecast relevant in determining the timing of orders for generating capacity at that time. (Deposition of Ernest C. Gaston, vice president, The Southern Company, Electrical Equipment Antitrust Actions, in all U.S. district courts, Birmingham, Alabama, January 27, 1964.)

[19] In The Southern Company it was testified that *revisions* of the peak loads forecast were associated with revisions of the turbine generator order rate. (Deposition of Ernest C. Gaston.)

sibility of delaying orders; (4) the possibility of accelerating orders; (5) the perceived need to get into the manufacturer's production schedule; and (6) interutility communication.

First there is the fundamental need perceived by each utility: to meet its exponential extrapolation of peak loads. Fluctuations in historical load growth, which become translated into fluctuations in anticipated loads, are generated by variations in the weather[20] and in the economy.[21] Variations in utility perceptions of peak load growth will obviously have an impact on their order rate for turbine generators.

Another variable with a pervasive—and perhaps perverse—impact upon utilities' ordering behavior in the turbine generator market is the degree to which various utilities can exchange electrical energy through transmission interconnections. According to utility executive testimony, increased interconnection capability has an impact upon the *timing* of orders, the *level* of orders, and the *unit ratings* being ordered. These are discussed in turn.

In planning system generating needs, considerations of "buy" versus "make" are important to utility management. Through interconnection with adjacent utilities, and through the energy purchases which are thereby made feasible, the need for generation capacity can be postponed. Power pooling further permits the procurement of larger units less frequently.[22] The number of options increases, and planning appears to become more flexible.[23] A

---

[20] Particularly down south, peak loads are very much dependent on climate conditions, and if you had a protracted period in which they had real hot summers and were making load projections on that background of information and then come to a summer where the average temperature was five or ten degrees lower, why obviously you are going to be off on your load growth projection.
(Deposition of William Henry Colquhoun, President of Ebasco Services, Inc., Electrical Equipment Antitrust Actions, in all U.S. district courts, January 6, 1964.)

[21] If things are booming, and everybody is using more and more electricity, you are really running fast trying to keep ahead. Along comes a depression and they all go under the table and wait for the load to build back up again. That has been going on for as long as I have been in the utility business and the manufacturers don't like it, but I don't think [it] will ever change.
(Deposition of Albert A. Casey, engineering vice president, Cleveland Electric Illuminating Company, Electrical Equipment Antitrust Actions, in all U.S. district courts, November 15, 1963.)

[22] When various power systems are interconnected, their combined capacity can be related to their combined loads. There is some diversity between loads usually, so the [required] total capacity is very often less than it would be if individually taken care of. When one company has installed a large unit and therefore has some excess power available, he will usually offer it to the other people that he is connected with, and perhaps they will defer their installations until that capacity is absorbed.
(Deposition of Ralph C. Roe, chairman of the board, Burns and Roe, Inc., Electrical Equipment Antitrust Actions, in all U.S. district courts, January 31, 1964.)

[23] Q. Do you recall any instances over the years in which clients deferred projects temporarily because the cost of any of the items of equipment going into it were too high?
A. Not the clients. These projects were scheduled by the demand for power and I think they were usually forced to go ahead at a particular time.
(Deposition of John R. Kiely, senior vice president of Bechtel Corporation, the large engineer-

planned expansion in capacity may even be postponed indefinitely by interconnection arrangements with an adjacent utility organization, depending
upon the economics of power supply. However, the impact of interconnection
on the demand for turbine generators may be perverse. The alternative of
purchasing power from a neighbor, instead of generating one's own, adds to
the uncertainty of a utility's future turbine generator needs. Future power
needs may be purchased—if it makes economic sense to do so—if one's own
supply is in short measure, and if such energy is available, even temporarily,
from an adjacent system. These added variables in the situation force a particular utility to consider both its own supply-demand situation and that of
its neighbors. The net effect of this added flexibility may be to amplify the
swings in turbine generator orders, as forecasting errors are compounded and
as perceived needs for added capacity are permitted broader latitude. Interconnections had another potentially volatile result over the historical period
of this study; they appeared to reduce the required reserve margin between
utility capacity and peak load.[24] With utility organizations temporarily persuaded that they could sail "closer to the wind" as between supply and demand, by such agencies as the Federal Power Commission and by their own
concerns to economize on investments, there was ample opportunity for
long-run mischief in the supply planning picture.

While elbow room might be provided by electric power interchanges, the
utility executives invariably agreed that capacity expansions could never be
postponed in the face of rising demand.[25] The electric power consumer had
to be served, regardless of price conditions in the turbine generator market
or anything else. There was a notable absence in utility management testimony of any reference to the long-term price elasticity of the demand for
turbine generator equipment. However, order *acceleration*—the purchasing

---

constructor firm, Electrical Equipment Antitrust Actions, in all U.S. district courts, January 29,
1964.)

[24] During the 1960s it was believed that interconnection lowered the utilities' overall reserves
requirements, thus lowering the level of required generating capacity, thus lowering the level of
turbine generator demand. (This belief was encouraged by the Federal Power Commission's 1964
National Power Survey, which had as its central theme an argument for a national power grid,
partly using the economic justification of reduced reserves requirements and lower generating
investment requirements which would, the FPC argued, thereby be feasible.) Testimony from
two representatives of prominent engineering consulting firms dwelt upon this point. (Deposition
of Kemp Reece, vice chairman of Ebasco Services, Inc., January 8, 1964, and William Henry
Colquhoun, President of Ebasco Services, Inc., January 6, 1964, Electrical Equipment Antitrust
Actions, in all U.S. district courts.)

[25] Q. On occasion did you ever advise your client, "Wait. This is not a good time to
buy," that you thought prices were going to go down?
A. I do not recall any such occasion. He had to buy a machine to be ready to meet
his schedules, so his buying period was determined by the demand for electricity and
not by the market.
(Deposition of Alf Kolflat, senior partner, Sargent & Lundy Engineers, Electrical Equipment Antitrust Actions, in all U.S. district courts, January 10, 1964.)

of turbine generators in advance of need—was perfectly feasible.[26] Among the many utility executives who offered their views, there was a diversity of opinion concerning the desirability of such order acceleration when supply considerations were favorable. Some utilities eschewed order acceleration, even when the turbine market offered exceptional buys.[27] Other utilities were delighted to take advantage of price-war conditions, as typified by the White Sale period.[28] In bringing exceptionally favorable buying occasions to utility attention, engineering consultants played an important role.[29] Many utility managers believed that if load growth projections and capacity needs did not mandate a turbine generator order, nothing the manufacturers could do, whether by price or by selling activities, could induce them to accelerate the purchase.[30] Arguing against purchase acceleration in response to favorable prices was the difficulty of fitting these purchases into the planning cycle,[31] the cost of financing equipment in advance of actual need,[32] and some ques-

---

26 Q. Do you advise your clients, "Now is a good time to buy?"
A. Oh, yes. We have done that when we knew that the price level was lower . . . .
He can order it *earlier* but he probably cannot order it later.
(Deposition of Frank V. Smith, senior partner, Sargent & Lundy, Electrical Equipment Antitrust Actions, in all U.S. district courts, January 6, 1964.)

27 [Concerning] the period of the White sale I could say not many clients of Bechtel Corporation bought during that period.
(Deposition of James Noble Landis, vice president, Bechtel Corporation, Electrical Equipment Antitrust Actions, in all U.S. district courts, January 27, 1964.)

28 Capital expansion of the system is on long-range planning so we know well in advance what we are going to require. If the market is soft, we make commitments which except for the market conditions we might have deferred.
(Deposition of Mark B. Covell, superintendent of Supply Service of Union Electric Company of St. Louis, Electrical Equipment Antitrust Actions, in all U.S. district courts, January 2, 1964.)

29 During the White Sale, Ebasco Services was particularly energetic in buying for utilities, as Kemp Reece (vice chairman of Ebasco Services, Inc.) testified:
Q. Can you give us the approximate number of turbine generators which you bought during this period?
A. I would speculate that we probably made two to three dozen such purchases.
(Deposition of Kemp W. Reece, Electrical Equipment Antitrust Actions, in all U.S. district courts, January 8, 1964.)

30 There's just so much business available in one of those periods, and usually it is split certain ways. Somebody gets this, somebody gets that, and somebody gets the other piece. Now, I don't believe the manufacturer goes out and offers a nice, fancy price hoping you'll buy a turbine, because he just cuts his own throat when he's through. I don't think the thing lends itself to churn up a bunch of turbines, going out and selling them if the guys don't want them.
(Deposition of Albert A. Casey, engineering vice president of Cleveland Electric Illuminating, Electrical Equipment Antitrust Actions, in all U.S. district courts, November 15, 1963.)

31 We ordered very little equipment in the White Sale or any other sale; and one reason was that we didn't believe in buying except as demand appeared on the horizon, and we had clearly indicated projects into which we could put equipment.
(Deposition of Philip Sporn, president of American Electric Power, Electrical Equipment Antitrust Actions, in all U.S. district courts, February 14, 1964.)

32 There is considerable reluctance on the part of the financial management of most utilities to order equipment before they need it [but] the engineer likes to order for delivery the year before he is reasonably sure he is going to use it.

tion as to the feasibility of incorporating such forward-looking investments into the utility rate base.[33]

The degree to which orders were accelerated during one notable price-cutting period, the White Sale of 1955, can be appraised in Chart 3.3. This shows *monthly* data on *unit* orders placed by a sample of 170 large investor-owned utilities over 1952–1959. In the short run, the orders stimulating impact of the White Sale was impressive: during all of 1954 these utilities purchased only 26 turbine generators; during January-February 1955, at the height of the White Sale, these same utilities purchased 38 turbine generators. However, any final judgment must await an assessment of the other demand factors in the situation.

In the writer's judgment, some of the utility arguments for *not* buying in advance under the stimulation of price were not very convincing. The point that specific project plans are not usually well enough along can be rebutted by the Ebasco testimony that only very general technical specifications were established for White Sale purchases. The point that the financial officers discouraged advance purchasing can be rebutted by the fact that such commitments seldom (it appears from the data) involved any commitment for progress payments before the units were actually under production. This same reason refutes the argument that advance-ordered units would not enter the utility rate base.

Strong factors do exist to discourage advance buying, even if market prices are low: ignorance as to the actual availability of bargains, the obsolescing impact of rapid technical change, the perennially underforecasted condition of most utility organizations and their consequent inability to plan or procure more than a few years ahead, and, finally, the pricing escalation policies of the manufacturers over this period, which tended to negate any price concessions which appeared to be granted during White Sale periods.[34] These factors provided ample reason not to accelerate a procurement; they are not, however, the factors cited by the utilities themselves.

There is another peculiar imbalance between utility and manufacturer testimony: the impact of announced price *increases* upon demand. While some manufacturers were apparently convinced of the potency of a *book* price increase announcement as a weapon for "scaring in" orders, the utilities hardly mentioned this factor at all.[35] It is conceivable that manufacturers

---

(Deposition of Abbot L. Penniman, Jr., vice president of Baltimore Gas and Electric, Electrical Equipment Antitrust Actions, in all U.S. district courts, June 10, 1963.)

[33] Materials bought ahead of time would be carried in stores and we are not permitted
    to earn as well on materials and supplies as we are on equipment actually in service.
(Deposition of H. N. Ramsey, president of Philadelphia Electric Company, Electrical Equipment Antitrust Actions, in all U.S. district courts, February 19, 1964.)

[34] For a discussion of price escalation from time of order until time of delivery, see Chapter Eight.

[35] The sole reference was in a speech by the Director of Purchasing and Stores of Cleveland

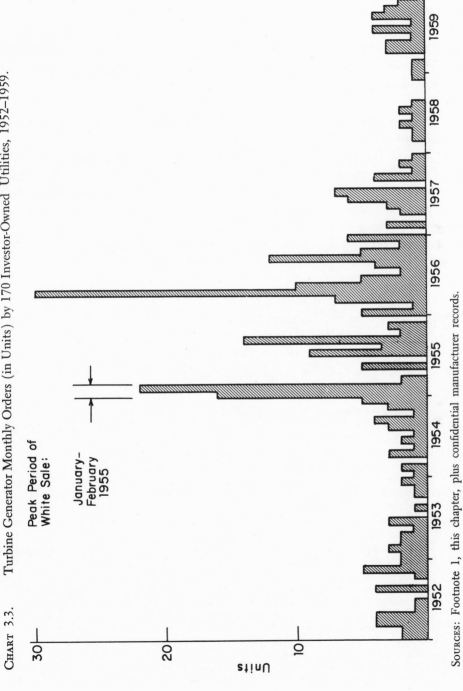

CHART 3.3.   Turbine Generator Monthly Orders (in Units) by 170 Investor-Owned Utilities, 1952–1959.

SOURCES: Footnote 1, this chapter, plus confidential manufacturer records.

were deluding themselves concerning their power to manipulate the order rate.

Two other important factors which emerged from utility and consultant testimony were backlogs (the need to "get in line"),[36] and interutility communication which leads to bandwagon behavior.[37] These factors combined to induce a periodic surge of utility orders. Cyclical expectations of future capacity shortages, mongered from one utility executive to another, and fanned by manufacturer representatives carrying tales of everlengthening delivery times,[38] would push the order rate into a periodic explosion. However, the bubble would eventually burst, and a combination of overcapacity (or adequate capacity) in generation and shortening delivery times would then lead to a quiescent period of ordering. And then some perceived shortage would commence the cycle all over again.

It is clear from the evidence that, throughout the period of this study, most utility managers were concerned only with the medium term (four or five years), and not with the long term, in supply planning. From this perspective it was therefore appropriate for them to assess the future demand for electric power as a problem which could be solved by extrapolating their immediate load growth experience. Price elasticities in the demand for electric power were not a factor in these considerations.

PLANNING MODELS EMPLOYED BY THE INDUSTRY

Other clues as to the determinants of short-term turbine generator demand may be discovered in the computer models which industry executives employ to assist their decision making. The manufacturers have built computer models which describe the decision-making processes for individual utilities, with emphasis upon decisions to add new capacity.

Electric Illuminating Company. ". . . I do know that in numerous cases the salesmen's friends are tipped off to buy ahead of expected price increases. . . ." (Talk entitled "Measures of Performance for Purchasing," delivered to EEI Purchasing and Stores Committee, National Exhibit 1342, deposition of Raymond P. Snow, Electrical Equipment Antitrust Actions, in all U.S. district courts, November 29, 1963.)

[36] A letter from the president of San Diego Gas & Electric to Pioneer Service & Engineering Company begins as follows: "We have lately been importuned by representatives of both Westinghouse and General Electric to file an order and get a place in line for a generating unit." (Letter from L. M. Klauber to A. C. Bull, dated April 3, 1951, National Exhibit, Electrical Equipment Antitrust Actions, in all U.S. district courts.)

[37] The private utilities field is one where communication within the field is very excellent, resulting from the business being relatively noncompetitive, and I am under the impression that the cycles [in turbine generator purchases] are largely due to executives keeping pretty well informed on what each other are doing. (Deposition of James N. Landis, vice president of Bechtel, Electrical Equipment Antitrust Actions, in all U.S. district courts, January 27, 1964.)

[38] It was not uncommon for the electrical manufacturers to endeavor to crystallize business by coming around and saying, "There is a whale of a demand and lead time now, 24 months, but if you don't get in pretty quick, it will be 30 months or 36 months." (Deposition of R. E. Shillady, New England Electric Power Service Company, Electrical Equipment Antitrust Actions, in all U.S. district courts, January 9, 1964.)

At one extreme of simplicity were the trend extrapolation models of General Electric, wherein *each* utility was modeled on the basis of (1) its historical load growth, which is forecasted some 10 years into the future according to its exponential trend, combined with (2) an arbitrary reserve margin, such as 15 percent, to arrive at a projection of required generating capacity ten years in the future, and (3) converting the required increment in generating capacity into an annual schedule of probable purchases, based on the likely size of unit which each utility will order. The result was a future schedule of required capacity *in service,* year by year. There was no apparent attempt to predict, at the level of individual utilities, the timing of the purchase commitments.[39] It is clearly easier to predict when new capacity will be required *on-line,* rather than when utilities as a group will choose to *order* new capacity from the turbine builders. For our purposes we need to understand *ordering* behavior, not on-line capacity increments.

At the other extreme are attempts to explain individual utility decisions to add new capacity, using complex models of the technical and business characteristics of the utility. One such approach, described by David Reps of Westinghouse, suggests that electric utility planning consists of two activities: policy making and systems planning.[40] The Reps model deals with the business forecasting problem and is mathematically structured in terms of earnings and revenues projections which are in turn functions of such variables as operating income, investment, energy sales, taxes, capital and operating costs, and electricity price. Annual forecasts of earnings and revenues provide a basis for policy making. At the system planning level, the uncertainties of load growth, future costs, and future technologies serve as inputs. Systems planning and policy making interact to generate the future investment program of each utility.

Even more detailed computer simulations are employed by manufacturers and utilities alike, to test alternative system configurations, and to project generating equipment needs. One typical approach was that developed by Westinghouse and Public Service Gas & Electric Company.[41] This consists

---

[39] Description provided by Charles Kilbourne, manager, marketing research and product planning, large turbine generators, General Electric Company, in Ohio Valley Electric, 62 Civ. 695 (S.D.N.Y. 1963) and San Antonio litigation, Civil Action 3064 (W.D. Texas 1963), in the Electrical Equipment Antitrust Actions.

[40] David N. Reps, Westinghouse Electric Corporation, "An Econometric Model for Electric Utility Forecasting," *Proceedings of the American Power Conference,* March 1962. For a similar approach see also John M. Kohlmeier, "An Investigation of Some Aspects of Capital Budgeting Policy, A Simulation Approach," unpublished doctoral dissertation, Harvard University, Graduate School of Business Administration, Boston, Mass., 1964.

[41] Baldwin, Hoffman, DeSalvo and Plant, Westinghouse Electric Corporation and Public Service Gas and Electric Company, *AIEE Transactions, Power and Apparatus Systems,* August 1960, cited in *The Methodology of Load Forecasting,* Technical Advisory Committee on Load Forecasting Methodology, for National Power Survey, 1969 (report to the Federal Power Commission, Washington, D.C., 1969), p. C-5.

of an econometric model for simulating *daily* operating performance for a utility, for as much as 20 years into the future. The model was essentially a representation of the utility and the power pool to which it was interconnected, and described the reactions of the power system, and the pool, to such external stimuli as load growth, and also such variables as spinning-reserves policy and maintenance programs. Human decisions which affected power system operations and development were included in the model. Submodels generated daily loads which confronted the simulated system capacity, which was described probabilistically, in terms of the amount of capacity *forced* out of service at any moment, and the amount of capacity which was scheduled out of service for maintenance. A long-term trend of June peak loads was the starting point. Seasonal, daily, and probability factors were applied in order to derive daily peaks. Analysis was conducted in terms of the demands upon the system, versus available capacity.

Such models are intended to be used by a single utility organization in analyzing the tradeoffs between the engineering characteristics of the utility system, capital investments, and the expected system reliability. They are not really devices for the forecasting of cycles in utility investment behavior. One common theme emerges, however: in determining the rate of addition of new capacity, forecasts of peak load growth are obviously dominant.

A Simple Model of Turbine Generator Orders

We may build a simple model of turbine generator orders, which does explain the cyclical ordering behavior of the industry adequately, merely by subjecting to statistical test those various factors which manufacturer and utility executives have testified to have an influence on short-term utility ordering behavior. A list of possible short-term demand factors, drawn up on this basis, follows:

(1) *Load Growth.* The fundamental determinant of turbine generator demand is peak load growth; more specifically, forecasted load growth in relationship to existing generating capacity of the utilities. Aggregate estimates of peak load are available for the United States.[42]

The first, and most obvious, variable to test statistically is the forecasted increment in peak load. Utility testimony suggests a typical three-year lead time from procurement to "on-line" capacity status, during the study period. One should therefore test the statistical significance of the forecasted change

---

[42] Every six months, for example, the Edison Electric Institute publishes estimates of the aggregate peak load for the United States, both for the summer peak and for the winter peak. These are the sums of the individual utility peaks, whenever those peaks occur, and do not represent the instantaneous peak of the aggregate utility industry. Since the utility industry is not totally interconnected, the actual aggregate instantaneous peak is irrelevant for demand forecasting purposes. It is the sum of the individual utility peaks, regardless of when those peaks occur, which counts.

in peak kilowatts load from the current year to three years into the future. The assumption is that utilities forecast the three-year load increment, and order some capacity multiple of that increment, such as 120 percent.

(2) *Current and Forecasted Margin Conditions.* Instead of being influenced by *load* forecasts, it is possible that the utilities are fundamentally persuaded to order turbine generators according to either current or forecasted percentage *reserve margins.* This becomes a second hypothesized variable in determining short-term orders.

(3) *Capacity Retirements.* Generating facilities eventually wear out physically, or become inefficient in relation to new capacity. At some point this obsolete capacity is no longer kept available even on a standby basis. The amount of capacity retired each year is minor by comparison with capacity additions: utilities retire three kilowatts of capacity for every hundred they add, on the average. Nevertheless, mandatory or forced retirements (measured in kilowatts of capacity) may be one determinant of turbine generator orders. Unfortunately for the test, it is likely that retirements are more often discretionary as to timing, and that the causation runs from new capacity additions to retirements, and not vice versa.

(4) *Price.* The hypothesis to examine is whether the price level may influence the *timing* of orders. Or whether a *change* in the actual price level may stimulate orders.

(5) *Changes in List Price.* Manufacturers (but not utility executives) often seemed convinced that announced changes in the list price (book price plus multiplier) could "drive in" orders.

(6) *Backlog.* There was ample testimony concerning the need to "get into line." The length of the queue was measured in two ways: both by the total industry kilowatts of backlog, and also by total kilowatts backlog in relation to the total industry manufacturing capacity; in other words, by the years of backlog. Such variables may account for bandwagon or follow-the-leader ordering psychology.

(7) *Forecasting Modifications, Euphoria, and Disappointment.* The ordering of turbine generators is a complex decision, subject to obfuscation because of forecasting errors, with complexities compounded by interconnection flexibilities, and subject to delay or acceleration within the utility organization itself. To explain the historical cyclicality of orders, one must somehow account for the pure psychology of the situation: are capacity needs unfolding as originally contemplated, or are special speed-up measures called for?

The state of the utility manager's mind, in response to the uncontrollable events around him, may be approximately measured by his *updating* of load forecasts, a measure of his "surprise." Downward revisions in the load forecast may then induce concern that too much capacity has been ordered. This may cause a slowdown in the letting of new orders. Upward revisions in the load forecast may cause panic, and plans and orders may be rushed forward in time.

All of the foregoing variables were tested in relation to the quarter-by-quarter kilowatts order rate, over 1951–1969. (Chart 3.4.) Statistical results are summarized in Appendix 1.

CHART 3.4.   Total Kilowatts Orders, Steam Turbine Generators.

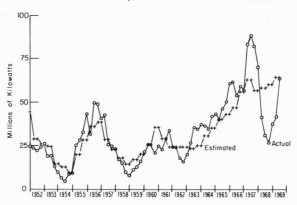

Short-Term Ordering Behavior: Statistical Results

Three variables are clearly related to the short-term (quarterly) order rate: (1) the forecasted peak load three years into the future; (2) the up-dating of the three-year-out load forecast, as it becomes the two-year-out forecast; and (3) the industry backlog condition, expressed in years of unfilled orders. These results confirm the importance of forecasted peak loads, the importance of bandwagon backlog effects, and the importance of management "surprise" as indicated by forecast revisions.

It is equally interesting to discover that the following variables do not demonstrate any strong statistical relation to the quarterly order rate: (1) current reserve margin conditions; (2) current capacity retirements; (3) price level, or changes in price level; and (4) announced changes in book price.

Some of the results are unexpected. The reserves condition of the utilities *must* influence their turbine generator orders. And certainly obsolete capacity must be replaced with new equipment. These factors undoubtedly have short-term influence, but via circuitous routes yet to be analyzed.

Whereas the announcement of an increase in *list* (book) prices was viewed by some manufacturers as being a potent device to stimulate the order rate, it apparently was not.

From a statistical point of view, *actual* prices were equally impotent. The fact that price effects were not distinguishable in the short-term order rate tends to be unexpected in view of the ordering surge which coincided with the 1955 White Sale. It appears, however, that other forces were at work on that occasion to stimulate demand. The influence of price alone was overrated by everyone. The price cuts probably triggered a surge of orders which was building up in any case. Once backlogs had lengthened, further orders were stimulated. The fact that price cuts have a minimal effect upon the timing of orders is further substantiated by the post-1959 price decline, which was not accompanied by any parallel surge in orders.

Other Studies: Long-Run Demand

The impact of price upon the growth rate of turbine generator demand is obviously a very long-term phenomenon. For insight into the nature of long-run demand, studies and commentaries by others have been reviewed. These studies have tended to concentrate upon the utilities' total dollars of capital expenditure, or else they have focused upon the more narrow issue of the nature of the production function or mix of investments in nuclear or fossil-fueled electric plants. Roos and Von Szelikski, for example, concluded that utilities' demand for new equipment was a function of their energy production, their current generating capacity, and a trend.[43] Morehouse discussed the benefits which would be achieved through smoothing out the cycles in the utilities' equipment building programs, and discussed the qualitative reasons such cycles are generated, reaching conclusions to parallel this study.[44] Kisselgoff and Modigliani published an econometric analysis of private investment in electric power in which they hypothesized that the major factor controlling the rate of investment was an attempt by utilities to maintain the rate of utilization of their capacity at some optimum level.[45]

Other studies examine the investment in electric power generation facilities according to per capita income, and stress the income elasticity of demand for generating facilities which is apparent. Statistical summaries by Edwin Vennard[46] and N. B. Guyol[47] fall into this category. What is missing from all of these analyses is any estimate of the long-run price elasticity of demand for generating equipment.

---

[43] C. F. Roos and Victor S. Von Szelikski, "The Demand for Durable Goods," *Econometrica*, Vol. 11(2), April 1943.

[44] Edward W. Morehouse, "Regularization of Business Investment in the Electric Utility Industry," in National Bureau of Economic Research, *Regularization of Business Investment* (Princeton: Princeton University Press, 1954).

[45] Arram Kisselgoff and Franco Modigliani, "Private Investment in the Electric Power Industry and the Acceleration Principle," *Review of Economics and Statistics*, November 1957, pp. 363–379.

[46] Edwin Vennard, *The Electric Power Business* (New York: McGraw-Hill, 1962).

[47] N. B. Guyol, *The World Electric Power Industry* (Berkeley, Cal.: University of California Press, 1969).

John Vernon speculates that "in the long run, the demand for power plants may be inelastic to price,"[48] but others, including Philip Sporn,[49] Jules Backman,[50] and Guy Suits,[51] seem to disagree. On several occasions Philip Sporn has chastised the equipment manufacturers and utility executives alike, for forgetting the historical role of price in stimulating investment in the industry.[52] The magnitude of the investment which is required under alternative technologies, and, by implication, the price of that capital equipment, is a key variable in the models of John Vernon[53] and Paul MacAvoy,[54] concerned with the economics of nuclear power generation. The demand for replacement equipment, as well as equipment to serve the growth in electric power demand, is said to be price sensitive. Turvey presents a theory of optimizing the capital investment in generating facilities, and indicates how the timing of replacements of obsolescent equipment will be determined by the investment cost of new equipment.[55] However, none of these researchers offer empirical estimates of the price elasticity of demand for generating equipment.

Empirically, the most promising mode of analysis may be cross-sectional. MacAvoy estimates the demand for electrical generating capacity as a function of the average selling price of *electricity*, on a cross-sectional basis in different regions of the United States. He concludes that, whereas the income and population elasticities of the demand for generating capacity are less than 1.0, "the price effect is somewhat more pronounced, since the price elasticity of demand is 1.24."[56] Unfortunately, for our purposes, the price at which electrical energy is sold to the consumer is a sum of many operating costs to the utility, of which the generating facility capital costs (price) is only one component.

---

[48] John M. Vernon, *Public Investment in Civilian Nuclear Power* (Durham, N.C.: Duke University Press, 1971), p. 40.

[49] Philip Sporn, *Technology, Engineering, and Economics* (Cambridge, Mass.: The M.I.T. Press, 1960), Lecture II.

[50] Jules Backman, *The Economics of the Electrical Machinery Industry* (New York: New York University Press, 1962), Chapter 2.

[51] C. Guy Suits, "The Age of Energy," *Speaking of Research* (New York: John Wiley, 1965). Guy Suits was in charge of General Electric's corporate research and development activity.

[52] Philip Sporn, "Load and Load Growth Foundations," Citrine Lecture, British Electrical Power Convention, Torquay, England, June 18, 1963; reprinted in Philip A. Sporn, *Vistas in Electric Power* (London, England: Pergamon Press, 1968), Vol. 1.

[53] Vernon, *Public Investment in Civilian Nuclear Power.*

[54] Paul W. MacAvoy, *Economic Strategy for Developing Nuclear Breeder Reactors* (Cambridge, Mass.: The M.I.T. Press, 1969).

[55] Ralph Turvey, *Optimal Pricing and Investment in Electricity Supply* (Cambridge, Mass.: The M.I.T. Press, 1968).

[56] Paul MacAvoy, *Economic Strategy for Developing Nuclear Breeder Reactors*, Appendix C. But MacAvoy also notes that other studies of electric power demand suggest a lower price sensitivity, or even inelastic demand with respect to price changes. See: Carl Kaysen and Franklin Fisher, *The Demand for Electricity in the United States* (Amsterdam: North-Holland Publishing Co., 1962).

To sum up, there are opinions that many factors influence the long-run demand for generating capacity, but on the key question of the long-run influence of the price of the equipment itself, no hard estimates. I therefore apply some judgmental estimates of my own, building upon MacAvoy's results.

Tables 3.1 and 3.2 are composite balance sheets and income statements for the private utility industry in the United States. The prices that are

TABLE 3.1.
COMPOSITE BALANCE SHEET: PRIVATELY OWNED ELECTRIC UTILITIES
IN THE UNITED STATES, DECEMBER 31, 1969.
(In Billions of Dollars)

Assets	
Electric utility plant[a]	$83.7
Accumulated depreciation	18.7
Net electric utility plant	$65.0
Current assets	4.8
Net "other" assets	8.5
Total assets	$78.3
Liabilities	
Equity	30.9
Long-term debt	37.1
Current liabilities	6.9
"Other" liabilities	3.4
Total liabilities	$78.3

[a] Details of electric plant: production: steam		$25.1
	other	5.2
	total	$30.3
	transmission	13.9
	distribution	29.1
	construction in progress	7.7
	other	2.7
	total	$83.7

SOURCE: U.S. Federal Power Commission *Statistics of Privately Held Utilities in the U.S., 1969*, Tables 1 and 5.

analyzed have their major influence on the utilities' investment in steam electric plants, about $25 billion of the total $83.7 billion of assets represented by electric utility plant (see Table 3.1). About one third of the steam electric production investment or about $8 billion will represent turbine generators—but to be generous, assume that *all* of the production investment will be affected by a price change, to a degree which corresponds to the price of the turbine generators alone. The cost to the utility of this investment may be approximated by the depreciation charge on the assets, plus

TABLE 3.2.
COMPOSITE INCOME ACCOUNT: PRIVATELY OWNED
ELECTRIC UTILITIES IN THE UNITED STATES,
DECEMBER 31, 1969.
(In Millions of Dollars)

Electric utility operating revenues		$18,022	100.0%
Expense:	operating and maintenance[a]	8,304	46.1
	depreciation	2,011	11.1
	taxes	3,701	19.9
	total	$13,899	77.1%
Net operating revenues, electric utility operations		4,123	22.9
Net "other" nonelectric utility items		474	2.6
Total income before interest charges		4,597	25.5
Interest charges		1,401	7.8
Net income		3,195	17.7

ᵃ See Table 3.1.

the interest charge on the debt, plus dividend payments on the equity, or approximately $5 billion per year on total assets of $78 billion (see Table 3.1), or approximately 6.4 percent annually, on utility assets. If steam electric generating plant prices were dropped one percent, a crude approximation of the savings to the utilities would be 6.4 percent of 1 percent of $25 billion, or $16 million per year. If the savings were passed through completely to the consumer, utility operating revenues would decline from $18.022 billion to $18.006 billion, a reduction in electricity prices of .09 percent. According to MacAvoy's elasticity estimate, a one percent decrease in electricity prices would result in a 1.24 percent increase in kilowatts of generating capacity demanded. Under our extremely crude assumptions, this means that a one percent decline in steam electric plant prices, which would permit a .09 percent decline in electricity selling prices, would result in a .11 percent increase in the kilowatts of generating capacity demanded. In other words, the price elasticity of demand for electrical generating equipment is —.11 in the long run. This is a low elasticity. It is no surprise that manufacturers tend to avoid price-cutting if they can, preferring instead to stimulate industry demand through improvements in product technology.

The full benefits of a price cut are not immediately realized, of course. Utility generating plants have an approximate life of 40 years. However, capacity doubles every 10 years, so after 10 years of a new, lower price structure, one half of the utility asset structure may benefit from the lower level of prices. Thus, assume one half of the benefits are enjoyed after 10 years, or an elasticity of —.06 by year 10. Obviously, the impact upon demand of an equipment price cut is modest indeed. Both John Vernon and Charles Kilbourne are close to the practical realities when they speculate that the long-run price elasticity of demand for generating equipment is nearly zero. The demand equation of our model will not be jeopardized if price elasticity effects are ignored in the short run.

To the utilities, the important cost factor is not the original cost, but the fuel expense and the related operating costs, as the expense statements (Tables 3.2 and 3.3) illustrate. Once again, the importance of the *technology* of the turbine generator units, and the relative unimportance of the *initial*

TABLE 3.3.
DETAILS OF OPERATION AND MAINTENANCE EXPENSES,
PRIVATELY OWNED ELECTRIC UTILITIES IN THE UNITED STATES, 1969.
(In Millions of Dollars)

Steam power production:	fuel	$2,909	35.0%
	other	410	4.9
	maintenance	434	5.2
	total	$3,753	45.1%
Hydro, nuclear, purchased power expense		1,360	16.5
Total power production expenses		$5,113	61.6%
Transmission expense		263	3.2
Distribution expense		1,139	13.7
Customer accounts and sales expense		754	9.1
Administrative and general		1,034	12.4
Total electric operation and maintenance		$8,304	100.0%

SOURCE: Federal Power Commission, *Statistics of Privately Owned Electric Utilities in the United States, 1969*, Table 4.

price of the units, is emphasized. It is largely the gain in efficiency which permits the cost reduction which permits the price reduction of electricity, as hypothesized in Chapter Two.

Other Studies: Short-run and Interactive

There are two noteworthy short-run simulation models of generating equipment demand. One was built by Alexander Pugh, using industrial dynamics techniques.[57] Pugh's colleague, Jay Forrester, described the problem as follows:

> The curve of electric power consumption in this country is one of the smoothest time series in our economic life. At the same time the placing of orders for electric generating equipment . . . [is] a classic case of one of our most unstable industries.

> The equipment companies feel that the trouble arises primarily from the manner in which the utilities place orders for equipment. However, the

---

[57] Alexander L. Pugh, III, *Utility-Electrical Machinery Manufacturers Study*, Massachusetts Institute of Technology, School of Industrial Management, Memo D-437, August 20, 1962.

instability of the industry appears to require the interaction of: (1) Deferrability of demand for equipment at the utilities. (2) Variable advance ordering by the utilities in response to changes in procurement lead time at the manufacturer. (3) The technological nature of the product which requires a long manufacturing period, and the practice of the industry which stresses equipment that is designed and made to special order. (4) The practices of the electric utilities in load forecasting. (5) The existence of excess manufacturing capacity in the equipment supplying industry. (6) The time delays inherent in increasing and decreasing production rates at the manufacturers.[58]

Pugh built a model in the spirit of Forrester's remarks.[59] His objective was to determine how to overcome severe cyclicality in the manufacturing sector.[60] His model consisted of a utility sector and a manufacturer sector, with the demand for electric power as an exogenous input. The price discount on generator prices was determined by the number of the unprocessed orders at the manufacturer level, and whether that number was falling. Discounts were a linear function of backlogs expressed in years. At 0.4 years backlog, there is a zero discount; at zero backlog, 25 percent discount.[61]

According to Pugh, utilities order their new equipment based on their forecast of demand, the number of generators on hand, and the current price of equipment. Changes in price might affect either the size of the "pool" of potential orders, or the length of time which potential orders remain in this reserve pool (without being released to the manufacturers) or both. Price also influences the utilities' views concerning the desired margin of power generating reserves. The smallest margin of reserve considered safe by utilities is 15 percent. This margin may be increased if low prices prevail, thereby inducing utilities to order additional equipment.

Pugh concluded that orders for new generators fluctuated more violently than did the growth rate in demand for electricity, due to two phenomena: the forecasting behavior of utilities and variations in manufacturing lead time. The effect of varying manufacturing lead times was to increase variations in orders by as much as a factor of two over what they would be under constant lead times. Pugh's model was a good beginning. Its chief limitation was that the parameters seem to have been assigned judgmentally.

---

[58] Jay W. Forrester, *Industrial Dynamics* (Cambridge, Mass.: The M.I.T. Press, 1961), students' edition, pages 341–343.

[59] Alexander L. Pugh, III, *Utility-Electrical Study* (1962), and Alexander L. Pugh, III, *Turbine Utility Model*, Massachusetts Institute of Technology, School of Industrial Management, Memo D-589, April 26, 1963.

[60] Pugh, *Utility-Electrical Study* (1962).

[61] More precisely, the Pugh schedule of discounts is linear along one path between 0.4 and 0.1 years backlog, according to the equation discount = 20 percent minus (backlog in years × 50%), and linear along another path below 0.1 years backlog, attaining 25 percent discount at zero backlog. This is not a very realistic depiction of actual discounting behavior in this industry. It implies the manufacturers are content to operate with 0.4 years backlog. In fact, panic ensued when backlogs dropped below two years.

The Pugh model was further refined by Donald Mack, a General Electric engineer at Schenectady, New York. Mack observed:

> The traditional fluctuations are caused by a positive-feedback loop, in which the variable manufacturers' backlog is included in the lead time of the power companies' forecasts of their generating requirements. Modifications of the manufacturers' policies found to be effective in reducing the fluctuations are (1) determination of the desired manufacturing capacity on the basis of the power companies' forecasts rather than on orders already placed, (2) timing plant expansions so that manufacturing capacity stays below the ordering rate just enough to keep the backlog constant, and (3) quoting a fixed delivery time. Of lesser effectiveness are (4) discounts offered to the power companies to stimulate ordering when the backlog is low, and (5) a proposed system of manufacturing parts for inventory, to be assembled after receipt of an order.

Mack's forecasting time horizon was a critical variable.[62] Utilities' forecasts had to be sufficiently far into the future to encompass (1) the average delay by power companies in making their annual forecasts (assumed .5 years), (2) the power companies' delay in ordering (average of 1 year), (3) the delay of orders in the manufacturers' backlog (average of .5 years), and (4) the remaining time required for engineering, manufacturing, and installation of the generating units (assumed 3 years). The steady-state value of the total forecasting lead time was approximately five years. The incorporation of backlogs information into the forecasting time horizon was a major factor in inducing oscillations in industry orders.

Mack hypothesized that the release of orders from the "unordered pool" could be accelerated if the price was low enough. However, price did not affect the rate at which new equipments were added to the unordered pool, except via the circuitous route of influencing the forecasting time horizon.[63] Thus, only the *timing* of orders was price elastic.

Like Pugh, Mack's model lacked empirical calibration. Nevertheless, his simulations of alternative policies were illuminating. Both a "conservative" discount policy, and a "panic" discount policy reduced the amplitude of orders and backlogs oscillations. However, upon reflection, it appeared that neither policy represented very practical business advice, since: ". . . the eight percent discount would be offered and withdrawn so many times during these periods that misunderstandings between the manufacturers and power companies would almost certainly occur . . ." and backlogs would tend to "chatter" as prices swung back and forth. Furthermore: "Discounts cost money. . . . The conservative and panic discount policies cost the

---

[62] Donald R. Mack, "A Study of the Large Turbine-Generator Business Using Control Theory," a dissertation submitted in June 1969 for the degree of Doctor of Philosophy (System Science) at the Polytechnic Institute of Brooklyn.

[63] Mack, ibid., p. 68.

manufacturers 440.5 and 431.7 megadollars or 1.9 percent of their no-discount income sales revenue during the simulated twenty-year period."[64] Mack finally concluded that manufacturers should plan their factory capacity based upon utility forecasts of load, and not the utilities' actual equipment orders, in order to compress the time delays inherent in the system.

Mack also observed that the real source of instability was that utilities had *too much information* about manufacturers' backlogs, and that this "loop with a positive feedback" led to oscillations in the system. The remedy therefore was for manufacturers to stop reporting actual backlogs to the utilities, telling them instead that backlogs were a constant six months, and, surprisingly, this would actually come to be the eventual state of affairs. Mack called this the process of "making a statement come true, by stating that it was true."[65]

Underlying both the Pugh and the Mack studies was the industrial dynamics credo that oscillations are per se bad. Hence the goal of policy analysis is to dampen the oscillations, eliminate delays, and snip the feedback circuits. But one should hesitate before embracing policies aimed merely at smoothing out the waves. We shall see that the waves helped in the implementation of oligopolistic strategy.

SUMMARY

Turbine generator demand responds to changes in the utilities' anticipated growth in peak electric power loads. Orders for turbine generators tend to be bunched together, coinciding with periods of upward revision of expectations. While orders are cyclical, shipments are less so. Thus, backlogs of unfilled orders at the manufacturer level fluctuate. When backlogs become extended, additional orders are placed by utilities as a precaution to insure a place in the manufacturers' production schedules. Thus, orders beget orders in an unstable fashion.

Close communication among industry executives contributes to the forming of a consensus view. Increased interconnection among utilities also removes some of the perceived pressure for autarkic supply planning. The increased complexity of turbine generator design has lengthened the manufacturing cycle, and pushed the required forecasting horizon ahead by many years. All of these factors contribute to cyclicality.

The bandwagon psychology merits further comment. Managers of different utilities operating in different markets, with different weather patterns, should develop rather diverse and randomly varying expectations concerning future loads. While some uniformity of load growth is imposed upon all utilities by the state of the national economy, there is also great diversity

---

[64] Mack, ibid., p. 98.
[65] Mack, ibid., p. 27.

because of local conditions.[66] With no communication, it would be reasonable to expect a rather low correlation in utility expectations, and hence a somewhat smooth distribution of expansion plans, and turbine generator orders, over time. In fact there *is* extensive publicity and communication. The Federal Power Commission diligently collects and disseminates data, as does the Edison Electric Institute. The result is a sharing of expectations, leading to a common view and in the end, a follow-the-leader consensus. The result will be a periodic bandwagon rush. Any prophecy as to impending tight supply will tend automatically to be fulfilled. Thus, wide swings in the order rate have a psychological basis. We shall see in subsequent chapters, how these wide swings are translated into fluctuations in capacity planning, and in order prices.

---

[66] As evidence of this, there were remarkably large variations in the errors in actual versus forecast load growth by different regions of the United States, in forecasts in the 1964 Federal Power Commission *National Power Survey*.

CHAPTER Four   The Forecasting of Peak Loads

THIS CHAPTER WILL ANALYZE THE REASON for the cyclicality in turbine generator demand: the instability of utility management expectations. The results of the demand analysis of Chapter Three suggest that surges in orders for turbine generators arise, in part, through fluctuations in utility managers' forecasts of peak loads. Here it will be demonstrated that such forecasts tend to be shaped by the utilities' recent load-growth experience. That growth, in turn, depends upon many fluctuating factors, including the weather and the state of the economy. Continuing revisions of forecasts are necessary, and these revisions are highly correlated with turbine generator ordering spurts.

THE UNCERTAINTY OF GROWTH IN THE LONG RUN

The electric power industry seems to be one of the most consistent growth industries. Kilowatts peak load[1] growth is seldom below 7 percent annually. However, growth rates have actually varied by large amounts (see Chart 4.1).

---

[1] There are two common measures of the growth of power demand: peak load (in kilowatts) and energy output (in kilowatt-hours). Depending upon the "peakiness" of electricity demand over the year, peak loads may grow at a different rate from energy output. There has been a tendency for total energy production to increase at a faster rate than total peak loads, as loads have been smoothed over the year and over the day in most utility systems. However, since 1955, growth rates of peak kilowatts and kilowatt-hours have been similar. Peak loads occur at one instant during the year for each electric power system. The data examined in this study are the "noncoincident" peak loads for the entire United States electric power system. This is not the one-time peak load for the entire country; that figure is probably not known to anyone. Instead, the sums of the peak loads (whenever they occurred) of the individual utility systems are aggregated into the Federal Power Commission's figure for noncoincident peak load. This is the relevant variable for determining the utilities' needs for new turbine generator capacity, since it is the sum of the individual utilities' needs which are under examination here. As a determinant of the electrical generating capability which must be on hand, kilowatts peak load is the relevant demand variable.

CHART 4.1.   Capability and Peak Load Kilowatts, Total Electric Utility Industry
(Excluding Alaska and Hawaii).

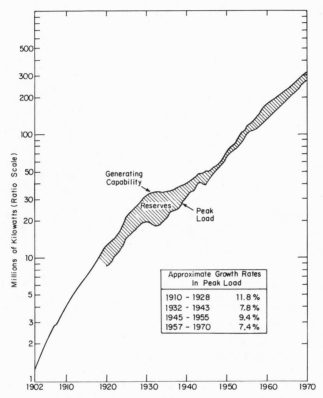

SOURCE: Edison Electric Institute Statistical Yearbooks.

Lack of knowledge of future markets is one source of long-range uncertainty. The utility industry has not grown twice as fast as the total economy, merely by serving its existing markets. There has been an incessant seeking of new markets. The first customers in lower Manhattan in 1882 used electricity for office building illumination only. By 1917, revenue from lighting had declined to 60 percent of the total, and power applications represented 35 percent of the total. Electric street railways represented about 5 percent of the 1920s total revenues.[2] During the 1930s, household appliances were a major source of load growth, plus the electrification of rural areas. The 1940s and 1950s saw a great expansion in industrial consumption of electric power. The 1960s were characterized by penetration of the space heating and cooling markets. Utility forecasters do not seem confident of their ability to predict the next markets to be conquered, and this is understandable.

---

[2] For a history of load growth in the early years, see: J. M. Gould, *Output and Productivity in the Electric and Gas Utilities, 1899–1942* (New York: National Bureau of Economic Research, 1946).

An important stimulant to long-term growth has been the steady price decline in electric power. The average price of electricity declined by one half over the 1902–1970 period, in spite of general inflation (see Table 4.1).

TABLE 4.1.
AVERAGE REVENUES PER KILOWATT-HOUR SOLD TO ALL CLASSES
OF CUSTOMERS, TOTAL ELECTRIC UTILITY INDUSTRY.

| Year | Cents per Kilowatt-Hour Average Revenue | |
	Current Dollars	Constant 1957–1959 Dollars
1902	3.36	10.68
1907	2.89	8.31
1912	2.48	6.71
1917	1.97	3.13
1922	2.54	4.91
1927	2.71	5.32
1930	2.66	5.54
1935	2.46	5.59
1940	2.06	4.40
1945	1.73	3.07
1950	1.81	2.18
1955	1.67	1.81
1960	1.69	1.67
1965	1.59	1.55
1970 est.	1.54	1.32

SOURCES: U.S. Department of Commerce, *Statistical Abstract of the United States*, 1930, U.S. Government Printing Office, for U.S. Census figures of 1902 through 1927. Edison Electric Institute, *Historical Statistics of the Electric Utility Industry*, New York, for 1930–1960 data and Edison Electric Institute *Statistical Yearbook for 1969*, for recent years. Constant dollar figures derived by deflating by the general wholesale price index.

In real dollar terms, prices have declined by one half since 1945. Forecasters sense that in the long run, demand for electrical energy is sensitive to the price of electric power relative to competing energy sources, and this has a deep impact on the pricing and technological response by utilities to their electric equipment suppliers.[3] "Intermediation" by the electric utilities in the energy market will be retarded if the utility industry cannot continue

[3] For a discussion of the "intermediation" role of the electric utilities in the supply of energy and the sensitivity of electric power demand to prices of competing energy sources see: J. C. Winger, J. D. Emerson, and G. D. Gunning, *Outlook for Energy in the United States* (Energy Division, The Chase Manhattan Bank, New York, October 1968). On the other hand, Fisher and Kaysen found that neither short-term nor long-term *residential* demand for electric power was price sensitive. For the *industrial* market, however, statistical evidence generated for 1956 indicated some price elasticity of demand. They also concluded, "Technological change was either neutral or acted to increase the importance of electricity for industry as a whole." (Franklin Fisher and Carl Kaysen, *A Study in Econometrics—The Demand for Electricity in the United States*, North-Holland Publishing Company, 1962). More recent econometric studies dispute the Fisher and Kaysen findings.

to offer relatively better energy values. In the past, technological advances in the product more than offset any inflation in the price of the utilities' capital equipment, permitting utilities to reduce prices, which in turn sustained their rapid growth. But forecasters cannot be certain that these accomplishments will continue.

Even though electrical energy price reductions characterized the past, the rate of reduction has steadily diminished. One can therefore understand the exhortation which pervaded many industry discussions of load growth. For example, Philip Sporn observed: "It is tempting to develop a feeling of confidence that substantially similar growth will continue in the future. But in an examination of the causes of the growth it is quite evident that many of the contributory factors to past growth have now disappeared, are disappearing, or have been substantially weakened. There is ample reason for concern that this growth may not continue."[4] Sporn lamented the "altogether too relaxed and non-probing attitude as to the likely future growth of the electric industry . . ." and expressed concern over the slowdown in the steady progression of price decreases which had stimulated demand in the past. The Federal Power Commission in its *National Power Survey* similarly noted that "in the face of increasingly strong competition from other energy industries, the electric power industry cannot afford to take its future growth for granted."[5] The Commission observed that the industry would have to develop new markets, such as the electric automobile, if it was to continue its historical trend.

In recent years, other developments have added to the uncertainty of utility load forecasting. Ecologists argue that growth must be discouraged. Fuel shortages and limitations on the siting of new plants create doubts as to the feasibility of expanding supply at the historical rate. And huge increases in fuel prices must now be passed through to the consumer.

The net result of this uncertainty as to the future course—or even the future feasibility—of load growth, was that planners confined their long-run extrapolations of electric power demand to the known, traditional markets. It is not surprising that long-term forecasts were nearly always biased toward the conservative; that long-range forecasts are perennially low. We have evaluated 54 long-term (10 or 15 years) forecasts of kilowatts peaks, or electrical energy consumption, or kilowatts capacity, for the United States electric utility industry. Overwhelmingly, the tendency has been to *under*forecast, often by huge amounts. This is true whether the forecaster is a utility executive, the Federal Power Commission, or an equipment manu-

---

[4] Philip Sporn, *Research on the Foundations of the Electrical Supply Industry: Load and Load Growth*, The Citrine Lecture, presented to the Fifteenth British Electrical Power Convention at Torquay, 18th June 1963.

[5] Federal Power Commission, *National Power Survey*, Part I (Washington, D.C.: U.S. Government Printing Office, 1964), Chapter Two, "Prospects for Growth."

facturer. The equipment makers have been *least* prone to err on the low side, and the Federal Power Commission has been *most* prone to underforecast long-term demand. (See Appendix 2.)

Partly because of this conservative bias in long-range forecasting, the utilities tend, on the average, to be in a perpetual "underforecasted" condition, with actual peak loads racing ahead of forecasts and outstripping the planned increments in supply. This tends to make for a taut market for electrical equipment. New equipment orders will be very responsive to each nuance of changing load-growth prospects.

Short-Run Fluctuations in Growth

Superimposed upon the longer term growth curve are year-to-year fluctuations in the growth of electric power demand, an additional source of uncertainty. Peak loads have increased by as little as 5 percent and by as much as 14 percent (see Table 4.2). An important determinant of such fluctuations was variation in the weather.[6] The growth of air conditioning shifted peak loads from the winter months to the summer, with increased demand sensitivity to "heat storms."[7] Fluctuations were also induced by cycles in economic activity, inasmuch as over one half of all electrical energy is used for industrial production.

How Utilities Forecast Short-Term Peak Loads

Given both this long-term and this short-term uncertainty in load growth, how do utilities forecast it? We have already determined that it is how the utilities *forecast* their short-term peak loads, and not actual peak loads, which has a direct bearing upon their cyclical ordering behavior. The forecasting task is obviously not simple. To ascertain just how difficult it is, a simple competition was run: three-year forecasts were simulated by projecting a simple exponential trend, and were then compared with the actual peak loads which were realized. The 1921–1970 exponential trend in national peak loads would have overforecasted peak loads for 1950–1953 and thereafter would have persistently underforecasted them. Average forecasting error would have been minus 4 percent and the maximum error an enormous 9 percent. Since utility reserves are only about 20 percent, this degree of error would have been serious indeed.

---

6 See, for example, Thomas and Drummond, "The Role of Weather in Load Forecasting," *EEI Bulletin*, August 1953; Clair and Einwechter, "How Philadelphia Electric Improves Accuracy of Daily Load Forecasting," *Electric Light and Power*, April 1968; Brosche, "Special Weather Forecasts Aid Utility Operation," *Electrical World*, August 14, 1967.

7 Summer versus winter peak loads are analyzed in: *Second Biennial Survey of Power Equipment Requirements of the U.S. Electric Utility Industry 1969–1978*, Power Equipment Division, National Electrical Manufacturers Association, New York, New York, February 1970.

TABLE 4.2.
ENERGY OUTPUT AND PEAK LOADS OF THE
U.S. ELECTRIC UTILITY INDUSTRY, 1946–1970.

Year	Energy[a] Output	Winter[b] Peak	Summer Peak	Change in Peak	Percent Growth Peak
1946	228	45.0	—	5.4	13.6
1947	260	49.6	—	4.6	10.2
1948	287	53.8	—	4.2	8.5
1949	296	56.5	—	2.7	5.0
1950	335	64.3	—	7.8	13.8
1951	378	70.4	—	6.1	9.5
1952	407	75.3	—	4.9	6.6
1953	449	81.1	74.6	5.8	7.7
1954	480	88.4	80.2	7.3	9.0
1955	554	101.1	91.1	12.7	14.4
1956	608	105.7	101.1	4.7	5.2
1957	638	110.1	110.0	9.0	8.5
1958	652	116.9	112.5	6.8	6.2
1959	720	125.4	125.3	8.5	5.0
1960	765	133.0	132.8	7.6	6.1
1961	800	140.7	141.0	8.0	6.0
1962	860	151.3	149.1	10.3	7.3
1963	922	161.3	159.5	10.0	6.6
1964	987	171.1	175.0	9.8	6.1
1965	1060	180.4	186.3	11.3	6.5
1966	1152	193.7	203.4	17.1	9.2
1967	1222	205.9	213.5	10.1	5.0
1968	1327	226.7	238.0	24.5	11.5
1969	1436	236.6	257.7	19.7	8.3
1970	1550	248.5	275.5	17.7	6.9

[a] Energy output in billions of kilowatt-hours.
[b] Peak loads in GW (GW = gigawatts = 1 million kilowatts).

SOURCE: *Semi-Annual Electric Power Surveys*, Electric Power Survey Committee of the Edison Electric Institute, and *Historical Statistics of the Electric Utility Industry*, Edison Electric Institute.

Not only this simple trend model was fooled. Charles Kilbourne, General Electric's manager of market research at Schenectady, observed that the utility industry experienced 12 years of rapid growth after World War II. When a slowdown in growth began in 1957–1958, it was difficult to perceive immediately whether the slowing was attributable to an unusually cool summer or a moderate winter, and not to an altering of the fundamental trend in the market. Utility organizations adjusted their expectations cautiously. However, "the second time that the peaks again fail to come up to expectations, one begins to wonder if this is a new consumption of electricity. By the time it happens three times in a row, you are pretty certain that a fundamental change has taken place."[8]

FORECASTING METHODOLOGY: SOME CASE HISTORIES

Clues as to forecasting methodology may be gleaned from the load fore-casting practices of four utilities over the 1950–1960 period.

Northern States Power[9]

Memoranda concerning kilowatts peak load forecasting at Northern States Power during the 1950s suggest that extrapolation of the historical exponen-tial trend was the basic technique. For example, Chart 4.2 shows the rather close correspondence of Northern Power's load growth to constant exponen-tial growth in three periods from 1910 to 1953, and a linear projection to

CHART 4.2.   Growth of Base Interconnected System Peak Loads, 1910–1963
(Northern States Power Company).

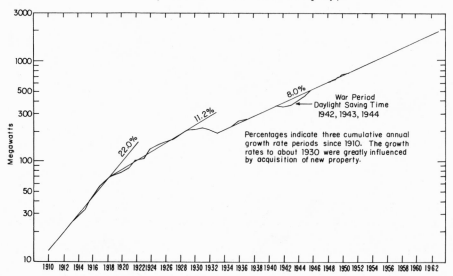

SOURCE: Exhibit material, Electrical Equipment Antitrust Actions.

---

[8] Testimony of Charles Kilbourne, taken from stenographer's minutes in the case of *Ohio Valley Electric* v. *General Electric*, 62 Civ. 695 (S.D.N.Y. 1963), p. 1,834.

[9] The information in this section is derived from documents on file at the U.S. Federal Court, Southern District of New York, in the matter of: *Responses of Plaintiffs Northern States Power Company and Northern States Power Company, In Cause No. 62 C 40 with regard to turbine-generator units and cause No. 62 with regard to power transformers, to Production of Documents as required by Pre-Trial Order No. 20,* Commonwealth Edison Company, et al., versus Allis-Chalmers Manufacturing Company, et al., in the United States District Court, Northern District of Illinois, Eastern Division, No. 61 C 1,277.

1963. The conversion of peak kilowatts *demand* into a schedule of required *supply* for the future, was fairly straightforward: about 15 percent reserves margin was targeted, taking into account the reserves which would remain should the very largest unit on the system suddenly fail. The load forecast, and the desired reserves position, defined the required increment in generating capacity each year (see Chart 4.3). The planning period was 10 years into the future. Forecasts from several sources were weighed: the predictions of consultants such as Stone & Webster, the forecasts of energy sales (kilowatt-hours) made by the operations department, and a range of possible growth rates extrapolated from history.

It was also necessary to retire plant capacity as it grew increasingly obsolescent. There was also uncertainty as to the amount of hydroelectric capacity available in any year, due to fluctuating water flows. In ordering its equipment, Northern States was highly conscious of the current manufacturing lead times for boilers and turbines. Estimated boiler and turbine generator lead times as of 1953, from one Northern States Power memorandum,[10] are shown in Table 4.3.

TABLE 4.3.
DELIVERY DATA: NORTHERN STATES POWER COMPANY
(As of September 1953).

Boilers	
Shipment after contract	20 months
Erection	10 months
Transit	1 month
Boil-out	1 month
Inquiry, bid and analysis	4 months
Total	36 months
Turbines	
Shipment after contract	22 months
Erection	7 months
Circulation, roll, etc.	1 month
Total	30 months

SOURCE: Commonwealth Edison v. Allis-Chalmers, 61 Civ. 1277 (No. D. Ill. 1963).

Authorization for an increase in capacity to meet the 1957 peak load was required from the Northern States board of directors as early as 1953. By the standards of the 1970s these lead times were modest—six to ten years would later become a common planning horizon.

---

10 Letter from H. H. Watson, vice president in charge of operation, Northern States Power Company, to B. F. Braheney, president, Northern States Power Company, dated September 28, 1953. Also, Memorandum from Seth N. Witts, system planning engineer, to Mr. Hibbert Hill, chief engineer, Northern States Power Company, dated March 28, 1956. National Exhibits introduced in the Electrical Equipment Antitrust Actions, all U.S. district courts. On file at S.D.N.Y.

CHART 4.3.   Generating Capabilities and Forecast of Peak Loads Based on Guaranteed Ratings (Northern States Power Company).

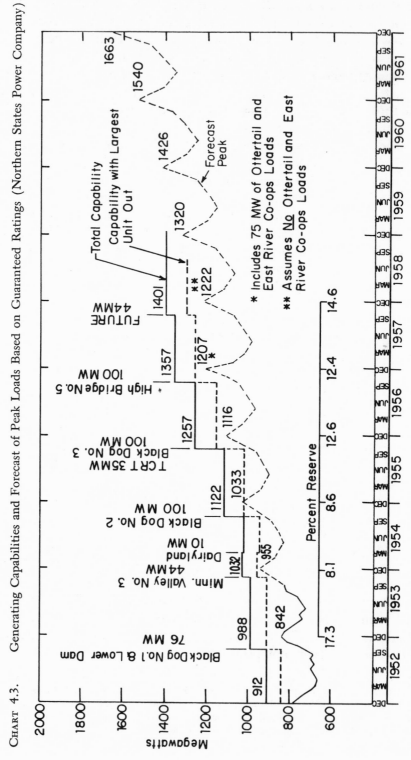

SOURCE: Northern States Power Company, Engineering Department, System Planning Section, September 3, 1953.

Connecticut Light and Power[11]

Memoranda concerning load forecasting at Connecticut Light and Power in the mid-1950s reveal a similar pattern.[12] The heart of the forecast was "a straight line increase" over a 20-year future period. Diverse contingencies which had to be considered included the possible necessity of supplying power to two small contiguous utilities. In addition, there was an attempt to judge the possible impact of several industrial plants switching to purchased power, away from self-generation of power. New large industrial loads (a possible steel mill) were the subject of speculation in the forecasts.

Consolidated Edison

Data concerning load forecasting at Consolidated Edison, of 1950 vintage, reveal an extremely simple forecasting method, tantamount to drawing a straight line with a ruler on a piece of ordinary graph paper, and projecting the historical trend five years into the future.[13] Neither this particular Consolidated Edison forecast nor the mid-1950s forecast prepared by Connecticut Light and Power allowed for exponential growth. Growth was expected to come in constant *kilowatts* increments in the next three or four years, and not at a constant percentage rate. The consequence would surely be to underestimate the growth in electric power demand.

Southern California Edison

More recent case histories suggest considerable advances in forecasting sophistication.[14] Southern California Edison provided a detailed example of a 10-to-30-year forecast. The distinguishing feature of the forecasting method was its concentration upon energy sales (kilowatt-hours), broken down by various consumer segments and using regression analysis to relate loads to gross national product forecasts and other economic variables. The sum of energy sales for all segments combined was then converted into a

---

11 The documents referred to in this section are contained in the Deposition and Exhibits of Sherman R. Knapp (president, Connecticut Light and Power Company), in all U.S. district courts in which Electrical Equipment Antitrust Actions are pending, New York, New York, January 10, 1964.

12 "Report on Estimated Load Increases (and) Additional Capacity Requirements to Meet the Estimated Load Increases, 1950–1970," by E. J. Amberg, Connecticut Light and Power Company, January 23, 1951. National Exhibit, Electrical Equipment Antitrust Actions, in all U.S. district courts.

13 "Five-Year Load Forecast" submitted to L. B. Bonnett, vice president, March 22, 1950, electrical litigation National Exhibit 4NX 185, contained in deposition of Gordon R. Milne, assistant vice president, Consolidated Edison Company, in Electrical Equipment Antitrust Actions, taken in New York, New York, January 6, 1964.

14 *The Methodology of Load Forecasting,* by Technical Advisory Committee on Load Forecasting Methodology for the National Power Survey (Washington: Federal Power Commission, 1969), Appendix A-3.

peak loads forecast, through applying the 10-year average ratio between kilowatt peaks and energy sales for the total system. Despite the greater sophistication of approach, the dominant feature was again an extrapolation of the recent historical trend; that is, a linear extrapolation. The forecasting record might therefore be expected to resemble that achieved under the less complex procedures which characterized the other three utilities many years earlier.

The four case histories revealed the great diversity of factors countenanced in the four-to-ten-year load forecast. Many of these factors related to the possible restructuring of franchise territories and to the interchange of power, which enormously complicated load forecasting for the individual utility. There was a noticeable tendency to accept the conservative outlook.[15]

How Utilities Forecast Peak Loads: Statistical Evidence

The four case histories suggest that load-growth *experience* probably dominates load-growth *forecasts*. This hypothesis may be subjected to statistical test, using aggregate forecasting data for the total United States utility industry.[16] The results confirm the hypothesis. (See Appendix 3.) Three-year forecasts were examined.[17] This was the approximate historical lead time which applied throughout much of the study period.

Two different propositions were tested. First, that utility organizations must expect their recent *percentage growth rate* experience to continue in the future. Alternatively, that they must expect their growth rate in *kilowatts per year*, to continue in the future. The latter characterized the Consolidated Edison and Connecticut Light and Power method of extrapolating load growth into the future. The former method seemed more typical of Southern California Edison and Northern States Power.

It seems that utilities would logically forecast a continuation of their percentage rate of growth. Utility loads have obviously grown exponentially in the long run. However, the statistical results demonstrate that utilities in the aggregate do *not* forecast exponential growth; instead, in three-year forecasting they make a linear extrapolation of their most recent load-growth experience. Forecasting load growth according to this rule results in con-

---

[15] Typical of the conservative bias in forecasting was a report to the Connecticut Public Utilities Commission, suggesting that load growth would follow an S-curve, and "it was impossible to tell just where along such an S-curve load growth now is." The strong suggestion was for a steady decline in growth in the future, however. "State of Connecticut Power Supply and Load," report submitted by utility representatives to the Public Utilities Commission, Connecticut, June 19, 1952.

[16] The source of utility load-forecasts data is the Edison Electric Institute *Semi-Annual Power Survey*, representing a summation of individual utility load forecasts.

[17] Another reason three-year forecasts are examined is due to the availability of data. However, three years provided a roughly suitable "release" timetable for utility orders of turbine generators. Plans for new capacity obviously stretched many years into the future, beyond three years.

sistent underforecasting of loads when actual growth rates are accelerating, and consistent overforecasting when actual growth rates are slowing down.

The results of this three-year load-forecasting behavior may be viewed in Chart 4.4. The utilities' load forecasts for 1952 and 1953 (made in 1949

CHART 4.4.   Perceived Forecasting Error and Updating of Three-Year Forecast.

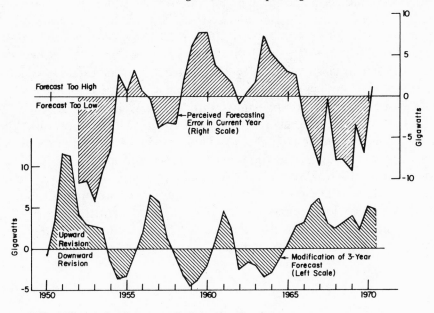

SOURCE: Edison Electric Institute compilations of utility forecasts.

and 1950) were too low by a wide margin—more than 10 percent. (The slow-growth environment of the 1930s continued to influence utility thinking for several years after World War II.) The rate of growth of utility loads declined after 1955, and gradually the utilities swung into a chronic *over*-forecasting condition. This became exaggerated in 1960, when the utilities overforecasted loads by more than 6 percent. From 1960 onward, the rate of growth of peak loads increased once again, and utilities gradually crept into an *under*forecasting condition once more, but, nevertheless, the earlier slow growth led to a dampening of equipment orders in the early 1960s.

How Utilities Update Their Load Forecasts: Statistical Results

We have also determined (in Chapter Three) that a second important determinant of turbine generator orders is the utility organizations' *updating* of their load forecasts. Again, using aggregate statistics of forecasts made by utility organizations in the United States, this "updating" behavior was analyzed.

The variable of interest is the amount of *modification* in the utilities' load forecast for the United States, as the forecast moves one year closer in time. It is the difference between the three-year-out forecast of peak loads, and the corresponding two-year-out forecast of peak loads, made one year later. Forecast revisions follow an adaptive control process. Utility organizations *revise* their forecasts by an amount which is correlated with the *degree of error* which their most recent actual experience tells them was built into their earlier forecasts. Specifically, the amount by which future load forecasts are revised, is a linear function of the difference between peak loads in the current year, and the forecast of those peak loads which was made some three years earlier (see Appendix 4). Their behavior follows a classical adaptive principle: modify your aim to the degree that your experience demonstrates that your aim has recently been off target.

Forecasters made very large *downward* revisions in their load forecasts in 1954, 1958, and 1963, all years which correlate with downward shifts in turbine generator orders (Chart 4.4). These might be termed years of maximum "disappointment." On the other hand, years of maximum "euphoria," perhaps, were 1956, 1960, and 1967, when forecasts were moved *upward* by large amounts. These were years when the immediate prospects for load growth began to look much greater than originally anticipated. And it is furthermore not surprising that it is under these circumstances that utility orders of new capacity are stimulated.

CHAPTER Five   Manufacturers'
Backlogs and Throughput

WE HAVE SEEN THAT BOOM FOLLOWED BY BUST characterizes the demand side of the turbine market. Now, the study turns to supply: to the manufacturers' response to these highly cyclical turbine orders. Of critical importance are the *time delays* in the system: first, the manufacturing delay—the time interval between the utilities' ordering of turbine generators and the manufacturers' shipment of that equipment to the utilities—and, second, the installation delay—the lag which occurs from the time the turbines are shipped from the factory until the equipment is finally installed in the generating station, tested, and ready to produce electric power.

MANUFACTURING DELAY

First, consider the delay from the time when an order enters a manufacturer's backlog, until the time of ultimate shipment. When a utility releases a turbine generator order or commitment, that order first enters the manufacturer's unfilled order queue or backlog, before any work is commenced. This queue is of variable length; backlogs tend to fluctuate widely. The actual building of the turbine will further contribute to the delay.

Unfilled Order Backlogs

The fact that a variable manufacturing queue was in operation may be seen clearly from Chart 5.1, which shows annual kilowatts of orders and annual kilowatts of shipments for the total industry over the 1945–1970 period.[1] Order rates were much more variable than shipment rates. The factories were motivated to stockpile orders so that they could better smooth their production rates. Furthermore, the utilities' actual needs for incremental

---

[1] Orders and shipments data, in kilowatts, have been derived from Edison Electric Institute reports, and from unpublished Association of Edison Illuminating Companies' data, obtained via the Electrical Equipment Antitrust Actions.

generating capacity were not as "lumpy" as their ordering behavior would indicate, and this also contributed to the stockpiling of orders.

The resulting fluctuation in "years of backlog" is shown in the lower curve plotted in Chart 5.1, a statistic computed by dividing total industry backlog (in gigawatts) by the total industry shipments rate (in gigawatts per year).

CHART 5.1.   Total U.S. Utility Turbine Generator Orders, Shipments, and Ratio of Backlog to Shipments.

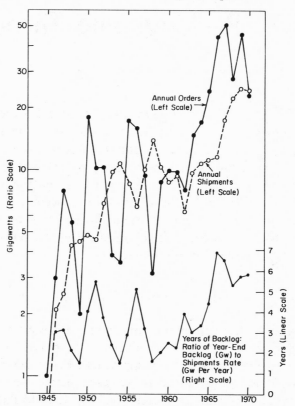

On three occasions, backlogs reached the reported "danger level" of 1.5 years at which actual work-in-process would begin to liquidate rapidly.[2] These were occasions for extreme alarm signals from the manufacturing organization to the marketing organization, signals which would lead to extremely competitive pricing.

___

[2] There are two alternative modes of specifying the magnitude of backlogs: gigawatts of backlog divided by current *throughput*, the statistic employed in Chart 5.1, and gigawatts of backlog divided by current manufacturing *capacity*, which is employed elsewhere in this chapter. The difference between the two measures is obviously the rate of capacity utilization. Both measures are useful indications of the degree of stress which is being imposed upon the marketing organization by the skimpiness or relative abundance of unfilled orders. Backlogs in years of *capacity* probably measure the severity of pressures more adequately, and are ultimately used in the price model of Chapter Seven.

CHART 5.2.   Total Industry Orders, Shipments, and Backlogs (Quarterly Data).

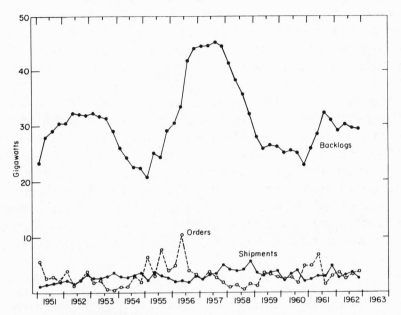

The backlogs phenomenon may be viewed in finer focus in Chart 5.2, which shows quarterly data on orders, shipments, and backlogs for the 1951–1963 period. Minor peaks and valleys in the order rate would accumulate to yield massive Alpine fluctuations of backlog. Shipments fluctuated as well, but the variations here were relatively modest. Thus "backlog buffering" absorbed the order rate cyclical shocks.

The stockpiling of orders was beneficial all around. The manufacturers were given a breathing spell in which to perform final engineering work on the units, consult with their customers concerning custom design features, and prepare production plans and workable engineering drawings. The average unit remained in backlog without any shop work being performed for about 18 months during the study period. Manufacturing efficiencies were thereby increased, last-minute scheduling panics were avoided, and costs were undoubtedly reduced.

The Manufacturing Lead Time

Once orders were drawn out of backlog and entered into the actual work cycle, further time was consumed by the required fabrication and assembly of the units. George Cox, marketing manager at General Electric, observed that the *total* elapsed time from order to shipment varied from a minimum of 11 months "almost to infinity."[3] The average order lead time for units

---

[3] George Cox, marketing manager for General Electric's Large Steam Turbine Generator Department, observed, "The average lead time has varied, but an average has been about two and a

ordered during 1952, from General Electric, Schenectady, for example, was 40 months.[4] John Peters, a marketing planner at General Electric, observed that for a typical order requiring shipment in 36 months, the first 18 months would be consumed with preliminary engineering design work and that the actual building of the unit would not be executed until the final 18-month period.[5] Daniel McLane of General Electric's marketing organization further explained that some of the components of a turbine generator, such as the machining of the forging for the generator field, had to be ordered from 12 to 14 months prior to the scheduled delivery date.[6] Another bottleneck was created by the fact that immense quantities of metal had to be removed from the forgings by time-consuming machining operations. One General Electric press release pointed out that a turbine rotor made from a 77-ton ingot, weighed only 22 tons after machining. Thus, 55 tons of steel were removed during lathe and milling operations on this one turbine part alone.[7]

Peters and Cox were describing large turbines built during the 1950s and

---

half years. This can be from a minimum of 11 months in which we have shipped a large steam turbine generator to a maximum of an almost indefinite time." (Testimony of George Cox, stenographer's minutes, *Ohio Valley Electric v. General Electric*, 62 Civ. 695, S.D.N.Y. 1963, p. 1,459.)

[4] "The average lead time in 1952 was computed by determining the shipment date for all units ordered from the General Electric Large Steam Turbine Generator Department in 1952, and then ascertaining the average lag between order date and shipment date. The average 'lead time' for all Schenectady-size units was 40.15 months, and for Schenectady-size cross-compound units, 35.78 months." (Plaintiffs' Post-Trial Brief, *Ohio Valley Electric v. General Electric*, 62 Civ. 695, S.D.N.Y. 1963, p. 103.)

[5] John Peters, a pricing specialist in General Electric's Large Steam Turbine Generator Department, observed,

> About 18 months before shipment we do some preliminary engineering work in order to purchase what we call limiting items. We [also] do whatever work is necessary to satisfy our customers' technical requirements, heat balance diagrams, engineering technical data, which we supply to our customers. As far as actual manufacturing, our lead times are predicted on the basis of what the time of shipment is and not on the date of the order. Now, this 18 months will depend upon different factors: the kind of unit that is involved, the availability of materials from our suppliers, our factory loading, we may want to advance machines in the schedule, and so forth. A generator which normally is to be built over three years could be obtained on an 18-month delivery.

(Deposition of John T. Peters, Electrical Equipment Antitrust Actions, in all U.S. district courts, New York, October 25, 1962.)

[6] According to Daniel McLane, of General Electric,

> The components of a large steam turbine generator take in the neighborhood of a year or more to produce—some of them. The field forging, or the rotating piece that goes in the generator, probably has to be ordered 12 to 14 months ahead of the time you are going to ship the turbine generator. And then in descending order of time other components have to be ordered. Then you have to schedule these things through the machine tools in your factory to be sure that they all meet at the subassembly and final assembly without any pieces missing so that you don't have enough to make a turbine generator.

(Deposition of Daniel J. McLane, Electrical Equipment Antitrust Actions, in all U.S. district courts, April 17, 1963.)

[7] "It Takes Time to Build Them," *Electrical World*, February 4, 1952, p. 23.

early 1960s, when a minimum delivery time of 18 months prevailed—although turbines could be delivered in a shorter period under emergency conditions. The estimated 18-month or 1.5-year minimum delivery time is significant; it meant that when the backlog of unshipped orders crept down to 1.5 years, the turbine factory was rapidly nearing a condition where work-in-process, as opposed to orders in the preparatory stockpiles, must dwindle. As the remaining unshipped orders were completed, machine tools and their operators would be idled, which had an immediate impact upon competitive behavior. When backlogs threatened to dip below 1.5 years, the management meetings became tense, alarm bells clanged in the sales department, and a general scurrying about for new business developed. This would inevitably lead to an undercutting of competitors' prices, in an attempt to rebuild backlogs. Backlogs, as measured in years of capacity or in years of throughput, were therefore an excellent indicator of the pressure being exerted upon the pricing decision makers in this oligopoly. It is not surprising, therefore (see Chapter Seven), that backlogs "pressure" was highly correlated with the degree of price-cutting in the marketplace, and this must be attributed to the organizational pressures exerted upon marketing management, responding to the load-scheduling needs of manufacturing management.

The Average Manufacturing Delay

The average manufacturing delay varied from year to year, because of the variable time delay of work in process, plus the variable time delay in the manufacturers' preparatory backlog. The number of years' delay between ordering and delivery was actually a frequency distribution, with a handful of orders being shipped in the same year as they were ordered, and other units not being shipped until as long as seven years after ordering (see Table 5.1). It is not surprising to notice that the longest *average* delay occurred with those batches of turbines which were ordered in years of high demand, whereas turbines were shipped most rapidly when they were ordered during years of lean demand.

A long "tail" on the frequency distribution of delivery times is evident. One unit ordered in 1956, for example, was not delivered until 1963. Some utility organizations were very cautious in advance ordering, while others were prone to panic when the backlog queue lengthened, or were prone to overestimate their load growth (and generating capacity needs), or were highly susceptible to supersalesmanship on the part of the manufacturers. Whatever the psychology, some utilities ordered far in advance of need. The consequence was a queue of variable length, as backlogs fluctuated in response to the periodic utility ordering spree.

The three competitors were far from equal in their ability to deliver turbines quickly, a fact which had deep competitive significance. In order to measure the average manufacturing time delay which was characteristic of

TABLE 5.1.
MANUFACTURING LEAD TIMES: TURBINE GENERATORS
(ALLIS-CHALMERS, WESTINGHOUSE, AND GENERAL ELECTRIC COMBINED).

Year Ordered	Number of Units Ordered	Number of Years to Delivery							
		0	1	2	3	4	5	6	7
1948	131	2	58	22	38	8	3		
1949	57	3	38	11	5				
1950	290	5	91	104	65	23	2		
1951	209	2	54	73	60	17	2	1	
1952	110		27	34	35	8	3	3	
1953	75		39	19	11	5		1	
1954	76	3	30	27	12	2	2		
1955	196	3	51	83	45	12	2		
1956	205	5	63	71	35	22	5	3	1
1957	74		25	13	23	7	5	1	
1958	33	2	15	9	6	1			
1959	63	1	21	29	5	6			1
1960	69	1	35	21	6	4	2		
1961	80	4	20	42	10	1	3		NA
1962	51	4	20	18	6	2	1	NA	NA
Totals	1719	35	587	576	362	118	30	9	2
Percent	100.0	2.0	43.2	33.5	21.0	6.9	1.7	0.5	0.2

SOURCE: Tabulated data on individual turbine generator orders, furnished by the manufacturers during the Electrical Equipment Antitrust Actions. File: U.S. District Court, New York. The data encompass both utility-sized and industrial-sized turbine generator units. "NA" indicates data not available.

each competitor, an analysis was conducted of the time delay for every turbine generator order (1,719 units) accepted by the United States manufacturers between 1948 and 1962, both large turbines and small, from both utility and industrial customers. This analysis is detailed in Table 5.3. The analysis is based upon the assumption that the frequency distribution of the time delay between order and delivery, for the individual firm, may be approximated by a Poisson distribution. The parameter "mu" of the Poisson distribution, which is the average years of delay, was then estimated for each firm, for each year, by use of the minimum chi-square method.[8]

[8] The discrepancy between observed and expected cell frequencies, according to the theoretical Poisson distribution, was tested with the chi-square statistic. Alternative "mu" parameters of the Poisson distribution were applied, and the chi-square statistic was minimized. See: W. F. Massy, David B. Montgomery, and Donald G. Morrison, *Stochastic Models of Buying Behavior* (Cambridge, Mass.: The M.I.T. Press, 1970), pp. 29–32. The fit to the theoretical distribution is a reasonable one. However, the distribution is not necessarily an exact description of the average delay times. The Poisson distribution assumption may be challenged through the lack of independence of the "arrival" at the shipping dock of each turbine generator unit; if one unit is accelerated through the factory, another unit may be delayed, and the arrival times may not be independent. See: Frank A. Haight, *Handbook of the Poisson Distribution* (Los Angeles: University of California, 1967).

Each competitor in the turbine generator market was seen to have a unique *average* delay. And the *variability* of this shipments delay was also unique to each firm. The average delay ("Mu") estimated by this procedure is shown in Table 5.2. General Electric had an average delay of 1.99 years

TABLE 5.2.
AVERAGE MANUFACTURING DELAY AND AVERAGE YEARS OF BACKLOG.

Average Manufacturing Delay		
Value of "Mu" for the best-fitting Poisson distribution fitted to years of shipments delay, using the minimum chi-square technique, 1948–1962.		
	Average Delay in Years (Mu)	Variability of Delay (SD of MU)
General Electric	1.99	0.29
Westinghouse	1.99	0.40
Allis-Chalmers	2.03	0.43

Average Years of Backlog		
At mid-year, 1948–1962, total kw backlog divided by total kw of manufacturing capacity as estimated by Ford, Bacon & Davis, consulting engineers, in the electrical litigation.		
	Average Years	Variability of Backlog (SD of Years)
General Electric	2.46	0.86
Westinghouse	2.29	1.03
Allis-Chalmers	1.59	0.66

NOTE: SD = Standard Deviation.

for orders taken in the study period. The comparable delay for Westinghouse was the same, 1.99 years, but Allis-Chalmers had a slightly higher average delay: 2.03 years.

The variance of the time delay was smallest at General Electric, and highest at Allis-Chalmers. It seems logical to assume that the delay between time of order and time of shipment might be related to the backlog situation of the firm, and the analysis proceeded under this assumption.

The average *years* of *backlog* for each competitor is shown in Table 5.2. Over 1948–1962, General Electric had the *highest* average backlog relative to its manufacturing capacity (2.46 years), Westinghouse was in an intermediate position (2.29 years), and Allis-Chalmers the lowest average backlog (1.59 years). Thus, Allis-Chalmers' longer average shipping time cannot be attributed to its higher average backlogs relative to the other two firms, but must be inherent in its manufacturing process or in the nature of its customers' ordering behavior.

Yet another complication is the fact that average delays which are estimated on the basis of *units* will tend to be lower than average delays computed for each firm on the basis of *kilowatts* of generating capacity. This is because large, complex turbine generators take longer to design and build than do small, standardized turbine generators. Thus, it is not surprising that an alternative "cut and try" attempt to find the best-fitting delivery delay, using aggregate kilowatts data, resulted in an average delay of slightly over two years for all turbine generator capacity. (This result tends to confirm Cox's estimate of an average *large* turbine delivery lag of 2.5 years.)

It was further hypothesized that, due to the secular increase in turbine generator technological complexity, manufacturing lead times might have gradually increased over 1948–1962, but this hypothesis was not supported by the data. (The truly phenomenal delivery delays which characterized the start-up of the nuclear era, in the late 1960s, were experienced subsequent to the data at hand, and may be attributed to technological bottlenecks in the steam supply system rather than in turbine generator manufacturing.)

Statistical Estimation of Factory Throughput: Individual Competitors

The time lag between orders and shipments is obviously not constant. In sum, it is subject to the varying risk attitudes of the utilities, as manifested in their tendency to order far in advance of immediate need. The time lag was further subject to the influence of the unique manufacturing equipment and organization of each competitor. Differences in the shipment delay over time, and among firms, may be attributed to (1) differences in the mix of customers' desired delivery dates, (2) differences in the ability of the firm to adjust their throughput rate in response to a heavy orders backlog, combined with the fact that some firms can build turbines faster than others.

It is conceivable that the first factor, that is, the degree to which customers, in their bandwagon fashion, periodically rushed to place orders at the factories for extended future delivery, was the major determinant of variable shipping delays. Furthermore, differences among competitors in this respect might just demonstrate the comparative skill of each competitor's marketing organization in selling their clients on the idea that they should order well in advance of need, and not differences in the utilities themselves. Differences attributable to the other factor, inherent manufacturing speed and flexibility, may be estimated by a regression analysis of "mu," the average shipments delay, as a function of the number of years of backlog at the time of order, for each firm (see Table 5.3). The residual or unexplained variance may be attributed to the first factor noted above.

The results of this analysis are illuminating. General Electric's average shipments delay of 1.99 years was apparently not influenced by the length of its backlogs. In other words, for General Electric, the estimated "mu" for each year was not correlated with the years of backlog which prevailed

TABLE 5.3.
REGRESSION RESULTS: AVERAGE MANUFACTURING DELAY.

Data: Estimated value of "mu" derived by fitting a Poisson distribution to the individual unit delays, 1948–1967 (Tables 3.2 to 3.4), via the minimum chi-square method. Years of backlog at mid-year of each year, for the individual firm, derived by dividing mid-year total kilowatts backlog by the current kilowatts annual manufacturing capacity of the individual firm, 1948–1962.

Description of Variables:

$$MU\ (I, T) = \text{parameter of the Poisson distribution for the Ith firm's shipments of orders received in year T.}$$

$$YBL\ (I, T) = \text{years of backlog of Ith firm in year T.}$$

Regression Results:

(a) General Electric: $R^2 = .10$ SEE $= .29$

$$MU\ (I, T) = 1.72 + 0.11\ YBL\ (I, T)$$
$$(t = 1.08)$$

(b) Westinghouse: $R^2 = .40$ SEE $= .33$

$$MU\ (I, T) = 1.43 + .25\ YBL\ (I, T)$$
$$(t = 2.45)$$

(c) Allis-Chalmers: $R^2 = .30$ SEE $= .38$

$$MU\ (I, T) = 1.45 + .36\ YBL\ (I, T)$$
$$(t = 2.1)$$

in that year. Throughput was adjusted according to backlogs, keeping the average delay constant. Allis-Chalmers, on the other hand, appeared to have the maximum sensitivity of its shipping delay to the length of the backlogs queue (the coefficient of the years backlog statistic was equal to .36). Westinghouse was in an intermediate position, with a statistically discernible sensitivity of shipping delay to backlogs, but not to the same degree as Allis-Chalmers.

These statistical results are evidence of the marketing and manufacturing scheduling and delivery advantages which accrue through scale. General Electric had the marketing capability to keep its average backlogs queue longer than the queue of either of its competitors. Furthermore, regardless of the length of that queue, General Electric's work flowed steadily through the shop with a relatively uniform speed or constant delay.

Allis-Chalmers was at the other extreme. It had the smallest average backlog, and when its backlogs climbed, so, inevitably, did its average delivery time. Allis-Chalmers' delivery delays were not only *more variable*, on the average, they were also *longer*, on the average. Uneven work flows are probably the inevitable consequence of being a small-scale competitor in a cyclical market, where business was acquired in a relatively few, discrete chunks. The marketing disadvantage to Allis-Chalmers would be great, since utilities placed a premium upon assured delivery to meet their projected peak loads. The manufacturing cost disadvantages would also be great, due to the "peakiness" of orders and the unevenness and uncertainty of factory work flows. With scale of operations there would accrue efficiencies of work flow, through smoothing of work schedules. Such smoothing would not be feasible at a very low volume of output. Lumpy throughput was attended by a manufacturing cost disadvantage, and these two factors alone could explain why Allis-Chalmers faded from the struggle in late 1962.

The statistical results demonstrate yet another interesting fact: the average delivery performance of the industry as a whole would be determined by the market shares of the three firms, because of the distinctive delivery response of each firm. As Allis-Chalmers' share of orders climbed, the industry's average delay would also climb.

An Aside: Modeling of Shipments

These results were incorporated into the final model of the utility-manufacturer system, for use in simulation analysis of the system. In the model, the kilowatts shipments of the ith firm in period t was computed according to:

$$S(i, t + n) = P(i, t, n) \cdot O(i, t)$$

where $O(i, t)$ equals the kilowatts orders of the ith firm in period t, and $S(i, t + n)$ equals that portion of $O(i, t)$ which is shipped n periods later. $P(i, t, n)$ is the Poisson probability which applies to firm i, in period $t + n$, calculated according to:

$$P(i,t,n) = \frac{mu(i,t)^n}{n! \; e^{mu(i,t)}}$$

where the parameter $mu(i, t)$ is defined according to the regression equation:

$$mu(i,t) = a_i + b_i \left[\frac{\text{kilowatts backlog } (i,t)}{\text{annual kilowatts capacity } (i,t)} \right]$$

In the simulation, therefore, the time spread of shipments which attends each batch of orders at each firm will be determined by the backlog and capacity situation of each firm when its orders were originally received.

INSTALLATION DELAY

Before a turbine generator can deliver electrical energy into the utility's transmission and distribution network, it must be erected and tested at the power plant site. This also consumes time, a secondary delay beyond that which attends the manufacturing of the turbine generator itself.

The turbine installation delay was important, because usually it was the turbine generator, and not the other power plant components, which was the bottleneck component determining how quickly a new power station could be brought to on-line status. For example, John P. Yates, executive vice president of Bechtel Corporation, noted that design and construction of power stations could be accomplished in 18 to 20 months under "forced draft," but that 2 to 4 years were normal. Primarily, it was the turbine generators which were the critical lead-time item.[9] Once a turbine had been shipped from the manufacturer's plant, between six months and a year and a half would elapse before the turbine achieved on-line status, according to Charles Kilbourne, manager of marketing research and administration at General Electric.[10]

Data on manufacturers' kilowatts shipments and on utilities' kilowatts additions to generating capacity were inspected to determine the average delay from time of delivery to on-line generating status.[11] Statistical analysis (see Appendix 5) suggests that additions to on-line generating capacity lagged behind manufacturers' shipments by six to nine months. From Chart 5.3 a one-year lag is apparent in annual data on shipments versus additions to generating capacity.

There was a noticeable tendency for the lag to increase in the late 1960s when manufacturer backlogs increased phenomenally, and when construction snarls, delays in the installation and licensing of nuclear plants, and nuclear pressure vessel problems caused start-up delays far in excess of historical experience—but this episode is outside of the time frame of this study. An average six-month delay was used in the final simulation model.

---

[9] "Design and construction under forced draft has been done in 18 or 20 months. At times when deliveries are slow, it sometimes.takes three or four years. It also varies with the size of the plant. It is a complex question." (Deposition of John Perry Yates, executive vice-president, Bechtel Corporation, Electrical Equipment Antitrust Actions, in all U.S. district courts, January 29, 1964.)

[10] Charles Kilbourne of General Electric observed,

> Our shipping time precedes the summer peak or winter peak [of the utility] by the erection period which the utility may need to get that machine from the received state after we have shipped it to the on-line state where they can use it. This is in the order of magnitude of six months, sometimes a year or a year and a half, depending on the particular utility, their erection schedules and their pressure that they put on getting the machine in service.

(Stenographer's minutes, Ohio Valley v. General Electric, 62 Civ. 695 (S.D.N.Y. 1963), pp. 1,839–1,840.)

[11] The data analyzed are quarterly kilowatts shipments, as derived from the Edison Electric Institute, and from the manufacturers' data directly, obtained via the Electrical Equipment Antitrust Actions. Annual increments to on-line generating capacity are as reported in the Edison Electric Institute's *Statistical Yearbook*, various years from 1950 through 1971, including early unpublished data obtained from EEI library in New York.

CHART 5.3.   Comparison of Manufacturers' Shipments and Additions to Utility
               Generating Capacity: Steam Turbine Generators for U.S. Utilities.

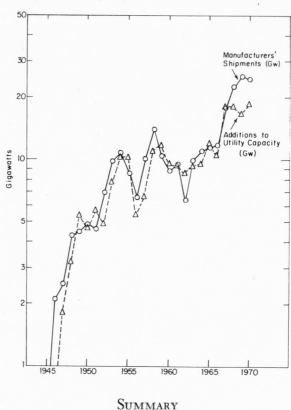

SUMMARY

In building a model of the power industry system, it is necessary to explain
the behavior of order backlogs, so that one may relate total industry orders
to total industry shipments. Total industry backlogs are modeled as being
the sum of the backlogs of Westinghouse, General Electric, and Allis-
Chalmers, variables which are in themselves important in explaining competitive zeal. Total industry shipments are likewise the sum of individual
firms' shipments. Orders trickle through the factories with a variable or
distributed delay. General Electric, Westinghouse, and Allis-Chalmers each
responded in unique fashion to the backlogs pressure upon them.

General Electric, it appears from the statistical results, had the most
flexibility in internal scheduling—the most "rubbery" production schedules
over the period of study. General Electric's backlogs were *not* correlated
with its manufacturing delay. Through having the largest scale of operations,
and given its apparently superior manufacturing resources, General Electric
was able to schedule a relatively smooth flow of orders through its shops.
When backlogs climbed, output would respond accordingly. Thus, Gen-

eral Electric could offer both faster and more predictable delivery than its competitors, which was a significant competitive advantage.

The Westinghouse manufacturing organization was comparable to General Electric in terms of its *average* delivery delay, over the period studied. But Westinghouse apparently had less inherent capability to maintain an unwavering delivery schedule, regardless of the magnitude of its backlogs. As a result, Westinghouse backlogs were correlated with its average manufacturing delay. Westinghouse would offer relatively fast delivery when its backlogs were low, but when backlogs were heavy—and this tended to occur for all competitors simultaneously—then Westinghouse's quoted delivery times would stretch farther into the future than did General Electric's. This would be a competitive disadvantage for Westinghouse at the height of a boom in utility orders.

Finally, Allis-Chalmers was least able to smooth its internal factory work flows. Delivery times quoted would depend very much upon the current backlog situation. Its scale of manufacturing operations permitted only modest production scheduling flexibility. Work would tend to come through the Allis-Chalmers' shop in large lumps. Costs would, as a consequence, be high, the marketing disadvantage extreme.

Another delay occurs between the time of shipment of the turbine generator units and their on-line availability. Because of these various delays, utility organizations would not have new generating capacity available until three and a half years after they placed their order. One corollary was the need for utilities to forecast peak loads at least three years in advance. Chapter Six will examine the procedures of utility generating capacity planning in more detail, to round out this analysis of turbine generator supply.

CHAPTER Six   Utility Generating Capacity and Reserves

WITH A CHARACTERISTIC DELAY, each manufacturer eventually delivers, and installs, the new generating capacity which utility organizations have ordered. However, this is only the first stage of the system. Equally critical, in the workings of the total system, is the supply of electric power to consumers. This chapter describes the utilities' planning of their generating supply.

THE TARGETING OF UTILITY GENERATING RESERVES

In planning their electric power supply capability—their generating capacity—utility organizations must build into their plans a certain excess of supply. Maximum generating capability, with all units operating, normally exceeds the utilities' peak load by a margin of 15 percent to 25 percent.

The Necessity of Generating Reserves

The necessity of having such a margin of supply capability, above expected demand levels, is perhaps self-evident. Several motivations are at work. Consider, for example, the 1970 reserves situation of electric utilities in the United States for the critical month of December: At that time, the "gross margin" of generating capability over peak load in the contiguous United States was 36.4 percent of peak loads.[1] The estimated annual gross margin for the whole of 1970 (that is, the relationship between peak loads and generating capability when each region within the country was measured at its own annual peak, whether winter or summer) was a much slimmer 18.4 percent.[2]

---

[1] Industry conventions as to whether to express margins as a percent of peak loads, or as a percent of generating capability, apparently varies. In the 1970 data cited, gross margins are expressed as a percent of peak loads.

[2] *1970 Year-End Summary of the Electric Power Situation in the United States*, December 31, 1970, Edison Electric Institute.

This 18.4 percent gross margin figure is a measure of the utilities' reserves of generating capacity available to meet: (a) unscheduled "outages," (b) scheduled "outages," (c) uncertainties of load growth, and (d) uncertainties in capacity expansions.

Reserves for *unscheduled outages* are the most obvious need. Unscheduled outages are random failures and accidents in generating (and transmission) equipment, which remove units from service. During the 1940s and 1950s, the "forced outage rate" for generating equipment on individual utility systems was generally below 2 percent (equipment not available due to unscheduled shutdown 2 percent of the time), whereas forced outage rates for the 1,000 megawatt and larger units placed into service during the late 1960s were expected to be 5 percent and higher, even after a two-year shakedown period. The very largest base-load unit often represents 10 percent to 15 percent of a utility's total capacity; should it fail in service there must be adequate stand-by capacity to pick up that amount of load.

Reserves for *scheduled outages* are necessary if maintenance work cannot be accomplished in the off-peak season. On the average, base-load boiler-turbine generator units require about one month of scheduled maintenance work each year in order to assure a long life and continued high reliability operation.[3]

Reserves for *uncertainties of load growth* are also necessary. Chapter Four analyzed the load-forecasting track record of United States utilities, using aggregate EEI *Power Survey* data. Errors of from 4 to 5 percent in the 3-year peak loads forecast have been fairly common in the past; with utility reserves margins of only 18 percent, an error of even 5 percent on the low side would cut into almost a third of planned reserves margin.

Finally, utility system planners must allow some margin for *misestimating future generating capabilities*. In the past, this was apparently not considered to be a grave source of misjudgment, but delays in digesting new technologies (both nuclear and conventional), delays in receiving licensing approval for nuclear plant operation, delays in construction, and extended "shakedown" periods for the very large new turbine generators, even after installation, have combined to disrupt forecasting confidence levels. Furthermore, as the time delay to place new capacity on-line stretches out in years, the year and the month of final availability have become more difficult to predict.[4]

Clearly, only the most astute planner will be fortunate (or lucky) enough to meet his planned reserves margin precisely. The penalties for underestimating required reserves can be, at the extreme, such spectacles, which oc-

---

[3] Federal Power Commission, *National Power Survey* (Washington, D.C.: U.S. Government Printing Office, 1964).

[4] As recently as 1964, the Federal Power Commission asserted, ". . . four years . . . represents the usual time for planning and construction of generating capacity . . ." but double this time period is probably more relevant for the late 1970s and capabilities forecasting errors are bound to multiply as a consequence. (*National Power Survey*, Vol. I, p. 195.)

curred during 1970 and 1971,[5] as Consolidated Edison pleading with its consumers in New York City to reduce their intake of power or, at the extreme, "load shedding," which is a euphemism for cutting off the power. The penalty for overestimating reserves requirements is temporarily excess capacity, the burden of which might not seem to be crushing to the utility managers, with their guaranteed return on capital. However, excess capacity is a condition which utility managers would prefer to avoid since huge amounts of capital would be tied up, unproductively, which might provoke rate-base questions from the regulatory agencies. Furthermore, utility managers of the recent past, with their engineering penchant for load growth, did not like to incur the cost penalty of carrying extra capacity. Finally, the rate of increase of power demand kept the system planners, engineers, and financiers busy even in the slackest of demand environments; they would not normally seek to accelerate their work load further by building far in advance of need. Thus, utility managers planned to build sufficient capacity to yield adequate reserves, but no more than that.

There are cushions which may soften the impact of underestimating one's reserve requirements. Two principal cushions are the deferred retirement of obsolescent capacity from service, and the purchasing of power from neighboring utilities. Unfortunately, since utilities tend to purchase their incremental capacity *en masse*, and are subject to similar load-growth patterns in any one part of the country, shrinkage in available reserves tends to be experienced by all adjacent utilities in unison, which decreases the opportunities for very large-scale borrowing from one's neighbors.

Targeted Reserves and Forecasting Error

The actual reserves position of utility organizations at any point in time is the result of the combined actions of three variables:

(1) its *targeted* reserves position; the kilowatts margin it was striving to maintain between peak loads and generating capability;

(2) its peak loads forecasting error, which will cause reserves to be greater or less than planned for; and

(3) its error in forecasting its generating capability.

Appendix 6 is an examination of this relationship. One may infer from

---

[5] See, for example, "One-Third of New York's Subways Halted as Power Shortage Hits Northeast U.S.," *Wall Street Journal*, July 29, 1970; "An Appeal to Reason," advertisement by Charles F. Luce, Chairman of the Board, Consolidated Edison Company of New York, in *Wall Street Journal*, August 7, 1970; "Utilities Cut Voltage on Sizzling East Coast But Rain Eases Pinch," *Wall Street Journal*, July 30, 1970; "Face to Face with the Power Crisis," *Business Week*, July 11, 1970; "U.S. Facing Its Darkest Hour," *The Star*, Johannesburg, Wednesday, June 17, 1970; "FPC Chief Sees More Power Cuts," *The New York Times*, July 28, 1969; "Talk of Power Crises Called 'Sheer Nonsense' by Trade Officials Group Official," *Wall Street Journal*, January 15, 1970.

an examination of actual peak loads forecasting errors, and generating capability forecasting errors, what the trend in the desired peak loads seems to have been. (The basic assumption is that forecasted reserves three years into the future is an approximation of where utilities want to be.) Surprisingly, utility organizations appear to have been striving to *increase* their reserves margin over the long run. This is contrary to views in some quarters, such as the Federal Power Commission, which has argued for a slimming of reserves margins in the long run. Utility managements, confronted with rising expectations of customers concerning standards of service, an increasingly demanding public, and knowing well the consequences of power interruptions in an electric-power-based economy, have increasingly attempted to widen the safety margin of their operations. In many years, these goals were not attained, because of load or capabilities forecasting errors; nevertheless, the long-term trend in the utilities' desired position is strongly evident. One consequence is to further stimulate primary demand for power generating machinery.

Load forecasting errors have already been studied in depth in Chapter Four; suffice to say, the long-term trend is for utility organizations to underforecast peak loads, and the short-term trend is for very cyclical overforecasting and underforecasting of peak loads.

Capabilities forecasting is the other topic to consider.

Utility Forecasts of Generating Capability

Utilities forecast both peak loads and their capability to meet those loads: their future on-line generating capability. Generating capabilities forecasting is really a summary of the utilities' own scheduled increases in production capacity. Errors in these forecasts are one key factor in determining whether the ultimate reserves of the utilities are ample or tight.

The utilities' forecasting *behavior*, and their forecasting *track record*, are observable in the EEI[6] *Semi-Annual Power Survey*, which contains forecasts of generating capacity for the total United States, built up from the forecasts of generating capacity by individual utilities. Chart 6.1 shows the utilities' forecasts of generating capacity increases made during the years 1949–1970. This chart also shows the forecasting track record: usually, the forecasts were for *less* capacity increase than actually occurred. Thus, the forecasting had a conservative bias.

Statistical analysis (Appendix 7) suggests that utilities forecast their increase in generating capability in proportion to the level of outstanding backlogs of unshipped orders at the turbine manufacturers. This result is eminently reasonable; the utilities forecast to have on-line and in-service what they know to be already on order with the turbine builders.

---

[6] EEI denotes the Edison Electric Institute, the private utilities' trade association.

CHART 6.1.   Utilities' Track Record in Forecasting Their Generating Capability
Three Years into the Future.

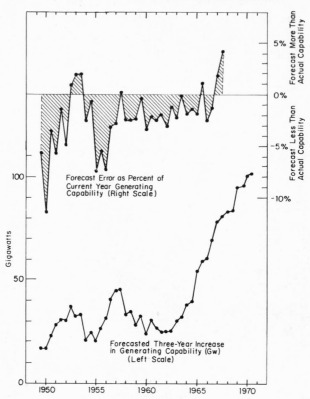

SOURCE: Edison Electric Institute data.

    While this is clearly *how* the utilities tend to predict their future gen-
erating capacity, what is less easy to understand is the poor forecasting
accuracy which such behavior leads to. Errors in the vicinity of 5 percent
of current capacity have been common, and given total reserves equal to only
15 percent or 20 percent of current capacity, an error of this magnitude
could create a precarious reserves position for the utilities. Now, in contrast
with the problem of forecasting peak loads or market demand, the forecasting of supply (three-year on-line generating capacity) should be child's play.
The capabilities forecast is based upon the utility's construction schedule.
The utility has most likely ordered its turbine generating equipment, and
power station planning must be well under way. If there are large deviations
from planned capacity only three years in the future, this would be unusual.
Nevertheless, sizable deviations from forecast do occur regularly, despite
pleadings and chastizing from the EEI statisticians who oversee the collec-
tion of these data. EEI minutes suggest that one reason for capabilities fore-

casting "errors" is a deliberate slowing down of capacity expansion plans in periods of sluggish load growth.[7]

A review of the historical forecasting record (Chart 6.1) shows that for only two brief periods between 1952 and 1970 were actual generating capacities less than forecasted. On the average, actual capability was about 2.5 percent *more* than it had been forecasted to be. When the utilities forecasted a very *large* increment in added generating capacity, they tended to forecast more than they actually put into service; contrariwise, when they forecasted a small increment in capacity, they would tend to be too conservative and forecast less than the actual capacity put into service. The latter was the typical case.

Since utilities (in the EEI survey) so seldom were caught with less capacity than they had forecasted, one might conclude that power shortages were unheard-of over this period. This would be a premature conclusion. Utilities indeed tended to underestimate their capacity additions, but they also tended to underestimate demand growth. Whether the net effect of these two forecasting biases resulted in perennially slim reserves, or fat reserves, remains to be examined.

The Impact Upon Utility Reserves Margins

Utility reserves margins consist of what generating capacity is left over after the utility's planned reserves have been buffeted about by miscalculations in load forecasting and errors in predicting when their new construction would be completed. It is thus the end result of load forecasting error, capabilities forecasting error, and targeted reserves margins. From time to time margins will become eroded, and, at other times, reserves margins have been grossly inflated. For example, testimony by Lindseth of Cleveland Electric Illuminating[8] and by Dillard of Westinghouse,[9] demonstrated how

---

[7] Nevertheless, sizable deviations from capacity plans do occur. Witness the pleading for greater accuracy recorded in the minutes from the May 1954 meeting of the Statistical Committee of the Edison Electric Institute:

> The Semi-Annual Electric Power Survey was then discussed. Mr. Payne said that as usual, it appeared the companies had overestimated the peak demand for the current year. [Also] the companies have been predicting they would install, each succeeding year, much more capacity than they actually installed, and he predicted that for 1954, only 10 million of the 14 million kilowatts scheduled for installation would actually get in.
>
> . . . He also pointed out that the manufacturers' backlogs are very low for the years 1955–56, due to the companies having brought their margins of reserve up and the loads developing slower than was first predicted they would.

(Deposition of John Thornborrow, Electrical Equipment Antitrust Actions, in all U.S. district courts, February 13, 1964.)

[8] Lindseth, president of Cleveland Electric Illuminating Company, observed:

> For the size units we had [in 1958] and the interconnections we had, the [safe] reserve ratios were essentially those we have today, but that doesn't answer the whole

the combined effect of long equipment order lead times, and load forecasting errors, resulted in higher-than-desired reserves margins in the early 1960s. One consequence was a tendency to revise forecasts downward, and therefore to adjust equipment orders downward.

Current and forecasted margins of reserve for United States utilities over the 1949–1970 period, are plotted in Chart 6.2 (the percentages are computed as a percent of peak loads). Actual reserves have ranged from an estimated low of less than 8 percent in 1951, to a high of almost 28 percent in 1958–59.[10] Over this 20-year period the average margin was approximately 19 percent.

Forecasted percentage reserves three years into the future (plotted on Chart 6.2) are not as volatile as are actual reserves: the forecasts have ranged from 15 to 25 percent. The upward trend is obvious, an indication of progressive upward shifts in the reserves targets.

From 1949 to 1961, actual percent reserves and forecasted percent reserves tended to move in unison. Since 1961, however, forecasted percentage reserves have rather consistently moved upward, while actual reserves have rather consistently moved downward! At first glance this may seem to be very peculiar forecasting behavior. It reflects the fact that actual reserves climbed to an unusually high level in the late 1950s, due to capacity expansion based upon overoptimistic load forecasts. Almost simultaneously, in the early 1960s, lower reserves margins became fashionable, as "interconnection" became favored public policy and as transmission technology and capabilities appeared to leap ahead; thus, the *forecasted* reserves margin, a strong clue as to utilities' *desired* reserves, plummeted.

Later, throughout the latter 1960s, the utilities were gradually working down their actual reserves, and modifying upward their forecasted reserves—

---

question, in view of the fact that our reserve ratio today is somewhat higher than we had anticipated that it would be because the rate of load growth has not been as rapid as we designed for . . . .

(Deposition of Elmer L. Lindseth, Electrical Equipment Antitrust Actions, in all U.S. district courts, December 20, 1963.)

[9] J. K. Dillard, manager of Electric Utility Engineering Department, Westinghouse, observed:
. . . along about the end of the Korean War the margin of the utility systems was down fairly low, about 10 percent or 11 percent . . . . And then as they were able to expand their systems and buy more generators—during the early '50s their loads expanded rapidly, and they built up some margin on their systems, and reached an all-time high in 1961 . . . of 28.8 percent. Since 1961 this margin has been falling off. Now, the reason for this high point in 1961 is because the utilities were buying turbines very heavily up through about 1957 and these . . . were the machines that were being installed on their systems building their generation up at the same time that the load on their systems was growing much slower than they had anticipated, so the margins got out of control and got much too high.

(Testimony of J. K. Dillard, stenographer's minutes, San Antonio v. General Electric, Civil Action No. 3064 (E.D. Texas, 1964), pp. 7,081–7,087.)

[10] These are EEI current-year *estimates* of the actual reserves margin, and not necessarily the actual reserve as finally determined; however, the difference is very slight.

CHART 6.2.   Current and Forecasted (Three Years Ahead) Percentage Margins of
Reserve: Electric Utility Industry.

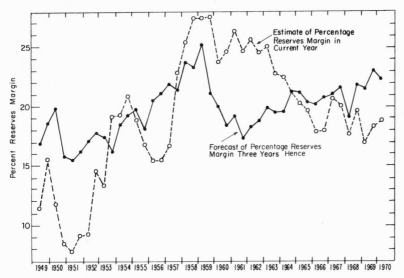

SOURCE: Edison Electric Institute data.

deliberately at first, until the ratios passed one another with a rush in the
late 1960s (see Chart 6.2), and it no longer became a matter of discretionary
taste. After 1965, the utilities simply could not install capacity fast enough
to keep margins from sliding downward further, while hoped-for margins
three years into the future continued to rise as the vision of lower margins
through interconnection was abraded by reality, and as utilities adjusted their
reserves targets upward accordingly.

CHANGES IN GENERATING CAPABILITY

To complete this analysis of utility planning for generating supply, the
impact of two "other" sources of change must be considered. The first is
utility behavior in the retiring of obsolete generating capacity. The second
is the addition of generating capacity from sources such as hydroelectric
dams and gas turbine sources.

Retirement of Obsolescent Capacity

The volume of retirements of obsolescent turbine generators, by year, is
shown in Chart 6.3. Retiring obsolescent generating capacity affects utility
reserves just as directly as does the addition of new capacity. However, compared with new installations, the magnitude of turbine generator retirements
is minuscule. Retirement of capacity is discouraged by the special nature of
utility capacity needs. Older equipment may be profitably used only once or

twice a year, to help meet the annual peak load, while remaining idle the rest of the time. In fact, the older equipment may never be used, but remains, nevertheless, as part of a utility's "last resort" stand-by reserves.[11] The design of some of the earlier models made them ideally suited for such stand-by "peaking" purposes.[12]

Given the disincentive to remove obsolescent capacity from service, and the highly discretionary circumstances surrounding the retirement decision,

CHART 6.3.   Retirements of Steam Turbine Generating Capacity from U.S. Utility Service.

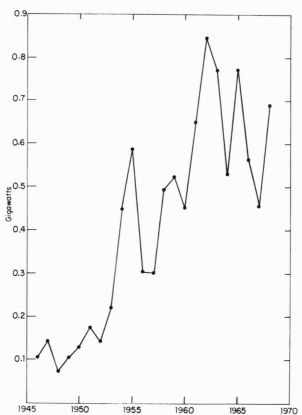

SOURCE: Edison Electric Institute *Statistical Yearbook*.

---

[11] "Utility-reserve margin figures include many units which would not be called into service except in the most extreme and unfortunate circumstances." (Testimony of Joe H. Burrus, Allis-Chalmers Company, stenographer's minutes, Ohio Valley Electric v. General Electric, 62 Civ. 695 (S.D.N.Y. 1964), p. 2,717.) So the obsolescent units remain nominally on-line, even though some are museum pieces. It is costly to tear them out from their foundations, and one never knows when they may be needed again.

[12] A Federal Power Commission Advisory Committee observed: "Most of the generating units [installed] prior to World War II [had] generous clearances and substantial design margins [and] were ideally suited for peak load and standby service after they had been superseded by more efficient base-load units." (*National Power Survey*, op. cit., Part II, p. 28.)

it is not surprising that analysis reveals that retirements are highly correlated with new additions to capacity (the utilities retire old capacity only when they add a large volume of new capacity) and with the utilities' current percentage reserves (when the utilities have ample reserves, they retire their old machines from service). This statistical analysis is presented in Appendix 8.

"Other" Sources of Generating Capacity

The *orders* analysis of this study (see Chapter Three) pertains only to steam turbine generators. Turbine generators are not the sole source of the generating capacity which has been studied in this chapter. Other sources of generating capacity include hydroelectric plants, gas-turbine peaking units, and internal combustion (e.g., diesel) plants. For sake of completeness of analysis, it will merely be pointed out that these other sources of power represent a relatively minor share of total industry capacity, and they can be considered in the total systems model which is being built as strictly exogenous inputs.

In 1968, conventional steam turbine generators accounted for 82 percent of total generating capacity in the electric utility industry, hydroelectric power represented another 16.8 percent, nuclear power 0.9 percent, and internal combustion engines 0.3 percent.

SUMMARY

We have now examined utilities' forecasted peak loads and actual peak loads, forecasted generating capabilities and actual generating capabilities; and finally the net result of these variables upon the generating reserves of utilities. (See Chart 6.4.) Utilities periodically grow into a power shortage (or surplus) situation, through the interaction of these variables.

It is a truism that a utility's current reserves position is the net result of where it had *planned* to be, and its misjudgments of load growth and capacity expansions. Utility peak load forecasts are highly cyclical in nature, as

CHART 6.4.   Utilities' Forecasted Loads and Generating Capability v. Actual Loads and Capability for Year T (Forecasts Made in Year T-3).

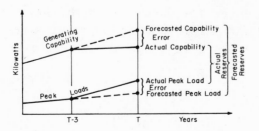

the analysis of Chapter Four demonstrated. Utility capability forecasts are also highly cyclical, because they depend upon the cyclical backlogs position of the manufacturers.

On the average, utility organizations tend to forecast less increase in capacity than they actually install. They also tend to underforecast peak load growth. The net result tends to be wide departures of actual margins from the apparent desired margins position. In the long term, periods of extreme shortage and periods of extreme surplus have been experienced.

A major balance wheel which helps to keep the whole system functioning is utility decisions to retire generating equipment. Capacity retirements are influenced by the volume of new capacity additions, and by the current percentage reserves position of the utilities. When reserves are high and new additions are heavy, then retirements will be accelerated.

The consequences of this utility behavior for turbine generator marketers are of fundamental importance. It has been demonstrated how load forecasts and forecasting errors will influence the turbine generator order rate, thence backlogs, thence prices. Simultaneously, it may now be seen, load forecasting errors have their obvious impact upon utility reserves margins. If load forecasts were too low, margins will be pinched, and upward forecast revisions will be the rule. This will lead to heavy ordering of additional turbine generator capacity, higher backlogs, higher forecasts of generating capability additions, and higher prices.

In this *homeostatic* fashion, the utility organizations endeavor to keep their generating capacity growing in line with the growth in their peak loads. Their effort is obviously hobbled by the long lead times involved. They cannot install new generating capacity without a two-to-four-year delay—even longer in the 1970s. As the utility organizations attempt to "fine tune" their supply needs, the stage is set for violently cyclical phenomena. Almost inevitably, it appears, the utilities will periodically enter the turbine market *en masse*, and then leave it again. More importantly from the perspective of the electrical energy consumer, the cycles are bound to be propagated into the reserves planning process itself. Periods of power shortage are surely bound to be experienced from time to time, as will periods of power surplus.

From the manufacturer's perspective, what this behavior implies is continued cyclicality in orders, in backlogs, and in price levels. The manufacturer is at the amplified whip-end of a system which is investing huge amounts of capital in response to minor fluctuations in the electric power growth rate. Those growth rate fluctuations seem hardly destined to cease. Therefore, even broader oscillations in supply response—and in pricing—are the necessary lot of the turbine builders.

CHAPTER Seven   Order Prices

THE UTILITIES' TURBINE GENERATOR ordering behavior has been defined. The manufacturers' supply response has been defined as well. It remains to be seen how these demand and supply factors interact to determine prices in the short run.

This chapter describes how *average order* prices are determined in the short run. It does *not* deal with the *relative* price charged by each turbine builder, above or below that average. Nor does it deal with the differential prices charged for different units in the product line. Nor does it consider the *final* price which is paid once the turbine has been delivered. These equally important dimensions of pricing will be dealt with in individual chapters.

THE "VALUE" PHILOSOPHY OF PRICING

My earlier companion study[1] described how the roots of pricing behavior may be traced to a philosophy which has the following characteristics.

The absolute upper limit on price increases is determined by "value" considerations—the decline in real costs of power generating equipment which is the fruit of technological change. Through technological change, both the investment cost per kilowatt and the operating cost per kilowatt-hour, for power generating equipment, have been steadily reduced by the manufacturers. The manufacturers may try to:

(1) *recoup all* of this added value from the utilities, through price increases, in effect keeping the utilities' real costs constant, or

(2) at the other extreme, *pass along all* of these technological gains to the utilities in the form of continually lower real costs and, thus, lower the effective price, or

(3) establish some intermediate price change, whereby both the utilities and manufacturers share the rewards of technological progress and cost reduction—the utilities through continually lower prices, and

---

[1] Ralph G. M. Sultan, *Pricing in the Electrical Oligopoly, Vol. I: Competition or Collusion* (Boston: Harvard Business School, Division of Research, 1974). See also Chapter Two of this Volume II for a formal statement of the theory.

the manufacturers through enhanced earnings which accrue largely to the technological leaders.

The "fair" or conscionable rate of increase has tended to be established with reference to the rate of inflation in labor wages, and in material prices (i.e., the rate of factor price increases). This provides a benchmark of equity which utility customers perceive as being acceptable and reasonable. It has little to do with actual cost behavior. As revenues diverge from costs, there is a growing likelihood of sharp adjustment: a price war. Direct costs set a lower bound upon price. It is seldom that manufacturers will sell at prices which result in an out-of-pocket loss.

Between the upper bound on price changes (established under the "fairness" doctrine) and the lower bound of price (established by direct costs), there is a discretionary zone of varying band width, in which price levels will be determined by managements' competitive zeal. Competitive zeal, in turn, will be determined by pressures operating upon line management from top management, and by budget goals and performance measures, all of these being reflected in "operating statistics" arising from current operations of the business.

Some of the short-run operating statistics which may activate or lull managers' competitive instincts are hypothesized to be: (1) the rate of incoming orders, (2) the utilization of factory capacity, and (3) backlogs of unfilled orders, in absolute amount or else relative to factory productive capacity.

Other "special events" may inflate or depress price levels, within the bounds of "fairness" and direct cost. Such special events are hypothesized to include:

(1) collusive agreements among competitors to raise prices jointly,
(2) government price controls (e.g., the 1952–1953 experience under OPS), and
(3) the threatened entry of foreign competition.

This model of pricing behavior may be subjected to statistical test in a two-step procedure: first, the bounding considerations of "value" and of direct cost may be inspected, manually as it were, to establish that price increases have indeed been below the rate of increase in value, and that price dips have indeed been limited by direct costs. On both counts, the model passes muster. As for the topside limit, the real cost of power generating equipment has continually descended, and price increases have been kept below their maximum "value" limit; and, considering the price inelasticity of demand, far below their monopoly limit. As for limits on the underside, it is clear that during the 1955 White Sale and during 1959–1961, Westinghouse and Allis-Chalmers were forced to sell at prices which approached their direct costs, while General Electric had its earnings margin greatly diminished.[2]

----

[2] See Volume I, Tables 6.3, 6.4, and 6.5.

However, direct costs acted as a lower bound on price. This constraint would be encountered first by the marginal highest cost competitor.

The Data

Prices of turbine generators have been computed on an index number basis, as plotted in Chart 7.1. This price curve is the careful reconstruction of the quarter-by-quarter aggregate dollar value of all turbine generator orders,

CHART 7.1.   Test of Conspiratorial Impact: Results of Fitting Regression Model to Data for Nonconspiratorial Period Only, and Then Using the Resulting Model to Estimate Prices for the Conspiracy Period.

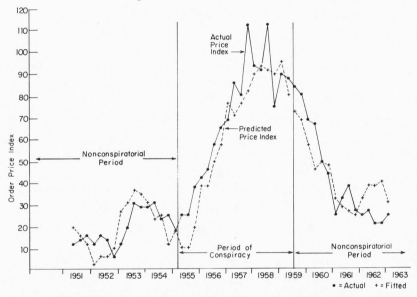

in current dollars, as a ratio to the aggregate value of the same units priced at 1961 handbook levels. The result is an index of the actual order price level compared with 1961 handbook price levels, automatically weighted to accommodate shifts in technology and in product mix. This is the price index statistic to be explained.

Inflation in the economy—as a proxy for the inflation in factor prices, the U.S. Bureau of Labor Statistics Wholesale Price Index for all industrial commodities was employed.[3]

Orders inflow data for the three firms are shown in Volume I (page 207). For purposes of statistical analysis, both the quarter-by-quarter actual megawatts of

---

[3] After the statistical work was completed, several reviewers pointed out that it would have been better to use the BLS wage data for this 3-digit SIC industry, combined with the wholesale price index for metals products. I concede this oversight. However, since the price index performs largely as a trend variable in the regression equation, I do not think the difference in results would be substantial.

orders for each firm, and the moving four-quarter average megawatts of orders for each firm, were tested. In addition, the rate of aggregate industry inflow of orders was tested for pricing impact. In the end, none of these proved to be significant.

Backlogs data for each firm are plotted in Volume I (page 203), in aggregate megawatts. The manufacturers said that when backlogs of unfilled orders were low, then prices weakened. Kilowatts backlog of unfilled orders were therefore introduced as an explanatory variable. However, large backlogs are not necessarily equated with firm prices; it is "backlogs relative to capacity" which is important, according to manufacturer testimony. Therefore, kilowatts backlogs were also divided by kilowatts manufacturing capacity, yielding "years" of backlogs; that is, the number of years of orders being held, at current rates of productive capacities. Backlogs in years are shown in Volume I (page 204), for each competitor.

Initially the backlog, in years, was computed at the total industry level. However, due to General Electric's prominent market share, this tends to be unduly weighted by General Electric's backlogs performance. It was apparent from manufacturer testimony that Allis-Chalmers or Westinghouse could exert severe pricing pressure downward, even though they were lesser factors in the total market. From this developed the idea that it might be the *minimum* backlog in years, among the three competitors, which is the relevant stimulant to price-cutting in the marketplace. The backlog in years for General Electric, for Westinghouse, and for Allis-Chalmers, individually was computed, and then the lowest number, quarter by quarter, from among the three was selected. In the majority of periods, it was Allis-Chalmers which had the minimum in years.

The percentage *factory utility utilization rate* for each of the three competitors (moving four-quarter average) is depicted in Volume I (page 204). In the final statistical model, capacity utilization was computed at the industry average level: total industry kilowatts shipments per quarter, divided by total industry kilowatts manufacturing capacity in that quarter, based on the sum of shipments and capacities of the three manufacturers.

The impact of *special events* can be tested through the use of dummy variables. It was assumed for purposes of statistical test that:

(1) The meetings among competitors were effective in the period up through the second quarter of 1959, when they were revealed, and not effective thereafter. It was also assumed the meetings in the 1955–1959 period had a specially intensive character. The question was whether these meetings resulted in an upward shift in the order price index.[4]

---

[4] Statistically, one can treat such a shift in price levels with a "dummy variable" which has a value of 1.0 during the conspiratorial period, through the second quarter of 1959, and zero thereafter. It is assumed that this effect was continuously present up to the summer of 1959,

(2) The OPS government price controls were present from the first quarter of 1951 through the first quarter of 1953, for a total of nine consecutive quarters, and thence nonexistent.

(3) The impact of foreign competition was felt in proportion to the 13.3 percent of domestic (kilowatts) orders acquired by Brown Boveri and Parsons in 1959, and in proportion to the 3.8 percent of domestic orders acquired by Brown Boveri in 1961, and not felt in the remainder of the 1948–1963 period, when no foreign bids were successful. (Of course, the actual volume of orders taken by foreign manufacturers is no measure of the *threat* posed by them in other years in addition to 1959 and 1961.)

Results: A Model of Turbine Generator Prices

Regression analysis revealed those economic factors which moved in unison with the quarterly average order price level in this industry. Three variables were jointly related to quarterly movements in the level of turbine generator order prices over 1951–1963 (see Appendix 9):

(1) factor prices—a trend variable,
(2) the average industry percentage utilization of capacity, and
(3) the *minimum* backlog, measured in years of productive capacity, measured across all three competitors.[5]

The following factors were apparently *not* relevant, according to these tests at least, in determining the order price index over this period:

(1) the rate of incoming orders,
(2) foreign competition, as measured by the fraction of business taken,
(3) conspiracy, and
(4) OPS price controls.

Thus, prices rise rapidly when inflation is heavy, when the three manufacturers (General Electric in particular) are working overtime to produce turbines for shipments, and when all three manufacturers have a "balanced" backlogs situation. If any single competitor has low backlogs relative to his

---

when, according to manufacturer testimony, the meetings ceased. Thereafter, it is assumed the conspiratorial factor was not present. There is evidence that the meetings did not really get organized until after the White Sale, in mid-1955. Therefore, another statistical test was performed, utilizing two dummy variables: one for the "really organized" meetings period of mid-1955 through mid-1959, and a second one for those infrequent meetings of a different character, which occurred prior to mid-1955. One, both, or neither of the dummy variables might display statistical significance.

[5] One reviewer has suggested that the "weighted average backlog" would probably be a superior explanatory variable. The weighted average backlog, in years, is the equivalent of the total industry backlog in years. This variable was tested, in both ordinary and log linear form. While it is a statistically significant factor, the industry backlog, in years, is clearly inferior (on t-test and contribution R^2 grounds) to the *minimum* backlogs, in years, variable in the price equation.

capacity, prices will be driven down for all. Pricing is therefore a factory load-balancing phenomenon.

This explains why the orders inflow may be heavy, yet the order prices depressed. Prices will not climb until backlogs and work-in-process are built up. Similarly, orders may be low, and prices high. The White Sale and its aftermath was a classic example of low backlogs and a low volume of work-in-process leading to price-cutting, in late 1954. The subsequent influx of orders meant heavy backlogs, heavy work-in-process loads, and rapidly climbing prices during 1955–1957.

In most time periods, Allis-Chalmers—the smallest competitor—had the minimum backlog. Westinghouse and General Electric could raise industry average price levels by yielding share and permitting Allis-Chalmers to load its factory. However, on several occasions (1954, 1959), Allis-Chalmers expanded its factory capacity greatly—beyond any scale of market share its larger competitors were willing to concede. Thus, only rarely was the Allis-Chalmers factory heavily backlogged, and it was during these periods that industry prices climbed rapidly.

In retrospect, the sharp price rise of 1957–1958, which figured so prominently in the damage suits against the electrical conspirators, was due in large measure to Allis-Chalmers at last being able to operate its expanded factory capacity with a comfortable backlog. This occurred, despite a downturn in total industry demand, largely because General Electric yielded share of market to Allis-Chalmers. The subsequent dramatic 1959–1961 plunge in price levels was the consequence of increased industry capacity, lower utilization rates for everyone and, most particularly, the declining Allis-Chalmers backlog and consequent Allis-Chalmers price-cutting. This interpretation fits well with management testimony on why a 1961 General Electric attempt to announce higher prices failed. Westinghouse managers said they supported the new General Electric price levels for a time, but found themselves undercut in the marketplace by an even hungrier Allis-Chalmers. The least-backlogs firm set the industry price, despite book price announcements by the leader firm.

The rate of inflation in factor prices may be interpreted as the "just" or "conscionable" rate of increase in turbine generator prices. This has little correlation with turbine generator manufacturing costs; it is an upper bound, determined by perceptions of fairness and operative when backlogs and demand are strong. The conclusion that prices were apparently not measurably affected by the impact of foreign orders taken in 1959 and in 1961 is surprising, but at that time prices were heading down in any case. This result finds support in the post-1963 experience, when foreign orders for turbine generators increased, at the same time there were rising order prices.

Prices were not measurably affected by OPS price controls. Prices, it seems, would have been relatively stable in any case over 1951–1953. (This result seems to be substantiated by the price controls experience of the early 1970s.)

The problem with price controls in 1951–1953 is that they applied to *book* prices. As has been demonstrated,[6] during the period of the study, book or list prices had little relevance for actual order prices.

The Impact of Conspiracy

There is no support in these statistical results for the proposition that the meetings, or electrical conspiracy, had a measurable impact on price levels. This conclusion—surely to be greeted with disbelief—deserves further comment. Some may argue that the meetings were very effective *over 1955–1958* when prices soared at their maximum rate. Others might embellish this argument with the observation (with some empirical basis), that in the electrical equipment meetings generally there were no meetings during the depressed price periods, such as 1954 and early 1955. Many meetings happened to coincide with the *high* price periods only. Therefore, it has been argued, the meetings affected prices.

It seems to this writer that any argument which runs in directional causality from meetings to price levels may just as well be turned around, to run from price levels to meetings. All of the historical evidence suggests that the meetings were enthusiastically endorsed by all when prices were high, and that they fell apart when prices dropped. As a consequence, the meetings might be perceived as highly successful about 50 percent of the time. Participants in the meetings could readily delude themselves into believing that they were having a significant impact on the price level, at least a significant fraction of the time. This alone would be sufficient motive for them to continue with the conspiracy. The fact that the meetings continued is not evidence that the meetings had any impact.

The only reasonable test of impact is whether prices were somehow contaminated in the *entire* period prior to July 1959, when meetings were once and for all suspended. It would be specious to select only the high-price periods, and to correlate them with meetings, and then to ask whether there is a correlation. In response to the question of whether the meetings affected prices throughout the entire pre-July 1959 period, these statistical results answer "no."

Some have argued that it was mainly the meetings over 1955–1959 which influenced prices. That proposition has also been tested statistically. Even the meetings of 1955–1959 alone failed to have observable impact, when measured with the dummy variable technique.

Meetings to Balance Backlogs?

In pricing, it is important to note that the balance of loads among the competitors' factories will influence price levels. Certainly at some of the meetings there were pleadings that one company or another was in special

---

6 See: Sultan, *Pricing in the Electrical Oligopoly, Vol. I.*

factory loading difficulty, and should receive "position." To the degree that the meetings resulted in some balancing of the available backlogs among competitors, through position agreements on specific contracts, then the meetings *would* affect price.

The only problem with this conclusion is that detailed and exhaustive discovery and cross-examination during the 1960s could turn up only 19 out of some 1,700 turbine generator transactions in which "position" was even discussed, let alone achieved.[7] And in some of these, a competitor without "position" wangled the order in the end. Even if this tally grossly underestimated the number of jobs on which position agreements were attempted, the overall impact of position agreements in the turbine generator business must have nevertheless been trivial indeed. The empirical fact of severe load imbalance suggests that any load balancing which was achieved must have been modest too. In fact, other criteria received more weight in the "position" discussions which were recorded in the conspiracy; for example, a competitor which was "close to" a particular utility generally ended up in the favored "pole position." Pleadings for position on the grounds of need received short shrift according to the court records.

The resulting "years" of backlog were hardly uniform among the three competitors:

	Average years of backlog 1948–1962	Standard deviation of years of backlog
General Electric	2.46	0.86
Westinghouse	2.29	1.03
Allis-Chalmers	1.59	0.66

As further evidence, a model of Allis-Chalmers' percentage market share, incorporating a dummy variable for the conspiracy period, failed to disclose any measurable impact for the conspiracy period. If the conspiracy resulted in load balancing of the competitors' factories, the degree of balancing must have been extremely slight.

An Alternative Test of Conspiratorial Impact[8]

An alternative test of conspiratorial impact is to fit the basic three-variable model (incorporating the wholesale price index, average capacity utilization,

---

[7] The search for evidence concerning the frequency of meetings in the turbine generator conspiracy is documented in *Vol. I*. See also Appendix 18, pp. 344–349.

[8] I am indebted to Professor Jesse W. Markham of the Harvard Business School for suggesting this additional test. It is based, according to Markham, on a statistical test employed by a General Electric consultant, on transformer price data during the electrical antitrust litigation—with remarkably similar statistical results.

and minimum years of backlog as the explanatory variables), to order price data for the years 1950 through 1963, *omitting* the observations or data points for the period from the first quarter of 1955 through 1959, when the conspiracy was at its alleged maximum impact. The resulting equation can then be fitted to the missing observation data points for 1955–1959, to yield the estimated order price for that period. When compared with the actual order prices of that period, any artificial gap between the two plots will be suggestive of conspiratorial impact.

Chart 7.1 shows the results of this test. The fitted price data for 1955 through 1959 are strikingly close to actual price data for that period. This suggests the model itself is robust, and that the conspiratorial period did not display unpredictable or unexplainable price changes.

The Sensitivity of Pricing Response

One may employ the statistical results to assess the sensitivity of pricing response to inflation and the two operating factors.

Sensitivity estimates are as follows:

A 10 percent rise in the wholesale price index would have resulted in about a 25 percent rise in the turbine generator order price index.

A decrease in capacity utilization from 115 percent to 80 percent would have resulted in an order price decline of about 13 percent.

A decrease in the minimum backlog from 2.5 years to 1.0 year, would have resulted in an order price decline of about 13 percent.

Together, the hypothetical reduction in utilization rate *and* backlogs combined, as posited above, would just about cancel out the posited 10 percent rise in wholesale prices; the net result of all three posited changes would be a zero change in order price levels.

These sensitivity estimates demonstrate that when the backlog and capacity utilization environment was favorable, turbine prices could climb much more rapidly than the rate of ambient inflation. However, when backlogs turned down, capacity utilization would also turn down eventually, providing a subsequent double-barreled depressant to turbine order price levels. This helps to explain the volatility in turbine prices over this time period.

Strategic Implications

Some strategic implications for manufacturers and for utilities are readily apparent from this analysis of price determination:

(1) Backlogs are a buffer stock, not directly proportional to immediate turbine generator orders inflows or shipments outflows to the utilities. If the manufacturers can keep a well-stocked larder of unfilled orders, regardless

of the immediate demand or shipments situation, then prices will tend to be high. Thus, it pays the manufacturers to encourage the utilities to order far in advance of need—for delivery many years hence, thereby building up backlogs. If prices are weakening, rumors of impending shortages may help to drive in orders, and backlogs, once they are lengthening, will tend to create additional orders from utilities anxious to obtain a place in the queue.

(2) If the utilities wish to depress price levels, they should order their turbines at the last minute, under crash schedule circumstances, thereby shrinking manufacturer backlogs and driving down the price level. If they wish to be even more diabolical, utilities may, from time to time, choose to withhold orders from just one of the competitors. This will assure their turbine generator supply and, concurrently, a desperate assault on the established price level by the one competitor which is starved for backlogs. This is about what happened in 1962, when Allis-Chalmers was ultimately driven from the market, but it is unlikely that this result occurred because of anyone's scheme. With the marginal competitor actually driven out, the entire plan will backfire in its intended result.

(3) Production delays, such as Westinghouse encountered due to strikes and manufacturing problems during the 1950s, will tend to swell backlogs and raise average price levels. Manufacturing bottlenecks can therefore be highly profitable for the manufacturers.

(4) Since pricing is a load-balancing phenomenon, among all competitors, it is clear that the manufacturers sink or swim together. It therefore behooves *each* manufacturer to make sure that his competitors have their *pro rata* "share" of whatever backlogs may be available. Greediness in this respect will lead to price collapse. It would be extremely short-sighted for General Electric to grab all of the orders available in order to maintain its own backlogs. General Electric's competitors will pull down prices for all. Every manufacturer should therefore ponder the fact that price levels depend not only on how well *he* fills up his own "order board"; but also on how well his competitors fill up theirs. In prosperity or adversity, it pays the manufacturers to "share the load."

(5) This line of reasoning leads to another interesting conclusion: if each competitor believes it is desirable, on pricing grounds, to adjust his market share until *each* manufacturer has a balanced share of total industry backlogs (relative to each manufacturer's capacity) then conditions are ripe for a bit of oligopolistic blackmail. If Allis-Chalmers came to believe that its competitors were compelled to give Allis' factory capacity its due, then Allis was greatly tempted to expand its factory capacity. Its competitors had powerful priced-based incentives to let Allis fill up that capacity with an orders backlog. Allis' market share would increase. Thus, any firm may bludgeon its competitors into yielding market share, through the vehicle of expanding factory

capacity, combined with the threat of a price war. The average industry utilization rate will decline, but when a smaller firm is involved, the pricing impact of utilization rates will be negligible.

(6) It may be reasoned that this type of competitive behavior will lead inevitably to the strategy of expanding capacity vigorously, in order to expand market share. But this is not necessarily the case. Each competitor has a difficult choice. By expanding factory capacity, thereby to blackmail competitors into yielding share, a manufacturer runs the risk that the others in the industry will choose lower prices over lower market share, and refuse to permit him to load his factory adequately. The competitor with expanded capacity may well discover that his orders are languishing. He cuts price. Industry prices tumble, and all suffer. But the competitor who has expanded capacity will suffer most of all, since he is now operating at a new and higher level of overhead costs. This is what happened to Allis-Chalmers in the late 1950s.

(7) Further, competitors will probably retaliate by expanding factory capacity of their own, to restore an "equilibrium level" of capacity shares.[9] Subsequent analysis in this study will substantiate this premise. Therefore, there is no assurance that a competitor can wedge himself further into the marketplace by expanding factory capacity recklessly; the odds are that he will only succeed in driving down industry utilization rates, backlogs (in years) for all, and his own backlogs (in years) in particular. There is no economic gain, unless the competitors are particularly sleepy or acquiescent to losing share—which they have historically not been in this industry. One concludes that the strategy of a capacity expansion as a bluff to expand market share will be embraced gingerly by major competitors. The ploy might fail—and bring prices down to direct cost levels.

(8) Even in the absence of capacity expansions for market share purposes, manufacturers must continuously plan to expand their capacity. If expansion plans go awry, if demand forecasts and capacity plans are grossly overoptimistic, then prices will surely descend, as utilization rates and backlog years shrink. (This is essentially what happened during the price decline of 1959–1961. New capacity plus diminished backlogs and orders resulted in very low price levels—frequently as low as the incremental cost floor.)

Utilities can encourage such overcapacity in the manufacturing sector (and low prices) by promulgating rosy demand forecasts. Manufacturers can respond in kind with gloomy demand forecasts, to discourage overcapacity.

---

[9] On the fight for capacity shares, see: William Fruhan, *The Fight for Competitive Advantage* (Boston: Harvard Business School, Division of Research, 1972), which describes analogous behavior in the airlines industry.

(Perennially, these roles appear to be reversed in real life; the manufacturers overestimate long-term demand and the utilities underestimate it.)

In all of this, meetings and agreements among competitors will tend to be useless, except when demand is strong and supply is tight. And on those occasions agreements are not necessary. Conspiracy cannot be recommended as a means to sustain market prices.

CHAPTER Eight   Escalation

THE ORDER PRICE WAS NOT THE FINAL PRICE which the utility paid. The order price—the individual discount off the book price—was negotiated, and was susceptible to the market forces described in Chapter Seven. However, beyond this, between the date of order and the date of final shipment (which could be several years later) "escalation" was imposed.

TYPES OF ESCALATION

Three pricing arrangements were common in the industry: "firm price," "price in effect at time of shipment," and "indices escalation."

(1) Under a firm price contract, the price the customer ultimately paid was the price which was negotiated originally.

(2) Under price in effect at time of shipment, or "PETS," the customer paid the *current* book price which was in effect at the time his turbine was shipped from the factory (which could be several years after the turbine was ordered), less the percentage discount from book price which had *originally* been negotiated at the time of the order.[1]

(3) Under indices escalation, the customer paid the originally negotiated price, plus an increment proportional to some published index of general inflation, such as the U.S. Bureau of Labor Statistics price index for labor and materials.

Turbine generator marketers generally argued that the reason for having escalation was to protect the *purchaser* from inflation. Their reasoning was: Turbine generators were purchased with a long lead time, often two to four years before delivery. Under a firm price contract, without any escalation at

---

[1] A General Electric manager explained:

We took the relationship of the orders received price to the published price at the time of the order, and then we reduced the published price at time of shipment by the same percentage.

Q. He buys at 12 percent off 1955 book, shipment is made in '58, you charge him 12 percent off '58 book?

A. That's right. Provided it does not exceed the ceiling.

(Deposition of John T. Peters, Electrical Equipment Antitrust Actions, in all U.S. district courts, October 25, 1962.)

all, it was argued that the seller would have to increase his order prices to *anticipate* future inflation in factory costs, with something extra to cover uncertainty; that is, to cover any possible margin of error. Thus, their argument went, ". . . in an inflationary period the highest price that a utility would pay . . . is when you quote a firm price . . . ."[2]

From customers, a different line of reasoning was heard: the reason manufacturers charged escalation was not altruistic; it was actually a device to protect the manufacturer from the pressures of inflation. When pressed on this point, one turbine generator marketer conceded that *current* prices were established with some view toward future inflation, which, it was pointed out, would have led to the "double-counting" of inflation in the oligopolistic pricing decision—a form of behavior which some customers suspected.[3] The facts of the situation may be better appraised through a capsule history of escalation in this industry.

History of Escalation

There is some confusion in the record, but it appears that PETS-type escalation was employed by the turbine manufacturers prior to World War

---

[2] John Peters of General Electric explained:

The basic reason [for escalation] is to provide protection for the purchaser and the seller against inflationary pressures. If there is deflation the purchaser and the seller should also be protected.

If at the time of the order there is a certain cost level, and then if there is an inflation, the seller is protected and he is able to recover all or part of the inflationary increases in cost due to that special provision.

It protects the buyer because if there is no escalation provision and you have firm prices, the seller would have to anticipate what future inflation would be, and factor that into his determination when he was making the quotation.

In an inflationary period, the highest price that a utility would pay is when you quote a firm price, because we would have to assume the highest rate of inflation you can imagine, and also the longest shipment.

The level of published prices is determined by current production, what you have just produced, or what you have got designed, and what you expect to produce within the next year or so. Some period later you make another examination of the cost of your current production, and what you are going to ship just immediately in advance of this period of time, so you have accurate cost data. You may have some machines with increased prices more than on other ones, because of some miscalculation.

It is my judgment that [with PETS] customers would generally pay the lowest orders received price, and generally they would end up with perhaps the highest amount of dollars of escalation.

There is the general economic condition, the volume of orders, backlogs and all kinds of factors which influence the price which you charge, so it is not just a matter of costs.
(Deposition of John T. Peters, Electrical Equipment Antitrust Actions, in all U.S. district courts, October 25, 1962.)

[3] Even when you have escalation, as contrasted with firm price, you are adding into your price your estimates of future increases in costs which will not be adequately taken into account by the indices that you employ?

A. That is correct, sir.
(Deposition of John T. Peters, ibid.)

II, and that indices escalation was introduced during the war. After World War II, "Electric Charlie" Wilson, the president of General Electric, briefly imposed firm prices on his company, in a patriotic attempt to thwart inflation—but this was a short-lived policy. By 1950, PETS escalation was the rule.

Indices escalation reappeared at the time of the White Sale (January 1955) as an extra competitive inducement offered to customers by General Electric to increase its market share. This practice continued until 1959. Beginning in 1959, the first 2.5 percent of escalation was "forgiven"—in response to collapsing prices. Later it was eliminated in bidding on the TVA Paradise contract by General Electric. This policy was then extended to General Electric customers generally, and was copied by General Electric's competitors.

During the price collapse of 1959–1961, it appears that the escalation tradition was broken down by hard bargaining on individual contracts. For a time, escalation disappeared completely. However, with the restoration of firmer order prices in 1963, escalation according to indices was restored.

LIMITS ON ESCALATION

In the boom (and highly inflationary) period immediately after World War II, there was apparently no contractual limit on the amount of total escalation which the manufacturers could charge under the PETS-type contracts which prevailed in the turbine generator market. Some customers objected, observing that this was tantamount to "we will ship it to you and charge you whatever we please."[4] In response to such negative feelings on the matter, the manufacturers imposed a ceiling for PETS-type contracts, limiting maximum escalation to 10 percent on shipments within one year, 20 percent within three years, and 30 percent on shipments beyond three years.[5]

Even with this limit on escalation which could be charged, questions remained. For example, some observers wondered about the wisdom of utilities being cajoled into purchasing turbine generators to "get in under the wire" immediately prior to a book price increase. This was a common tactic —which seemed to work! But with hindsight, neither buyers nor sellers could give a sound explanation for such buyer behavior.[6] (Customers would pre-

---

[4] Observation of Amasa C. Bull, vice president and director, Pioneer Service and Engineering Company, delivered at a meeting of the Public Utilities Group of the National Association of Purchasing Agents. Mr. Bull added that, with this remark, a Mr. Sugge of General Electric "lost his temper." (Deposition of Amasa C. Bull, Electrical Equipment Antitrust Actions, in all U.S. district courts, January 21, 1964.)

[5] Testimony of George B. Cox, stenographer's minutes, Ohio Valley Electric v. General Electric et al., 62 Civ. 695, U.S. District Court, S.D.N.Y., p. 1,653.

[6] As to the rationality of "buying flurries" by utilities prior to an announced increase in book price, Peters testified:

Q. You said "Let's have two 5s because if it becomes known that we have a ten percent increase under consideration, we will get a lot of new business, people coming in under the wire?"

sumably pay the book price in effect at the time of shipment of the order, regardless of what book price happened to prevail at the time the order was taken.)

Indeed, given the realities of order prices in the marketplace, as analyzed in previous chapters, one can argue that the optimum time to order under PETS-type escalation was immediately *after* a book price increase. This is because book prices rise in a stair-step pattern. The step increases in book prices are patterned so as to stay just above order prices, which are going up on a steady incline. Thus, the percentage discount off book has its greatest magnitude immediately *after* a new book price goes into effect—during periods of price increase. However, since we have seen that utility purchasers did *not* time their orders to take advantage of this fact, one may question how well they had thought through the implications of PETS-type contracting or how deeply they really cared about gaining a few extra percentage points of price reduction. In defense of his seeming ignorance of this point, one marketing manager observed that by ordering just *prior* to a book price increase, "the *ceiling* on escalation was approached sooner than it would have been if we started at the higher price,"[7] and this was indeed one justification which made some sense.

PETS-type escalation contracts became a point of contention at meetings of utility purchasing managers. In response to these murmurings of discontent, General Electric began to offer indices escalation as an alternative to PETS-type escalation in January 1955 (during the White Sale). An internal General Electric memorandum written just prior to the White Sale argued that indices escalation should be based upon publicly available government price series, available to all, easily understood, and "usable by competition"—presumably in order to afford the greatest opportunity for market leadership in matters of escalation as well as in matters of order prices generally.[8]

A. Yes.

Q. I want you to explain to me what difference did it make under a price in effect clause, because the new increased price would be applicable at the time of shipment, and therefore you would get this increase from all orders placed at the lower price.

A. I don't know the answer to that question right now, sir.

(Deposition of John T. Peters, Electrical Equipment Antitrust Actions, in all U.S. district courts, October 25, 1962.)

[7] Testimony of George B. Cox of General Electric, stenographer's minutes, Ohio Valley Electric v. General Electric et al., 62 Civ. 695, U.S. District Court, S.D.N.Y., pp. 1,651–1,653.

[8] Excerpts from a General Electric memorandum concerning escalation:

It is essential that any escalation indexes which are used should fulfill the following conditions:

    (1) Indexes should be published by the Bureau of Labor Statistics.

    (2) Indexes should be available upon request to all concerned.

    (3) Labor and material indexes should reflect changes in labor and material costs for the particular department involved.

    (4) Indexes used should have a broad selection of reporting establishments to avoid possible adverse fluctuations due to local conditions of one or two reporting establishments.

The memorandum also contained the erroneous judgment that most customers, with the exception of government agencies, would continue to prefer PETS-type escalation if given a choice.[9] As it happened, most customers switched to indices escalation when given the opportunity, apparently preferring to place their confidence in the exogenous economic inflation, as opposed to the inflation of book prices as controlled by the manufacturers.

Early in 1956, Westinghouse attempted to gain business by relaxing its escalation provisions, but reportedly there was little customer response.[10] Westinghouse then seems to have returned to the escalation policies followed by the other manufacturers, although during the conspiratorial meetings among competitors of 1956–1957, there was often acrimonious debate over the accusation that General Electric's competitors were not charging escalation, in violation of what they had promised they would do.

The first significant *public* departure from the policy of escalation occurred in 1959, at the time of bidding on the Paradise power station of Tennessee Valley Authority. In its bid, General Electric eliminated the first 2.5 percent of escalation. This was apparently part of General Electric's campaign to ward off foreign competition on the Paradise job.[11] The Paradise escalation

---

(5) Material index should rapidly reflect changes in material cost and not be subject to considerable time delay.

(6) Selected indexes must be usable by competition.

"Price in effect" method of escalation has a 20 percent ceiling whereas the "Index" method has the advantage of no ceiling.

It will be necessary to adjust handbook prices more frequently if escalation is based on the "Index" method in order to keep prices and costs within a reasonable relationship. On "Price in effect" cost would increase 10% before a 10% increase in price was made.

One advantage of the "Index" method is in meeting foreign competition because the purchaser cannot increase our bid price to the maximum ceiling level as is the case on "Price in effect" bids.

"Price in effect" method requires less accounting but requires considerably more sales effort in justifying escalated prices.

Many purchasing agents feel that they are at the manufacturer's "mercy" with the existing clause and would prefer escalation to be based on factors not "solely controlled" by the manufacturer.

The "Index" method will assist in selling progressive payments because the earlier payments will not be escalated as much as the payments at shipment in a rising market.

In those areas where we have had an opportunity to check, it has been found that the "Index" method will result in approximately the same return or escalated price as the "Price in effect" method.

(National Exhibit NX 171, Electrical Equipment Antitrust Actions.)

[9] Deposition of John T. Peters, October 25, 1962.

[10] In January or February 1956 at a utility buyers' group meeting in Chicago, Mr. Lagrone of Westinghouse said that they averaged their index from the date of order to the date of shipment, whereas General Electric did not, and they had this clause for six months, but they didn't get any plus business, so they discontinued it and adopted the clause which was similar to General Electric's. (Testimony of John T. Peters, stenographer's minutes, City of San Antonio v. General Electric et al., Civ. 3064, W.D. Texas, 1964, pp. 5,453–5,454.)

[11] John T. Peters, San Antonio, pp. 5,456–5,458.

terms became a general provision on all orders, and merely reflects the softening demand situation of 1959, which was reflected in a slump in the order
price itself, as well as in the other terms of sale.

Escalation terms had an indirect impact on book prices, as became evident
in 1959. As prices plunged downward in 1959–1961, book prices were *not*
adjusted downward immediately. This was apparently not done because of
the understanding with some customers that their delivery price should be
pegged to book prices under PETS contracts—even if the book price itself
was no longer a legitimate barometer of market prices.[12]

The seeds for much disagreement and customer ill will were thereby sown.
The signers of PETS-type contracts had apparently never considered the
possibility that list prices might not be adjusted downward by significant
amounts, if that is what happened to actual prices in the market. As a result,
some utility customers concluded that escalation was a one-way street, operating only to the benefit of the manufacturers.

However, customers had other weapons at their disposal when faced with
the prospect of paying final prices which were clearly above the current
market level, as was the case in 1959–1961. They simply refused to honor
their purchase commitments. They canceled their orders, or they rescheduled
the shipping dates to some remote and unlikely time in the future. Astonish-
ingly, the contract penalties for doing so seem to have been insignificant or
nonexistent.[13] The rewards for breaking gentlemanly understandings were
reaped by buyer and seller alike.

Manifestly, buyer-seller relations in this industry had been rooted on the
understanding that the final price to be paid would reflect price levels at
time of shipment, and not at the time of order. During the price depression
of 1959–1961, the utilities were merely exercising this understanding. Thus,

---

[12] Q. You indicated that one of the reasons you did not reduce the book price in 1963
was that you would have to give the benefit of that reduction to those people who
had bought under this type of a deescalation provision? Wasn't it contemplated in
1959 and thereafter, at the time these orders were taken, that these customers would
receive the benefit of a decrease in book price?
A. No, it was not.
(Testimony of George B. Cox, stenographer's minutes, Ohio Valley Electric v. General Electric
et al., 62 Civ. 695, U.S. District Court, S.D.N.Y., pp. 1,754–1,755.)
[13] William Henry Colquhoun, president of Ebasco Services, explained:
[There were] normally either six-month or one-year cancellation clauses. If the market
had changed substantially from the original date of commitment and if the desired
trial operation of that piece of equipment was out beyond the period of time that the
original commitment would cover, [the customer] might well think of cancelling [the
order].
Q. So that during a price declining market price conditions, it was essentially open
to the utility on threat of cancelling the contract to renegotiate the prices continuously
until its original commitment was down to the then current market price?
A. That is correct.
(Deposition of W. H. Colquhoun, Electrical Equipment Antitrust Actions, in all U.S. district
courts, January 6, 1964.)

final delivered prices were renegotiated downward, but not without much wrangling along the way. The attempt of the manufacturers to wriggle out of the understanding, by sticking to the letter of the contracts, generally failed.

IMPACT OF ESCALATION ON PRICES

What was the net impact of escalation on the actual prices paid? It is clear from the testimony that when demand was strong, the manufacturers wrung very favorable escalation terms from their customers; when demand was weak, many utilities were "hard-nosed" about renegotiating contract prices downward. Thus, escalation was continuously modified in accord with supply and demand conditions. The final price paid might tend to reflect supply and demand conditions *in the period immediately preceding shipment.*

Escalation policies which were designed to exploit firm market conditions would tend to fall apart during soft market conditions. The alert utilities would be expected to balk at the tough escalation provisions of outstanding contracts, once they perceived a trend toward drastically lower prices. Renegotiation would then prevail. However, it is evident that many utilities did *not* renegotiate their contracts when prices collapsed in 1959–1962. The manufacturers encouraged such behavior by not adjusting book prices downward immediately. In a sense, the manufacturers were repaid in kind, when the utilities later used the huge percentage discount from book which resulted during 1960–1962, as a club with which to belabor the manufacturers during treble damage litigation.[14]

The extent to which price escalation occurred, in defiance of external market forces, has been measured statistically. The relationship between the rate of escalation on orders not yet delivered, and the rate of inflation on new order prices in the marketplace "outside," was tested for 1,567 turbine generators purchased in the United States over 1948–1963, for which both original order prices, and final delivered prices were available. (See Table 8.1.) The extent to which the manufacturers exploited those utilities which did not renegotiate their contracts during the post-1959 price collapse, is quite evident. The average escalation of existing orders over the entire 1948–1963 period was about 6.7 percent; however, the average price change in the external marketplace (for 1,567 transactions—the bulk of which overlapped the price collapse episode during manufacturing) was a *minus* 19 percent! Escalation pricing did *not*, therefore, reflect the identical market forces of supply and demand as did *order* prices originally. The central con-

---

[14] As the history of the civil litigation in my companion book points out, one far-fetched but legally devastating damage theory of the utility plaintiffs was based upon applying the "percent discount off book" which prevailed during the "competitive" period of 1960–1962, to contract prices which prevailed during the "conspiratorial period" of the 1950s. See: Sultan, *Pricing in the Electrical Oligopoly, Vol. I* (Boston: Harvard Business School, Division of Research, 1974), Chapter Four.

TABLE 8.1.

RELATIONSHIP BETWEEN ORDER PRICE ESCALATION AND THE CONCURRENT
CHANGE IN MARKET PRICE LEVEL: INDIVIDUAL UNIT ORDERS.

(1)   *Definitions*

$$\text{Escalation (I)} = \frac{\text{Final delivered price of Ith unit}}{\text{Original order price of Ith unit}}$$

$$\text{Delta Price (I)} = \frac{\substack{\text{Market price index at} \\ \text{time of delivery of Ith unit}}}{\substack{\text{Market price index at} \\ \text{time of order of Ith unit}}}$$

(2)   *Mean Values (1,567 transactions)*

Escalation	1.0667
Delta Price	.812

(3)   *Correlation Coefficient*   .26

(4)   *Regression Results*

Escalation (I) = .96 + .13 (Delta Price (I).)

$F = 110.$
$R^2 = \quad .07$
$SEE = \quad .07$

Sample size = 1,567 transactions (based on census of U.S. turbine generator orders for 1948–1963).

clusion is that order prices were determined by the pricing mechanism described in Chapter Seven; that is, they reflected the general trend in inflation, the rate of factory utilization, and minimum backlogs. However, escalated prices would rise from that negotiated figure, often in defiance of the external forces of supply and demand.

Can this divergence, the unlinking of the trend in market price and the trend in final contract price, be attributed to conspiracy? Unfortunately for the conspiratorial interpretation of electrical industry pricing, the unlinking was most obvious in the period *after* the conspiracy was revealed in 1959. This is hardly evidence of conspiratorial impact. It is instead evidence of the inability or unwillingness of the bulk of utilities to renegotiate their purchase prices downward, after 1959. The original conclusions about the nonimpact of conspiracy, and the lack of price sensitivity of the utility purchases, stand without modification.

VARIATIONS IN ESCALATION PRACTICE AMONG MANUFACTURERS

Manufacturers were not uniform in their escalation practices. For example, Westinghouse relaxed its escalation charges as a competitive weapon during

1956. The differences in escalation practices among Westinghouse, General Electric, and Allis-Chalmers, have been assessed through statistical analysis.

Variations in escalation could be an important competitive weapon, at least as important as cutting the order price directly. They were a hidden form of price cut and, as such, less susceptible to retaliation. By softening their escalation terms, Westinghouse and Allis-Chalmers could compete with General Electric, with less risk of dragging down the market level through overt pricing warfare.

It is possible to construct a statistical model of manufacturer sales revenues, using data on the physical volume (kilowatts) of manufacturer shipments, and the order price index. One cannot predict sales revenues as being the mere *product* of physical shipments and the relevant order price index; this would ignore escalation.[15]

Each manufacturer's escalation and sales revenue accounting policy was assessed statistically. Annual kilowatts shipments were weighted by the order price index with a varying lag, and compared with the dollar sales billed in each year, for each manufacturer. It was assumed that *billing* prices in any quarter approximated the *order* prices of some other quarter (perhaps the current quarter), regardless of when the order was taken. This corresponds to the hypothesis that final delivered prices were escalated in unison with the trend in actual market prices. The timing of the relevant price index was shifted consecutively all the way from date of order to final date of shipment, as a means of estimating which time delay provided the best statistical fit to the net sales billed data. (See Table 8.2.)

If the best fit is one wherein the relevant order price index is that *of the period in which final shipments were made*, this is evidence of 100 percent escalation in line with the trend in the market.

On the other hand, if the best fit is one wherein the order price index is that *of the period in which the original order was placed*, then this is strong evidence of zero escalation.

Finally, the best fitting price index may be that for some intermediate lag period, between order and delivery date.

---

[15] There is yet another complication: manufacturers took progress payments for work in process, and each progress payment was escalated separately, according to the time of payment. Other payments were not recorded until *after* date of shipment. Thus, accounting data on *orders invoiced*, was a blend of past, present, and future shipments from the factory.

Buehler, finance manager at Schenectady, explained:

> Output and shipments are the same. To compare that with sales, you have to analyze all the contracts that we shipped. Quite frequently we would ship a machine in a year and not be able to bill it for as long as two years afterwards, but usually it would be six to twelve months afterwards. A sale couldn't be billed until the job was complete, and there might be a big variation between partial shipments at the end of one year with partial shipments at the end of another year. This would show up in the unbilled shipments account.

(Testimony of C. F. Buehler, stenographer's minutes, *Ohio Valley Electric v. General Electric et al.*, 62 Civ. 695, U.S. District Courts, S.D.N.Y., pp. 2,899–2,900.)

TABLE 8.2.
REGRESSION RESULTS: FINDING BEST-FITTING ESCALATION PERIOD.

Data: Annual sales volume for turbine generator operations, in thousands of current
dollars, 1948–1963.
Annual kilowatts shipments, turbine generators, in thousands of kilowatts,
1948–1963.
Annual average of 4-quarter order price index (1961 book price = 100).
Total of 15 observations per firm.

Description of Variables:

GESALES(T) = General Electric sales revenue in year T
WESALES(T) = Westinghouse sales revenue in year T
ACSALES(T) = Allis-Chalmers sales revenue in year T
GESHIP(T)   = General Electric kilowatts shipments in year T
WESHIP(T)   = Westinghouse kilowatts shipments in year T
ACSHIP(T)   = Allis-Chalmers kilowatts shipments in year T
PRICE(T)   = Order price index as of year T

Regression Results: (The asterisk between two variables means multiplication of the two
variables.)

(a)   *General Electric:*

$$GESALES(T) = 83{,}615 + .157 GESHIP(T)*PRICE(T) \qquad R^2 = .90$$
$$(t = 11) \quad (t = 9.9)$$

$$GESALES(T) = 82{,}447 + .163 GESHIP(T)*PRICE(T\text{-}1) \qquad R^2 = .80$$
$$(t = 6.3) \quad (t = 6.3)$$

$$GESALES(T) = 89{,}919 + .152 GESHIP(T)*PRICE(T\text{-}2) \qquad R^2 = .46$$
$$(t = 3.2) \quad (t = 2.8)$$

$$GESALES(T) = 133{,}153 + .070 GESHIP(T)*PRICE(T\text{-}3) \qquad R^2 = .06$$
$$(t = 2.9) \quad (t = 0.8)$$

(b)   *Westinghouse:*

$$WESALES(T) = 17{,}694 + .167 WESHIP(T)*PRICE(T) \qquad R^2 = .77$$
$$(t = 2.2) \quad (t = 6.1)$$

$$WESALES(T) = 18{,}612 + .167 WESHIP(T)*PRICE(T\text{-}1) \qquad R^2 = .85$$
$$(t = 2.7) \quad (t = 7.5)$$

$$WESALES(T) = 12{,}461 + .195 WESHIP(T)*PRICE(T\text{-}2) \qquad R^2 = .91$$
$$(t = 2.0) \quad (t = 9.7)$$

$$WESALES(T) = 12{,}547 + .203 WESHIP(T)*PRICE(T\text{-}3) \qquad R^2 = .86$$
$$(t = 1.4) \quad (t = 7.0)$$

(c)   *Allis-Chalmers:*

$$ACSALES(T) = 6{,}146 + .222 \; ACSHIP(T)*PRICE(T) \qquad R^2 = .84$$
$$(t = 2.2) \quad (t = 7.7)$$

$$ACSALES(T) = 6{,}301 + .218 \; ACSHIP(T)*PRICE(T\text{-}1) \qquad R^2 = .87$$
$$(t = 2.3) \quad (t = 8.3)$$

$$ACSALES(T) = 5{,}189 + .240 \; ACSHIP(T)*PRICE(T\text{-}2) \qquad R^2 = .86$$
$$(t = 1.6) \quad (t = 7.7)$$

$$ACSALES(T) = 5{,}510 + .254 \; ACSHIP(T)*PRICE(T\text{-}3) \qquad R^2 = .82$$
$$(t = 1.3) \quad (t = 6.1)$$

For General Electric, a zero lag on the price index provided the optimal fit. This implies that General Electric was likely to apply full escalation; that final billed prices tended to be equivalent to the order prices which were current as of the date of shipment. (See Chart 8.1.)

CHART 8.1.   General Electric Annual Dollar Sales: Turbine Generators.

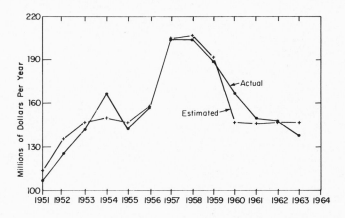

For Westinghouse, a two-year lag on the price index provided the optimal fit. This implies virtually zero escalation. The billed price tended to be the order price at the time the order was taken. (See Chart 8.2.)

CHART 8.2.   Westinghouse Annual Dollar Sales: Turbine Generators.

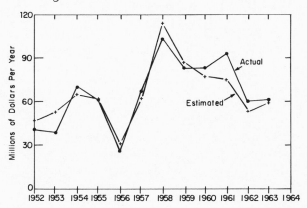

Finally, for Allis-Chalmers one obtains an intermediate result: a one-year lag. This suggests partial escalation, billed prices equivalent to the order price of some intermediate point in time between order date and shipment date. (See Chart 8.3.)

These are crude and approximate results, which apply only to the 1948–1963 period. Nevertheless, they are consistent with impressions of escalation

CHART 8.3.   Allis-Chalmers Annual Dollar Sales: Turbine Generators.

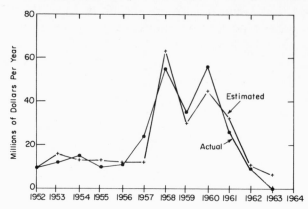

practices as garnered from testimony on the bickering of the electrical conspirators.[16]

A Note Concerning Differences in Product Mix

One may also discern from the statistical analysis the impact upon revenues of differences in product mix of each firm. From the statistical revenue equations, we have an estimate, on the margin, of the dollars of sales revenue produced per kilowatt of shipments. The three competitors are ranked as follows:

	Marginal Revenue Dollars per kw Shipped
General Electric	$15.70
Westinghouse	$19.50
Allis-Chalmers	$21.80

These are expressed in 1961 dollars. Differences among the three firms may be attributed largely to differences in product mix. The smaller the average size of the turbines produced, the higher the revenue per kilowatt yield, due to the economies inherent in producing large turbine generators. Differences in escalation practices, and/or differences in order price (holding product

---

[16] A further note of caution: a transaction-by-transaction analysis of all the turbine generator units purchased from domestic manufacturers during the 1950–1963 period reveals that, on the average, Allis-Chalmers escalated the lowest percentage of its units, Westinghouse the highest percentage of its units, and General Electric was in the middle. These contradictory results may be a consequence of when the large volumes of orders were taken by each competitor, and subsequent industry escalation experience. In other words, a large volume of Allis-Chalmers units was ordered immediately prior to a period of minimal escalation for the industry. The analysis presented in this chapter gives equal weight to each year of experience; in contrast, the transactions analysis reported in Volume I gives equal weight to each unit order of experience. See: Sultan, *Pricing in the Electrical Oligopoly, Vol. I* (Boston: Harvard Business School, Division of Research, 1974), Table 8.38.

mix constant), were much more modest among the three competitors, and could not account for such large variations.

Thus, General Electric produced the largest units, and received the lowest yield in dollars per kilowatt. Because of this product mix factor, General Electric was, in a sense, underpricing its competitors. Westinghouse had an intermediate revenue yield and an intermediate product mix. Thus, its product mix yielded more dollars, per kilowatt, than that of General Electric. Allis-Chalmers sold the smallest turbines and received the most dollars per kilowatt, because of the product mix factor.

CHAPTER Nine   Long-Term Trends in Value

IN THE TURBINE GENERATOR BUSINESS, the dollars-per-kilowatt cost has been steadily reduced. This has presumably been achieved through the combined workings of capital investments in highly productive plant and equipment, better work methods and a more highly skilled work force, continuous cost-reduction programs, and sheer learning and experience in the factory. In addition, a large measure of the downward trend in cost must be attributable to product innovation and redesign. Since large turbines are priced lower on a dollars-per-kilowatt basis, than are small turbines, this is strong *prima facie* evidence that economies are available through product technology. Such technological advances are quite independent of productivity advances in the factory.[1]

We are interested in assessing the character of the long-term cost trend. Unfortunately, one cannot assess this directly because our detailed *cost* data encompass only some 15 recent years.

For the very early periods of history, cost data are not to be found; but price data are readily available. And within the confines of our theoretical model, one may assess the long-term trend in unit costs by analyzing the long-term trend in selling prices. The virtue of this approach is the availability of price data for turbine generators spanning 66 years of history.

The purpose of this chapter is therefore to examine the nature of the

---

1 For related literature, see: W. Fellner, "Two Propositions in the Theory of Induced Innovations," *Economic Journal*, Vol. 71, 1961; Robert M. Solow, "Technical Change and the Aggregate Production Function," *Review of Economics and Statistics*, August 1957; Kenneth J. Arrow, "The Economic Implications of Learning by Doing," *Review of Economic Studies*, Vol. 29, 1962; Robert M. Solow, "Some Recent Developments in the Theory of Production," *The Theory and Empirical Analysis of Production*, National Bureau of Economic Research, 1967; T. P. Wright, "Factors Affecting the Cost of Airplanes," *Journal of Aeronautical Sciences*, Vol. 3, February 1936; Neil E. Harlan, *Management Control in Airframe Subcontracting*, Harvard Business School, Division of Research, 1956; A. R. Gallant, "A Note on the Measurement of Cost/Quality Relationships in the Aircraft Industry," *Journal of the American Statistical Association*, December 1968; E. W. Pike, "A Note on Learning Curves," *Journal of the American Statistical Association*, December 1969.

long-term trend in prices, in order to gauge the nature of the long-term trend in costs. Costs will then be analyzed directly, in Chapter Ten. As a check upon our results, the measured rate of decline in prices, assessed over the long run, may be compared with the measured rate of decline in costs, measured over a shorter period.

The Trend in Prices of Other Electrical Equipment

To provide even further substantiation, one may examine data on related products in this industry, under the hypothesis that the long-term trend in steam turbine generators has its counterpart in other items of electrical equipment. If the configuration of the long-term trend is similar for other industry products, then one can proceed with added confidence.

Three electrical industry products are examined: turbine generators, power transformers, and power capacitors, representative of the generating, transmission, and distribution segments of the industry, respectively.

Power transformers are the massive units which step up and step down transmission voltages at power station and major switching sites. They bear scant resemblance to the smaller distribution transformers on utility poles. Selling price data were obtained from the manufacturers, for 35 years of history. Power capacitors alter the capacitance of a distribution system, reducing distribution losses. They are off-the-shelf items, in contrast to turbine generators and power transformers. Price data are available for 47 years.

All three products share some common technologies, are marketed to utility customers, and are manufactured by more or less the same manufacturers.

Empirical Results: Long-Term Trends in "Value"

Price data, literally speaking, are not available for long time periods, and would be irrelevant even if they were. What is important is the long-term trend in *value* per unit, which is the combined result of price reductions and product mix shifts. Values are defined in this chapter as the *average* dollars of revenue per unit of physical output shipped by the industry. For example, one may divide total dollars by aggregate kilowatts of industry shipments for turbine generators. (This is different, it may be noted, from the more expansive use of "value" in the model of Chapter Two.)[2]

Steam Turbine Generators. Data on the average *value per kilowatt* of

---

[2] At the risk of pushing into a semantic bog, it seems important to emphasize the special meaning of "value" as it has been employed in this chapter. "Value" per unit, as employed in the statistical analysis of this chapter, is literally the average dollar value per kilowatt (or per KVAR, or per MVA) of industry shipment in each year. This may seem confusing in the context of the theory of Chapter Two which also refers to the rate of *increase* in value. However, that model is based upon a different meaning of the word "value": it refers to value to the customer in the full sense of the term; that is, the *increase* in values per kilowatt attributable to longer lived, more reliable equipment; and, in particular, turbine generators which will produce more kilowatt hours with fewer thermal units of coal.

steam turbine generator shipments are plotted against *cumulative kilowatt shipments* in Chart 9.1 for selected years over the 1904–1970 period. The dollars have been deflated by the wholesale price index (base 1957–1959 = 100).

This is a plot of dollar value per kilowatt. It is not an index of relative price for a constant "bundle" of goods, which would be a meaningless exercise, because the bundle of goods has changed continuously. The shift from units rated at 5,000 kilowatts in 1904, to units rated at 500,000 kilowatts in 1970, permitted an enormous reduction in the average dollars-per-kilowatt value. Thus, we are here looking at "revenue yield," what has been termed "price per unit of capacity" in the context of the theory in Chapter Two. Chart 9.1 reflects the composite result of changes in product mix *and* of changes in manufacturing efficiency.[3]

The cumulative kilowatts of *throughput experience* which are plotted in Chart 9.1 are those of General Electric, not those of the total industry. The reasoning here is that it is the market leader's experience or cumulative ship-

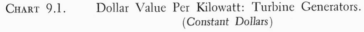

CHART 9.1.   Dollar Value Per Kilowatt: Turbine Generators.
(*Constant Dollars*)

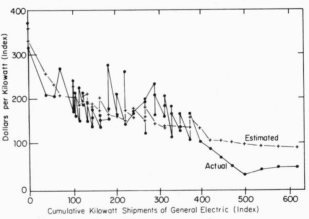

SOURCE: Electrical litigation data and unpublished company data.

ments which are most relevant in determining price trends in the long run, following the theory expounded in Chapter Two. It is assumed that the interchange of technological "experience" among competitors is limited. Thus, the experience of the firm which has the largest cumulative experience is most relevant. We are interested in the trend of costs for the most efficient producer, the market leader, since it is the costs of the market leader, in the long run, which will set the market price.

---

[3] As one reviewer has pointed out, to use the terminology "model" for these results would be to imply an elegance beyond what the simple tests in fact achieve. But an even tighter testing of the long-term cost model of Chapter Two is not feasible for the data availability reasons outlined.

On the other hand, the dollars-per-kilowatt values which are plotted on Chart 9.1 are estimates drawn from data for four individual "firms"; Westinghouse Philadelphia, Allis-Chalmers, General Electric Schenectady and General Electric Lynn (two quite separate businesses within General Electric). These estimates yield a total of 72 observations.

Recall the cost hypotheses of Chapter Two. If an aircraft-industry-type "learning curve" applies, one expects the points in a log-log plot to lie upon a straight line. One can test competing trend lines through regression analysis. The four alternatives tested were:

(1) log-log: the aircraft-industry-type learning curve. Logarithm of value is a linear function of the logarithm of cumulative shipments.

(2) semi-log: value is a linear function of the logarithm of cumulative shipments.

(3) linear: value is a linear function of cumulative shipments.

(4) trend: value is a linear time trend.

The detailed results of this statistical competition are shown in Appendix 10.

Power Capacitors. We used the same approach to assess the trend in average values per kilovar of power capacitors, for shipments over 1921–1968. Dollars per kilovar[4] (deflated to constant 1957–1959 dollars by the wholesale price index) versus cumulative kilovars shipments (at the total industry level) are plotted in Chart 9.2. Regression results are shown in Appendix 11.

CHART 9.2. Price Per Kilovar: Power Capacitors.
(Constant Dollars)

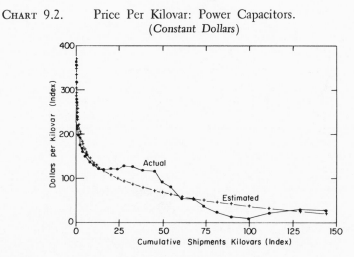

SOURCE: Data made available to the author by General Electric.

For capacitors, the log-log trend line is the clearly superior specification. As with the previous turbine generator data, the downward trend in dollars per

---

[4] Kilovar is an engineering measure of capacitor capacity.

kilovar power capacitor values reflects a strong component of technical change in the product. The average size of power capacitors increased from 2½ kilovars per unit in 1921 to over 100 kilovars in 1968.

Power Transformers. As a final check upon the long-term trend in electrical equipment values, data were examined for the average value of large power transformers shipped by domestic manufacturers in the United States. Chart 9.3 shows estimates of the average dollars per MVA value of power transformers shipped, plotted against estimates of the cumulative MVA shipments for the domestic industry, for the period 1933 to 1968.[5] Again, this was a period of rapid technological advance. For example, the average size of unit shipped by the power transformer industry increased from about 8 MVA in 1958 to over 18 MVA in 1969. As before, the dollar values have been deflated by the general wholesale price index.

Regression test results are shown in Appendix 11. The log-log model was far superior in depicting the trend in values per MVA for power transformers.

CHART 9.3.   Dollar Value Per MVA: Power Transformers.
(*Constant Dollars*)

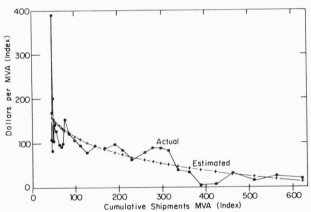

SOURCE: Data made available to the author by Westinghouse.

My conclusion is that, in depicting the revenue yield for turbine generators, capacitors, and transformers, the conventional learning curves best capture the long-term trend. However, yet to be disentangled are the separate influences of (a) technological *product* changes, and (b) the influence of other "learning" in the *factory*, which may be attributable to plant and equipment investments, experience, and improved production technology.

COMPARING THE RATES OF PROGRESS: THREE PRODUCTS

Now compare the rates of progress for all three products. The parameter of interest is the slope of the learning curve, from which one may estimate the

---

[5] MVA = MegaVolt-Amp, which is a measure of power transformer throughput capacity.

cost reduction elasticities; that is, the cost reduction achieved with each doubling of throughput experience.[6] The statistical results for the three products are shown in Table 9.1.

TABLE 9.1.

LONG-TERM TREND IN VALUES PER UNIT OF ELECTRIC EQUIPMENT SHIPMENTS, BASED UPON LEARNING CURVE ANALYSIS

Product	Time Period Encompassed	Unit of Measure (In Constant Dollars)	Ratio of Costs per Unit with Each Doubling of Output Experience[a]
Steam Turbine Generators	1904–1970	$ per KW	87%
Power Capacitors	1921–1968	$ per KVAR	68%
Power Transformers	1933–1968	$ per MVA	75%

[a] Interpretation: If total output of steam turbine generators, on a cumulative throughput basis, climbs from 6 million to 12 million kilowatts, costs per kilowatt will decline from an index of 100 to an index of 87.

The principal findings are: *With each doubling of historical output, unit prices have declined by 13 percent for turbine generators, by 32 percent for power capacitors, and by 25 percent for power transformers.* An 80 percent learning curve has been touted as applicable to aerospace projects. By comparison with the aerospace industry, it seems that a remarkably high rate of cost reduction was achieved by the electrical equipment industry.

ADJUSTING LONG-TERM VALUES FOR PRODUCT MIX

It remains to be determined whether the cost reduction which has occurred is mostly attributable to product technology (i.e., through introducing larger and more complex steam turbine generators), or whether it is attributable to advances in manufacturing technology, quite apart from product changes.[7] One can isolate the impact of *product* technology by introducing

---

[6] The underlying form of the learning curve relationship is:
$$y_i = ai^b$$
where y_i is the cost of the ith unit, and "a" is the cost of the first. The parameter "b" is a measure of the rate of learning. The slope of the learning curve is expressed in percentage terms as:
$$S = 2^b \times 100\%$$
A slope of S percent means that each time the total quantity of units produced is doubled, costs per unit decline by $100 - S$ percent.

In conventional fashion, parameters a and b were estimated through regression analysis, using the transformed equation:
$$\log (y_i) = \log a + b (\log i)$$

[7] This is similar to the issue examined in a study by Solow in which the rate of productivity

a proxy variable for product technology, in the statistical analysis: the average size per unit (average kilowatts per unit shipped). The results are presented in Appendix 10.

The statistical estimates suggest that price reductions have taken place through increases in the average size of unit shipped, *as well as* through cumulative experience. Investments in *product* technology and investments in *manufacturing* technology must simultaneously be credited with the sustained downward trend in unit prices. The elasticity estimates are:

	Steam turbine generators	
	Product technology variable (average size of unit)	Experience variable (cumulative kilowatts production)
Ratio of prices with each doubling of size, or of experience	about 93%	about 93%

Doubling the size of the average unit (from 250,000 to 500,000 kilowatts, say) had the effect of reducing the price per kilowatt by about 7 percent. Meanwhile, doubling the cumulative production experience had the quite independent effect of reducing the price per kilowatt by another 7 percent. (At the historical rate of growth of this industry, doubling of production experience occurs approximately every ten years; thus, in the absence of technological change, real selling prices per unit could be expected to decline 7 percent every ten years.)

The overall 87 percent learning curve for turbine generators has therefore been split into two components: a 93 percent curve for product technology and a 93 percent curve for cumulative production experience. Let me emphasize again that these are estimates of two special kinds of "elasticities": of value per kilowatt with respect to the size of unit, and of value per kilowatt with respect to production experience.

The observed elasticities are a reflection of discretionary pricing decisions by managers. While this pricing behavior is in part the consequence of the long-term trend in costs, and competition which forces prices to maintain some relationship with costs in the long run, it is also a consequence of deliberate product-line pricing *strategy*. In other words, the revenue figures will be shaped by managerial decisions—particularly with respect to the prices to be charged for advanced-technology versus low-technology machines.

increase for the total economy was decomposed into one component attributable to technology, and another attributable to capital intensiveness, etc. See: Robert M. Solow, "Technical Change and the Aggregate Production Functions," *Review of Economics and Statistics*, August 1957. For an analysis which embodies all productivity change in the product variable, *see* Robert M. Solow, "Technical Progress, Capital Formation and Economic Growth," *American Economic Review*, Vol. 52, 1962.

Product-line pricing strategy will determine how rapidly any decline in costs due to technology will be transferred to customers, through reductions in the per-unit revenue yield. This topic will be analyzed further in Chapter Ten when the magnitude of product-technology related *cost* trends will be contrasted with product-technology related *pricing* trends, as a means of determining what proportion of cost reductions is reflected, subsequently, in revenue yield reductions, and what proportion is withheld from the customer in the form of a quasi-rent.

Differences Among Firms

Regression analysis might also detect differences in the trend line in value per kilowatt among General Electric, Westinghouse, and Allis-Chalmers. One firm, Allis-Chalmers, had a higher average value per kilowatt shipped, even after adjusting for the smaller sized units which Allis-Chalmers manufactured over this period of time. In addition, there is some slight tendency (hardly statistically significant) for Westinghouse average values to be biased in the same direction. This result was completely unexpected (Appendix 10).

One may immediately dismiss the possibility that Allis-Chalmers was selling steam turbine generators at *markedly* lower prices; there is too much evidence that price differentials were, at most, a few percentage points. The most plausible explanation of this phenomenon is that General Electric, the price leader and the producer of the largest sized units, was systematically and continually forcing a modification of the price schedule (i.e., the published book price schedule of dollars-per-kilowatt versus kilowatts size of unit) so that eventually a product mix "bundle" consisting of *smaller* units was *priced higher for competitors* than a similar product mix "bundle" had been priced for General Electric itself, at some earlier time when General Electric was producing such a bundle of smaller sized units. Of course, over time, due to the gathering cumulative experience, units of *all* sizes are decreasing in price. But the larger sized units are being decreased in price faster than are the smaller sized units.

Of what strategic sense is this? It implies a particularly "soft" form of product-line pricing strategy. The continued advance toward more experience and larger sized units gave the market leader an opportunity to force *downward* the realized prices of the follower firms, to, in effect, handicap them for being followers in product mix. But it appears that General Electric passed this opportunity by. Instead, *it appears that the leader firm actually permits its competitors to charge higher-than-anticipated prices for their product mix—the opposite of any conjectured price "squeeze."*

If this is indeed the case (and one must stress the frailty of the statistical evidence) such a product-line pricing strategy could make sense on the ground of (a) the necessity of keeping relatively high-cost competitors in business, which gives General Electric an incentive not to exercise the maximum price competition of which it is capable by virtue of its advanced technology, and (b) the desirability of motivating customers to switch to the more economical large-sized units. The second result could best be achieved by permitting a large price differential to emerge between the older, obsolescent and smaller machines, and the advanced machines where General Electric was temporarily in a monopoly position. This result would permit the leader firm to exercise selectivity in jobs taken and some greater measure of control over the flow of orders in the marketplace. *An additional result would be reduced incentive, in terms of prices and margins, for the follower firms to wean themselves from the smaller sized units, even though by marketing smaller units they surrendered some measure of market control. The arrangement could be symbiotic.*

These results are consistent with the findings of the "tipping the curve" strategy, to be discussed in Chapter Twelve. In that chapter is presented further evidence of systematic product-line pricing actions by the market leader, which actions have the consequence of providing temporary shelter for the obsolescent technologies of follower firms. In sum, the market leader does not impose, through overt product-line pricing, any short-run "technology squeeze" upon the follower firms in the revenues they receive; quite the contrary, the squeeze is upon unit revenues for the higher technology units. The "squeeze" on the follower firms comes in the longer run, as customers are given maximum incentive to shift out of the older, obsolescent technologies.

CHAPTER Ten   Direct and
Overhead Costs

THE COST ACCOUNTING SYSTEMS of both Westinghouse and General Electric reveal that these two firms recorded, and managed, their costs in two broad categories: direct costs and overhead costs. Direct costs included hourly labor, material, purchased components, and indirect factory expense. Overhead costs included general and administrative expense, financial charges, corporate assessments, and advanced engineering and marketing. Any analysis of cost behavior is most appropriately divided on the same basis.

This chapter contains an analysis of *direct* costs for each competitor, as well as an analysis of *overhead* costs. First, let us explore what line managers had to say about the subject.

DIRECT COSTS

During the electrical equipment litigation, the operating managers of Allis-Chalmers, Westinghouse, and General Electric were quizzed as to the determinants of their manufacturing costs. Their answers provided a rich vein of information concerning management perceptions as to the reason for cost variations in the factory. That testimony provides a list of the factors which were then employed as a source of hypotheses for statistical testing.

Variation in Direct Cost: Management Testimony

The first source of manufacturing cost variation cited in the managerial testimony was the degree of capital expenditures on new plant and equipment. William Kuyper, manager of manufacturing engineering of General Electric, testified that large productivity gains were achieved through investments in new plant and equipment.[1] As a rule of thumb, according to

---

[1] William Kuyper, manager of Manufacturing Engineering in General Electric's Large Steam Turbine Generator Department in Schenectady, observed:

We spend all our energies in getting the best tools that could be gotten, as good business practice. In the analysis of putting the tools in place, developing the methods

Kuyper, a doubling of plant space, accompanied by modernization of machine tools, could lead to a quadrupling of output. In addition, special purpose machine tools led to vastly increased productivity in the shop.

"Programmed" cost reductions were a second source of cost variation in the factory. These cost reductions were singled out as explicit targets in the budget. Buehler of General Electric explained that over 40 cost-reduction committees had been organized, involving over 400 engineering and manufacturing personnel. Achievements relative to the cost-reduction budget were audited at the end of each year.[2] Annual reductions on the order of 2 to 5 percent of manufacturing cost were common.[3] Other less formal efforts reduced costs by 6 to 8 percent per year.[4] It is important to note that these cost reductions were *cumulative*; that is, the reductions of one year were in addi-

---

and the time standards [we had] about 50 men. This grew to about 80. Above that, we wanted the most efficient [facilities] that we could afford, in order that we would be in the best position to compete in the future. Beyond that, we wanted to displace the old facilities. You try to get the most output per investment, you try to get the lowest labor cost per unit of investment, you try to get the lowest cycle time, all of these things are not necessarily consistent, but you can often arrive at a very fine optimum.

. . . (in 1954) . . . most of the large tools at least were pre-war tools of older standard types . . . we found that the most favorable things we could buy were special tools, tools ideally adapted to the work to be done . . . . These were largely metal cutting tools. We seldom, almost never came to less than two to one, and we obtained three to one and better in terms of time cycle and man hours. . . .

(Testimony of W. Kuyper, stenographer's minutes, Ohio Valley Electric v. General Electric et al., 62 Civ. 695, S.D.N.Y. pp. 2,135–2,136.)

[2] Buehler, manager of Finance at General Electric's Large Steam Turbine Generator Department, describes the cost-reduction program at Schenectady:

By 1935 we had an annual budget of cost reduction in each department in Schenectady and lists of projects and monthly reports of accomplishments.

The engineer in charge of the program would discuss the total budget for the coming year with the section managers of the department, and we would arrive at a total budget. Then he would allocate this budget to all of the various committees which he had organized. Each had a target to shoot at for the coming year.

He added: A very substantial "hope factor" which was supposed to, and did, encourage new ideas to come in.

Each project, upon completion by the committees, was turned over to the cost accounting section and they audited it to make sure it was accurate. There would be disputes. Sometimes I had to referee them.

(Testimony of C. F. Buehler, stenographer's minutes, Ohio Valley Electric, pp. 2,735–2,742.)

[3] Testimony of Buehler, Ohio Valley Electric, p. 2,743.

[4] William Kuyper of General Electric Schenectady, observed:

The bogeys for the cost-reduction activity were increased gradually from 1957 until they were pretty high, stabilized at six percent, and then going up to about eight percent.

(Testimony of W. Kuyper, stenographer's minutes, City of San Antonio v. General Electric et al., Civ. 3064, W.D. Texas, pp. 6,215–6,216.)

At Lynn, the General Electric organization reported a 15 percent cost reduction accomplished within two years, or about 7½ percent per year.

(Testimony of W. Kuyper, San Antonio pp. 6,141–6,142.)

tion to the reductions of the year before. Thus, over time, a progressive lowering of costs was achieved.[5]

The intensity of cost-reduction effort was apparently inversely proportional to the current rate of manufacturing output.[6] When the plant was busy, attention was diverted away from the cost-reduction program, but when work in the shop was slack, cost-cutting received more attention.

In view of our adoption of the concept of "learning," it is important to note that the ongoing cost reduction program was unrelated to new capital investments. Learning may result in better manufacturing methods, cost-saving ideas, and greater worker skill. Management testimony just cited suggests that annual cost reductions ranging from 2 to 7 percent were attained on this basis.

A third factor, inflation in labor and materials prices, tended to offset the efficiency gains achieved through capital expenditures or by the annual cost-reduction programs. One manager observed ". . . wage increases, material increases, all of these things offset what you do on a cost-reduction program."[7]

Fourth, manufacturing managers perceived that there was some relationship between the plant utilization rate and average costs in the short run. According to Herman Hill of General Electric, "Once you exceed approximately 85 percent of normal capacity, you are not at the optimum point cost-wise." Costs would rise because of seven-day overtime manning of bottleneck plant facilities, night-shift premiums, reworking of mistakes in machining, excessive materials waste, and the hiring of less-skilled workers, as output climbed beyond rated capacity.[8]

---

[5] Kuyper, Ohio Valley Electric, pp. 2,107–2,108.

[6] Herman Hill, manager of Manufacturing at Schenectady, observed:

> In the early fifties, most of our top skilled people, management and labor, were aimed at getting production out. This is where they were needed, where they were used, as supervisory personnel. When our volume was reduced in 1958, 1959, started down, we took some of our top people and devoted them principally to new tooling, new methods and new procedures to see if we could become more productive.

(Testimony of Herman Hill, stenographer's minutes, Ohio Valley Electric v. General Electric et al., 62 Civ. 695, S.D.N.Y., p. 2,075.)

[7] Brown, manager of the General Electric Lynn manufacturing engineering organization, asserted:

> The cost-reduction activity is only one-half of the story. There are other elements that continuously have the effect of increasing it: wage increases, material increases, all of these things offset what you do on a cost-reduction program.

(Testimony of T. Brown, Jr., stenographer's minutes, City of San Antonio v. General Electric et al., Civ. 3064, W.D. Texas, pp. 6,149–6,150.)

[8] Herman Hill, former Manufacturing manager at Schenectady, testified:

> . . . The first thing that happens, you attempt to man your equipment, particularly those limiting pieces of equipment, on a seven-day basis around the clock. As a result of this you incur additional losses and machine interferences as a result of the skills you have to bring into the shop that are not the true skills that you would have on a standard basis.

A fifth factor which, according to manufacturer testimony, influenced costs, was engineering in its nature: a steady advance in the state of the art in manufacturing. Two examples cited by General Electric managers from the 1950s pertained to defect-free castings and "clean" forgings.[9] Managers were continually learning new ways to improve upon their complex manufacturing technologies.

A sixth factor which, managers said, influenced costs, was the feedback of external business conditions upon costs and productivity. Efficiencies deteriorated and internal costs climbed when the pressures of highly competitive market conditions were relaxed.[10]

On the other hand, any such slackness would tend to disappear, once there was a restoration of strong competition in the marketplace—in the period 1959–1963, for example.[11] This cyclical fluctuation in costs was attributed

---

This causes your costs to go up, it also causes your machine times to go up and you barely find the time to perform the maintenance that you need on the equipment.

The night shift bonus goes up, the overtime premium goes up, you have to work long shifts to cover for those people who have to have a day off for the Sunday work, which causes additional overtime premium, so your costs skyrocket.

It causes rework, because of the people who are brought in who do not have the kind of skills that you would like to have on a normal basis, you have machining errors and inaccuracy in the drawings. When you get to the assembly plates the parts will not fit, and they have to go back to be remachined. Almost without question, any operation that works a high percentage of overtime will have a loss curve that will be in direct proportion to the overtime.

(Testimony of Herman Hill, stenographer's minutes, Ohio Valley Electric, pp. 2,048–2,050.)

[9] Hill of General Electric testified:

In the early fifties, we were rejecting, either at the steel mills or at the turbine plant, 35 percent of the forgings. In the early sixties, this number had shrunk to five percent.

Q. These examples that you have given of the castings and forging problems had to do with the state of the art at that time?

A. That is correct.

(Herman Hill, stenographer's minutes, Ohio Valley Electric, pp. 2,051–2,054.)

[10] Peters of General Electric cited the "lack of control of labor and labor demands" in the pre-1958 period, and:

You had very high demand; you had inflation that we were very conscious of, in increasing materials and labor costs, and you had high backlogs in all manufacturers' shops and demand of such a nature that we were forced to work six and seven days.

[But] along in that period we were hit with foreign competition and Parsons got an order at TVA for two-thirds of what we had quoted, and Brown and Boveri did the same thing at the City of Los Angeles. This, let us say, shot gave the manufacturing people the lever to get across to the man on the floor, to the working man, to the direct laborer, that their jobs were really jeopardized, their continuity of employment was really jeopardized if they didn't get out and really give us a good day's work for a day's pay. And they really began to become more productive and give a better day's work.

(Deposition of John T. Peters, Electrical Equipment Antitrust Actions, in all U.S. district courts, April 17, 1963.)

[11] Bill Ginn, vice president of the General Electric Turbine Division, made a similar point:

Q. Did you in point of fact pursue cost-reduction policies with the same vigor in 1957 that you did in 1960 and 1961?

A. Personally, yes.

to declining worker and management productivity during prosperous business conditions, followed by a tightening of work standards during the lean years. The phenomenon has been noted by others, notably C. Northcote Parkinson and Cyert and March.[12]

A seventh factor which could cause variations in costs, was the unique technology of each competitor, and the speed with which this technology was transferred among firms. Leader firms in other respects also tended to set the pace in manufacturing technology. With a time lag, other firms would adopt these lower cost manufacturing techniques. In the long run, all of these firms would be forced to adopt a lower cost technology, in response to price competition in the marketplace. The feedback from the technological leaders to the follower firms could be direct, and not necessarily induced via competition in the marketplace; that is, product-design technologies were cross-licensed, and machine tool and other suppliers created a communications link to disseminate manufacturing technology. On rare occasions, managers were even invited to tour their competitors' factories. Although manufacturers would seldom expose all of their proprietary manufacturing methods during such tours, knowledgeable observers could glean an impression of the pace of technological change and new cost-cutting techniques.[13]

To summarize, management testimony points to seven factors which shaped turbine generator costs, beyond the product technology variable.

Q. Did your department?
A. No.
Q. You were unsuccessful in getting them to reduce costs?
A. I didn't say I was unsuccessful. I was not so successful, to the extent that once the foreign machines began to arrive on the shores then I was more successful in motivating the people in the shop.
(Deposition of William A. Ginn, Electrical Equipment Antitrust Actions, in all U.S. district courts, January 14, 1963.)

12 A General Electric memorandum, for example, complained about "the 200 to 300 percent increase in the profit markup percentage made effective on January 1, 1952, by most of our principal internal suppliers." (Cited during testimony of Buehler, stenographer's minutes, Ohio Valley Electric, p. 2,831.) See also: Richard M. Cyert and J. G. March, *A Behavioral Theory of the Firm* (Englewood Cliffs, N.J.: Prentice-Hall, 1963).

13 Herman Hill reports as follows:
I kept getting reports that the European manufacturers were fast equipping themselves to build any kind of turbine generator sets that we could. So in 1958, I took a trip. I visited and talked with the English Electric people, I visited with WTH plant in Rugby, the Metropolitan Vickers Company in Manchester; BTH's plant in Larne, Ireland; AEG in Berlin, also one of their plants in Muelheim, Siemens in Berlin; Brown Boveri in Switzerland; Alsthon in Belport, France.

Most of these plants had new, modern, up-to-date equipment. It would take them two to three years to equip themselves skillwise to produce the same kind of designs and size machines that we were producing.

They could do these at less cost than ourselves because of the basic difference in the cost of materials and labor.

[As a result of this trip] I launched a program . . . aimed at reducing our cost, to become competitive with what I thought the cost level would be in Europe.
(Testimony of Herman Hill, stenographer's minutes, Ohio Valley Electric, pp. 2,068–2,073.)

Three of these produced a long-term trend toward cost *reduction*: (1) investment in new plant and equipment, (2) programmed cost reduction in the factory ex-capital investments, and (3) other inspirational advances in the state of the art in manufacturing technology. These three factors could be managed differently or there could be different opportunities for realizing various economies across the three firms. This could produce cost differentials across firms, as well as a long-term cost decline for the industry as a whole.

Another key cost determinant, according to manufacturer testimony, was the plant utilization rate. Very high output would lead to increased costs, because of bottlenecks and inefficiencies.

There were two factor-related cost phenomena: the obvious impact of factor *prices* (e.g., direct labor wages per hour; copper prices per pound) upon manufacturing costs; and the less obvious impact of factor-utilization *efficiencies* upon total factor cost. Under boom conditions, prices would tend to rise; efficiencies would drop as well. Under this joint impact, total factor costs would rise.[14]

Finally, one discerns in the testimony a connecting link which prevents any competitor from being completely unaware of competitors' manufacturing and product technologies: "Technological transfer" among competitors would tend to keep all of the firms operating with the best available methods, constrained only by the asset and scale capabilities of each individual firm.

A Model of Direct Costs

The weight of management testimony on the subject of costs, plus the theoretical and empirical research of other economists, suggests that the following variables may have some statistically measurable impact upon the level of direct costs per kilowatt for each of the *individual* turbine builders:

(1) Cumulative production experience of the firm.
(2) General factor price inflation.
(3) Product technology (average size of unit shipped).
(4) Rate of utilization of factory capacity.
(5) Technology transfer among competitors.
(6) Feedback of order prices upon costs.

First, it is hypothesized that the long-term trend in direct costs for *each* competitor follows a learning curve trend, and that the rate of learning is

---

[14] One referee has observed that he would have expected the managers to testify as to high costs due to underutilization of people and equipment during business *slumps*, further observing that if this was not the case, then it must be due to "strange bookkeeping." My explanation is that the managers were possibly thinking of performance relative to standard unit costs in this testimony, and not of the actual total cost-versus-total revenue situation in the factory. Costs relative to some norm could be climbing, even as costs relative to revenues were dropping.

correlated with the rate of accumulation of production experience of each firm. Cumulative throughput must be a proxy for the cumulative productivity gains of sheer learning, improved manufacturing knowledge, capital investment in manufacturing, cumulatively improved work methods, cumulatively increasing worker skill and education, and the like. Thus, cumulative production throughput since the year 1900, for each of the three competitors, becomes a key explanatory variable for their respective direct costs.[15]

The theoretical model of Chapter Two allowed for *both* learning and economies of scale to co-exist. In our crude statistical measures, we shall be unable to discern the blend of the two. My final choice of learning, as opposed to absolute scale, may raise a few eyebrows. It is possible that any "learning" phenomenon which we may perceive is *entirely* attributable to the current scale of operations, and not to any blend of historical learning combined with current scale.

Clearly, there are major economies of scale in this industry, combined with a significant tendency for a continuous secular increase in productivity. The issue, in empirical measurement, really boils down to a choice between two specifications of the cost model: the classical economies of scale hypothesis from micro-theory, combined with secular productivity growth; or, alternatively, wrapping both productivity change and scale together, into a single "learning" phenomenon. These are really not opposing theories of cost; one is simply an hypothesis of greater order in economic affairs than is the other. The learning hypothesis is a subset of the economies of scale plus secular productivity change hypothesis, and, if it fits empirical experience, it is a much neater and more useful definition of the behavior of direct costs.

The costs of this business are hardly immune from the effects of general inflation in the economy. To remove the influence of the general inflation in labor and materials prices (factor prices), all of the cost data to be studied were first converted into constant 1957–1959 dollars.

A third variable which surely influences direct costs is product technology. It has already been demonstrated in Chapter Nine that product technology —as measured by the average rating of units shipped, in kilowatts-per-unit— has a measurable effect upon the trend in *prices*. It would therefore be astonishing if product technology did not also have some impact upon *costs*. This is strongly supported by the long-term trend toward reduced unit prices

---

15 One referee observed that cumulative production throughput at any point in time is equivalent to the current annual rate of production, if market shares are constant, so that any statistical test of "learning" is tantamount to a statistical test of simple economies of scale. My rebuttal: this is true, insofar as a comparison of the costs of competitor A versus B versus C *at one point in time* is concerned. However, when the costs of A in 1937, and the costs of A in 1963, the costs of B in 1950, and the costs of C in 1960, all lie upon the *same* learning curve, then it would be awkward to demonstrate with a simple economies-of-current-scale model that something else (i.e., an underlying secular downshift in costs) was not simultaneously present. For want of a better term, call it "learning."

as technology has advanced, and in view of the typical price-size curve which manufacturers offer to their customers at any point in time.[16]

A fourth variable, which both management testimony and economic theory (but not very often economists' empirical cost studies) suggest should influence the level of direct costs, is the rate of factory utilization. It was asserted that the optimum level of factory usage is about 85 percent of capacity in this business; that beyond 85 percent utilization, marginal costs rise. There is yet another reason to test for the impact of factory utilization upon costs: we previously concluded that turbine *prices* are influenced by average industry factory utilization. It now should be possible to ascertain whether this pricing behavior is cost-based, or whether it is more in the nature of a psychological response by managers to perceived demand conditions.

It is hypothesized that the transfer of manufacturing and engineering knowledge from the pioneering firm to the follower firms, the next factor, should result in lower average costs for the follower firms, *given comparable levels of cumulative experience.* The reason should be intuitively obvious: they do not have to "re-invent the wheel" if they have access to the manufacturing technology of the leader firm. The transfer of manufacturing technology will be manifested in a downward shift in follower firms' costs, relative to the leader.

Finally, it appears that there are rather good prospects for the discovery of some feedback from demand conditions in the marketplace, to manufacturing costs. An inflation of manufacturing costs may well occur during periods of heavy backlogs, high order prices, prosperity, and general management euphoria. Such euphoria invariably leads to a reduction in management pressures for efficiency, leading in turn to softness in bargaining with the various factors of production, for example, particularly raw materials suppliers and the workers themselves. The drive for programmed cost reductions may likewise be relaxed. However, with a decline in prices and a return to harsher business conditions, managements' cost-paring knife may return, and internal efficiencies should rise.

---

[16] Some idea of the relationship between the direct manufacturing costs *for a specific point in time*, between various sized turbine generator units, may be obtained from the following data showing direct labor and material costs, by rating, in the 1960s:

Cross-Compound Units (General Electric)

Rating (in Kilowatts)	Cost Per Kilowatt
150,000 to 199,000	$14.51
200,000 to 249,000	$11.76
250,000 to 299,000	$11.02
300,000 to 599,000	$10.56
600,000 and larger	$ 7.66

SOURCE: *Defendants' Post-Trial Brief and Proposed Findings,* Ohio Valley Electric v. General Electric et al., 62 Civ. 695, U.S. District Court, S.D.N.Y.

Such a feedback from market conditions to manufacturing costs may be manifested in some correlation between the level of order prices in the market, and direct costs, even after direct costs have been stripped of any influence of general factor price inflation. Some observers may argue that such an effect, even if statistically present, merely reflects the impact of inflation in factor prices *upon* costs and therefore upon the turbine generator price level. Such direction-of-causality debates are seldom resolved one way or the other. In the present context, *order* prices will not be matched against some factory costs until two to three years after the order has been taken. It therefore seems unlikely that the direction of causality is other than in the direction suggested: from selling prices to factory costs, and not vice versa.

Perhaps the most potent factor of all, in explaining differences in the costs of Allis-Chalmers, Westinghouse, and General Electric—and hence their vast differences in profitability—is the difference in their respective accumulated manufacturing "experience," and all the various phenomena which that variable stands for. One fundamental question, therefore, is the degree to which the costs of these three firms do lie upon a *single* learning curve when the direct cost data for each are plotted versus *each* firm's corresponding manufacturing experience since the time it entered the business some 75 years ago.

The adherence of direct costs for each firm, to one common underlying trend line may be appraised from Chart 10.1. This is a graph of direct costs

CHART 10.1.   Direct Costs Per Kilowatt (in Constant 1957–1959 Dollars) v. Cumulative Kilowatt Shipments for General Electric, Westinghouse, and Allis-Chalmers.

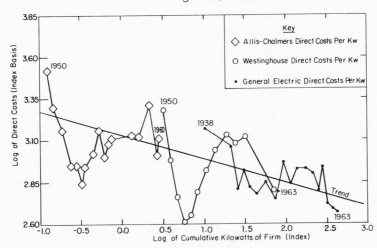

per kilowatt (on an index number basis) versus the cumulative kilowatt shipments of the individual competitors. (All costs have been deflated to constant 1957–1959 dollars.) The goodness of fit of one common learning curve to the pooled direct cost data seems to be fairly good, but any conclusions are best derived from statistical analysis.

Summary of Statistical Results

The statistical results of applying the direct cost model to data on three "firms" (General Electric Schenectady, Westinghouse Philadelphia, and Allis-Chalmers) are presented in Appendix 12. The learning hypothesis is accepted.

Statistical analysis also reveals a second variable which is strongly correlated with direct costs: this is product technology, as measured by the average unit rating of turbine generators shipped. This result was expected. Big units can be built for fewer dollars per kilowatt, albeit at the cost of overhead spending in order to create new technology. This finding applies to the average unit rating of a shifting bundle of products over time, and is merely the time-series counterpart of a fact already demonstrated to hold true at any single point in time: the progressive reduction in direct manufacturing costs as unit ratings increase.

Next, consider the statistical results as they pertain to the basic learning curve hypothesis: *direct costs per kilowatt appear to be related to the cumulative kilowatts production experience of each individual firm.* This result is highly significant. The learning curve in manufacturing appears to apply to the *individual* manufacturing experience of each competitor. The results imply that the leader firm, with some 60 percent of historical production experience, has an almost uncatchable advantage in manufacturing costs. Allis-Chalmers, with less than 10 percent of historical experience, and Westinghouse, with the remaining 30 percent share of experience, seem locked into a perennially higher cost position, unless they can thrust ahead of General Electric in the market for a sustained period of time.

(An aside: if readers want to interpret these statistical results as merely proving the existence of economies of scale, I agree with their conclusion— as long as they admit also to the presence of a strong secular productivity increase, which by coincidence fits the shape of the economies of scale function to produce the net result reported above.)

The magnitude of the follower firms' cost disadvantage may be crudely estimated. As of 1963—the last year in which all three competitors were active in the marketplace—General Electric had accumulated about 138 million kilowatts of throughput experience, Westinghouse 70 million kilowatts, and Allis-Chalmers about 17 million kilowatts of experience in the domestic utility market over the period 1898–1963. Assume for the purpose of a hypothetical illustration that a goal is established by Westinghouse managers to catch up with the level of General Electric direct costs within ten years. Total industry shipments are growing at 7 percent annually. By 1973 cumulative industry throughput will be in the neighborhood of 415 million kilowatts, according to these assumptions. If Allis-Chalmers drops out of the race, this means that Westinghouse and General Electric must each have accumulated about 207 million kilowatts of experience by 1973. However, General Electric in 1963 had already slightly exceeded that throughput. The implied result is that, in order for Westinghouse to catch up with General Electric's level of direct costs, it must acquire 100 percent market share for the next ten years. The scenario is fantastically unreal, and illustrates why any shift in the direct cost hierarchy is unlikely to occur.

The third variable which appears to have a statistically significant impact upon direct manufacturing costs is demand conditions in the marketplace, as measured by the proxy variable: order prices. What is apparently going on here is a relaxation of cost-cutting pressures by management when backlogs are heavy, when the factory is busy, and when order prices are high. Contrariwise, when market conditions turn sour for the turbine builders, cost-cutting returns with a vengeance, bargaining with the unions stiffens, materials and components purchasing practices toughen up, and efficiency rises in the factory.

Factory Utilization

The factory utilization data for this study were unusually good, the product of a year-long engineering study by the consulting engineers Ford, Bacon & Davis.[17] However, the statistical results do *not* support the hypothesis that direct costs per kilowatt were affected by the rate of utilization of factory capacity.[18] This, one of the key short-run variables of usual microeconomic theory, is statistically impotent.

This unexpected empirical finding leaves dangling the management testimony concerning the cost-inflating impact of factory overcrowding, scheduling problems, and the like, when factory utilization climbed beyond 85 percent. My conclusion is that management certainly perceived costs to be

---

[17] The Ford, Bacon & Davis team of consulting engineers was commissioned to collect data on the rate of factory utilization in each quarter of each year, for the study period, as part of the background data for the Electrical Equipment Antitrust Actions. The results of their study were presented in the action: Ohio Valley Electric v. General Electric et al., 62 Civ. 695, S.D.N.Y. Their approach was to measure kilowatts of shipments in each quarter, and to appraise kilowatts of manufacturing capacity for each of the five plants of the industry (two each for General Electric and Westinghouse, and one for Allis-Chalmers) based upon machine tool records, labor records, and overtime and other wage payments.

[18] This held true whether the percentage utilization rate (for individual firms) was employed directly, whether it was introduced as a squared term, or whether both "utilization" and "utilization-squared" were introduced simultaneously into the regression analysis. I therefore gave utilization rate the opportunity to behave in quite an imaginative curvilinear fashion, and it failed. Direct costs per kilowatt remain constant over the output range almost as low as 50 percent to almost as high as 125 percent.

rising when the factory was very busy, but that this was in fact attributable to the relaxation of market pressures upon workers and management, and not so much attributable to crowded conditions in the factory. But again, the direction of causality is open to debate.

It is perhaps significant that management testimony concerning the impact of the factory utilization rate upon costs was trotted out to support a litigation theory of *pricing* which was founded upon classical microeconomic theory—rising marginal costs leading to rising prices and the like (see the OVEC case analyzed in Chapter Four of my companion book, particularly the pricing testimony of Professor M. A. Adelman).[19] Certainly, *prices* climbed when factory utilization climbed. The defendants in the electrical litigation attempted to demonstrate that this was because *costs* climbed when the percentage utilization rate climbed. However, this writer can find no empirical support for the theory, and, indeed, none was forthcoming during the electrical litigation either.

In sum, when percentage utilization of factory capacity climbs, this provides the psychological uplift necessary for marketing managers and their salesmen to negotiate higher order prices in the marketplace. But this is not happening because of higher unit manufacturing costs. As a result, price-direct cost margins will tend to rise when factory utilization is high.

Technology Transfer

The final factor which was appraised for statistical impact was the transfer of manufacturing technology from leader to follower firms in this market. No such transfer could be discerned in the cost data. Manufacturing costs are neither higher nor lower than they would be expected to be, given the level of manufacturing experience of each competitor.[20]

Relative to General Electric, costs are higher for Westinghouse, and very much higher for Allis-Chalmers, even after correcting for product mix. These cost differences are largely explainable by the respective differences in cumulative production experience. The follower firms do not seem to benefit from any transfer of manufacturing knowledge from the leader. Instead, *manufacturing* technology appears to have been proprietary and highly compartmentalized. (This need not be true of *product* technology, created through overhead spending.)

Thus, while the analysis of Chapter Nine suggests that follower firms benefit from a "reverse price squeeze" in terms of the average *revenue* yield

---

[19] See: Ralph G. M. Sultan, *Pricing in the Electrical O'igopoly, Vol. I: Competition or Collusion* (Boston: Harvard Business School, Division of Research, 1974).

[20] This conclusion was reached through discovering that direct costs per kilowatt for Westinghouse and Allis-Chalmers cannot be better explained by introducing dummy variables for these firms into the regression model.

achieved by their product mix, no additional benefit accrues through adopting a follower role on the direct cost side of their operations.

Direct Cost Elasticities

In Chapter Nine, the rate of change or elasticity in price per kilowatt was compared with respect to cumulative experience and with respect to the average size of unit produced. It is now possible to present parallel estimates of the elasticities on direct costs (see Table 10.1).

TABLE 10.1.
ELASTICITIES BEARING UPON DIRECT COSTS OF STEAM GENERATORS.

	Product Technology Variable (Average Size of Unit)	Experience Variable (Cumulative Kilowatts Produced)	Selling Price Variable (Index of Orders Prices)
Ratio of Costs with Each Doubling of the Explanatory Variable	62%	93%	125%

These results imply that direct costs (in constant dollars per kilowatt) will be 62 percent of what they originally had been, with each doubling of the size of the unit; that is, costs will decline by 38 percent. This leads to another important conclusion:

Questions of the expense and risk of getting there aside, in terms of the required research and development investment, it obviously paid to engage in rapid product evolution. The historical pricing strategy was to reduce prices per kilowatt by about 7 percent with each doubling of the size of unit (see analysis of previous chapter). However, direct costs are estimated to decline by approximately 38 percent per kilowatt, with each doubling of the size of unit. The residual 31 percent was an "untransferred" gain or quasi-rent. The quest for larger and larger units seems to have been profitable.

The results imply that the turbine competitors were able to achieve a continuous shift of product mix, in a manner which approached steady state conditions. Recall that our statistical analysis is both cross-sectional and over time. At any instant, looking at a cross-section of units, the larger units were more profitable. However, over time any given size of unit would become less profitable, as the total product mix of the industry shifted to the more advanced and larger sizes. A permanent high-profit niche at the high end of the size scale could be perpetuated, even amid rapid product evolution.

We can now appreciate the forces which drove these oligopolists to innovate. The statistical results suggest that the most profitable strategy was to lead a zealous search for the most advanced technology, in order to build the most advanced, largest units. Furthermore, it points out why, once the leadership position in technology had been gained, it should be tenaciously held, in the face of the dislodging efforts of competitors. The building of advanced technology units provided higher margins, and, so long as the required dollar outlays on overhead, and the risks involved in technology, were not prohibitive, leadership could be a very high-profit strategy.

It is equally notable that these statistical results show that: *Cost reductions attributable to increased cumulative experience were apparently all passed along to the customers.* According to the table of elasticities, with each doubling of cumulative kilowatts throughout, direct costs are 93 percent of what they originally had been. Previously, it was determined that with each doubling of experience, *prices were 93 percent of what they had been also. Thus, prices and costs, insofar as they are influenced by cumulative production experience, seem to have moved in unison.* This result is consistent with competitive pricing in an industry where all competitors are increasing their output at about the same rate, and bringing prices down parallel to the cost reductions available through experience.

Demand Euphoria

We also have an estimate of the direct cost impact of what might be termed "demand euphoria" or just plain sloppy operations, when market pressures are relaxed. If selling prices are doubled, then it is estimated that costs will be 125 percent of what they had been, due to what we interpret as a relaxation of effort and efficiency by workers and by management. *Thus, about one quarter of the gains from higher prices are passed along to the factors of production (workers, components suppliers, raw materials suppliers, etc.),* either in factor price increases or reduced efficiency. Contrariwise, one quarter of any *decline* in prices will be recovered through negotiation with factors of production and tighter factory efficiency. It obviously helps earnings to have strong demand conditions—but not by as much as one might anticipate. Only three quarters of any price increase remains after the induced internal inflation of costs.

Summary

In sum, four variables have a statistically discernible impact on direct manufacturing costs per unit: general inflation in the economy and in factor prices, the cumulative throughput experience of each firm, product technology as manifested in the average unit rating of the turbines manufactured, and the degree of euphoria generated by strong demand and price conditions in the marketplace. Two other variables: the rate of utilization of factory capacity, and the transfer of manufacturing technique among firms, do not appear to affect direct costs materially.[21] (However, the rate of factory utilization does affect *prices*.)

We may now see that a major proportion of the difference in profitability among the three competitors must be attributed to differences in their direct costs. The advantage of a vigilant leader firm in this respect appears to be "uncatchable" by any follower firm, except under the most severe of assumptions.

OVERHEAD COSTS

Having just analyzed one portion of expenditures: direct costs, we will now turn to the other: overhead costs. In the turbine generator oligopoly, overhead expenditures are small by comparison with direct costs, but they play a highly strategic role. It is important to have some understanding of their strategic role, if one is to understand the forces of competition in this industry. Such expenditures are one of the fundamental variables under short-run management control.

Overhead spending tends to be more discretionary than is spending for labor and materials and other items in the category of direct costs; that is, overhead costs are more readily managed in the short run. Furthermore, overhead spending is often in the nature of an investment for competitive strength in the future. It is largely from overhead dollars that future technologies are funded, and product superiority or inferiority acquired. The firm which has both the capacity and the will to invest the most in technology will tend to dominate the market, all other competitive factors being equal.

The Level of Overhead Spending

Overhead expenditures include such "period costs" as advanced engineering, marketing, general administration, financial charges, corporate assessments, and the like. Some of these are fixed charges in the short run, regardless of volume; others are quite variable. What is of interest to us is their overall *level*, not their short-run fixity. Once again, our empirical analysis is at the mercy of the accountants insofar as the comparability of data across firms is concerned. The writer has made an effort to homogenize the data, but there is surely some unknown degree of variation in the categorization of costs from one firm to the next. Such arbitrariness in the data should not

---

[21] A referee has submitted a telling argument on the other side, which may be summed up as follows: while statistical analysis did not produce any evidence of rising marginal costs, the managers *did* perceive themselves to be operating with rising marginal costs. In pricing decisions, should we not be governed by what the management decision makers think is the situation, regardless of the facts of the situation? My reply: "Agreed! And that is exactly what the observed *pricing* behavior tells us they did. So it boils down to beliefs, not facts—to metaphysics, not marginal analysis."

seriously weaken any attempt to understand the motivating forces and *directions* of overhead cost movements; but one should be cautious in the degree of finality which is attached to differences in the *level* of expenditures which appeared on the profit and loss statements of each competitor's turbine division.[22]

As a fraction of the total sales dollar, overhead expenses are less important than direct costs. Expenditures on labor, materials, and purchased components, and the costs of indirect factory expense[23] and application engineering,[24] that is, what tends to be designated by the accountants as "direct expenses," typically consume from 65 to 75 percent of total sales revenue, leaving 25 to 35 percent of sales revenue as the gross margin which will pay for overhead items, and for profits. It is illuminating to consider overhead spending in proportion to sales revenue, for the three turbine generator competitors. First, consider each competitor's revenue base, from which overhead spending must be funded. Over 1946–1963, the *average* net sales of steam turbine generators billed annually for the three firms was roughly of this order of magnitude:[25]

General Electric	$130 million
Westinghouse	$ 70 million
Allis-Chalmers	$ 20 million

Over 1946–1963, General Electric's average annual overhead outlays were in the vicinity of 16 percent of sales revenues. Westinghouse, in contrast, spent about 24 percent of its sales revenues on overhead items. Even at that higher *rate* of overhead expenditure, Westinghouse's total dollar outlays would fall short of the total dollar outlays of its principal competitor, General Electric. This brutal fact is a key to understanding the competitive process in this industry: Westinghouse was in a competitive struggle to match General Electric's technology and marketing investments but had only one half the

[22] The data are derived from the annual operating statements of the turbine divisions of each of the three competitors, as culled by me from the exhibit material of: Ohio Valley Electric v. General Electric et al., 62 Civ. 695, S.D.N.Y. The major homogenizing activities by the author involved: (1) separating engineering expenditures into the overhead category; (2) adjusting for items expensed, but not yet invoiced; (3) estimating, from fragments of other concurrent accounting data and marketing reports, the bare outline of an earnings statement for several years for which the original profit and loss statements were missing for one of the firms.

[23] It is assumed that indirect factory expense, which encompasses such costs as supervision in the manufacturing areas, janitors, sweepers, crane operators, cutting oils, minor shop tools, and other items not charged to specific customer orders, are nevertheless mostly variable with the rate of factory throughput.

[24] It is assumed that the engineering work which is performed on specific turbine generator contracts is more or less directly proportional to the volume of contracts; draftsmen and lower level engineers will be laid off if the volume of work slackens.

[25] Sales at the beginning of this 18-year period were obviously much lower; sales in 1963 were obviously much higher. Because of variations in product mix, shares of total industry sales revenue are not proportional to shares of kilowatts orders.

sales revenue base from which to fund that struggle. The businesses had long since reached such massive proportions relative to the rest of the corporation, and such a state of maturity in the market, that continued funding from *other* divisions of the parent corporation was not appealing to management; instead these businesses were expected to finance their own overhead. This is common practice. Since Westinghouse had about one half the sales revenue base, it would have to spend at double the rate of General Electric if it were to match General Electric's dollar outlays. A rate of expenditure which would "catch up" with General Electric might have been tolerable, except for one handicap: the higher costs (i.e., lower gross margin) of Westinghouse. This alone provides ample explanation for General Electric's product leadership in this industry over those years.[26]

Even so, in order to be somewhat competitive in technology and in marketing, it was necessary for Westinghouse to spend a higher proportion of its sales dollar on overhead items, 24 percent versus General Electric's 16 percent. A "matching" 32 percent was unthinkable. This just about sums up the entire profit story insofar as Westinghouse was concerned: higher percentage overheads applied to a lower percentage gross margin.

The third participant in the struggle, Allis-Chalmers, had average overhead expenditures over the 1946–1962 period which averaged out to about 29 percent of sales. In total dollars, Allis-Chalmers' outlays were only one third as large as those of Westinghouse, and one quarter as large as those of General Electric. The dilemma confronting Allis-Chalmers' management in endeavoring to keep pace with the technical and marketing outlays of its

---

[26] Some reviewers have questioned my reference to General Electric's product leadership in this industry over the 1948–1963 study period. General Electric's leadership in size is documented in Chapter Twelve (page 204). A parallel record in having the minimum heat rate units exists (page 205). As for other dimensions of technology, one revealing report was a 24-page evaluation of competing bids prepared for the Southern California Edison Company, on the Alamitos power station, units no. 3 and 4. This engineering report was prepared by the consulting and construction firm of Bechtel Corporation. The covering letter stated: "Your organization had on hand proposals on 50 turbines from Allis-Chalmers Manufacturing Company, General Electric Company, and Westinghouse Electric Corporation for 200 MW, 250 MW and 300 MW size units for a variety of steam conditions and various style turbines." In the comparison, the following historical performance on other central stations units was cited:

Company	Number and Percentage of Units with Ratings Above or at Guarantee	Number and Percentage of Units with Rating Below Guarantee	Average Percentage by Which Units Bettered Guarantee	Average Percentage by Which Units Did Not Meet Guarantee
General Electric	47 units 88.7%	6 11.3%	1.3%	0.8%
Westinghouse	29 units 72.5%	11 27.5%	0.81%	1.5%
Allis-Chalmers		(No data seem to be available)		

SOURCE: Report by Bechtel Corporation to W. L. Chadwick, vice president, Southern California Edison Company, March 27, 1957, p. 7; National Exhibit 2NX 450, Electrical Equipment Antitrust Actions, in all U.S. district courts.

larger (and lower cost) competitors is obvious. But even at 29 percent, Allis-Chalmers' overhead consumed virtually all of its available dollars of gross margin, leaving Allis-Chalmers with zero profits, or a loss, in the majority of years. (See Volume I, Chapter Six.)

Relationship to the Long-Run Theory

The theoretical model in Chapter Two suggests that, in the long run, the available gross margin between prices and direct costs will be determined by the rate of product innovation and perceived gain in value, working through the price level, to influence the available margin for profits and overhead spending. There will be a rate of product innovation which is consistent with any given gross margin, and any given level of technological spending. The split of this margin between profits and overhead was, however, a discretionary judgment for managers, and an equilibrium-type decision need not happen automatically. Nevertheless, the proportion of the available gross margin which could be extracted in the form of accounting profits, in any single year, was in real life sharply constrained by management's longer run goals of being superior to, or at least equal to, competitors in the oligopoly in marketing and in product technology.

We see in these profit and loss statements of Westinghouse, Allis-Chalmers, and General Electric one set of management spending decisions which would tend to result in a long-run equilibrium situation: that is, (1) a fairly high proportion of overhead spending (as opposed to accounting profits) chosen by General Electric managers; (2) a forcing of the number two competitor, Westinghouse, to spend on overhead at a rate which produced only a marginal level of profitability and which gave the parent corporation little incentive to pour further resources into the business to challenge the leadership of General Electric; and (3) a third competitor, not really a threat to either of the two larger firms, which could be tolerated as merely being a nuisance factor in competition (but not in pricing), and a useful competitor in terms of helping to maintain customer harmony as a third source of supply. In a sense, the industry over 1948–1963 was operating in an equilibrium mode.

Short-Run Fluctuations in Overhead Spending

Aside from the long-run equilibrium averages, how can we account for the short-run fluctuations in overhead spending? Such fluctuations were considerable, as demonstrated in Chart 10.2, which shows unit overhead spending, in dollars per kilowatt, plotted against the cumulative kilowatts shipments of each firm. In addition to the economies of scale which are obviously present, there are considerable year-to-year variations in the unit overhead spending rate—and these variations cannot be explained by fluctuations in

CHART 10.2.   Overhead Costs Per Kilowatt (in Constant 1957–1959 Dollars) v.
Cumulative Kilowatt Shipments for General Electric,
Westinghouse, and Allis-Chalmers.

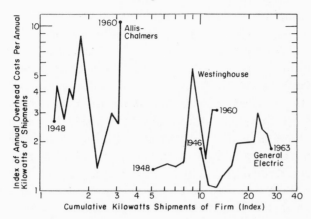

unit output alone. The purpose of this section is to explain the short-run decision-making process by which managers adjust their overhead expense from year to year.

In our model of managerial behavior, overhead expenditures are budgeted in the long run as some fraction of total sales revenue. The fraction which is selected by each firm is set by the available gross margin, and management judgment, as discussed. What is now desired is an explanation of the short-term fluctuations. Fluctuations in sales revenue, plus lethargy in policy implementation, are the keys to understanding these decisions.

Appendix 13 reports the statistical results for simple models of overhead expenditures adjustment, following an approach employed by Koyck[27] and by Lintner.[28] The Lintner-type model is apparently the most appropriate description of managerial behavior.

Lintner first used this model to explain *dividend* "spending" decisions by managers. It now also seems true that managers budget their *overhead* outlays in a fashion akin to their behavior when paying dividends. In the Lintner model, developed in 1956 to explain the dividend policy of firms, managers have the goal of paying out a fixed percentage of earnings to their stockholders. However, they do not immediately adjust their dividend outflows— the payout percentage is just a target for them to work toward. The amount of inertia in the decision-making system is rather predictable. Each year the managers close the expenditures gap, from where they are to where they want to be, by some constant proportion. It is necessary to estimate em-

---

[27] L. M. Koyck, *Distributed Lags and Investment Analysis* (North-Holland Publishing Company, 1954).

[28] John Lintner, "Distribution of Incomes of Corporations Among Dividends, Retained Earnings and Taxes," *American Economic Review*, May 1956.

pirically two fractions: the target payout ratio, and the proportion of the gap between actual and desired dividends which will be closed during the year.

The application to overhead expenditures is straightforward. Instead of assuming some target payout ratio for dividends, assume there is some target overhead expenditures ratio: some percentage of current sales revenue which management thinks it is normal and desirable to allocate to overhead items. Further assume that for good reasons (the undesirability of a stop-and-go hiring policy, the time lag in decision making, the delays inherent in finding new people in an upturn, or delays inherent in reducing the size of staff in a downturn), there is inertia in the system. Budget decisions are determined first by the targeted expenditures ratio, and, second, by the speed of closing the gap between desired and actual expenditures.

In addition, there may well be a built-in upward bias in overhead expenditures—an annual inflation which continues quite independently of the targeted expenditure decisions. One can test for the presence of such a built-in annual increment in spending. The resulting model is summarized in Table 10.2.

TABLE 10.2.
THE OVERHEAD EXPENDITURES MODEL.

$$\begin{bmatrix} \text{Year-to-Year} \\ \text{Change in} \\ \text{Overhead} \\ \text{Spending} \end{bmatrix} = \begin{bmatrix} \text{Built-In} \\ \text{Annual} \\ \text{Increment} \\ \text{in Overhead} \\ \text{Spending} \end{bmatrix} + \begin{bmatrix} \text{Speed of} \\ \text{Adjustment} \\ \text{Coefficient} \end{bmatrix} \times \begin{bmatrix} \text{Targeted} \\ \text{Change in} \\ \text{Overhead} \\ \text{Spending} \end{bmatrix}$$

and also:

$$\begin{bmatrix} \text{Targeted} \\ \text{Change in} \\ \text{Overhead} \\ \text{Spending} \end{bmatrix} = \begin{bmatrix} \text{Target} \\ \text{Spending} \\ \text{Ratio:} \\ \text{Overhead as} \\ \text{Percent of Sales} \end{bmatrix} \times \begin{bmatrix} \text{Expected} \\ \text{Sales} \\ \text{Revenue} \\ \text{Next Year} \end{bmatrix} - \begin{bmatrix} \text{Actual} \\ \text{Overhead} \\ \text{Spending} \\ \text{for Year} \\ \text{Just Ended} \end{bmatrix}$$

This target expenditures model becomes a simple ratio model, wherein overhead expenditures are a constant percentage of sales revenue, if the speed-of-adjustment coefficient is 100%; that is, if the targeted spending rate *is* fully achieved each year.

From the statistical analysis, these parameters of managerial behavior were obtained (see Table 10.3 and also Charts 10.3, 10.4, and 10.5):

Westinghouse, according to the results indicated in Table 10.3, adjusts overhead expenditures fully each year; a constant ratio model explains its budgeting policies adequately. Westinghouse, it appears, must budget with a close eye to current business conditions. This would be an appropriate

TABLE 10.3.

STATISTICAL RESULTS: OVERHEAD SPENDING BEHAVIOR BY THREE FIRMS, 1948–1963
(Turbine Generator Divisions Only).

	E Annual Built-In Inflation of Overhead Expense	c Target Expenditures Ratio as Percent of Sales	d Speed of Adjustment Coefficient (Annual Amount of Adjustment Toward Target)
General Electric	(Not Statistically	12%	30%
Westinghouse	Different from Zero for Any	20%	100%
Allis-Chalmers	of Three Firms)	16%	52%

CHART 10.3.   Annual Change in General Electric Turbine Generator Overhead:
1948–1963.

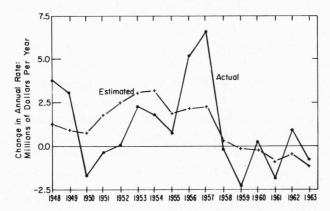

SOURCE: General Electric profit and loss statements, large steam turbine generator department,
Schenectady, New York.

CHART 10.4.   Annual Change in Westinghouse Turbine Generator Overhead:
1947–1961.

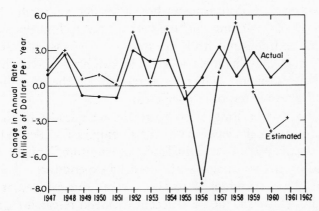

SOURCE: Westinghouse profit and loss statements, large turbines, South Philadelphia Works.

CHART 10.5.   Annual Change in Allis-Chalmers Turbine Generator Overhead:
1947–1962.

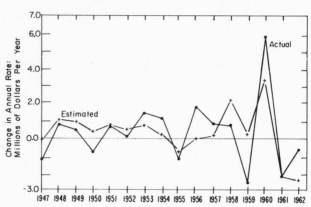

SOURCE: Allis-Chalmers profit and loss statements, steam division, West Allis, Wisconsin.

stance for a follower firm which is spending a high proportion of its available gross margin on overhead, with slender residual profits.

General Electric displays a more phlegmatic budgeting posture, budgeting a target 12 percent of sales on overhead expense items, and adjusting only 30 percent of the way toward that goal in any one year. Given the size and complexity of the General Electric organization (and consequently, the time lag in moving that organization), given its availability of resources to ride out minor year-to-year fluctuations in net sales, and given its strong market position, General Electric's "smoothed" response seems to have been an appropriate overhead spending strategy.

Finally, Allis-Chalmers seems to be in a somewhat intermediate position. It is targeting to spend 16 percent of sales on overhead items—between the General Electric and Westinghouse percentages—and its speed of adjustment is 52 percent in a given year—again between the Westinghouse and General Electric rates of response. We perceive here a smaller competitor that realizes the impossibility of matching the marketing and technological outlays of the larger firms, and does not really try to. As in the case of Westinghouse, it is important for Allis-Chalmers to keep its overhead outlays in trim with the sales revenue situation, which is suggested by the magnitude of the Allis-Chalmers' speed-of-response coefficient.

As an aside, it is interesting to compare the magnitudes of the estimated speed-of-adjustment coefficients with those empirically derived in broad-based dividend policy research. Dividend "expenditures" might be easy for managers to adjust in comparison with overhead expenditures. Therefore, one may expect overhead spending to display a more sluggish response than do dividend outlays. However, the most recent dividend research suggests speed-of-adjustment coefficients in the range of 28 to 30 percent.[29] General Electric's overhead spending speed-of-adjustment of 30 percent is consistent with general dividend adjustment practice. Allis-Chalmers and Westinghouse overhead adjustments are much *less* sluggish by comparison. It seems that overhead expenditures, in our sample of three oligopolists, are relatively responsive to the target. That the range of values for these widely differing decisions should be of the same magnitude lends credibility to the findings.

Summary

Overhead spending in this industry is much smaller in magnitude than the outlays on direct costs, but in many ways it is much more "strategic." Overheads are highly susceptible to management control, and frequently consist of investments in *future* product and marketing strength. Overhead expenditures are cut to fit the cloth of available gross margins and managements' future strategies, so to speak.[30]

It is apparent that General Electric, given its larger market share, and its lower direct costs (and consequently, its higher percentage gross margin), could readily outspend its smaller competitors in such critical overhead areas as engineering development, cost-reduction studies, manufacturing engineering, and marketing, while still showing a good profit return. Westinghouse attempted to match the overhead outlays of General Electric, and in the process suffered reduced profits. Allis-Chalmers was hard-pressed to keep abreast of the overhead outlays of either larger competitor, even when spending at a rate which effectively absorbed all of its available gross margins. The available pool of gross margins dollars for each firm was determined by (1) the market price level, (2) the direct cost level of each firm, and (3) the market share of each firm. The size of this pool would, in the long run, establish the competitors' comparative standing, in terms of current earnings performance, and also in terms of future market strength. Overhead dollars constituted the fund from which would be purchased advanced technologies, management depth, and marketing skill; and these determined the competitive hierarchy.

Given their unique gross margin situation, and their inclination—or lack of it—to secure or to challenge vested market positions, managers will develop an implicit "target" percentage of sales in their overhead budgeting decisions. They attain this target over the short run with a lagged response which is also unique to each firm. General Electric displays the most sluggish, or

---

29 Eugene F. Fama and Harvey Babiak, "Dividend Policy: An Empirical Analysis," *Journal of the American Statistical Association*, Vol. 63, No. 324, December 1968.

30 Richard B. Heflebower, "Full Costs, Cost Changes, and Prices," National Bureau of Economic Research, conference report, *Business Concentration and Price Policy* (Princeton: Princeton University Press, 1955), p. 365, reaches similar conclusions.

most "smoothed" response; Westinghouse displays the least. These are appropriate spending strategies, given the comparative ability of each competitor to pay. Thus, comparative advantage in direct costs is translated into comparative abundance and stability in overhead spending, and for the leader a permanent advantage in product technology and in marketing spending. As long as there is some minimum management competence in the leader firm, these advantages will tend to secure for the leader a permanent advantage in product technology and in marketing. Such advantages cannot be easily or economically overcome by a competitor's direct assault upon that market position; instead, it seems the natural advantage of the market leader can only be whittled away in those relatively rare situations of overconfidence, complacency, and creeping senility in the dominant firm's management, or by a sudden and unforeseen breakthrough in technology by the follower firms.

CHAPTER Eleven   The Strategy of Manufacturing Capacity

ELECTRIC UTILITIES ARE ALWAYS CONCERNED that the expansion of their generating capacity will be outstripped by the growth of their peak loads. Periodically, such concerns are heightened; that is, when manufacturers' backlogs become extended such as during the late 1960s when four-year to five-year delivery became commonplace. On such occasions, the manufacturers take pains to assure their utility customers that adequate manufacturing capacity is in place to meet their future needs.[1] However, the competitor with the least backlogs relative to manufacturing capacity, will be in the best position to promise rapid delivery, and this will increase the likelihood of his increasing his market share.

In this chapter we shall develop the argument that a firm's decision to invest in added manufacturing capacity parallels in many respects a nation's decision to invest in military capability. Rivalry in manufacturing capacity expansion can resemble rivalry in arms spending. If a firm is not to be shoved slowly out of the marketplace, it must maintain some semblance of parity in manufacturing capability, to thereby enforce long-term "norms" of market position, vis-à-vis its principal enemies.[2] Understanding the mechanics of

---

[1] For example, in 1968 Donald E. Craig, vice president and general manager of General Electric's Large Steam Turbine Generator Division, inserted this advertisement in the trade press (excerpts):

> TO OUR ELECTRIC UTILITY CUSTOMERS: Can U.S. manufacturers meet your turbine generator needs? Speaking for General Electric, we can still commit delivery of large steam units in 1971, either fossil or nuclear. I know of no case in the past two heavy-order years when a utility could not place an order with a domestic manufacturer for delivery to meet anticipated needs.
>
> It is on the basis of a planned investment of more than $200,000,000—solely for large steam turbine generators—that General Electric will have the necessary capability, when you need it. You have a vital interest in our present and future manufacturing investments. If you have any suggestions, questions or criticisms, we would very much like to get together with you for an in-depth discussion.

Electric World, May 20, 1968.

[2] See, for example, the arms race models of Kenneth Boulding, *Conflict and Defense*, a

such interdependent expansion decisions is a key to the understanding of oligopolistic rivalry.

MANUFACTURING CAPACITIES: THE HISTORICAL RECORD

It has sometimes been suggested by economic theorists that one of the defects of competition in the concentrated industries, is a tendency to chronic overinvestment in manufacturing capacity.[3] However, only periodically has total capacity greatly exceeded total capacity needs in this oligopoly. Chart 11.1 shows estimates of annual manufacturing capacities for the three com-

CHART 11.1.   Estimated Annual Manufacturing Capacity: Domestic Turbine Generator Manufacturers, 1946–1963 (in Kilowatts Per Year).

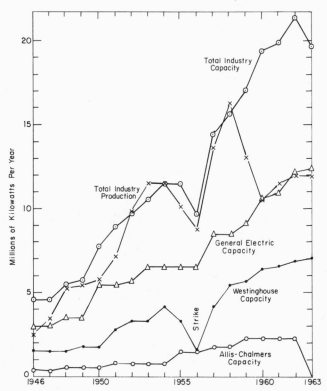

SOURCE: Ford, Bacon and Davis.

petitors and for the total industry, compared with total industry production rates, for the period 1946–1963.

General Theory (New York: Harper and Row, 1963); also, Thomas Schelling, *The Strategy of Conflict* (Cambridge, Mass.: Harvard University Press, 1960).

[3] See, for example, the discussion in John M. Cassels, "Excess Capacity and Monopolistic Competition," *Quarterly Journal of Economics*, May 1937 (Cambridge, Mass.: Harvard University Press). The excess capacity hypothesis was a prominent feature of Professor Edward Chamberlin's work on monopolistic competition of the 1930s.

These data provide one approximate basis for assessing supply and demand balance. We cannot find here any evidence of a tendency toward chronic excess industry capacity, although such behavior has been hypothesized for oligopoly. Brown Boveri also leveled this charge at the United States manufacturers in the 1960s. Utility plaintiffs in the electrical equipment antitrust actions went so far as to propound, with curious logic, that the excess industry supply of the 1960–1963 period was proof of the beneficial impact of the electrical conspiracy concerning price, upon the prosperity of the marginal producers, and therefore upon their expansion of manufacturing capacity.[4] Unfortunately for these various assertions, the periods of excess manufacturing capacity have been quite rare. For the period up to 1958, industry output was very close to five-day, three-shift manufacturing capacity, even rising above that in 1953–1954, and again in 1958. Over 1959–1963, total industry capacity greatly exceeded output, but even this was a temporary situation. By the late 1960s the industry was operating close to capacity once more.

A revealing definition of "capacity" was provided by the manufacturers in the EEI survey;[5] they viewed their capacity as being rather elastic. Capacity would depend as much upon lead times, and the size of the engineering staffs (which fluctuated with demand) as it did upon any succinct measure of physical facilities. Defining plant capacity in relation to bricks and mortar, and machine tools, would be a vast over-simplication.

---

[4] During the Electrical Equipment Antitrust Actions, plaintiff utilities asserted that the capacity expansion plans of the turbine builders had been "tainted" by conspiratorial forces, so that post-1959 supply and demand conditions were not the same as those which existed in the earlier years. One brief asserted, for example:

> The capacity of the industry to manufacture turbine generators, and the utilization thereof, were distorted by the conspiracy so that the capacity situation in the years following 1959 was not the same as it would have been had the conspiracy not existed.

Accordingly, capacity and its utilization cannot properly be used to explain price behavior. (Plaintiffs' Post-Trial Brief, Ohio Valley Electric v. General Electric, et al., 62 Civ. 695, U.S. District Court, S.D.N.Y., pp. 85–88.)

The consequence of the price umbrella of conspiracy, according to this line of reasoning, was an unwarranted expansion of manufacturing capacity during the alleged conspiratorial period:

> Assuming there were non-competitive high prices and that Westinghouse was not the low cost producer and was less efficient than General Electric, the high conspiratorial prices could be the cause of Westinghouse's expansion. (Ibid.)

The logic was that (a) during the alleged conspiracy, there was a price umbrella held over the market, which allowed the higher cost and less-efficient competitors to expand, and that (b) the excess capacity condition after the alleged conspiracy had ended proved this was so.

[5] The estimated amount of open manufacturing capacity available at a given time for a particular future year is a measure of the additional delivery possibilities including allowances for the necessary lead time; that is, the time required for normal engineering, procurement of materials, manufacturing operation, and fabrication up to the point of shipments. Unless the full manufacturing potential for a future year is entirely committed, the open manufacturing capacity for that year will start to decrease, after a certain point, due to loss of lead time. Finally, the open capacity will cease to exist. (Edison Electric Institute, 48th Semi-Annual Electric Power Survey, October 1970, p. 24.)

The elastic nature of supply is evident from a plotting of EEI data concerning "percent of capacity schedule" for "this year," "next year," "two years out" and so on, as shown in Chart 11.2. We see here that *estimates of future industry capacities invariably shrink over time, as they approach the present*, while the present year's output invariably is close to 100 percent of "capacity." Thus, in appraising how stretched or how slack the manufacturers feel themselves to be at any moment, it is best to examine the percent of capacity which they have scheduled for "next year," before their actual capacities shrink to meet their current demand.

The incidence of *cyclical* excess capacity may be appraised from the EEI data for the years 1949 through 1970. Over these 21 years, the proportion of *next* year's capacity which has been committed ranges from 60 to 100 percent. The slack years correspond to previously noted cycles in demand. However, on a "next year's" basis, the normal situation is to operate close to 100 percent of capacity—again, far from the picture of chronic excess capacity painted by some oligopoly theorists.

INDIVIDUAL COMPETITORS' MANUFACTURING CAPACITIES

Consider next the individual competitors' expansion programs. Over 1946–1963, each increased his production capability enormously: General Electric from an estimated 3 gigawatts to 12.5 gigawatts annual capacity; Westinghouse from 1.5 to 7; and Allis-Chalmers from less than 0.3 to almost 2.5 gigawatts annual capacity.[6] There was a tendency for manufacturing capacity to expand, even in the absence of bricks and mortar investments, through the alternative route of product engineering investments. For example, William Ginn of General Electric observed that the Schenectady facility had originally been designed for a capacity of 50 turbine "shafts" a year. As the average size of a turbine generator (one shaft) increased from about 30,000 kilowatts in the immediate post-World War II period, to almost 200,000 kilowatts by the beginning of the 1960s, the total capacity of the shop increased accordingly. Ginn related, "Through innovation and through development, by building bigger units, you were releasing capacity to make the overcapacity problem even that much more serious."[7]

Since kilowatts of manufacturing capacity varied according to product design, a corollary was that capacity for each competitor was highly dependent upon product mix. For example, Eikner of Westinghouse explained, "Our kind of business is a job shop, custom-built product, and the capacity

---

[6] Some of the increases in capacity were particularly rapid; Allis-Chalmers increased its capacity from 1954 to 1959 by over 200 percent. Westinghouse increased its capacity from 1953 to 1961 by 100 percent. (Plaintiffs' Post-Trial Brief, Ohio Valley Electric v. General Electric, et al., 62 Civ. 695, U.S. District Court, S.D.N.Y., pp. 85–88.)

[7] Deposition of William S. Ginn, vice president of the General Electric Large Turbine Division, in Electrical Equipment Antitrust Actions, all U.S. district courts, January 16, 1963.

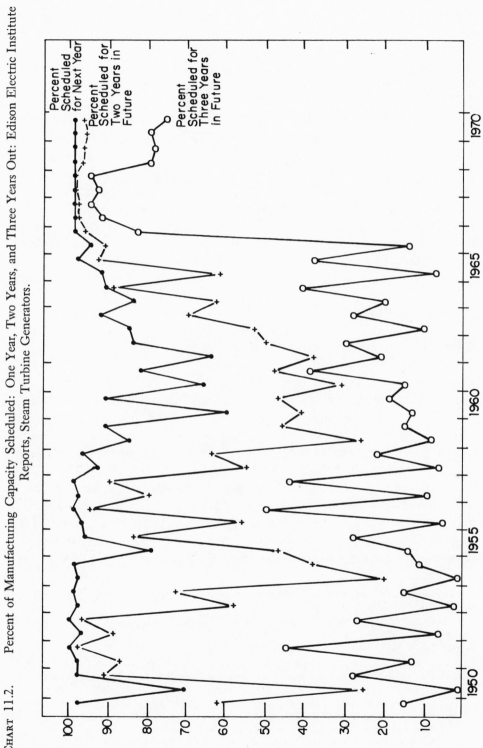

CHART 11.2.   Percent of Manufacturing Capacity Scheduled: One Year, Two Years, and Three Years Out: Edison Electric Institute Reports, Steam Turbine Generators.

of that plant is in terms of facilities and mannable work stations. We almost have to define the mix of product that we want, in order to determine whether we have the capacity for producing it."[8]

The interrelationship of manufacturing capacity and product technology (product mix) had important strategic consequences. We have seen that the market leader was also the firm which tended to set the pace in product innovation. Through influencing the rate of introduction and market adoption of new technologies, the market leader could exercise some influence over the required manufacturing capabilities of the industry. Knowledge of the probable required future manufacturing capabilities gave the market-technological leader an edge in the planning of its own manufacturing facilities, and it also contributed to planning uncertainties for the follower firms. Follower firms would be tempted to hold back on their investments until the trend in industry product mix—and their own facilities requirements—became clear. This was, in fact, the historical behavior of these firms:

(1) General Electric

Immediately following World War II, manufacturing capacity planning at General Electric proceeded on the assumption that the 1930's growth trends would continue. Facilities projections in 1946 envisioned a plant which could produce about four 40,000 kilowatt machines a month, plus two or three 100,000 kilowatt machines each year, or about 2.5 million kilowatts annually.[9] At that time, General Electric's principal turbine generator manufacturing facility, located at Schenectady, New York, was housed in four main buildings, one of which was approximately 50 years old (the parent manufacturing facility was Edison's original machine works, built during the 1880–1900 period—portions of which were still in use). General Electric also manufactured medium-sized turbines for utilities in Lynn, Massachusetts (the original Thomson-Houston works which was merged with Thomas Edison's company to form General Electric in the 1890s).[10]

---

[8] Deposition of L. M. Eikner, in Electrical Equipment Antitrust Actions, all U.S. district courts, March 7, 1963.

[9] Testimony of John Peters of General Electric Company, stenographer's minutes, City of San Antonio v. General Electric, Westinghouse, and Allis-Chalmers, Civil Action 3064, U.S. District Court, West District of Texas, San Antonio Division, p. 5,415.

[10] Herman Hill, manager of manufacturing, Large Steam Turbine Generator Department of General Electric, described the first postwar expansion at General Electric in the following terms:

> In 1946 the operation was converting from wartime production to building land sets. There were not many machines in production. Two things happened: volume and the size of the machines were both increasing. It became obvious that the new designs would not be able to be produced in these facilities.
>
> The cranes were inadequate. I think the major crane they had in the late '40s in this building was 100 ton, and we had to use two cranes to lift the generators. They

Even if General Electric planners were aiming as low as 50 percent market share, their 1946 plans suggest a postwar market on the order of 5.0 million kilowatts annually. However, 1946 orders were actually over 7 million kilowatts. Capacity needs thinking had to be hastily revised. By 1950, annual industry *shipments* were in the neighborhood of 5 million kilowatts, from which level they kept on growing.

Charles Wilson, president of General Electric, was convinced that a boom in the demand for electrical equipment was in the offing. Wilson pushed for a new modern manufacturing facility—later designated Building 273—which would constitute about 20 acres under one roof, and cost about $30 million by the time it was completed in 1949.[11] The facility was immediately dubbed "Wilson's Folly" because of its grand scale.[12]

Another factor gave General Electric incentive to invest in a new manufacturing facility: its intensive product design effort and the attendant new manufacturing capability needs. The old GE buildings were equipped with cranes, for example, with maximum lifting capability of 100 tons.[13] The size and mass of the advanced turbine generators on the drawing boards would exceed those capabilities. As the technological leader firm, General Electric was in an advantageous position to forecast future turbine and generator design characteristics. A rapid increase in unit ratings was probable; hence, the need to invest quickly in new manufacturing facilities. (It will be noted later that Westinghouse was far more conservative in forecasting its manufacturing capability needs, perhaps because it was concentrating upon producing standard machines.)

Despite General Electric's aggressive capacity expansion of 1947–1949, it was apparent by 1950 that even these facilities would be inadequate. An additional three acres of space were added in 1951–1952.[14] Capacity to produce 5.5 million kw annually was installed.[15] (GE's capacity was about equal to total industry shipments in 1950.)

---

planned a new building, Building 273. We started moving into the building in 1949 and I believe the move was completed in 1950.

(Stenographer's minutes, Ohio Valley Electric v. General Electric et al., 62 Civ. 695, S.D.N.Y., pp. 2,031–2,035.)

11 Testimony of Herman Hill, San Antonio, pp. 6,049–6,050.

12 Partly as a result of the expansion into the new Schenectady facilities, General Electric's turbine business operated "in the red" in 1946 and in 1947. (Testimony of Buehler, manager of finance at General Electric Schenectady, stenographer's minutes, Ohio Valley Electric v. General Electric, p. 2,748.)

13 Testimony of Herman Hill, San Antonio.

14 Everyone just nicknamed [the new building] Wilson's Folly, [but] Mr. Wilson knew a lot more than the rest of us, and when we moved in the facility in 1950 it was not large enough. So we shoved out the back end and increased the floor space by another three acres.

(Testimony of John T. Peters, San Antonio, pp. 5,414–5,415.)

15 A March 1951 appropriations request at General Electric recognized that earlier facilities planning had been too conservative:

Despite this relative abundance of new capacity, manufacturing operations were still extremely busy at Schenectady, even after the second-round expansion of facilities. General Electric was reportedly barely able to meet its production requirements.[16] One manufacturing manager observed, "It was a continual congestion from 1949 when I first joined the manufacturing gang until I left in 1953. . . ."[17]

To aid the congested Schenectady facility, the line of demarcation between "Schenectady-sized" units and "Lynn-sized" units was continually raised, and some production was transferred to Lynn, Massachusetts.[18] In view of the increasing Lynn workload, plans were formulated in 1956 to expand the Lynn turbine generator facilities as well. A $25 million expansion program was launched, to be completed by 1960.[19] There is a hint that the magnitude of planned expansion of the Lynn works may have been understated in press releases—possibly to lull competitors into complacency concerning General Electric's growth in manufacturing capabilities.[20] By 1957, Lynn was increasing its capability to produce up to 60,000 kw units.

The future utility demands from the Schenectady turbine division indicate that this division will be required to produce five and a half million kilowatts of turbo-generator units annually. This not only involves a large number of units, but also larger sizes than Building 273 was laid out to produce.
(Testimony of Herman Hill, Ohio Valley Electric v. General Electric, p. 2,043.)

[16] An internal General Electric memorandum of June 1951 states:
The manufacturing operations in Schenectady, although still on a normal five-day week basis to permit us the requisite flexibility of operation, have actually been working almost continuously on a three-shift six-day basis for the past year, with limiting operations carried on on the seventh day. As a result, our overtime and night shift bonus charges are very heavy, but we see no way at the moment of overcoming this situation.
(Testimony of Herman Hill, Ohio Valley Electric v. General Electric, p. 2,046.)

[17] The new facilities at Schenectady, even after the 1951 expansion, were barely adequate:
The average size of the turbine generator sets had grown appreciably since the initial planning for that building (273) took place. We had to straighten out the flow lines and the assembly and test areas in the back end of the building were so congested we couldn't complete the product in time. It was a continual congestion from 1949 when I first joined the manufacturing gang until I left in 1953.
(Testimony of Herman Hill, San Antonio v. General Electric, pp. 6,051–6,053.)

[18] While capacity was being expanded at Schenectady, a parallel expansion was under way at Lynn, Massachusetts, where General Electric produced medium-sized turbines for land and marine use. In 1950, General Electric transferred the production of 15,000 kw turbine generator sets to Lynn from Schenectady. (*Electrical World*, January 9, 1950.) In September 1953, the demarcation between Lynn-sized and Schenectady-sized units was increased to 44,000 kw. (*Electrical World*, September 14, 1953.) This was continually repeated, as the scale of units steadily increased over time.

[19] Testimony of T. A. Brown, manager of manufacturing engineering, Lynn Works, describing the plans which were formulated early in 1956 to double manufacturing capacity for Lynn turbine generators. The plan contemplated the expenditure of $25 million. The program of expansion was completed in 1960, with expenditures beyond that amount. (Testimony of T. A. Brown, San Antonio v. General Electric, pp. 6,089–6,092.)

[20] A March 1957 press release indicated the physical facilities which were involved in expanding Lynn production capabilities. (*Electrical World*, March 18, 1957, p. 126.) Significantly, the press release understated the magnitude of the contemplated capital expenditures program—for

With the Lynn expansion under way, a study was launched at Schenectady in 1956 with the aim of forecasting 20-year turbine orders and required plant capacity. The results of the study may be viewed in Chart 11.3, which shows the forecast of Large Steam Turbine Generator Department kilowatts orders for the period 1957–1976, presented as of December 1956.[21]

The immediate outlook was bullish: forecasted total orders for General Electric in Schenectady to exceed 15 million kilowatts by 1960. (In actuality, as Chart 11.3 demonstrates, Schenectady orders in 1960 were only 7 million kilowatts.) However, under the impetus of this rosy demand forecast, the planners at Schenectady set in motion another capacity expansion program.

The surge of 1955–1956 orders meant several years of backlog for the turbine builders. Hill, in General Electric manufacturing management, reported that when he returned to Schenectady in 1957, "We were just straight out."[22]

In 1957, the Schenectady works was further expanded with an additional 300,000 square feet of manufacturing area.[23] Plans were formulated to have 10 million kilowatts of capacity installed to meet an expected flood of orders during the early 1960s.[24] Beginning in 1958, the order rate slackened. Nevertheless, sophisticated custom machine tools which had been ordered during the frenzied 1950s were delivered and installed throughout the early 1960s, greatly adding to fixed capacity and diminishing the need for an expanded work force.[25]

Beginning in January 1959, General Electric announced a planned reduc-

---

reasons we can only surmise; however, lulling the competition into complacency may have been the motive.

[21] It is interesting to compare the 1956 General Electric forecast for 1970 for Schenectady with actual results for 1970. Chart 11.3 projects orders of 32 million kilowatts for 1970, and indicates 1970 will be a cyclical peak year. In actuality, it is estimated that Schenectady received orders around the magnitude of 15 million kilowatts in 1970—about one half of the forecasted amount. Perhaps the long-term trend is a fairer statistic to compare. The forecasted long-term trend is about 21 million kilowatts for 1970; the actual was probably about 17 or 18 million kilowatts orders for Schenectady. On either count, the long-term forecast was overly optimistic. One reason total orders did not meet the forecast was the sharing of orders with the Lynn works, which was equally hard-pressed to obtain new business in the early 1960s.

[22] Hill added, "We were working almost a hundred percent of our people on Saturdays on manufacturing and working a good 20 to 25 percent of them on Sunday." (Testimony of Herman Hill, Ohio Valley Electric v. General Electric, pp. 2,058–2,060.)

[23] In 1957 it was even worse from a standpoint of the plant and equipment that we had to produce the needs of our customers and it was a rat race. We were working complete six-day weeks and in many operations, seven days a week, three shifts, around the clock.
(Testimony of Herman Hill, San Antonio v. General Electric, pp. 6,054–6,055.)

[24] Testimony of Herman Hill, Ohio Valley Electric v. General Electric, p. 2,060.

[25] Unfortunately, the time cycle on much of this large equipment was four to five years from the time you plan it until you actually have a productive facility available. Much of this did not come into useful being until 1962, 1963, [when] the volume dropped, the new equipment came into play; and as a result we had more capacity than was needed.
(Testimony of Herman Hill, San Antonio v. General Electric, pp. 6,055–6,057.)

CHART 11.3.   Orders Received, General Electric Company Large Steam Turbine
                   Generator Department.

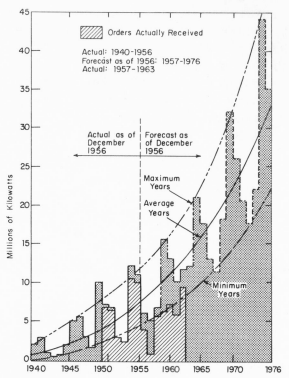

SOURCE: Defendants' Post-Trial Brief and Proposed Findings and Conclusions, Ohio Valley
Electric Corporation v. General Electric Company, et al., 62 Civ. 695, U.S. District Court, S.D.N.Y.,
Appendix B.

tion in the Schenectady work force, because of the reduced backlog of work.[26]
The magnitude of the adjustment was severe. By 1963, the level of employment had been reduced by 40 percent. Many of the workers who were fur-
loughed were highly skilled machinists and assembly workers, who would be
difficult to replace. An attempt to bring outside work into the shop was not
successful.[27] In spite of these layoffs, General Electric's capacity still greatly
exceeded its production requirements throughout the early 1960s.

———————
[26] General Electric Company announced plans to lay off 800 employees in its department
  of large steam turbine generators and attributed the proposed move to a drop in orders
  for the generators. The department now employs about 10,000. General Electric noted
  there's around a two-year cycle between receipt of these large turbine orders and shipment. Because 1956 was a good year for obtaining orders, the department had "good
  production" last year. In a capital goods recession the heavy equipment maker is the
  last to recover, the company spokesman noted.
(*Wall Street Journal*, January 8, 1959.)
  [27] Hill gave this graphic description of the adjustment of Schenectady operations to the
downturn:
  We backed off many of the third-shift operations. The employment level was down

It was not until the latter portion of the 1960s that General Electric productive capacity again became stretched to the limit; in the interim, machinery and men were idle.

In summary, one notes from manufacturers' testimony that the estimated capital expenditures by General Electric on its turbine generator business in Schenectady over the 1948–1960 period totaled approximately $75 million: $30 million for the Building 273 project, and $45 million in other appropriations. In Lynn, Massachusetts, it appears from various published sources that capital expenditures over a similar period totaled about $25 million for the medium turbine generator business. Thus, in total, capital commitments by General Electric to the turbine generator business over 1948–1960 were about $100 million, for new physical plant.

(2) Westinghouse

The nature of Westinghouse's capacity expansion over 1946–1963 was quite different from that of General Electric. Westinghouse emerged from World War II with its manufacturing facilities for the turbine generator business divided between South Philadelphia (turbines) and Pittsburgh (generators).[28]

Westinghouse's first capacity expansion move resulted in further geographic dispersion of effort: in 1948 it acquired the Joshua Hendy Iron Works in Sunnyvale, California, which were converted to turbine manufacturing operations.[29] It appears that this facility was best suited to the manufacture of small turbine generator ratings. (Possibly the Westinghouse planners did not anticipate the unprecedented upward shift in the average size of turbine

---

40 percent by 1963. Almost on a daily basis I reminded them (in marketing) that we had been instructed to equip ourselves to produce ten million kilowatts by the early sixties, we had this investment in place, we were losing our skilled people, if we ever had to do this we were going to have problems getting our skilled people back. We put people on to go out and contact people on the outside to see if we could bring in work to keep our people busy. This was not very successful, however. We produced several units ahead of our customers' needs and held them in inventory. In general the people were still going out, and the reason for this was simply the fact that our new facilities were coming into play, and the combination of higher productivity because of the new equipment with the lower volume was causing us to lay people off right and left.

(Testimony of Herman Hill, Ohio Valley Electric v. General Electric, pp. 2,065–2,067.)

28 Pricing was included in our responsibility in the large turbine department in South Philadelphia. The generator is manufactured at a division in our East Pittsburgh Works, but this is a manufacturing and design function. The marketing function of generators is incorporated in the marketing of turbine generator units at South Philadelphia. It was a matter of mutual agreement between South Philadelphia and East Pittsburgh as to the allocation of the value of the total job to the turbine division and the generator division, and that was in the general range of 65 to 70 percent for turbine, the remainder electrical.

(Testimony of L. M. Eikner, Ohio Valley Electric Co. v. General Electric, p. 2,266.)

29 *Electrical World*, November 13, 1948, p. 21.

generators which was about to occur.) Furthermore, this was a conversion of an existing factory, what one Westinghouse manager referred to as "the old Joshua Hendy plant" and not a new, custom-designed turbine factory such as General Electric at that time was creating at Schenectady.[30] In defense of the decision, one may note that the practice of reciprocity in purchasing decisions by utilities provided some inducement for the manufacturers to decentralize geographically their electrical apparatus manufacturing facilities, and the West Coast represented a rapidly growing utility market. However, weighed against the economies of scale which are manifest in turbine generator product design, and the economies attained via throughput experience—best fostered in one core facility—the Sunnyvale plant of Westinghouse appears to have been destined to be a minor strategic force in the industry.

The pending leap in sophistication and complexity of turbine generator design and manufacturing was not immediately evident in the early post-World War II years. In counter-direction, there was a strong and partially successful "standardization" movement, which simplified turbine generator configurations and permitted some simplification of manufacturing processes. This was of particular interest to Westinghouse. In 1950, for example, about 54% of Westinghouse throughput was in such standardized ratings.[31] However, shortly the percentage of standard units dropped to 22%, and, later, virtually to zero. The standard machines were obsolete.

The movement away from standardized designs, toward custom-designed machines which were more complex to engineer and to build—but also of greater intrinsic value to the customer—was led by General Electric. By the time of the Korean War (1951), Westinghouse managers had come to realize the magnitude of the engineering and production technology problem

---

[30] Testimony of L. M. Eikner, general manager of the Large Turbine Division at Westinghouse, *Ohio Valley Electric v. General Electric*, p. 2,267.

[31] Shortly after the Sunnyvale expansion (a facility largely suited to the manufacture of smaller, less complex units), there was a shift in demand away from small, standardized units, toward larger, nonstandard, more complex, reheat turbine generators—a shift fostered by aggressive General Electric offerings of such units to the utilities. This development thrust new and possibly unanticipated loads upon Westinghouse manufacturing and engineering. Morgan, former manager of manufacturing of the Westinghouse Steam Division, related:

> In 1950 our production on standardized turbines represented about 54 percent of our capacity. We dropped down to about 22 percent.

> The standard machine was an ordinary single-cylinder high-pressure and single-cylinder low-pressure turbine. When we get into the higher pressure, higher temperature machines, we have much more difficult problems. Even in 1946 I became concerned as to the percentage of that kind of business, realizing that it carried with it very substantial increases in cost, not only increases in cost of the article itself, but enlargement of our engineering and drafting work in the research departments that would be required.

> Following the outbreak of the Korean War, the real desires of the power industry became more apparent. It placed a very substantial load on our engineering group.

(Testimony of D. W. R. Morgan, general manager of Westinghouse steam division, 1948–1953, *Ohio Valley Electric v. General Electric*, pp. 2,224–2,227.)

they faced. One manager observed, "Oh golly, that is when the real desires of the power industry became more apparent with respect to demanding turbines of larger capacity, extremely high pressures and high temperatures . . . and we simply had to put on a crash program to find out the behavior of these materials, so that we coud keep our stresses within the bounds of what would be acceptable."[32]

The required engineering outlays increased sharply—by an estimated factor of seven to ten times.[33] Westinghouse was understandably hard-pressed to meet these challenges since Westinghouse does not appear to have deliberately planned to foster such a design and manufacturing approach. Westinghouse instead was responding to competitive pressure from General Electric and customer demand.

Westinghouse's engineering resources were further diluted by a jet engine program for the U.S. Navy (a rather unsuccessful effort),[34] strategically vital nuclear propulsion studies which were to be a forerunner of the currently strong Westinghouse position in nuclear power, and—amazingly—the technically challenging but apparently limited-commercial-value engineering of an enormous wind tunnel for the U.S. Air Force. Inevitably, at least some of these activities must have resulted in a whittling away of the resources available for turbine engineering.[35]

Westinghouse manufacturing capabilities were also stretched. By the early 1950s, it was clear that neither the existing Westinghouse manufacturing facilities at Philadelphia-Pittsburgh, nor the West Coast Sunnyvale facility, were adequate to meet production requirements. But rather than building a new plant, Westinghouse leased a Merchant Marine plant which Westing-

---

[32] Ibid.

[33] Carlson, division engineering manager at Lester for Westinghouse, commented on the severe engineering load created by the rapid evolution in turbine generator designs:

> Beginning with these newer, larger, more advanced reheat machines, generally each one was a new design and an advancement in the art and it multiplied our engineering costs many times over.
>
> It became an exceedingly difficult time to procure enough engineers to do the job, particularly 1950, 1951, 1952.
>
> Overtime was a way of life. We worked every Saturday and we worked, particularly in our drafting department, sometimes two nights a week plus the Saturday, in some cases Sunday.

(Testimony of John R. Carlson, Ohio Valley Electric v. General Electric, pp. 2,971–2,972.)

[34] See: F. M. Scherer, *The Weapons Acquisition Process* (Boston, Mass.: Harvard Business School, Division of Research, 1964). This contains an account of the unsuccessful development of the Westinghouse jet engine.

[35] The Westinghouse Engineering manager testified, with ill-concealed pride, "The United States Air Force wished to build this large wind tunnel at Tulahoma, and we were picked as the ones for that job. That was a huge undertaking requiring a great deal of engineering and development. As a matter of fact, that compressor on that wind tunnel required a motor of 216,000 horsepower and the blades in the compressor were placed on a drum that was 18 foot [sic] in diameter, the blades were six foot [sic] long and about two foot [sic] wide. Incidentally all the engineering was done within the Steam Division." (Testimony of D. W. R. Morgan, Ohio Valley Electric v. General Electric, pp. 2,228–2,229.)

house had laid out and operated during World War II, at South Philadelphia. This provided ". . . more sit-down space and a very desirable layout so far as the test stands were concerned. . . ." A sum of $17 million was budgeted for the rearrangement of facilities, plus tools and fixtures.[36] In 1952 a $6 million outlay for a new development laboratory was also announced.[37] In similar fashion to General Electric, the Westinghouse facility was busy six and seven days per week during the early 1950s.

It appears that the planned expansion in manufacturing capability at South Philadelphia did not go smoothly as had been anticipated. By mid-1953, customer orders were delayed, because of labor problems, there were delays in obtaining the necessary machine tools, and there were also production scheduling problems.[38]

One Westinghouse manager wrote to a field sales manager, "You are familiar with the long delay we have had on the new machine tools we are installing in our expanded facilities. Until we can realize the full output of these tools, we will have to continue the heavy subcontracting program that we now have." The cost of the expansion program crept upward to $32 million.[39] Costs were probably inflated owing to the heavy dependence upon subcontracting.

As if there were not problems enough, during 1955–1956 Westinghouse endured a 10-month strike at its manufacturing facilities. Turbine generator shipments dropped to a trickle (although the flow of new orders was maintained through a remarkably successful marketing effort). Backlogs of unfilled orders soared, and a heavy volume of costly overtime payments and subcontracting was required in order to achieve a normal delivery situation again, once the strike ended.[40]

---

[36] We had come to the conclusion that the test stands that we had in our plant were insufficient but rather than build a new building, we then set about in 1951 to lease the Merchant Marine plant, which we had previously engineered and laid out and operated from 1942–1945; it provided some 600,000 additional square feet, and we laid that out to give us more sit-down space and a very desirable layout so far as the test stands were concerned for our large turbines.
(Testimony of D. W. R. Morgan, Ohio Valley Electric v. General Electric, p. 2,230.)

[37] *Electrical World*, June 2, 1952, p. 142.

[38] A June 1953 letter to all Westinghouse district managers outlined delays in acquiring machine tools as originally scheduled, and asked sales personnel to ascertain which utility orders might be rescheduled: "In preparing a realistic schedule, we need your help and assistance." The letter stated, "We should appreciate your quietly checking the customers' requirements, utilizing both your Sales and Service Departments, if advisable." (DXWE-5022, Letter from Westinghouse Electric Corporation Steam Division, dated June 15, 1953, stenographer's minutes, San Antonio v. General Electric, p. 5,072.)

[39] November 1953 letter to a Westinghouse district manager, San Antonio v. General Electric, pp. 5,090–5,091.

[40] We utilized all of the facilities that we had in our plant, we got as much of a running start as we could by working in 1957 against our 1958 backlog and we did subcontract and work overtime heavily to get by this period of time.
(Testimony of L. M. Eikner, San Antonio v. General Electric, pp. 6,569–6,574.)

Throughout 1956 and 1957 the Westinghouse planners, as did their counterparts at General Electric, continued to revise upward their estimates of the capacity requirements for the early 1960s.[41] Plans for yet another round of factory expansion were laid.[42] A task force was assigned responsibility for forecasting the future product mix, and of planning future product mix, and of planning future manufacturing needs in detail, in order to forestall further manufacturing and delivery problems. The task force presented its first set of recommendations in late 1956, proposing a brand new plant, built around the product design concepts of the "building block" program —a redesign effort which had achieved some standardization of turbine components. This engineering effort had been one beneficial end product of the pause in work created by the lengthy Westinghouse strike.[43]

The investment cost and the contingent uncertainties of the task force proposal seemed too high. The task force was asked to come up with an alternative less ambitious plan, based upon the rearrangement of existing facilities at Lester, Pennsylvania, and incorporating the most modern machine tools within the existing "bricks and mortar."[44] The alternative plan was submitted in the autumn of 1957 amid continuing ebullient demand forecasts. Facilities planning work was accelerated.[45]

Throughout 1958 some rearrangement of facilities and the ordering of new machine tools was begun. It had already appeared that some of the earlier demand forecasts for the early 1960s might have to be adjusted downward, but the "postponement" of demand appeared to be slight.[46]

A capital appropriation request of $20 million for the Westinghouse expansion program was finally approved in February 1959.[47] At this time,

---

[41] Ibid., pp. 6,564–6,578.

[42] Ibid., p. 6,577.

[43] Ibid., pp. 6,577–6,579.

[44] The total cost to bring this about was such a large amount of money that the company just was unable to accept this recommendation. We had to provide an answer to this problem of indicated growth of our business, and the need to have more capacity to fulfill this growth need. Another approach then was identified. The assignment was to come up, as quickly as possible, with a plan of rearrangement of our existing facilities which would optimize the ability to utilize the existing bricks and mortar, whether new, large or any size tools should be installed in order to take advantage of the latest manufacturing techniques. In other words, to come as close to doing the job that the new plant would do, but keeping it in mind that we had to do it for a lot less money and we had to end up with something that was going to put us in as competitive a position, costwise, that we could possibly achieve. (Testimony of L. M. Eikner, *San Antonio v. General Electric*, pp. 6,579–6,580.)

[45] Ibid., pp. 6,562–6,580.

[46] Throughout 1958 specific plans were formulated for rearrangement of the Lester facilities, and the procurement of new machine tools. In January of 1958 a load forecast prepared by an independent Westinghouse group suggested that factory load might not materialize as rapidly as originally contemplated; the 1961 peak factory load was now expected to be pushed forward into 1962. Nevertheless, 8.5 million kilowatts of throughput was foreseen for 1967—a very bullish forecast. (Testimony of L. M. Eikner, *San Antonio v. General Electric*, pp. 6,564–6,578.)

[47] Ibid., pp. 6,580–6,582.

Westinghouse managers reportedly believed that their historical shipping performance was about to improve greatly. Furthermore, heavy product engineering investments were approaching fruition. At the American Power Conference in April 1959, Westinghouse announced, by means of a technical paper and an elaborate turbine generator model display, a completely new line of machines. Unfortunately, Westinghouse's investments in manufacturing and in product development were being executed immediately prior to a lengthy industry recession.

The Westinghouse expansion program was substantially completed by 1961—timed to coincide with the very bottom of the business slump.[48] The bulk of the investment went toward purchasing new tools and to rearrange manufacturing flows at the Lester works.[49]

In summary, public sources indicate that the major items in the Westinghouse 1948–1960 capital expenditures program, related to the turbine generator business, were:

1948:	Sunnyvale	$ 3.5 million
1951:	South Philadelphia Merchant Marine Plant	17.0 million
1952:	Laboratory, So. Philadelphia	6.0 million
1956:	Expansion, So. Philadelphia	5.0 million
1959:	Expansion, So. Philadelphia	21.0 million
Total		$52.5 million

Comment

The contrast between the Westinghouse and the General Electric capacity expansion strategies in the postwar period is striking and, with the benefit of hindsight, instructive.

In the full dozen years between 1948 and 1960, General Electric committed about $100 million of capital funds to the business, and Westinghouse about $50 million, or in the ratio of 2:1. It also happens that in turbine generator sales revenues, the ratio between the two competitors over these same years was about 2:1. Thus, capital dollars were expended about in proportion to sales dollars, for both businesses. However, one cannot leave this history of strategic facilities commitments without somehow feeling that General Electric acquired more manufacturing "bang for the buck" in the long term.

For most of the 12 years, General Electric operated from a modern, specially designed turbine generator facility—a facility which aided immensely its push for larger units and superior product technology, better delivery, and lower costs.[50] One senses that Westinghouse, on the other hand, had to

---

48 Ibid.

49 *Electrical World*, July 27, 1959, p. 76.

50 The first General Electric aircraft turbine work was at Lynn, Massachusetts, and not at Schenectady. General Electric's work on nuclear power and submarine propulsion was centralized

struggle to "make do" in less-than-ideal facilities. If Westinghouse had made a large commitment to a new plant *early*, as General Electric did, its competitive position—particularly its cost position—might have been stronger, even without spending any more money in the long run.

Perhaps the most important contrast is that between the apparent "crash efforts" of Westinghouse engineers to be competitive in product engineering, and the leadership which General Electric could—and apparently did— exercise over the pace and direction of product technology. General Electric could exercise this leadership only by pushing technology ahead very rapidly.

Possibly the contrast in expansion strategies is in large measure attributable to the greater uncertainty which plagues follower firms. The type of facilities required, particularly the type of complex machine tools, was very product-design dependent. Westinghouse planners were handicapped by the fact that continued and rapid evolution in product design meant that a facilities study, or a forecast of needed manufacturing facilities in the future, was really a projection of future product designs (e.g., the Westinghouse task force of 1956). However, the pace and the direction of change in product technology were strongly influenced by the current strategy being followed by the leader firm. In the absence of some insight into the long-range product strategy of the leader firm, it was difficult to plan capacity needs accurately.

As a consequence, it is understandable that Westinghouse seems to have been caught rather unprepared for the rapid, determined, and unyielding switch by General Electric away from the less-efficient, simpler, standardized units after World War II, toward highly sophisticated, complex, reheat machines which capitalized upon General Electric's superior engineering development resources. One can sympathize with the problems facing the Westinghouse facilities planners, since they were forced to estimate the future path of product evolution when that path was largely controlled by a competitor.

There are interesting contrasts in the *timing* of the capacity expansion decisions. Westinghouse seemed to lag one or two years behind General Electric in recognizing the shape of upcoming order cycles. General Electric moved to greatly expand kilowatts capacity, beginning in 1948. Westinghouse made its move around 1950. At the end of the period, General Electric, according to Herman Hill, set capacity expansion plans into motion in 1957–1958, looking forward to the boom that never came in the early 1960s. Westinghouse, making the same rosy forecasts, made a decision to expand its capacity as late as January 1959. Both companies were caught off base, with demand forecasting errors of major magnitude. However, General Electric seems to have caught sight of the true orders trend about a year earlier

---

initially at Schenectady, but at a different facility some miles apart from turbine generator engineering (Knolls Atomic Power Laboratory).

than did Westinghouse and was tapering off its expansion plans even as Westinghouse was still launching its expansion.

Concerning the apparent decision-making lag at Westinghouse, relative to General Electric, there is yet another plausible explanation: possibly Westinghouse managers set their capacity plans according to the publicly announced plans of General Electric—thereby following the same expansion path but lagging by a dozen months or so (the lag time for the capital expenditures appropriation process). This would explain the observed behavior, and would be in keeping with a strategy which says "maintain a constant share of industry manufacturing capacity." This would be an understandable strategy, since there is a strong tendency for market shares to follow capacity shares in this industry. These ideas will be developed further in the statistical modeling to be reported in the next section.

Explaining the Capacity Expansion Decision

The data suggest three phenomena: long-term stability in competitors' shares of total industry manufacturing capacity; "long cycles" in capacity shares; and short-term fluctuations from year to year.

(1) *Long-term stability in capacity shares.* Each domestic competitor's *share* of total industry manufacturing capacity, is plotted in Chart 11.4.

Westinghouse has rather consistently maintained about 32 to 35 percent of industry capacity, with the exception of the strike period.

Chart 11.4.   Average Share of Industry Manufacturing Capacity: General Electric, Westinghouse, and Allis-Chalmers (Quarterly Data).

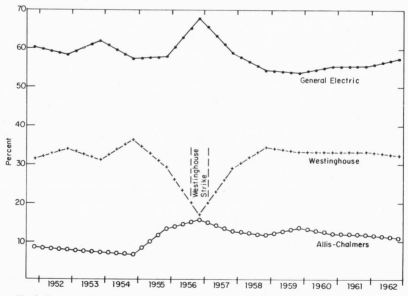

Source: Ford, Bacon and Davis data.

General Electric slowly allowed its share of total industry capacity to slide downward over the 1952–1959 period (the Westinghouse strike period aside). Following 1960, there was a perceptible tendency for General Electric's share of total industry capacity to rise once more.[51]

The really aggressive capacity moves were made by Allis-Chalmers, which in 1955–1956 increased its share of industry capacity from the 7 or 8 percent level to over 15 percent. Allis-Chalmers was lucky in its timing, inasmuch as Westinghouse was forced to withdraw its capacity from the market just as Allis-Chalmers' large capacity expansion was completed, thereby easing the absorption of this new capacity by the market.

Shifts in manufacturing capacity shares are obviously less volatile than the shifts in market shares. Allis-Chalmers' 1955 play is the solitary interesting feature in an otherwise dull landscape.

The paramount fact of life is the long-term stability in the share of total capacity held by Westinghouse and by General Electric. The phenomenon cannot be coincidental; it must reflect the deliberate strategic choice of Westinghouse and General Electric managers, facilitated by the goldfish-bowl planning environment of this industry. Any "model" of capacity expansion must take this into account.

Capital investment programs are announced in the trade press with maximum press coverage, to trumpet among utility customers the added capability to serve. Even in the absence of press announcements, plans for new long lead-time machine tools, plant rearrangements, and bricks-and-mortar invest ments, are rather well known throughout the industry. The Edison Electric Institute surveys each competitor semi-annually for his future capacity estimates, and publishes the total as part of its equipment information service for the utilities. In all, a competitor's capacity intentions are seldom a secret.

It is interesting to observe that it was apparently common to underreport capacities, in the hope that competitors might thereby be dissuaded from expanding their own capacities aggressively.[52] One can only presume that such capacity-reporting biases were duplicated at Westinghouse, Allis-Chalmers, and General Electric. Clearly, competitors monitored one another's capacity

---

[51] Chart 11.4 shows shares based upon moving four-quarter average capacity figures (kilowatts throughput capability per period).

[52] The strategic importance of data on manufacturing capacities is apparent from litigation testimony. John T. Peters of General Electric observed that capacities reported to EEI for the semiannual power survey were usually biased on the low side, in order to deceive competitors:

> We made sure that when we gave them (EEI) backlog information that we did not want to tell Westinghouse and Allis-Chalmers all of our capacity data and therefore we did not, at that time, give them accurate information on capacity. We have an economist who meets with Mr. Campbell (of EEI) and his associates, as I say, every spring, and they also modify this information semi-annually. This economist gives to EEI estimates of our capacity, and it is this figure, this estimate of capacity, that we generally try to understate.

(Testimony of John T. Peters, San Antonio v. General Electric, pp. 5,705–5,709.)

expansions, for strategic purposes. This tended, in the long run, to produce stability in capacity shares.[53]

(2) *Long cycles in share of capacity.* While there has been great long-term stability in capacity shares, it is also true that both Westinghouse and General Electric were forced to concede a share of capacity to Allis-Chalmers during the 1950s. Given the public nature of capacity planning, it seems certain that Westinghouse and General Electric managers must have been aware of what had happened. Perhaps they intended to give Allis-Chalmers every opportunity to consolidate its competitive beachhead.

However, there were apparently limits beyond which the two market leaders would not be pressed. When General Electric's share of industry capacity approached 50 percent, it acted to bring its capacity share back in line with its long-term market share expectations. Westinghouse appears to have had even narrower tolerance limits, beyond which it could not be nudged.

(3) *Short-term variations.* Short-term variations in share of industry capacity obviously coincide with the varying dates upon which competitors brought new capacity "on-line." The specific timing of a plant expansion may be influenced by operating factors. Current profitability, for example, might dampen or fuel capital investment appetites. Or, a high utilization rate could trigger an expansion move, as could high backlogs or a high rate of incoming orders. Fluctuations in these operating variables could therefore account for some of the short-term variation of capacity shares, within the "control limits" set by each firm.

Various speculations concerning the decision to expand manufacturing capacity may be subjected to statistical test. Given the fact of relatively stable capacity shares, for the two larger competitors, and the somewhat "maverick" behavior of the smallest competitor, it seems likely that quite different decision rules might be governing the behavior of the two larger firms, in contrast with the behavior of the smallest firm.

Westinghouse and General Electric

As for the two largest firms, a long-term decision rule which may implicitly govern their behavior is: "Maintain share of total industry manufacturing capacity at X percent, plus or minus Y percent, in accordance with long-term market share norms." This logic suggests that the two largest firms estimate future industry demand and future industry capacity requirements, and then build their own share of it accordingly. This is probably a rather close

---

[53] Fruhan has analyzed the close relationship between market shares and capacity shares in the airline industry, and notes that the carriers' tendency to maintain market share at any cost results in chronic wasteful overinvestment in airline capacity on individual routes. See: William E. Fruhan, Jr., *The Fight for Competitive Advantage: A Study of the United States Domestic Trunk Air Carriers* (Boston, Mass.: Harvard Business School, Division of Research, 1972), Chapter 5.

approximation of how General Electric and Westinghouse in fact determined their long-term capacity needs. However, if capacity expansion decisions were strictly determined in this fashion, it is not evident that the result would be long-term stability of capacity shares. The reason is very simple: each firm's estimates of future industry demand varied greatly. This would lead to great variation in their plant construction schedules.

An alternative decision guideline is suggested—a close relative of the preceding one. Each of the two major competitors may increase his own manufacturing capacity in proportion to the perceived amount of expansion of his major rival. General Electric managers may be stimulated to add capacity merely because Westinghouse is adding capacity, and vice versa. Such an interdependent mode of expansion would be consistent with theorizing concerning strategic behavior in oligopoly.[54]

Appendix 14 reports the statistical results of an analysis based upon data for Westinghouse and General Electric, in which each firm's capacity is determined as a *fixed ratio* to his rival's capacity of four quarters earlier.[55] According to this reasoning, the two large competitors struggle to maintain their share of industry capacity in the long run, a capability which must be maintained for the defense of market share. The resulting behavior resembles an "arms race" in military rivalry terms.

When Westinghouse increased its capacity, General Electric did likewise. It might be argued that, given the decision lag one discerns between General Electric and Westinghouse, the sequence was likely to be that General Electric initiated the capacity expansion and Westinghouse followed. However, in a spiraling arms race it is futile to seek to identify the initiating participant; instead, one observes a series of upward-ratcheting investments in round-robin fashion, by both participants. Some exogenous market force triggers an expansion by General Electric, which triggers an expansion by Westinghouse, which triggers an expansion by General Electric, and so on, as each competitor acts to restore his "normal" capacity share. The spiral may end only when manufacturing capacity has clearly exceeded market requirements.[56]

---

[54] See Fruhan, *The Fight for Competitive Advantage*. Knickerbocker has also analyzed the checkmating investment propensities of oligopolists when entering markets overseas, and the follow-the-leader behavior which results. He also notes, "The intensity of checkmating investment is in part determined by the breadth of a firm's product line. Narrow product-line firms, because they have few options, tend to respond in kind when a rival makes a foreign direct investment." In Knickerbocker's terminology, the turbine generator businesses are narrow-line "firms," for which the investment response may be predicted to be very direct. See: Frederick T. Knickerbocker, *Oligopolistic Reaction and Multinational Enterprise* (Boston, Mass.: Harvard Business School, Division of Research, 1973), p. 195.

[55] Note that it requires two to four years to have capacity in place, from the time a decision is made to add capacity. However, the plans to add capacity are not kept secret in the interim. (See, for example, the earlier account of the Lynn expansion which reached fruition in 1960–1961, after being announced in *Electrical World* in 1957.)

[56] For a somewhat parallel model based upon the problem of anticipating the output of a

Such a ratcheting arms race model explains the trend in General Electric and Westinghouse capacities adequately, particularly if kilowatts backlog is included as a secondary, modulating influence (see Appendix 14). Adding backlogs as a secondary determinant of manufacturing capacity prevents an uncontrolled spiral from occurring. As soon as capacity expands in extreme fashion, backlogs will decline, and capacity itself will eventually shrink.

Allis-Chalmers

Allis-Chalmers, it appears (see Appendix 14), expanded manufacturing capacity more in accord with its own current utilization rate in the factory. In its own capacity expansion decisions, it was less influenced by the manufacturing capacity actions of its two larger rivals. Such an inward-looking interpretation of Allis-Chalmers' behavior seems intuitively sound, given Allis-Chalmers' diminutive size. However, such inward-looking behavior also led Allis-Chalmers to expand its share of manufacturing capacity beyond a point which could be sustained. In retrospect, a parity rule such as General Electric and Westinghouse seem to have followed might have served Allis-Chalmers better.[57]

In sum, while General Electric and Westinghouse capacity expansions could be explained by a modified arms race model, Allis-Chalmers seemed to be less motivated by such rivalistic concerns, and instead added to its manufacturing capacity in accordance with its own factory utilization rate and its own backlogs position. The picture of two large rivals eyeing one another and making their capacity decisions accordingly, and one smaller competitor being chiefly concerned with its private internal operating statistics (disregarding its larger rivals), is intuitively appealing as a description of competitive behavior in this oligopoly.

---

rival firm, in duopoly experiencing a business cycle, see: A. Smithies and L. J. Savage, "A Dynamic Problem in Duopoly," *Econometrica*, Vol. VII, 1939, pp. 130–143.

[57] One reviewer objects to my implicit characterization of the Allis-Chalmers' expansion as "reckless," and makes the valid observation that:

> As turbogenerators got bigger and bigger and as special design became more important, AC must have found itself in an increasingly difficult position. Given its small market share, it was hard-pressed to swallow necessary, partially fixed research, development, and engineering costs; and the infrequency of very large orders lent a precarious instability to its operations. I suspect AC's management recognized that they either had to increase their market share or "go down the tube." They did two things then: tried to jump ahead technically, and they built up their capacity so they could win a disproportionate share of new orders when backlogs were large and time of delivery a significant marketing advantage. If that was inward-looking and mindless, I'd like to know what a right-minded company ought to do. To be sure, the gamble failed. But what would have happened if demand and prices (and the conspiracy) hadn't collapsed? The risk certainly *could* have been successful, and in my opinion, it was probably AC's only chance of achieving viability.

Benefits from Scale in Manufacturing: Backlogs and Throughput Smoothing, and Capacity Utilization

Consider next the benefits, beyond market share, which accrue through scale. Principal among these are the benefits which derive from backlogs and throughput smoothing. However, one obvious drawback to adding manufacturing capacity is the risk that not all of that capacity might be used.

Backlogs

Total kilowatts backlogs are plotted in Volume I (page 203), for General Electric, Westinghouse, and Allis-Chalmers. The time series is volatile. Obviously, *backlogs* buffering is the principal means by which the fluctuating flow of orders is accommodated by this industry. Now, the relative variability of each competitor's backlogs may be interpreted as a measure of the degree of backlogs buffering which each pursues. Such a comparison is summarized in Table 11.1.

TABLE 11.1.
MEAN AND STANDARD DEVIATION OF BACKLOGS OF UNFILLED ORDERS
(QUARTERLY DATA), 1951–1963.

	Mean Value (000 kw)	Standard Deviation (000 kw)	Standard Deviation as Percent of Mean Value
General Electric	18,598	3,706	20%
Westinghouse	9,905	2,274	23
Allis-Chalmers	2,368	1,195	51

General Electric had the least variation in backlogs, relative to the size of its average backlog. Allis-Chalmers had the most (taking one standard deviation around the mean as the relevant measure of variability).

The fact that Allis-Chalmers worked its backlogs up and down much more than the other two firms is not surprising, in view of the previous findings concerning the relative variability of Allis-Chalmers' orders inflows.[58] Allis-Chalmers had no other choice, given the volatility of its orders inflow, and the necessity to smooth out the factory production rate as much as possible.

However, another factor could potentially contribute to Allis-Chalmers' higher degree of backlog fluctuation: a very minimal backlog relative to demand. However, this is not the case. All three competitors maintained backlogs which were rather alike relative to shipments. See Table 11.2:

[58] See Ralph G. M. Sultan, *Pricing in the Electrical Oligopoly, Vol. I: Competition or Collusion*, pp. 210–211.

TABLE 11.2.
AVERAGE KILOWATTS BACKLOG DIVIDED BY AVERAGE
KILOWATTS SHIPMENTS PER QUARTER, 1951–1963.

General Electric	10.6 quarters
Westinghouse	11.0 quarters
Allis-Chalmers	11.6 quarters

We conclude that one of the competitive advantages of scale in this industry was probably the ability to operate with a slightly lower average backlog while still maintaining a smooth work flow through the factory. This would tend to improve average delivery performance for the leader firm, an important competitive edge.

Backlogs Relative to Capacity

The manufacturers testified as to the importance of having a sizable backlog of unfilled orders, "in order to fill up the factory." It is therefore interesting to examine their backlogs in proportion to their manufacturing capacity. Volume I (page 204) shows, for each competitor, total kilowatts backlog divided by total kilowatts per year throughput capacity. The result is backlogs in "years" of manufacturing throughput. The minimum "years" of backlog among all of the competitors is an important determinant of price levels in this industry (as demonstrated in Chapter Seven).

General Electric often had a comfortable backlog, although the long-term trend, clearly, was to shorter and shorter backlogs relative to capacity, over a period when manufacturing lead times were actually *increasing*, as product complexity and size increased. Manufacturing managers would tend to feel themselves under increasing pressure in these low backlogs years.

The Westinghouse backlogs record, relative to capacity, is quite similar to that of General Electric, with the major exception of the strike period when Westinghouse backlogs soared.

Allis-Chalmers was a relatively weak competitor, in the backlogs-to-capacity sense. Allis-Chalmers seldom had more than two years of work in backlogs, and on several occasions (1955, 1961–1962) it had less than one year of work to look forward to. Allis-Chalmers' manufacturing schedulers must have been confronted with a virtually impossible production-smoothing task. Given the discreteness of orders and Allis-Chalmers' backlogs situation in 1954, and again in the 1959–1960 period, we speculate that the production schedulers' distress would be communicated to Allis-Chalmers' marketing staff, who would then be the first to cut prices in an endeavor to rebuild backlogs.

Shipments Smoothing

Manufacturing scale also influences the ease of smoothing factory production—an important factor in keeping costs down. Chart 11.5 shows aggregate

CHART 11.5   Quarterly Shipments of Steam Turbine Generators by General Electric, Westinghouse, and Allis-Chalmers.

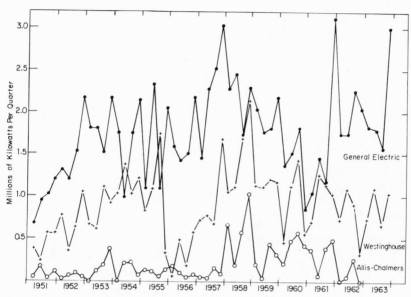

kilowatts shipped by each firm in each quarter. While not as erratic as orders, even shipments were quite fluctuating in nature.

While Westinghouse and General Electric had "peaky" shipments, at least they made *some* shipments in each quarter. This was not true for Allis-Chalmers, which experienced several quarters with no shipments at all, and many quarters when shipments were very close to zero. Allis-Chalmers was undoubtedly having extreme difficulty in smoothing its work flow throughout most of the 1951–1963 period.[59]

The statistical evidence for Allis-Chalmers' relative unevenness of work flow may be found in Table 11.3.

Capacity Utilization

Our final statistical measure concerns the utilization of manufacturing capacity: the ratio of actual throughput to throughput capability. The results are plotted for each firm in Volume I (page 204). These curves show the relative success of each competitor in keeping his factory in balance with his flow of production work.

---

[59] One reviewer suggested an analysis of *unit* production flows using the hypothesis of a Poisson process. An alternative to this was pursued: *kilowatt* production flows were assumed to be a Poisson process, with parameter (mean delay) determined by the degree of backlogs pressure on the individual firm. See Chapter Five.

TABLE 11.3.
QUARTERLY SHIPMENTS OF TURBINE GENERATORS, 1951–1963.

	Mean Value (000 kw)	Standard Deviation (000 kw)	Standard Deviation as Percent of Mean
General Electric	1,763	554	31%
Westinghouse	901	423	47
Allis-Chalmers	205	213	104

One measure of competitive success in balancing factory capacity with demand are the average percentage utilizations over 1951–1963:

General Electric	86%	Factory utilization
Westinghouse	84%	Factory utilization
Allis-Chalmers	52%	Factory utilization

Westinghouse's utilization of capacity seemed to lag behind General Electric's by a year or two. In other words, the Westinghouse factory was at its busiest a year or two following the time when General Electric was at its busiest; it was in the doldrums about a year or two behind when General Electric was in the doldrums.

This lagged relationship suggests that General Electric was more successful in winning orders during a demand upturn. It increased its share of the market when the order rate was rising, and filled its factory sooner than Westinghouse did. However, when industry orders were falling, General Electric was less successful in acquiring orders than was Westinghouse. Thus, Westinghouse kept its factories busy later into the downward phase of the cycle. This result is completely compatible with "buffering" behavior for the market leader.

Costs and Benefits

In choosing a manufacturing capacity strategy, the virtues of smoothing, achievable through scale, must be weighed against the cost of unused capacity, if the gamble of expanding capacity does not succeed.

From the perspective of a small nibbling competitor in the marketplace (an Allis-Chalmers for example) capacity expansion decisions which are essentially inward-looking, seeking to build upon historical success without regard to the ponderous reactions of the major industry suppliers, may seem eminently sound, given the direct cost reductions, overhead spreading advantages, and other production smoothing benefits which may be attained. However, Allis-Chalmers' managers probably underestimated the financial risk of living with unused capacity.

From the perspective of major competitors such as Westinghouse and General Electric, an essentially reactive strategy, aimed at blocking one's rival from achieving even a temporary advantage in delivery capability—that is, in capacity—would seem to be sound long-term strategy. It insures market position. While rivals may experience cyclical excess capacity from time to time, and incur reduced earnings as a consequence, neither firm will gain at the expense of the other, in market share, and this is a cornerstone of the leading firm's strategy. The larger firm will benefit from superior smoothing, in addition to the other economies of scale and learning in his operation, and has the option of employing his added gross margin to fund advanced technologies, and to engage in a superior marketing effort. If the leader plays his cards well, he can both drive the industry forward in technology, and preserve his hegemony.

It should now be abundantly clear that manufacturing capacity strategy is linked to product technology, another major strategic variable under the direct control of management. This will be the subject of Chapter Twelve.

CHAPTER Twelve   Technological Strategy

THIS CHAPTER IS CONCERNED WITH MANAGEMENT'S second major strategic weapon: the product itself and the technological change which is embodied in the product. Of the three principal elements of managerial strategy: market share, manufacturing capacity, and technology, this is the most complex to manage. It is also the most potent, in the sense of determining competitive strength in the marketplace.

Market structure helps to shape each competitor's strategy and, therefore, technological change is inextricably linked with market structure.[1] Economists from Schumpeter[2] to Galbraith[3] have argued that the link is positive; that is, that concentration and some degree of market power and monopoly position are preconditions for large-scale technological development in the modern industrial world. It is argued that an industry composed of a few large oligopolists will be technically more progressive than an industry composed of a larger number of smaller firms.[4] However, the situation is not as simple as Schumpeter and Galbraith would have us believe. It is *differential* technological capability—related to differentials in the size of firm —which is the key to the process of innovation, such differentials being important both on the demand and on the supply side of the marketplace.[5]

---

[1] See: Richard E. Caves, *Market Structure and Embodied Technological Change*, working paper prepared for the Brookings Workshop on Economic Regulation, Harvard University, 1973.

[2] Joseph A. Schumpeter, *Capitalism, Socialism, and Democracy* (New York: Harper, 1942).

[3] See: John Kenneth Galbraith, *American Capitalism* (Boston: Houghton Mifflin, 1952); and *The New Industrial State* (Boston: Houghton Mifflin, 1967).

[4] For a discussion, see: Edwin Mansfield, *The Economics of Technological Change* (New York: W. W. Norton, 1968), p. 93ff.

[5] The impact of regulation upon the scale and organization of the electric power industry has been analyzed by William R. Hughes. See: "Scale Frontiers in Electric Power," William M. Capron, ed., *Technological Change in Regulated Industries* (Washington: Brookings Institution, 1971). Hughes analyzes the influence of structure on the demand side of the marketplace and concludes that the diffusion of newly established scales and steam conditions would clearly have been more rapid in a "rationalized" industry structure; that is, a utility industry with fewer, larger organizations. I am not sure that Hughes is right. Under my thesis, it is *differential* technological competence, costs, and profitability which is the engine of technological change. If all

Disparity in scale, combined with a few very large firms, is helpful to progress, both among customers and among suppliers.

TECHNOLOGICAL CHANGE IN TURBINE GENERATORS

There has been rapid progress in turbine generator design. One utility executive commented upon the "progress in the size of units, in the pressure and temperature of steam at which units could be operated, the design of the generators, more particularly as to cooling (and) the improvements in operating speeds, occasioned by improvements in metallurgy."[6] This executive could fluently recount these factors from memory—testimony of his personal involvement in monitoring turbine generator technology. This was typical of top utility managers, for whom technology was very important. The reasons are readily discerned. The vice president of engineering of one utility observed that increasing turbine generator operating efficiencies permitted the utilities to offer rate reductions to their customers, a rapid increase in turbine generator investment costs notwithstanding.[7]

Three parameters of technological progress in turbine generator design are: (1) the increase in the "steam conditions"—the temperature and pressure of the steam when first entering the turbine unit; (2) the "heat rate," which is a measure of efficiency in converting fossil fuel into electric power; and (3) the increase in the size of the turbine and of the generator.

Steam Conditions: Temperature and Pressure[8]

The historical rise in maximum steam pressures is plotted in Chart 12.1. Another key parameter of the thermodynamic cycle, maximum initial

---

utility organizations were identical in scale and technical competence, there would be no laggard customer sector to keep alive the follower firms in the turbine generator oligopoly, and progress might suffer in the pricing environment which could ensue.

[6] Deposition of Elmer L. Lindseth, president of Cleveland Electric Illuminating Company, Electrical Equipment Antitrust Actions in all U.S. district courts, December 20, 1963.

[7] See, for example, the following dialogue:

Q. It is the efficiency in today's systems as compared with 1945 that has enabled the utilities to produce electricity today at a cheaper cost than they could 15 years ago?

A. Well, and thank God we can. Now you are talking about just out-of-pocket expenses? You are not talking about investment charges or anything else?

Q. Production costs.

A. If it wasn't for that, we might be bankrupt or else the rates would be so high nobody would use it.

(Deposition of Albert M. Casey, Engineering vice president, Cleveland Electric Illuminating Company in Electrical Equipment Antitrust Actions, all U.S. district courts, November 15, 1963.)

[8] For an analysis of steam temperatures and pressures see: R. O. Brown and J. E. Donahue, "Advancements in Large Tandem Compound Steam Turbines," Proceedings of The American Power Conference, April 27–29, 1965, Chicago, Illinois; J. E. Downs and C. H. Holley, "Progress in the Design of Large Steam Turbine Generators," National Power Conference, Albany, New York, September 19–23, 1965 (General Electric reprint GER-2303); Edwin E. Parker, "Recent Trends in Turbine Generator Unit Capacities, Steam Pressures, and Temperatures," Presentation to the Southeastern Electric Exchange, Richmond, Virginia, October 5, 1951.

CHART 12.1.   Maximum Steam Pressures, General Electric Turbine Generators:
1903–1936.

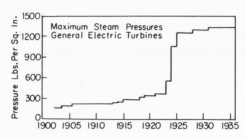

SOURCE: Ernest L. Robinson, "The Steam Turbine-Generator in the United States," *Mechanical Engineering*, April 1937.

temperature, is plotted in Chart 12.2. Progress here was much steadier, although there was a pause in progress, due to the 1930s Depression and World War II. If one extrapolated the trend, one would have predicted maximum temperatures to climb from 1100°F. level shown for 1953 to possibly 1500°F. by 1970. This would have been too optimistic a forecast; maximum temperatures had about reached a ceiling in 1953, because of metallurgical constraints.

While *maximum* temperatures encountered a ceiling, *average* temperatures for the entire industry (an indication of the breadth of *adoption* of advanced steam conditions), continued to rise (see Table 12.1). Improvements in the thermodynamic cycle were disseminated throughout the utility industry, while the advanced prototype units were becoming stuck on a technical plateau.

The major reason for this technological deceleration, insofar as steam temperatures were concerned, was metallurgical: the unsuitability of conventional ferritic steels for continuous operation at temperature in excess

CHART 12.2.   Maximum Initial Temperature, General Electric Turbine Generators:
1905–1953.

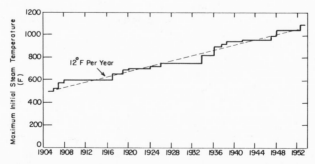

SOURCE: E. E. Parker, "Recent Trends in Turbine Generator Unit Capacities, Steam Pressures, and Temperatures," a paper presented to the Southeastern Electric Exchange, Richmond, Virginia, October 5, 1951.

of 1050°F., and the consequent necessity to employ austenitic (stainless) steels, or even more exotic alloys. While this was technically feasible, it was not economical. The increase in capital cost outweighed any savings in fuel costs which could be achieved through having a superior thermodynamic cycle.

TABLE 12.1.
AVERAGE PRESSURES AND TEMPERATURES FOR SHIPMENT YEARS 1947–1962.
(*Industry Total*)

Year	Initial Pressure	Initial Temperature	Reheat Temperature
1947	860 psi	875°F	875°F
48	870	880	975
49	930	890	990
50	1120	930	990
51	1150	945	995
52	1350	965	1005
53	1490	985	1005
54	1510	990	1010
55	1630	1000	1005
56	1660	1005	1010
57	1770	1007	1010
58	1940	1025	1010
59	1960	1017	1005
60	1990	1023	1002
61	2040	1015	1001
62	2080	1016	1000

SOURCE: Electrical litigation, National Exhibit NX 590.

Steam pressures also hit an economic ceiling. One prototype 4,500-pounds pressure unit was built by General Electric for American Gas & Electric (the Philo plant of 1956), but proved uneconomical. An even more advanced 5,000-pound pressure unit (Eddystone) had been built by Westinghouse, with similar results. The culprit in this case was not so much the economics of building a supercritical pressure turbine; it was the associated capital cost of the rest of the steam electric plant: the high-pressure boiler system and piping which was required. Inasmuch as boiler equipment costs constituted over one third of the total cost of a power station, any cost penalties here weighed heavily upon the economic feasibility of the total station.[9]

[9] For example, the 950,000 kilowatt Bull Run Station of TVA, typical of large modern plants, had a total plant cost of $150 per kilowatt, of which $22 was for the turbine generator, $60 for the boiler equipment, $21 for the structure, and the balance for land, accessory electrical equipment, the general overhead expense of construction, and other items. G. P. Palo, G. O. Wessenauer, J. R. Parrish, and E. Floyd Thomas, "Units 500 MW and Larger Found to Yield Savings," presented at World Energy Conference, Moscow, and published in *Electrical World*, March 31, 1969.

Boilers and piping (steam generation systems) are manufactured and installed by other contractors, not the turbine builders, and these other manufacturers have their own technological strategies, which may not always mesh the pace of change which suits the turbine builders.

Heat Rates[10]

The payoff from gains in thermodynamic cycle efficiency and other designs improvements may be measured in the "heat rate," in nontechnical terms the pounds of coal required to generate a kilowatt-hour of electricity. In 60 years (1905–1965) this declined from about 6.0 pounds of coal to less than 0.9 pounds of coal for all electric utility systems in the United States. The very best modern plants are today below 0.8 pounds in efficiency.

Engineers prefer to measure heat rates in "British Thermal Units per kilowatt-hour." The progress since 1938 is shown in Table 12.2. These data illustrate the consequences of the retardation of advances in the thermodynamic cycle (temperature and pressure). Diminishing returns in technology are shriveling the annual gains in heat rates. In 1969 the utilities not only did not gain, they actually slipped backwards a little. As progress slows on the technological frontiers, the "average" station has been catching up to the "best."[11]

Unit Size: Kilowatts[12]

A third parameter of technological progress is the *size* of turbine generator units. In 1902, the General Electric Company manufactured turbines with ratings of 500 to 5,000 kilowatts. (The 5,000-kilowatt machine was as powerful as the largest steam engine of the day.) As Chart 12.3 indicates, there

---

10 The best heat rates are usually attained by the larger units with the highest steam temperatures and pressures. However, many variables, including the loads carried during the year, the type of fuel burned, the number of turbine stops and starts, and turbine maintenance, have a direct bearing upon the annual heat rate performance. In 1964, the Federal Power Commission predicted a national average heat rate of 8,050 for the United States in 1990, a figure which now appears to be wishful thinking. Sporn, president of American Electric Power predicted in 1959 a national average heat rate of 8,500 to 9,000 for 1975 (clearly too optimistic), and of 6,400 to 7,000 for the year 2000 (which now seems unattainable). See: *Energy Resources and Technology*, Hearings, Subcommittee on Automation and Energy Resources, Joint Economic Committee, 86th Cong., 1st Sess., October 13, 1959, statement by Philip Sporn.

11 In 1938 the *best* U.S. thermal plant had a heat rate of 10,788 BTUs per kilowatt-hour, which was 65 percent of the average for that year; by 1969, the *best* plant had a heat rate of 8,707, which was 83 percent of the national average.

12 For scale considerations, see: R. R. Bennett, "Station Size, Where Are We Heading?" Proceedings of American Power Conference, 1968, Volume 30; C. E. Kilbourne and M. K. Morrison, "Factors Affecting the Unit Size Trend," Talk to Committee on Power Generation, Association of Edison Illuminating Companies, February 25–26, 1963; S. C. Barton, J. A. Massingill, and H. D. Taylor, "Design Features and Characteristics of Large Steam Turbine Generators," Proceedings of AIEE-ASME National Power Conference, Boston, Mass., September 29, 1958 (General Electric reprint GER-1549).

TABLE 12.2.

NATIONAL AVERAGE HEAT RATES FOR FOSSIL-FUELED STEAM-ELECTRIC PLANTS—
TOTAL ELECTRIC POWER INDUSTRIES—1938 TO 1969, INCLUSIVE.

Year	BTU Per Net Kilowatt Hour	Thermal Efficiency (Percent)	Year	BTU Per Net Kilowatt Hour	Thermal Efficiency (Percent)
1938	16,500	20.68	1959	10,970	31.11
1948	15,738	21.69	1960	10,760	31.72
1950	14,030	24.33	1961	10,650	32.05
1951	13,641	25.02	1962	10,558	32.33
1952	13,361	25.54	1963	10,482	32.56
1953	12,889	26.48	1964	10,462	32.62
1954	12,180	28.02	1965	10,453	32.65
1955	11,699	29.17	1966	10,415	32.77
1956	11,456	29.79	1967	10,432	32.72
1957	11,365	30.03	1968	10,398	32.82
1958	11,085	30.79	1969	10,447	32.67

SOURCE: Federal Power Commission, *Steam-Electric Plant Construction Cost and Annual Production Expenses*, 22nd Annual Supplement, 1969, Washington, D.C., 1969.

was a steady growth in the maximum size of ratings through the mid-1920s, culminating in an enormous leap to beyond 200,000 kilowatts size in 1928. Thereafter, further advance in the size of units ceased until after World War II. Not until 1955 did General Electric again put into service units which were larger than 200,000 kilowatts, striking evidence of the technological drought created by conditions of the Depression (and demonstrating, by the way, that rapid technological advances are hardly stimulated by adverse economic conditions).

The growth in unit ratings at Westinghouse is illustrated in Chart 12.4. In 1950 the largest tandem compound unit ordered was 200,000 kilowatts. By 1964 that figure had trebled. The annual rate of increase in maximum kilowatts size has been estimated at 8 percent for Westinghouse over the

CHART 12.3.   Maximum Size of General Electric Turbine Generators: 1902–1935.

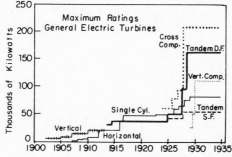

SOURCE: Ernest L. Robinson, "The Steam Turbine-Generator in the United States," *Mechanical Engineering*, April 1937.

CHART 12.4.   Growth Trends of Tandem Compound Steam Turbines.

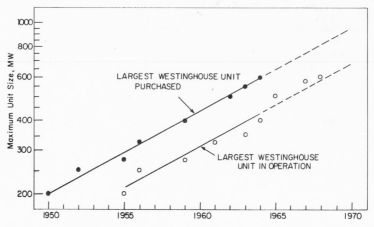

SOURCE: Westinghouse Corporation.

1950–1970 period;[13] and for General Electric for the 1935–1958 period, at 8.5 percent per year.[14]

It is not a coincidence that the annual growth in turbine generator size is similar to the long-term growth in utility peak loads (about 7.5 percent). A utility organization is constrained in the maximum size of turbine generators it can install, by the maximum kilowatts load upon its system.[15] Prudent engineering has dictated that the largest unit on a utility system should not exceed, say, 7 percent of total system load, so that the largest turbine could fail in service without placing undue strain on the utilities' 15 percent to 25 percent reserve generating capacity. As total system loads grow, so does the maximum feasible size of turbine. For the same reason, it is not surprising that the very largest systems, such as TVA and AEP, have usually been the systems to lead in the installation of the largest turbine generators.

By 1969 the annual growth in maximum ratings of two-shaft cross-compound units appeared to have accelerated to a 12 percent trend line, and 3,600-rpm tandem units to about a 10 percent trend line. The rate of introduction of new technology was speeded up.

To describe all of the generator and turbine design accomplishments would require a massive narrative. During litigation Westinghouse listed some 460 product and manufacturing technology innovations which it had introduced from 1946 through 1961.[16] General Electric, in responding to similar queries

---

[13] Brown and Donahue, "Advancements in Large Tandem Compound Steam Turbines."

[14] Barton, Massingill, and Taylor, "Design Features and Characteristics of Large Steam Turbine Generators."

[15] For an extended analysis see: William R. Hughes, "Coordination and Integration in the Electric Power Industry: A Study in Industry Structure and Performance," unpublished.

[16] Defendant Westinghouse Electric Corporation's Second Supplemental and Further Supplemental Answers to Set No. 2 of Interrogatories on behalf of Plaintiffs, Consumers Power

during litigation listed some 554 design improvements for the 1946–1961 period.[17] The individual steps were hardly dramatic, but each improvement, piled upon previous improvements, sustained rapid and continuous progress.

The Path of Technological Change

Historically, the path of technological change has varied. Sometimes emphasis has been given to increasing the scale of units; at other times there has been concentration upon improvements in thermodynamic efficiency. Two engineering managers, Schabtach of General Electric[18] and Carlson of Westinghouse,[19] described how the direction of their engineering programs was influenced by a combination of the following factors:

(1) the availability of materials to withstand higher temperatures and pressures, and their costs.

(2) fuel savings attainable through advances in the thermodynamic cycle, but subject to diminishing returns as temperature and pressures rise.

(3) the price of coal, which established a value for the gains in fuel-burning efficiency.

(4) the reduction in capital costs for the utilities achieved through increasing the sheer scale of turbines and of generators.

The future direction of engineering effort will be influenced by expectations concerning the future utility costs of capital. If fuel prices decline, relative to capital costs, this will discourage development efforts aimed at improving the thermodynamic cycle, and will tend to skew design efforts toward the scaling-up of designs, to minimize capital costs. On the other hand, should fuel prices climb relative to capital prices, this will encourage technological investments aimed at achieving further improvements in the thermodynamic cycle. Progress is disjointed. At any instant, the designers are imprisoned by the path of their previous efforts and led forward by current expectations of the future utility cost environment.

The historical track of design evolution therefore embodies, in part, the history of perceived future costs in the utility industry. However, non-economic considerations also shape the path of technological development, as indicated by such technological barriers as the "austenitic steel" barrier which may forestall continued design evolution along a particular path.

Company et al. v. Allis-Chalmers Manufacturing Company et al., 61 Civ. 4285, U.S. District Court, S.D.N.Y.

[17] Supplemental Answers of Defendant General Electric Company to Plaintiff's Priority Product Line Interrogatories Set No. 2, Atlantic City Electric et al. v. General Electric et al., 61 Civ. 4258, U.S. District Court, S.D.N.Y.

[18] Testimony of Carl Schabtach, manager of product engineering, Large Steam Turbine Generator Division, General Electric, in stenographer's minutes, Ohio Valley Electric v. General Electric et al., 62 Civ. 695, S.D.N.Y., pp. 4,146–4,163.

[19] Testimony of John R. Carlson, division engineering manager, Lester, Pa., stenographer's minutes, Ohio Valley Electric v. General Electric, 62 Civ. 695, S.D.N.Y., pp. 3,020–3,021.

The resulting evolution of designs is therefore a composite of economic and purely technical considerations.

When technological barriers are encountered along one dimension of the product, the rate of change may then be accelerated along another dimension of the product. Since technological risk is a function of the experience garnered through the operation of units along *all* dimensions of technology, the thwarting of progress along one dimension, and its acceleration along another, can increase technological risk in a sudden and unanticipated fashion.

THE DEMAND FOR NEW TECHNOLOGY: UTILITY COST STRUCTURES

Among utilities, innovation is in strong demand. During prebid qualification, it was each supplier's technological competence which was often at issue.

The incentives which derive from the economics of utility operation and regulation have been the subject of much speculation. One observer reasoned as follows:

> The turbine generator is the starting point for any given power plant. By far the most expensive item of electrical equipment in a power plant, the turbine generator, necessarily has the greatest impact on the utility's rate base. Around it, and based on its characteristics, is added the ancillary equipment necessary to the complete plant. The efficiency of the generator in large part controls the operating costs of the plant. Since operating costs, unlike equipment costs, cannot be capitalized (fed into the rate base), improvement in such efficiency is of vital concern to the utilities. By seeking to reduce operating costs (per kwh) on the one hand, while increasing asset values (through equipment purchases and revaluation) on the other, utilities can justify continuance of existing rates and at the same time keep, as profit, revenue formerly paid out for operating costs. This impact is magnified many times by the fact that such equipment has an extremely long service life; it is not uncommon for utilities to have in service today generators installed in the 1930's.[20]

One notes here a similarity to the currently popular Averch-Johnson theory of public utility behavior under regulation; that is, if the regulatory authorities permit a percentage return on the utility rate base which exceeds the current cost of capital, then the utility will be excessively capital-intensive. The less elastic is demand, the more the capital-intensiveness will be distorted above the socially optimal level.[21]

---

[20] Memorandum of Allen-Bradley Company with respect to recall of Elmer F. Lindseth for Further National Discovery, January 17, 1964; Atlantic City Electric Co. et al. v. General Electric Company et al., 62 Civ. 686, U.S. District Court, S.D.N.Y.

[21] Harvey Averch and L. L. Johnson, "Behavior of the Firm under Regulatory Constraint," *American Economic Review*, December 1962; also Frederic M. Scherer, *Industrial Market Structure and Economic Performance* (Chicago: Rand McNally, 1970), Chapter 22. It is further suggested that regulation can block innovation by setting constraints upon prices. See: William M.

However, utility managers in fact seemed to be more concerned about their historical rapid growth being jeopardized if utility costs, and electric power prices, escalated. An engineering culture dominated utility organizations, a culture in which technological efficiency was appreciated for its own sake, and where simple profit-maximizing behavior could be scorned.

Given this bias toward price-induced growth, and new technology, there were strong fiscal incentives to innovate rapidly, because:

(1) Within the category of *generation* expense, fuel costs are almost 80 percent of the total. Maintenance and other operating costs are small by comparison.[22] Fuel consumption (the "heat rate") would be a major preoccupation.

(2) The industry is extremely capital-intensive. Total investment in electric utility plant is $65 billion after accumulated depreciation, or almost $4.00 for every $1.00 of sales. Interest and depreciation consume one fifth of revenues.[23] Utility executives therefore placed a high priority on technical advances which promised reduced capital costs as well.

Fuel Efficiency: Long-Term Trend

Consider first the long-term trend in fuel consumption. For decades the utility industry successfully offset inflation through the advance to higher steam pressures and temperatures, plus the widespread adoption of the reheat cycle in power generation, which increased fuel-consumption efficiency. Chart 12.5 shows how the utilities, until the mid-1960s, offset an increase in fuel prices by a steady rise in the efficiency of their new steam electric plants. Remarkably, utilities achieved, on balance, a steady *decline* in fuel costs (dollars-per-kilowatt hour) despite continuous inflation in the economy. Thus was fostered a general hubris among utilities and turbine builders alike.[24]

By the early 1960s dramatic reductions in cost were becoming increasingly difficult to accomplish through improvements in the thermodynamic cycle. The path of technological change therefore switched to more rapid scaling-

Capron, ed., *Technological Change in Regulated Industries* (Washington: Brookings Institution, 1971).

[22] Federal Power Commission, *Steam-Electric Plant Construction Cost and Annual Production Expenses*, 22nd Annual Supplement (Washington, D.C.: U.S. Government Printing Office, 1969).

[23] Ibid. See also Chapter Three, Tables 3.1 and 3.2.

[24] From 1946 to 1969, the national average heat rate for fossil-fueled steam electric plants declined by a third. At 1946 thermodynamic efficiencies and 1969 fuel prices, the private sector of the industry would have spent $4.5 billion for fuel in 1969, instead of $3.0 billion. Many factors contributed to this $1.5 billion annual rate of fuel savings, but the thermodynamic efficiency of the turbine generator and associated steam generation system was one of the most important.

CHART 12.5.   Effect of Fuel Price and Efficiency of Use Upon Cost of Fuel Per
Kilowatt-Hour Generated.
(*Total Electric Utility Industry—Including Alaska and Hawaii
Since 1963*)

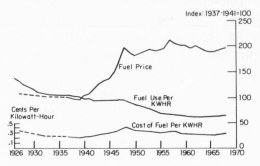

NOTE: Data based on all fuel used in electric generation, and expressed in units of equivalent coal.

SOURCES: Edison Electric Institute, *Statistical Yearbook of the Electric Utility Industry for 1968*,
New York, 1969, Chart VII-A.
    1927–1932, U.S. Census of Central Electric Stations.
    1937–1958, Federal Power Commission.
    1959–1968, Federal Power Commission and EEI.

up of the size of units, as a means of continuing the steady reduction in
power generation costs.

Investment Costs: Long-Term Trend

Remarkably, the historical reduction in *operating* costs was accompanied
by a parallel reduction in *capital* costs for the utilities. This may be demonstrated in various ways. Table 12.3, for example, shows the investment cost
for the various steam electric plants in the Commonwealth Edison system in
1969. The cost per kilowatt of the most recent plant, Kincaid, initially
operated in 1967, was less than the cost per kilowatt for the oldest-equipped
plant, Powerton, initially operated in 1928—even ignoring the over 100 percent inflation in the purchasing power of the dollar over that time period.[25]

Over the long term, therefore, manufacturers could offer compelling economic inducements to the utilities to adopt advanced technologies. Even at a
fixed point in time, utility planners were enticed toward advanced technologies
by the obvious economies of power plant scale. Such economies were realizable
both in operating expense and in investment cost, given the typical price and
technology offerings of manufacturers.[26]

---

[25] The cost of new capacity averaged $320 per kilowatt in 1951–1953, and only $230 per
kilowatt in 1965–1967, for the total industry. See EEI, *Statistical Year Book*, 1968.

[26] During 1969 the investor-owned segment of the industry added about 15 million kilowatts
of steam electric capacity; the economies may be very conservatively valued at about $1 billion
per year at current rates of capacity expansion, even disregarding the forces in inflation. Thus,
the net accomplishment of the electric power industry, utilities and manufacturers together, has

TABLE 12.3.

STEAM ELECTRIC PLANT CONSTRUCTION COST AND ANNUAL PRODUCTION EXPENSE
IN THE COMMONWEALTH EDISON COMPANY SYSTEM, 1969.

Name of Plant	Installed Generating Capacity Megawatts	Average BTU Per Kwh of Net Generation (Heat Rate)	Number of Units Total	Reheat	Cost[a] Per Kw of Capacity ($)	Total Production Expenses (Mils/Kwh)
Powerton	320	13,933	4	—	115	6.15
Fisk	571	10,752	3	1	195	4.82
Saybrook	146	11,365	4	1	191	4.33
Ridgeland	690	10,920	4	2	183	4.23
Crawford	701	10,257	3	2	149	4.23
Waukegan	1042	10,282	7	3	132	3.75
Will Cty.	1269	9,788	4	4	128	3.66
Joliet	1862	10,444	8	3	112	3.19
Kincaid	1319	10,139	2	2	106	2.97

[a] Land, structures and improvements, and equipment, initially plus all additions less all retirements, at initial cost.

SOURCE: Federal Power Commission, Steam-Electric Plant Construction Cost and Annual Production Expenses, 22nd Annual Supplement, 1969, Washington, D.C.

The Impact of Plant Scale

At any point in history, the larger plants were the more efficient plants. For many years, the manufacturers could offer efficiency improvements (operating cost reductions) as turbine generator size increased. For example, one set of representative calculations, made in the early 1960s, examined the economic merits of a utility moving from a 200-megawatt generating plant to a 1,000-megawatt generating plant. With this change of plant scale, fuel costs declined approximately 0.2 mils per kilowatt-hour, operating costs 0.15 mils, and maintenance costs 0.10 mils. Total savings (0.45 mils per kilowatt-hour) added up to about 10% of power generation costs, even before any consideration of investment savings.[27]

In addition, savings in investment cost could be realized as unit ratings increased. The representative calculation of the early 1960s suggested that total plant investment costs (turbine plus boiler, piping, housing, land and all other equipment), might decline by one quarter ($32 to $42 per kilowatt) as one moved from the 200-megawatt to a 1,000-megawatt unit.

been technological change which by 1969 had reduced utility demands upon the economy by at least $2.5 billion annually, compared to the costs which would have been incurred had technology stagnated at the 1946 level. For related discussions see: Philip Sporn, Nuclear Power Economics (New York: Kuhn, Loeb, 1966); Donald E. Craig, "Objective—Economical Power," Talk before The New England Conference of Public Utility Commissioners, Chatham, Massachusetts, June 24–26, 1963.

[27] This computation was based upon fuel costs of 30 cents per million BTUs; the more expensive the fuel, the more attractive the savings become as one moves to the larger units. Source: General Electric records.

In the total picture, capital cost savings loomed much larger than the operating cost savings. The reduction in investment cost in the example cited was almost three times as great as the estimated savings in operating costs. This was merely the economic manifestation of the diminishing returns in improvement in the heat rate, and the emerging dominance of investment costs savings as the path to lower generating costs.

Further illustration of these economic and engineering factors may be derived from a set of estimates prepared for the Federal Power Commission in 1964 (see Chart 12.6 and Table 12.4). The capital costs savings achieved

CHART 12.6.   Performance and Cost Characteristics: Coal-Fired Steam-Electric Plants.
(*Two-Unit*)

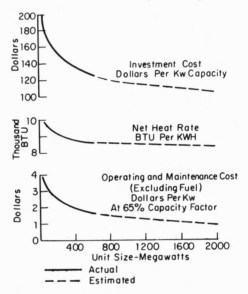

SOURCE: Figure 45, Federal Power Commission, *The 1964 National Power Survey*, Part II, Washington, D.C., U.S. Government Printing Office, 1970.

TABLE 12.4.
ESTIMATED POWER PRODUCTION COSTS.

	1–3,200 Mw Plant		8–400 Mw Plants		Savings	
	$1,000/Yr.	Mils/Kwh	$1,000/Yr.	Mils/Kwh	$1,000/Yr.	Mils/Kwh
Fixed charges	$47,520	2.61	$66,528	3.65	$19,008	1.04
Fuel expenses	24,490	1.34	26,824	1.47	2,334	0.13
Operation and maintenance expenses	3,300	0.18	7,760	0.43	4,460	0.25
Total	$75,310	4.13	$101,112	5.55	$25,802	1.42

SOURCE: Federal Power Commission, *National Power Survey, 1964*, p. 70.

through shifting to the largest sized generating unit were over one quarter of the original capital costs. Aggregate fuel, operations, and maintenance savings were less than one fifth of the original amount.[28] Identical conclusions obtain.

It is obvious that the magnitude of the utilities' cost savings hinged upon the manufacturer's schedule of price reductions with an increase in unit size, for the turbine generator portion of the project, and also upon the available economies of scale in the construction of the rest of the generating plant. For example, as one increased the scale of plant from 200 megawatts to 500 megawatts, about half of the savings in investment/cost were through a decline in the price of the turbine generators, and about one half was due to economies in the steam generator (i.e., boiler system), foundation and housing structure, and ancillary systems. However, as one continued to increase the size of plant, up to 1,000 megawatts, the pricing of the turbine generator had to carry an increased proportion of the savings, until finally it carried them all. In other words, the economies of scale in the "other" plant costs gradually disappeared.

Since capital cost savings outweighed operating cost savings, as plant scale was increased, this tended to emphasize the role of initial cost in the utilities' calculations of the marginal gains realizable under the new technologies. Their increasing preoccupation with investment costs therefore enhanced their sensitivity to differences in turbine generator prices among the available units. Price (or initial cost) sensitivity increased throughout the late 1950s and 1960s, as operating cost-reducing opportunities waned.

Because of the utilities' desire to achieve a continued reduction in power generating costs, tremendous pressures emerged to push rapidly toward the larger, advanced technology machines. *The net result was to give enormous leverage to the manufacturers' structure of the turbine generator price-size relationship, particularly in the larger ratings.* Manufacturers could influence utilities' purchasing behavior through price-technology strategy—the pricing of emerging versus obsolescent product designs.[29]

The emphasis in this discussion upon two variables only, capital costs and fuel efficiencies, is of course an oversimplified view of the many considerations affecting utilities' power generating economics. Other significant costs are incurred in adopting the larger ratings, one of the most important being an increase in the "forced outage rate." This would tend to favor the supplier who could convince the utilities that he had the maximum experience, in operation, behind his new product claims.[30]

---

[28] Assuming 15 percent cost of capital, and 60 percent load factor. See: Federal Power Commission, *National Power Survey, 1964* (Washington, D.C.: U.S. Government Printing Office, 1964).

[29] Although turbine generator costs are but a fraction of the utilities' total generating plant investment, they are one item in the plant most susceptible to strategic price management.

[30] The forced outage rate equals the total hours which a unit is, by necessity, unavailable on

LEADERSHIP-FOLLOWERSHIP ROLES IN TECHNOLOGY

There is convincing evidence that General Electric was the industry leader in technology, followed by Westinghouse, with Allis-Chalmers bringing up the rear. For example, over the period 1948–1962, General Electric had both more units, and also a greater proportion of its mix of orders, in unit ratings over 400,000 kilowatts, in comparison with Westinghouse (see Table 12.5).

TABLE 12.5.

DISTRIBUTION OF 1948–1962 ORDERS BY TURBINE GENERATOR SIZE.
(Maximum Mw Rating According to Manufacturers)[a]

Turbine Generator Megawatts Rating	Allis-Chalmers		Westinghouse		General Electric	
	Units	Percent	Units	Percent	Units	Percent
1 to 99 mw	118	76.1	391	66.7	620	62.4
100 to 199	26	16.8	134	22.9	253	25.5
200 to 299	6	3.9	37	6.3	75	7.6
300 to 399	5	3.2	19	3.2	29	2.9
400 to 499			1	0.2	8	0.8
500 to 599			4	0.7	3	0.3
600 to 699					2	0.2
700 to 799					1	0.1
800 to 899					—	—
900 and over					2	0.2
Total	155	100.0	586	100.0	993	100.0

[a] Units 2500 kw and larger.

Allis-Chalmers, according to the reported data, had no orders for units in this larger size range.[31]

The leadership-followership record on advanced steam conditions machines is similar (see Table 12.6). There was an orderly hierarchy among General Electric, Westinghouse, and Allis-Chalmers both in terms of the proportion of units ordered of 1000°F. temperature or greater, and of 1800 psi pressure or greater.[32]

an unplanned basis, divided by total service hours plus forced unavailable hours. In the 100,000- to 300,000-kilowatt size range, forced outage rates of 3 to 4 percent were regarded as normal; for the very large 1,000,000-kilowatt and over units, forced outage rates in excess of 7 percent have been experienced (FPC, 1964 *National Power Survey*).

[31] The Consolidated Edison "Big Allis" unit of Allis-Chalmers' manufacture (1,000,000 kw) was not tallied.

[32] One General Electric advertisement of 1961 recited these facts:

Since the electric utility industry first broke the 9,500 btu/kwh annual heat rate, 47 different steam-electric power plants in the U.S. have beaten this mark. Of these 47 plants, all but six are equipped with one or more General Electric large steam turbine generators. And G.E. steam turbine generators have been in the top five plants every year since 1951. Year after year, heat rates have dropped. In fact, the Federal Power

TABLE 12.6.
DISTRIBUTION OF ORDERS BY STEAM TEMPERATURE (°F.) AND
PRESSURE (PSI) OF TURBINE GENERATORS, 1948–1962.[a]

Steam Temperature °F.	Allis-Chalmers		Westinghouse		General Electric	
	Units	Percent	Units	Percent	Units	Percent
Under 700	8	5.1	46	7.9	74	7.4
700 to 799	24	15.5	122	20.8	138	13.9
800 to 899	14	9.0	47	8.0	115	11.6
900 to 999	58	37.4	157	26.8	230	23.2
1000 to 1100	51	32.9	208	35.5	430	43.3
1100 and over			6	1.0	6	.6
Total	155	100.0	586	100.0	993	100.0
Steam Pressure (Psi)						
Under 599	20	12.9	112	19.1	144	14.5
600 to 799	23	14.8	84	14.3	103	10.4
800 to 999	42	27.1	108	18.4	197	19.8
1000 to 1799	37	23.9	143	24.5	238	24.0
1800 and over	33	21.3	139	23.7	311	31.3
Total	155	100.0	586	100.0	993	100.0

[a] Units 2500 kw and larger.

Finally, it is not surprising that the leader firm in technology should tend more often to serve the very largest electrical utility systems. As Table 12.7 indicates, the competitors had the following proportions of their unit orders from "power pools" of 5,000 megawatts peak load, or greater:

General Electric	17.1%
Westinghouse	12.3
Allis-Chalmers	5.9

The largest utility organizations were the "early adopters" of new technologies, by virtue of their greater risk-incurring tastes, their greater engineering competence, and—most important of all—their greater scale, which permitted them to ingest large-scale units without undue risk to the total generating system.[33]

Commission's latest report shows that the three most efficient power plants for 1961 operated even below the 9,000 btu/kwh level!

Here again, four of the five steam turbine generators in these top three plants are General Electric units. The advanced state-of-the-art of steam turbine generators makes further improvements increasingly difficult. But advances will continue to be made . . . and General Electric intends to make them.

(National Exhibit NX 594, Electrical Equipment Antitrust Actions, all U.S. district courts.)

[33] See: Everett M. Rogers, *Diffusion of Innovations* (New York: The Free Press, 1962). The characteristics of early adopters in the utility industry tend to coincide with the traits

TABLE 12.7.
DISTRIBUTION OF ORDERS, 1948–1962.
(Among Manufacturers, By Size of Power Pool to
Which Utility Organization is Linked)[a]

Peak Megawatts of Power Pool in 1962	Allis-Chalmers		Westinghouse		General Electric	
	Units	Percent	Units	Percent	Units	Percent
1 to 99	13	15.2	37	10.7	47	8.1
100 to 499	30	35.3	79	22.8	110	18.8
500 to 999	7	8.2	55	15.9	97	16.6
1000 to 2499	19	22.4	89	25.6	103	18.0
2500 to 4999	11	13.0	44	12.7	125	21.4
5000 to 9999	2	2.4	5	1.4	18	3.1
10,000 and over	3	3.5	38	10.9	82	14.0
Total	85	100.0	347	100.0	584	100.0

[a] Includes power-pool connected utility organizations only, as of 1962, and turbine generators 2500 kw and over.

A familiar pattern was therefore repeated: a "pairing-off" among competitors, product technology, and size of the utility. These observable pairings of manufacturer size, of customer size, and of product technologies, were the natural outcome of the manufacturers' comparative advantages in technology, and their technological strategies.[34]

THE TACTICS OF INTRODUCING NEW TECHNOLOGY: THE PRICE-SIZE RELATIONSHIP

How does the leader firm exploit his advantage? This brings us to the heart of technological strategy.[35]

---

generalized in Rogers' research (perceived as deviants by other members of the system, higher social status, more favorable financial position, information sources in closer contact with the origin of the ideas, etc.). See pp. 311–315.

[34] One reviewer criticizes my depiction of the inevitability of General Electric's dominance of the industry:

First, is there no room for Yankee ingenuity and willingness to take risks? And second, isn't investment in innovation an investment, rather than an ongoing overhead cost? And if so, weren't Westinghouse and Allis-Chalmers, as good-sized, diversified corporations, quite able to make those investments IF their engineers came up with technically promising approaches? The technical laggardliness of Westinghouse and Allis-Chalmers may have been the result of a failure of imagination or nerve. The history of Westinghouse's investment behavior certainly suggested an unimaginative management unable to grab hold and decide where it wanted to go. Sultan never comes to grips with the question of causality—was it really GE's size, or the failure of rivals to have good ideas and invest in them—that explains GE's technical leadership?

My answer: It is clearly impossible to distinguish, ex ante, among these alternative possibilities. I prefer the obvious economic explanation, rather than the alternative explanation of differential management and engineering competence.

[35] Among competitors, according to the slopes of the total revenue curve, from the statistical

In this industry, the tool by which managers manage the price-technology relationship is the published handbook price schedule which defines the *relative* price of various types and sizes of turbines: those with advanced steam conditions,[36] for example, versus those with ordinary steam conditions. Among marketing managers, this is commonly referred to as the issue of product-line pricing.

A question of central concern to management is how to foster, through product-line pricing, the adoption of advanced-technology machines, while simultaneously funding the required development investments in yet-more-advanced technologies, while simultaneously preserving the health of competitors.

Managers must decide how rapidly to increase the average size of turbine generators being marketed; that is, how rapidly to introduce new technology. There is a bell-shaped frequency distribution in the size (rating in kilowatts per unit) sold in any year. A few of the largest, most-advanced units are purchased by large utilities of a pioneering bent. Some very small units are purchased by the smaller power system. The bulk of the machines are in the middle-size range. Over time, as utility system capabilities grow and as manufacturers' technological capabilities grow, there is a progressive shift upward in the average size of the unit ratings which utilities order; that is, an upward shift in "product mix." Such an upward shift in size distribution of ratings is illustrated in Chart 12.7.

CHART 12.7.   Histogram, Showing Shift in Size Distribution of Turbine Generators Marketed to Utility Organizations, Over Time.

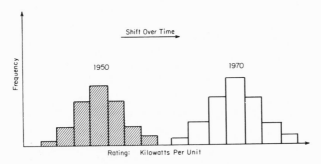

Although "large" turbines are not necessarily tantamount to "advanced-technology" turbines, they have tended to be synonymous through the choice of the market leader. This makes good competitive sense. It is also a natural consequence of the fact that it is the large utilities that are prone to risk-taking in all new technologies.

---

results of the previous chapters, the price was about $24, $22, and $17 per kilowatt for Allis-Chalmers, Westinghouse, and General Electric, respectively, in 1958.

36 "High" or "advanced" steam conditions means turbines which operate at high initial steam temperatures and high initial steam pressures.

Price-Size Relationships in Turbine Generators

Our basic proposition is that the *average* price level cannot be managed; it is exogenously determined. But the *relative* price of different types of machines *can* be administered, more or less, by marketing managers.

If one plots the published handbook prices in dollars per kilowatt against kilowatts size of unit, at any point in time, one obtains a pattern such as depicted in Chart 12.8. Larger units (in kilowatts) are priced lower than

CHART 12.8.   Typical Price-Size Relationship at One Point in Time.

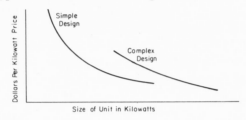

are smaller units.[37] Complex designs (with lower operating costs, size for size) are priced higher than are simple designs. Note that the complex units normally extend farther to the right, into a larger range, where dollars-per-kilowatt price tends to be lowest.

Consider the extreme case of the pricing behavior of a pure monopolist. If turbines lasted forever, price/kw would decline for larger units only in reflection of its incentive effect to induce utilities to order large rather than smaller units, and the turbine monopolist would capture the rents from scale economies in capacity. Because turbines can be scrapped, it might also be rational for the monopolist to lower price/kw for large units to accelerate retirement of older small units. But monopoly is prohibited by law; this is an oligopoly. Furthermore, the oligopolists are differentiated in their capability to create new and complex technologies, and differentiated with respect to unit costs. Thus, the strategic problem is how the leader firm may exploit his advantages, knowing that in the long run it will not be able to hold industry prices at the monopoly level. Any rents which he can extract from his customers will be transitory.

"Tipping the Price Curve"

"Tipping the price curve" refers to the conscious altering of the slope of the price curve. Two events typically provide management with a natural opportunity to change this slope: the announcements of new products, and inflation-induced adjustments in the book price of the entire product line.

---

[37] In 1951 a 100,000-kilowatt unit was priced at about $26 per kilowatt; a 200,000-kilowatt unit was $23 per kilowatt. These prices applied to tandem compound turbine generators operating at 2,400 pounds steam pressure, and 1000° to 1050° Fahrenheit steam temperatures.

An announcement of new and more complex products (or, more commonly, the extension of an existing product line into the higher size ranges—see Chart 12.9) alters the competitive position of various-sized units. There

CHART 12.9.   "Tipping the Curve" Clockwise.

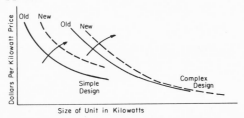

is an accelerated obsolescence of smaller units. Customers are induced to shift their purchases toward the larger size ranges to minimize their investment and operating costs. (See Chart 12.10.)

CHART 12.10.   Altering the Competitive Lineup of Products Through Product-Line Extension.

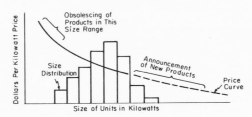

Inflation also provides a natural opportunity to adjust the price-size relationship. Given the passage of time, and the ubiquitous forces of inflation, *all* book prices of all models of machines are periodically adjusted upward. This is an ideal time to alter the slope or the "tilt" of the unit cost-size curve as well.

In this oligopoly—and, it seems, in others—the market leader typically decides to tilt the curve in a *clockwise* direction. At the extreme, the price of very large units may not be increased at all; that is, price increases may be confined to the smaller sizes, maximizing the clockwise rotation of the curve. This clear-cut case of the leader imposing his will upon the marketplace seems to be feasible only where follower firms are under considerable cost pressure.

We derive the following prescription: *"Tipping the curve" is the strategy of progressively reducing the prices of the newest, larger, and more sophisticated machines (or, at least, holding price increases for them to a minimum amount) while steadily increasing the prices of the older, smaller, and less-sophisticated machines.* There is much empirical evidence and explicit management testimony concerning this deliberate altering of the price-size curve.[38]

---

[38] The terminology "tipping the curve" originates with managers in this industry. See related

Price-size curve tilting may not be unequivocably clockwise. Medium-sized units may be increased more in price than are the very smallest units, in order to improve profitability. The bulk of orders consists neither of the very smallest nor of the very largest units in the price book. Short-run earnings can therefore be enhanced by increasing prices to the greatest extent in the intermediate size range, where the bulk of sales volume resides. This approach yields price changes which are at a minimum at the extremities of the curve, both in the very small and the very large sizes, and at a maximum in the intermediate size range (as indicated in Chart 12.11).

CHART 12.11.   Maximizing the Price Increase for the Bulk of Current Orders: An "Unbending-Type" Rotation of the Price Curve.

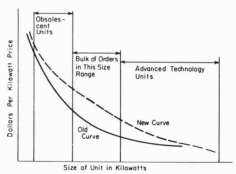

One may term such a price change a virtual "unbending" of the price-size curve, with the very smallest and the very largest units being relatively unchanged in price. Such a maneuver will maximize price increases for the products which constitute the bulk of sales volume, where they are most beneficial to *current* earnings, while preserving the *long-term* strategic benefit to the technological and cost leader which derives from inducing a consumer shift to the largest sizes of turbine generators.

To complicate the story further, the price curve of one product line may be tilted clockwise, and the price curve of another may be simultaneously tilted counterclockwise, as shown in Chart 12.12. Such complex maneuvers may induce product-mix shifts to a product design wherein the market leader has a cost and technological advantage. The pattern was to keep prices low on the high-technology machines, to promote a shift in demand toward the more advanced machines.

In adjustments to the book price there is also ample historical evidence of the leadership of General Electric, and sparse indication that West-

---

expositions: R. E. Donnelly and H. Ogilvie, General Electric Company, "A Discussion of the General Electric Steam Turbine Generator 1961 Price Structure," General Electric brochure GER-1790; F. A. Ritchings, "Effect of Changing Conditions on Steam-Electric Station Costs," Ebasco Services Inc., 29th Annual Executives Conference, The Roosevelt Hotel, New York, December 1958.

CHART 12.12.   Simultaneous Clockwise Tilting of More-Sophisticated Product
Line, and Counterclockwise Tilting of Less-Sophisticated
Product Line.

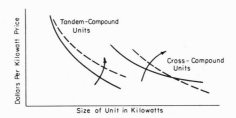

inghouse or Allis-Chalmers did anything but follow—at least according to the published price books of all three. Since General Electric had technological leadership, it would be natural that it also played the leadership role in announcing the shape of price-size curve.

As unit ratings climbed, diminishing returns in investment cost reductions set in with a given price-size relationship. This gave heightened leverage to any price changes for turbine generators in the higher ratings. Even slight modifications in the slope of the price curve would be seized upon by the most progressive utility customers in order to preserve their continually declining costs.

Motivations for Leadership in Curve Tipping

Significant profit payoffs accrued to the leader through switching customers into ever-larger turbine units. We have seen that *direct* costs per kilowatt declined about 38 percent with every doubling of the average size of turbine generators produced. As long as *price* reductions lagged behind, then manufacturer profits would be enhanced if customers were shifted briskly into the larger size ranges. This is because gross margins (price minus direct cost) would be higher on the advanced-technology, larger sized units.

This does not mean that greater profits automatically accrued to the manufacturers through rapid technological innovation. While gross margins, at any point in time, may have been greater on the advanced-technology units, it was also true that the new technology had to be paid for, and developing the new designs was a costly and risky venture. We must therefore distinguish *direct* costs from *overhead investments.* Thus, high profits through inducing rapid technological change were by no means assured. But if the engineering risks could be managed properly, and if market introductions were carefully paced, then this could be a highly profitable strategy.[39]

---

[39] One reviewer notes:

If Sultan really believes his firm's-own-learning-cycle hypothesis, he should note that GE would rationally tilt the curve clockwise even as a pure monopolist, to tip purchases toward larger-scale units where current orders amount to a greater proportional increase in cumulative output, and thus lead to greater learning gains. On the other hand, if

Motivations of Follower Firms

Leaders and followers alike recognized that in the rush toward advancing technology, it was in everyone's interest that havens of low-risk profitability be preserved, through systematic price *increases* on the less-sophisticated machines.

In this industry, the maintenance of these profit havens served four purposes:

(1) Inasmuch as the follower firms still had the bulk of their product mix in the less-sophisticated machines, their profitability was preserved, despite their higher overall costs.

(2) For the leader firm, which also had a large volume of business in the less-sophisticated machines, the raising of margins in the lower technology ratings helped to finance its thrust toward the higher technology ratings.

(3) The follower firms were given scant incentive to incur the high risks and high outlays required to challenge the leader's technological superiority.

(4) The leader was compensated for the risks of a leadership role through enhanced profitability.

To summarize, an appropriate price-size strategy for the leader firm embodies: deliberately low prices on the complex, very advanced technology and largest sized units, fostered by the market leader who is in the most advantageous position, by virtue of its lower manufacturing costs and higher reservoirs of technology, to assume this leadership role. At the same time, profitability is maintained in the higher sales volume, less complex and smaller turbine generator size ranges, both for the leader firms and also for the higher cost follower firms. This strategy insures maximum technological progress, the means to finance this progress from current revenues, continued market strength for the leader firm, and a profitable follower role for its other competitors.[40]

---

this phenomenon isn't important, or if the industry's productivity depends on the industry's cumulative output, the connection between the cost structure and pricing practices is relatively trivial and not worth stressing.

My comment in reply: Total kilowatts of shipments per year are constrained by total utility demand. And General Electric's market share is constrained by the Department of Justice. Within these limits, and granting that General Electric's costs were a unique function of its own learning curve, there was an optimal rate of curve tipping in the oligopoly. On the other hand, I agree that in a monopoly General Electric would have greater incentive to reduce its costs, therefore its prices, therefore the utilities' costs, and therefore electric power prices, in order to accelerate industry growth, General Electric's own rate of cost reduction, and General Electric's own profitability.

[40] One reviewer notes:

This seems to imply that GE's rate of technological advance was constrained by the need to keep its competitors in the game. Would a monopolist have attained faster progress? I don't think the evidence supports that at all. To the degree that innovations

Under certain circumstances, an aggressive "clockwise tilting" price-technology strategy may be unwise strategy:

(1) The follower firms may be pressed too hard, and (a) they may take a desperate plunge forward in technology (which *could* just succeed), in which case the leader has lost his position; or (b) they may resort to very aggressive pricing which would diminish the ability of the leader firm to fund its very necessary technology. In this sense, the leader has more to lose from price warfare than do the follower firms.

(2) The follower firms may be pressed too hard, and fail. This could bring intervention and forcible breakup from the Department of Justice, because of the monopoly structure which would tend to develop if too many competitors gave up the race.

Risks in innovating too slowly are equally apparent: permitting follower firms to gather strength for an assault on the leader, diminished profitability for the leader, diminished customer goodwill through slower or nonexistent cost reduction, and increased customer price sensitivities in the absence of rapid technological change.

TECHNOLOGICAL RISK

Consider next the managing of technological risks. Over the years, it may become increasingly difficult to achieve decreased costs without truly large leaps in the scale and sophistication of power generating machinery. Under these circumstances, customer demands for new technologies can get out of hand, particularly if nourished by wild engineering speculations and unrealistic promises by manufacturing firms. This behavior, in fact, seems all too common in high-technology businesses.[41]

---

affected large-scale units in which GE specialized, GE controlled through its own pricing decisions the extent to which its innovative gains could be taken through increasing its own market share versus increasing the extent to which it took the innovator's rents in the form of higher mark-ups on "frontier" units. Thus the premise of a competitive constraint on GE's innovation rate seems most dubious. Furthermore, I don't understand why it would ever be rational for the followers to try to seize technological leadership— isn't that the beauty of the strategy for GE? (My response: "Yes.")

[41] The most obvious manifestation of technological acceleration was reduced dependability of service and increased downtime. The value of turbine generator dependability is illustrated by the experience of (it seems) Tennessee Valley Authority which, in 1967, had in service two 500 MW units of British manufacture, and four units of comparable size or larger which had been supplied by General Electric. The British units had been in operation a total of 100 months, during which they had a forced outage of 640.5 days (Monday through Friday) or 29.2 percent of the time. The General Electric units had been on the line a total of 174 months during which time they suffered a forced outage of 182.5 days, or 4.8 percent of the time on a comparable basis. A reasonable evaluation of the worth of outage time, it was said, was $70,000 per day, which meant that the British units were costing the utility several million dollars per year in additional expense due to their abnormal forced outage rate. (Comments by General Electric Company before the Federal Power Commission in Docket No. R-345, Procurement Competition, March 13, 1969, Washington, D.C.)

Technological development is secured through spending money on engineering, and through operating experience. If either receives skimpy attention, technological innovation can only proceed at greater risk.

Two independent factors may accelerate the introduction of new technology which outruns the base of engineering development or operating experience: (1) Some technological barrier (e.g., the austenitic steel barrier) may emerge which forces the designers to switch paths, proceeding more rapidly along one dimension of design development, to compensate for blocked expansion along another. (2) Alternately, technological acceleration may be induced by increased competition in the marketplace, which forces each manufacturer to "play" more of his technological chips, so to speak, in an effort to stave off lower prices and earnings in the heightened struggle for market share. Both factors were at work during the 1960s to cause an acceleration of the introduction of new designs which emphasized sheer scale.

One may gain some perspective on the forced-draft nature of this historical push into larger ratings from Chart 12.13, which plots the *maximum* postwar turbine generator ratings versus the *average*, for 1947–1971. The ratio of maximum to average has tended to climb over the years, but there was one period in particular when maximum ratings "took off," far beyond any current operating experience: the period immediately following 1960. This happens to have coincided with the period of maximum price competition in the last 20 years in the turbine generator industry. The juxtaposition of the two events is hardly a coincidence. Under competitive stress, the announcement and initial marketing of new technologies were accelerated. Simultaneously, metallurgical barriers caused the acceleration to be concentrated in the "size" variable and not in thermal efficiencies.

Such an acceleration of the introduction of new technology may be of dubious economic benefit to consumers. The advancement to ever-larger ratings can reflect cautious extrapolations from both design and operating experience, or it can reflect a "leapfrogging" of experience at great risk—as Allis-Chalmers' well-publicized difficulties in the late 1960s with its pioneering Consolidated Edison 1,000,000 kilowatt Ravenswood unit illustrates.

There will be a discretionary lag from the time of development to the time of announcement of a new technology.[42] In examining the rate of introduction of new technology, and the attendant technological risk, it is therefore important not to be deceived into thinking that the *announcement* of new

---

[42] See: Morton I. Kamien and Nancy L. Schwartz, "Timing of Innovations Under Rivalry," *Econometrica*, Vol. 40, No. 1 (January 1972). Factors which must be taken into account by the firm in making its timing decision are increasing cost with compression of the development period, reduction of profit opportunities with prolongation of development period, and the probability of rival innovation and imitation. The inability of the innovating firm to appropriate all of the rewards tends to *retard* development, but also, the firm expects to receive a larger reward if it is the innovator, rather than the imitator, which accelerates development.

CHART 12.13.   Ratio of Maximum to Average Kilowatts Rating of Turbine Generators Shipped to U.S. Utility Organizations, 1947–1971.

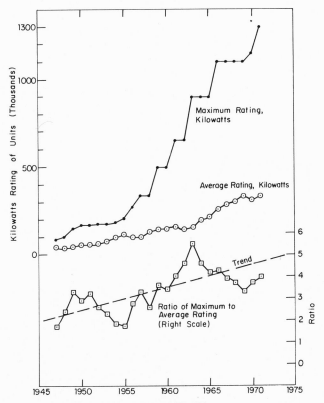

SOURCE: Edison Electric Institute and Litigation NX 591.

technology to the marketplace is tantamount to the *creation* of new technologies. Advanced designs are created through investment spending, and through experience. In the next section it will be seen that the funding of engineering development tends to rise and fall with the level of general overhead expenditures, not necessarily in unison with the rate of announcement of new technologies. The outlines of the complex interplay of technological change, competition, and pricing begin to emerge.

The Funding of Technological Change

We come, finally, to the question of how the new technology will be financed. The rate at which the creation of new technology is funded determines, in the long run, the feasible rate of technological change. The announcement of new technology may be accelerated in the short run for tactical reasons, but eventually, if risks are not to balloon out of control, the underlying development homework will have to be done. The amount of technical development homework accomplished will in the long run tend to be proportional to the size of the engineering and development budgets. In other words, the pace of innovation will be sharply constrained by the size of the available pool of dollars.[43]

(1) *Westinghouse Technological Funding.*[44] Litigation interrogatories yielded estimates of expenditures on research and development in the West-

TABLE 12.8.
WESTINGHOUSE EXPENDITURES ON RESEARCH AND DEVELOPMENT.

Annual expenditures for research and development for the Steam Division were as follows:

1948	$ 4,303,000
1949	3,643,000
1950	4,620,000
1951	5,822,000
1952	7,374,000
1953	10,084,000
1954	11,488,000
1955	10,068,000
1956	11,941,000
1957[a]	18,049,000
1958	16,822,000
1959	16,013,000
1960	14,702,000
1961	15,436,000
1962	12,799,000
1963	16,101,000

Annual expenditures for research and development for the Transportation and Generator Division were as follows:

1948	$4,945,000
1949	4,643,000
1950	5,246,000
1951	7,139,000
1952	8,331,000
1953	8,383,000
1954	8,588,000
1955	6,803,000
1956	7,266,000

[a] Peak year.

---

[43] Technology is obviously "produced." This fact, and the relationship between technological inputs and outputs has been subjected to extensive theoretical treatment in: William Nordhaus, *Invention, Growth, and Welfare* (Cambridge: MIT Press, 1969).

[44] It is not easy to quantify the manufacturers' investments in technological change, because part of the cost is incurred in "learning on the job." The manufacturers engage in advanced research and development activities, and budget data are available for these. Equally important are the funds spent in the course of executing specific customer orders: the engineering of specific turbines, and the development of new manufacturing methods. Such development expenditures tended to be submerged in the accounts.

inghouse Steam Division (Lester)—where the turbines alone were built—
and also at the Westinghouse Transportation and Generator Division (East
Pittsburgh)—where the generator portion of the set was built, commingled
with many other types of electrical machinery not directly related to turbine
generators.[45] These data are shown in Table 12.8. They encompass both
"standard" development work of a general nature, and customer order development work specific to particular orders.[46]

The turbine portion of a turbine generator represents about two thirds
of the total cost. One might, therefore, approximate Westinghouse research
and development expenditures on turbine generators by adding 40 percent
or 50 percent to the annual figures for the Steam Division. The Westinghouse rate of expenditure on research and development which is implied
bv these figures appears to range from 8 percent to 12 percent of net sales
billed, with a mid-range value in the vicinity of 10 percent of sales.

As an independent check there is information on the rate of Westinghouse development spending on the OVEC contract in the 1950s at standard
burden rates. On the OVEC job, $1.82 million was allocated to "customer
order development and engineering" under the standard costing rates in effect
at Westinghouse at the time.[47] This is equivalent to 9.6 percent of the total
order price of $19.0 million for the OVEC units sold by Westinghouse. Not
included in this 9.6 percent is any amount for "standard development" work,
but prior to the so-called Westinghouse "building block program" of the
later 1950s this might be expected to be much less than "customer order
development" in amount. One can safely conclude that Westinghouse may
have been spending slightly more than 10 percent of net sales on research
and development at the time of the OVEC shipment (1955), which checks
with the previous estimate.

(2) *Allis-Chalmers Technological Funding.* Data on Allis-Chalmers' research and development expenditures were similarly provided during the
litigation.[48] The results are shown in Table 12.9.

---

[45] Answers of Westinghouse Electrical Corporation to Interrogatories Nos. 12, 13, 15, 17 and
18 of Consolidated Plaintiffs' Local Interrogatories Served Pursuant to Local Pre-Trial Order
No. 1 (Set No. 1); Atlantic City Electric et al. v. General Electric Company et al., 61 Civ.
4358, U.S. District Court, S.D.N.Y.

[46] Testimony of J. P. Wearn, stenographer's minutes, Ohio Valley Electric v. General Electric,
op. cit., pp. 3,107–3,108.

[47] Testimony of H. T. Duff, stenographer's minutes, Ohio Valley Electric v. General Electric,
op. cit., p. 3,917.

[48] Answers of Defendant Allis-Chalmers Manufacturing Company to Consolidated Plaintiffs'
Local Interrogatory, Interrogatories 12 through 18 (Set No. 1); Atlantic City Electric Company
et al. v. General Electric Company et al., 61 Civ. 4258, U.S. District Court, S.D.N.Y. The reply
states, in part,

The research and development undertaken by Allis-Chalmers during the period in
question fell into two categories: research and development in connection with a specific
turbine generator unit, and general research and development not attributable to a
specific unit. The figures for the first type of research and development are merged and

TABLE 12.9.
ALLIS-CHALMERS EXPENDITURES ON RESEARCH AND DEVELOPMENT.
(Steam Turbine Department)

Year	Total	Percent of Steam Division Net Sales Billed
1948	$ 142,460	1.4
1949	296,266	2.3
1950	179,510	2.0
1951	278,817	3.3
1952	274,385	2.9
1953	261,194	2.1
1954	270,900	1.8
1955	807,621	8.2
1956	263,789	2.3
1957	475,313	1.9
1958	551,329	1.0
1959	619,509	1.7
1960	966,847	1.7
1961	1,446,259	5.5
1962	1,423,403	15.4
1963	74,027	—

(Motor and Generator Department)

Year	Total
1948	$ 43,909
1949	37,316
1950	36,692
1951	97,803
1952	237,181
1953	552,630
1954	238,307
1955	179,165
1956 (10 months)	207,508

These data encompass *general* research and development spending only.
If Allis-Chalmers' spending pattern followed the tendencies of Westinghouse
and General Electric, perhaps twice as much again was spent by Allis-
Chalmers on the engineering of specific turbine generator orders. Even with
such crude refinements in the data, one readily perceives that Allis-Chalmers'

reflected in the costs of the individual unit involved, and cannot be effectively extracted.
With regard to general research and development, it should be noted that prior to
October 16, 1956, the generator portion of steam turbine generators was manufactured
by the Motor and Generator Department. The research and development expenditures
in that department allocable to generators used in steam turbine generators are not
available. The figures submitted for the Motor and Generator Department are for the
entire department.
Subject to the above explanation, Table 12.9 presents the annual expenditure for research and
development by departments engaged in the manufacture of steam turbine generators.

spending on research and development scarcely exceeded 10 percent of sales
—and it was probably much lower. This conclusion, added to the fact of
Allis-Chalmers' limited sales volume base, means that Allis-Chalmers had
extremely limited technological resources to deploy. Allis-Chalmers was simply not a factor in the technological spending race with Westinghouse or
with General Electric.

Furthermore, it appears that in attempting to stay in the race, by pursuing
at least one notably large turbine order in the early 1960s (i.e., Consolidated
Edison's 1,000,000 kilowatts Ravenswood unit), Allis-Chalmers hastened its
own exit from the industry. The data reveal that Allis-Chalmers' research and
development spending soared to a $1.4 million annual rate for two consecu-
tive years, 1961 and 1962, at a time when Allis-Chalmers' two competitors
were retrenching their overhead spending in line with languishing business
conditions. The costly R&D effort, reaching 15 percent of sales in 1962,
must have contributed to management's final decision to get out of the
business.

(3) *General Electric Technological Funding.* General Electric research
and development spending was also reported during litigation.[49] The data
are shown in Table 12.10.

TABLE 12.10.
GENERAL ELECTRIC EXPENDITURES ON RESEARCH AND DEVELOPENT.
(Steam Turbine Generators)

1948	$ 7,991,000
1949	8,318,000
1950	9,085,000
1951	12,009,000
1952	12,224,000
1953	14,445,000
1954	16,370,000
1955	19,073,000
1956	23,884,000
1957[a]	24,085,000
1958	22,661,000
1959	21,326,000
1960	21,226,000
1961	20,458,000
1962	20,553,000
1963	18,779,000

[a] Peak year.

[49] General Electric said, "It is impossible to segregate Research and Development expense
per se, as General Electric records are not kept in this manner. Table 12.10 is the annual
expenditure for Engineering expense in steam turbine generators. Research and Development
is a major portion of the amount shown." Answers of Defendant General Electric Company to
Consolidated Plaintiffs' Local Interrogatories, 5, 12, 13, 14, 15, 17 and 18 (Set No. 1); Atlantic
City Electric et al. v. General Electric Company et al., 61 Civ. 4258, U.S. District Court,
S.D.N.Y.

General Electric's expenditure levels ranged from a low of 8 percent of sales, to a high of 18 percent of sales, with a typical mid-range value being about 10 percent of net sales billed. The foregoing data probably encompass General Electric's category of expenditures designated PECE (Product Engineering Cost and Expense), which included engineering and drafting work on specific jobs, as well as advanced development work.[50] While not all items of R&D spending are encompassed by these data, independent checks suggest that the percentage figures are reasonable approximations of the level of General Electric funding of the major portion of its technological effort.[51] The results for the turbine builders also tend to check with EEI[52] and National Science Foundation[53] estimates of research and development funding in the industry.

---

[50] Testimony of Buehler, stenographer's minutes, Ohio Valley Electric v. General Electric, pp. 2,889–2,910.

[51] Not included in the General Electric PECE totals is any credit for advanced and fundamental research in electric power generation conducted by the General Electric Company at the Knolls Laboratory at Schenectady. (See G. Guy Suits, vice president and director of research, General Electric Company, *Speaking of Research*, John Wiley & Sons, 1965.)

[52] See: Edison Electric Institute survey of research and development expenditures by electric equipment manufacturers. The scope of this survey varies from year to year, beginning with 5 major manufacturers and ending with 14. The products encompassed include all types of power distribution, transmission, and generation apparatus *including* atomic power research. The definition of research and development is that employed by the National Science Foundation. The results are:

1962	$76 million
1963	97.7
1964	105.5

It is clear from these totals, which are barely more than twice the amounts reported by the turbine manufacturers in the interrogatories, that the definitions employed by the turbine builders in response to litigation inquiries were broad, encompassing more dollars than "research and development" in the National Science Foundation usage of the term. (Reference: *Research and Development in the Electric Utility Industry*, reports for 1962, 1963 and 1964, Edison Electric Institute, New York.)

[53] See: National Science Foundation figures for research and development spending in the product category of SIC 351, "engines and turbines." Unfortunately, over one half of shipments in SIC 351 are *internal combustion* engines; most of the balance is turbine generator sets:

Year	Applied Research and Development (Millions of Dollars)	Industry Shipments (Millions of Dollars)	Percent
1959	87	1959	4.4
1960	98	1817	5.4
1961	100	1706	5.9
1962	121	1876	6.5
1963	124	2014	6.2
1964	126	2195	5.7
1965	138	2384	5.8

SOURCE: National Science Foundation, *Reviews of Data on Science Resources*, various publications, 1946–1969, Washington, D.C.: U.S. Government Printing Office.

Since both Westinghouse and General Electric spent comparable amounts as a percent of sales, the total dollar amount spent by these two competitors was in proportion to their market shares. Throughout 1948–1963, Westinghouse's market share was about 32 percent and General Electric's was about 60 percent. Thus, technological spending by the two firms was about in the ratio 2:1, and goes far to explain the apparent leadership role played by General Electric in technology. Allis-Chalmers was not a contender in this spending race.

It is important to note that the level of research and development funding was not constant. For General Electric, it peaked in 1957. For Westinghouse, there was a comparable peak of effort in 1957. The peak in Allis-Chalmers' spending came later, in 1960–1962. In part, fluctuations in the magnitude of spending merely reflect fluctuations in the level of work in the shop, that is, fluctuations in orders and shipments volume. However, the volume of spending was also influenced by the available gross margins in the business. When prices and earnings declined in the early 1960s, the percentage of revenues allocated to development was reduced.

Thus, as with other elements of overhead cost, spending on engineering development was very much a "residual funds" phenomenon. The turbine builders allocated to engineering development some portion of their available gross margin dollars. When that pool of available funds was cut back, so was the development effort.

Now we can readily appreciate why it was General Electric which appeared so often in the role of technological innovator in this industry, and the initiator of price curve "tilts." The direct cost savings realizable from leading a shift in the product mix were not available to all competitors on an equal basis. The direct costs savings were accessible only after the required fund of technological knowledge was in hand, and General Electric could outspend its competitors to acquire that knowledge first. The reason General Electric was in a leadership position, technologically, was no tribute to its cleverness —it was simply because of its significantly greater sales volume base, its larger gross margin percentage, and consequently its greater capability to sustain an ambitious technical development program. Westinghouse and Allis-Chalmers could not generate comparable financial resources from within their business.[54]

---

[54] One reviewer notes that the question of different organization productivities or capabilities associated with the R&D function is not broached. My answer: in view of the hard facts of the dollars of expenditure data, this alternative possibility was not explored—but it could have been a factor. I was also asked why the follower firms did not enter the capital markets in order to acquire the fund of dollars which might then be used to wrest leadership in technology away from General Electric. The reasons seem to be several: (1) there is no reason to suppose that General Electric would placidly permit leadership to be taken from it without a long and costly struggle; (2) the costs would be great, and the returns uncertain, when viewed incrementally from a projection of present strategies; and (3) the businesses were sufficiently large and mature

It is also important to note that development funding was *reduced* at the very time that the rate of announcement of new technology was *increased*. Inevitably, technological *risk* must have increased during the first portion of the 1960s.

The Utilities' Financial Inputs

The manufacturers did not carry the burden of technological funding alone; the utilities played a major role. However, the *financial* inputs of utilities were picayune; their key role was to offer cooperation, engineering advice, and a test bed for the manufacturers' advanced technologies.

This partnership arrangement, with most of the funding taking place through the manufacturers' internal budgeting, has often been criticized. Research and development spending has been a touchy subject among utility executives since Joseph Swidler (for example), chairman of the Federal Power Commission, publicly chastised the industry in 1963 for its failure to spend more on research. In response, the Edison Electric Institute itself estimated the magnitude of utility industry funding of research and development (of *all* types) at a measly $50 million in 1965.[55] The Federal Power Commission placed the level of utility spending on R&D even lower: a mere $5 million in 1969, using the FPC's strict bookkeeping definitions.[56]

It is reasonable to conclude that utility organizations are very, very junior partners in terms of what they spend on identifiable, budgeted research into turbine generator technology. The manufacturers play the principal role, serving as the conduit of utility funds and the managers of technological effort. Obviously, they recoup these expenses from their utility customers.[57]

---

within their respective corporations to make it necessary for them to find their own capital programs internally, from their own marketplace.

[55] Joseph C. Swidler, "The Special Research Problems and Opportunities of the Electric Power Industry," an address before the 31st Annual Convention of the Edison Electric Institute, Denver, Colorado, June 4, 1963. In 1969, after many similar exhortations, the electric utility companies were spending two tenths of one percent of revenues on research, according to the FPC.

Following the Swidler speech, the Edison Electric Institute conducted period surveys of its members. The utilities in 1965 were reported as spending $46 million annually for all types of research. However, some of the reported projects ("Development of Telescopic Scaffold on Top of Turbine Room Cranes for Inspection and Repairs to Underside of Roof") leave us with questions as to the utilities' definition of "research and development."

[56] The Federal Power Commission provides these estimates of expenditures for fossil-fuel steam power plant research and development by the utility organizations:

1966	$2.9 million
1967	3.2 million
1968	4.3 million
1969	4.9 million

Total utility research expenditures were $36.9 million in all areas in 1967 (including nuclear research of $4.7 million), an effort which was probably less than that of the turbine builders alone, in that year. (Federal Power Commission, *Statistics of Privately Owned Electric Utilities in the United States*, 1967, 1969, Washington, D.C.: U.S. Government Printing Office.)

[57] In 1948 all three manufacturers combined were spending about $15 million annually on

The Strategy of Follower Firms

Since Westinghouse and Allis-Chalmers had fewer gross margin dollars with which to fund the required engineering development, they attempted an alternative technological strategy particularly suited to their situation: the "standardization" strategy. Westinghouse managers conceded that General Electric, by virtue of its superior funding capability, could more readily afford to develop advanced-technology turbine generators.[58] Complex engineered products stretched the available engineering resources of follower firms.

Two alternative strategies evolved, aimed at easing the engineering burden created by the high rate of technological innovation: (1) the "standardization" movement of the early 1950s,[59] and (2) the "building block design" approach of the latter 1950s. Neither approach prevailed in the long run.[60]

One alleged reason the preferred standard movement died is that "engineers love to engineer," and they wanted no part of work-simplifying design standardization.[61] This argument seems spurious as the cause of failure.

The principal cause was that the preferred standard units were "no bargain," after evaluation of all fuel consumption factors.[62] Sporn of AEP, for example, asserted that, "We opposed standardization of turbines on the ground that turbine technology was moving far too fast for standardization to be anything but a retarding and, I would say, reactionary influence. We couldn't see how we could buy a standardized turbine. By the time it became standard, we would no longer be interested in it."[63]

Thus, the ultimate force working to destroy the "standardizing" strategy was the rapid rate of technological change. Everyone finally recognized that

---

new technology; in 1957 about $50 million annually; in 1963 about $40 million. Over the entire 1948–1963 period, manufacturers' cumulative expenditures on research and development were on the order of $0.4 billion in the turbine generator business. The payoffs are so large that refinements in the calculation are unnecessary. The value of technological change over 1946–1969, at the 1969 rate of savings, was perhaps $2.5 billion per year, and probably much more. This resulted from the combined efforts of utility organizations, turbine manufacturers, steam generator manufacturers, design engineers, and others. Credit must be distributed among a myriad of parties, but there is ample reward to be spread around.

[58] Testimony of Westinghouse engineer J. P. Wearn, stenographer's minutes, Ohio Valley Electric v. General Electric, p. 3,114.

[59] Testimony of D. W. R. Morgan, ibid., pp. 2,218–2,220. Trade association committees were formed after World War II to specify standard designs. The utilities were told this would cut costs.

[60] Testimony of John R. Carlson, ibid., pp. 2,956–2,968. By the 1960s the "preferred standard" designs were obsoleted by reheat designs. The peak year was 1954, when standard machines were 30 percent of the total. Notably, that is also the year when General Electric decided to become more competitive.

[61] Deposition of Albert M. Casey, Electrical Equipment Antitrust Actions, in all U.S. district courts, November 15, 1963.

[62] Ibid.

[63] Deposition of Philip Sporn, Electrical Equipment Antitrust Actions, in all U.S. district courts, February 14, 1964.

it simply was futile to go through the committee work to agree upon certain standard designs, when the half-life of an optimal turbine generator design was measured in months. The economies which could be attained by the utilities and the reductions in costs which could be achieved by the manufacturers through the *continual rapid evolution* of turbine generator designs, made standardization prohibitively expensive.

It is important to note that the period of maximum profitability for Westinghouse in the years under study coincided with the years in which the greatest proportion of industry units were "preferred standard."[64] As an alternative to standardization of the complete turbine generator design, Westinghouse in the latter 1950s launched an aggressive program of *components* standardization: the "building block" approach. This was really a variation of the standardization strategy. The building-block concept entailed freezing the design of certain key turbine components or modules, a selection of which could then be manufactured in batches and later assembled into turbines suited to specific customer needs.[65]

The motivation for the "building-block program," it is clear, was again the conservation of scarce technological resources for the follower firm. Both engineering and manufacturing would be simplified.[66]

It seems that the Westinghouse building-block program was substantially completed by 1959. Beginning in 1960, the increase in the size of turbine generators ordered "took off." In such an environment, turbine designs based upon standardized components would be hard pressed to maintain the leading edge in technology. Too many product variables were in motion, as the pace of technological change accelerated.

The conclusion is that a strategy of standardizing either complete turbine designs, or turbine components, is difficult to sustain in a fast-changing technical environment. Each design tends to be unique, not because of engineering peccadilloes but because this is the most economical way to build turbine generators. In recent years it has been said that a manufacturer cannot afford to deliver even *one duplicate* unit because of the rapid rate of design evolution and the need to offset inflation in labor and materials with ever-larger unit ratings.

In sum, in this particular technological and market environment, standardization strategies were hardly appropriate for technological leaders and could be little recommended even for the follower firms. There was really no easy alternative to attempting to keep pace with the technological leader firm.

Previous analysis suggests that expenditures on new technology are a unique function of sales volume for each competitor. They are a sub-category

---

[64] Testimony of L. M. Eikner, stenographer's minutes, Ohio Valley Electric v. General Electric, pp. 2,396–2,399.

[65] Testimony of Carlson, ibid., pp. 3,007–3,008. See also Chapter Eleven.

[66] Testimony of Wearn, ibid., pp. 3,059–3,112.

of overhead costs, budgeted as some fraction of the total overhead spending of each firm. The targeted level of overhead spending, and therefore technological spending, is obviously influenced by the relative scale and affluence of each competitor.[67] Given the appropriate market and technological opportunities, technological spending can be enhanced if total sales revenues swell. For example, if prices climb 10 percent and nothing else changes, then technological spending, after an adjustment delay, will also rise 10 percent. If prices drop by a third, such as characterized the early 1960s then technological spending will tend to drop by about a third.[68]

Thus, there is a direct feedback from competitive conditions in the marketplace to the funding of new technology, in the manner which Joseph Schumpeter posited 30 years ago. Technological change is promoted by "pockets of profitability" which are the result of monopoly elements in the marketplace.

---

[67] The data on research and development spending by each competitor, given in this chapter, are a composite of overhead dollars and direct cost dollars. Some research and development costs are incurred when working on specific orders. Other research and development expense is in the category of overhead spending, e.g., advanced research. It appears, based upon an examination of the data, that the bulk of spending should be categorized as "overhead," in the definition of costs used in Chapter Ten. As such, research and development expenditures are determined as some targeted fraction of total sales revenues, with the target being approached with a lagged response.

[68] There are parallels between these conclusions and the research of others. Mansfield has noted that the level of a firm's research and development expenditures can be explained reasonably well by a simple model which assumes that the distribution of expected returns from R&D projects, together with the firm's size, determines the firm's desired level of R&D spending. The firm's speed of response toward this desired level of expenditures depends on the extent to which the desired level differs from last year's spending and the percent of its profits spent last year on R&D. See: Edwin Mansfield, *Industrial Research and Technological Innovation* (New York: Norton, 1968).

CHAPTER Thirteen   Market
Share Strategy

IN OLIGOPOLY, THE IMPORTANCE of market share strategy is self-evident. Market share—as targeted by managers, and as eroded from time to time by the perennial grinding of oligopolistic rivalry—is the most visible barometer of competitive success. Thus, managers' attentions become riveted upon the market share statistics—and the managing of market share results.

THE KEY: MARKET SHARE OF ORDERS

The relevant strategy variable is share of orders, not share of shipments. Because of time lags, a decline in share of orders would not appear as a decline in share of shipments for several years. If managers focused their attention upon share of shipments in their strategic deliberations, they would be reacting to stale information—competitive intelligence several years obsolete.

Additional clues in this regard may be found in the internal management reports of General Electric and Westinghouse, which invariably referred to the "share of the available business"; which means the percentage share of the *orders* let by customers during some time period. The reports did *not* refer to share of sales billed, or share of orders processed. Thus, it is share of orders which is relevant to understanding strategic behavior in this industry.[1]

What is revealed about competitive standings by such share of orders statistics? General Electric had the largest market share (and also a product mix skewed toward the largest ratings and the most advanced technologies). Westinghouse was second in market share, and also second in its average unit size. Allis-Chalmers brought up the rear in both market share and in average unit size. (Table 13.1.) The correlation between market position and technological position was not coincidental; high market shares would permit low direct costs, which in turn would permit higher overhead spending, which tended to per-

---

[1] For further discussion of this point see: Deposition of L. M. Eikner, March 6, 1963, in Electrical Equipment Antitrust Actions, all U.S. district courts.

TABLE 13.1.
MARKET SHARE: STEAM TURBINE GENERATORS ORDERED BY U.S. UTILITY AND
INDUSTRIAL ORGANIZATIONS, 1948–1962 (2,500 KW SIZE AND ABOVE).

	Number of Units	Percent of Total
General Electric	993	57.1
Westinghouse	586	33.7
Allis-Chalmers	155	8.9
Foreign	6	.3
Total	1,740	100.0
	Aggregate Kilowatts	Percent of Total
General Electric	102,677,000	60.8
Westinghouse	53,121,000	31.4
Allis-Chalmers	11,256,000	6.7
Foreign	1,920,000	1.1
Total	168,974,000	100.0
	Average Kilowatts Per Unit	
General Electric	103,400	
Westinghouse	90,650	
Allis-Chalmers	72,620	
Foreign	320,000	
Total	97,110	

SOURCE: Tabulation of transactions data submitted to U.S. District Court, S.D.N.Y., in connection with Electrical Equipment Antitrust Actions.

petuate product leadership—and that was critical to retaining leadership in
market share.

Year by year, however, market shares were quite variable. General Electric's
market share fluctuated from a low of 44 percent to a high of 74 percent
(Table 13.2). Westinghouse attained a maximum market share of 42 percent;
its low was almost 10 percent. Allis-Chalmers experienced what might be
termed a "surge-followed-by-flameout." Allis-Chalmers began the post-World
War II period with a very small market share. Beginning in 1954 it expanded
capacity and surged ahead, ultimately to 15 percent. During the White Sale
(January 1955), it was beaten back. However, during the peak price period
of 1958, Allis-Chalmers achieved a 25 percent market share. Nevertheless,
its aggressive pursuit of share—and economies of scale—ultimately failed.[2]

One can best see the broad *trends* in share of orders in Chart 13.1. For
General Electric, the market share trend line was V-shaped: a long-term downward trend beginning in the early 1950s, reaching bottom in 1959, then trend-

---

[2] By this, we mean that Allis-Chalmers was forced to withdraw from the market. However, in
1970 Allis-Chalmers reentered the turbine generator business, utilizing German technology obtained under license agreement. Its first order was two 430,000 kw units, ordered by Louisiana
Power and Light Company.

TABLE 13.2.
PERCENT SHARE OF TURBINE GENERATOR ORDERS BY U.S. UTILITY AND
INDUSTRIAL ORGANIZATIONS (AGGREGATE KILOWATTS BASIS).

	General Electric	Westinghouse	Allis-Chalmers[a]	Foreign
1946	63.0%	35.0%	2.0%	0%
1947	57.0	38.0	5.0	0
1948	59.7	35.2	5.1	0
1949	56.2	39.1	4.7	0
1950	58.6	38.1	3.3	0
1951	62.4	35.1	2.5	0
1952	63.3	32.6	4.1	0
1953	73.7	23.2	3.1	0
1954	60.0	24.7	15.3	0
1955	62.9	33.4	3.7	0
1956	59.4	27.9	12.7	0
1957	48.5	38.1	13.4	0
1958	48.8	25.9	25.3	0
1959	52.5	25.5	8.7	13.3
1960	62.4	32.8	4.8	0
1961	55.2	26.4	14.6	3.8
1962	63.6	35.2	1.2	0
1963	60.3	34.3	5.4	0
1964	59.0	41.0	0	0
1965	57.7	41.0	0	1.3
1966	62.5	37.5	0	0
1967	44.0	42.2	0	13.8
1968	55.0	31.3	0	13.7
1969	60.0	28.7	0	11.3
1970	62.7	10.0	3.5	23.8

[a] Crediting 1,000,000 Kw Consolidated Edison unit to Allis-Chalmers in 1963, although commitment made late in 1962.

SOURCE: Tabulation of Electrical Equipment Antitrust Actions data, filed at S.D.N.Y.

ing upward into the 1960s. Westinghouse's market share trend was essentially flat over this period. Allis-Chalmers' market share trend was the mirror image of General Electric's: an inverted V, peaking in 1959 and sliding off to zero by 1962.

What follows is an analysis of why market shares followed such a pattern. Market share is the product of management strategies on the supply side, and of autonomous brand choices on the demand side, and both sides of the market warrant analysis.

CONSUMER PREFERENCE

First consider those market share factors operating on the demand side of the marketplace. In part, turbine generator market shares were determined by

CHART 13.1.   Moving Average Market Share of Steam Turbine Generator Orders Received, 1951–1963.

the loyalties and technological tastes of the utility customers. These supplier preferences were often rooted in years of mutually satisfactory relationships. Further, some utility organizations had entered into informal but nevertheless closely interlocking "partnership" arrangements with key manufacturer organizations, with the aim of advancing power generation technology. These technological "liaisons" were buttressed by some utilities' deliberate skewing of purchase awards to their chosen manufacturer allies, and by these manufacturers' price reductions in turn, for the benefit of their chosen partner utilities. To complicate the demand pattern further, some utility organizations deliberately rotated their awards among the three domestic turbine generator manufacturers, according to predetermined percentage allocations or quotas. All of these factors would influence market share.[3]

Large utility organizations tended to purchase turbine generators which were larger, of higher steam temperature rating, and of higher steam pressure rating (Tables 13.3 and 13.4). These were the advanced technology machines. General Electric achieved its maximum market penetration among the larger utility organizations through its lead in product technology. The facts are clear: large utility organizations would be the first to adopt new technology and they made their supplier choices accordingly. Thus was formulated one of several dimensions of "brand loyalty."

As utilities with differentiated loyalties entered the marketplace in random sequence, and since there were relatively few transactions in each time period,

---

[3] For an extended treatment of customer buying behavior, and the extent of differentiated brand loyalties, see: Ralph G. M. Sultan, *Pricing in the Electrical Oligopoly*, Vol. I (Boston: Harvard Business School, Division of Research, 1974), Chapter Nine.

TABLE 13.3.
Size of Turbine Generator Purchases, 1948–1962, According to
Size of Utility Organization.

Turbine Generator Maximum Rating	Purchasing Utility Size in 1968					
	Small (Up to 1 Billion Kwh/Yr.)		Medium (1 to 10 Billion Kwh/Yr.)		Large (Over 10 Billion Kwh/Yr.)	
	Units	Percent	Units	Percent	Units	Percent
Up to 100 mw	383	95.0	263	44.7	24	8.6
100 to 199	18	4.5	247	41.9	145	52.0
200 to 299	2	0.5	57	9.7	59	21.0
300 to 399			14	2.4	39	14.0
400 to 499			7	1.2	2	0.7
500 to 599			1	0.2	6	2.2
Over 600 mw					4	1.4
Total	403	100	589	100	279	100
Advanced Units Not Yet in Handbook	0		2		20	

Source: Tabulation of electrical litigation data, and compilations of the author.

TABLE 13.4.
Initial Steam Temperature of Turbine Generators Ordered, 1948–1962,
According to Size of Utility Organization.

	Purchasing Utility Size in 1968					
	Small (Up to 1 Billion Kwh/Yr.)		Medium (1 to 10 Billion Kwh/Yr.)		Large (Over 10 Billion Kwh/Yr.)	
	Units	Percent	Units	Percent	Units	Percent
Under 700	20	4.9	4	0.7	5	1.8
700 to 799	89	22.1	16	2.7	1	0.4
800 to 899	79	19.6	16	2.7	0	—
900 to 999	174	43.2	154	26.1	24	8.6
1,000 to 1,099	41	10.2	398	67.6	238	85.3
1,100 and over			1	0.2	11	3.9
Total	403	100	589	100	279	100

Source: Tabulation of electrical litigation data, and compilations of the author.

thus was created a certain random variation in market shares among the competing suppliers. But even greater movements in market share could be attributed to actions on the supplier side: to actions formulated according to manufacturer strategy. These will be considered next.

Manufacturer Strategy

Long-Term "Norms"

In the long term, General Electric's market share hovered in the vicinity of 60 percent. This was hardly a coincidence. One General Electric marketing manager testified that 60 percent was in fact the approximate General Electric market share goal.[4]

That market share "norms" would evolve seems inevitable. Long-term market share expectations were often written down as part of the long-range plans and budgets of each firm, and managers became committed to them. Once these expectations were backed up by historical experience, competitors would struggle fiercely to hold what they had come to believe was their proper and rightful share of the business. Norms were further reinforced by being built into the formal process of management appraisal, such performance reviews often stressing current share relative to the historical share. Larger firms would generally have the marketing strength to defend their market position, although prices and earnings could suffer as a consequence.

Short-Term Fluctuations

Short-term market share fluctuations, around the long-term norm, may be attributed to: variations in the "mix" of customers in the market in any particular year, as mentioned previously; shifting of orders dictated by some utilities' need for early delivery; and market share managing. That is, for strategic reasons, manufacturers might seek a short-run shift in their market share. These various factors were subjected to statistical analysis.

Statistical Analysis of Market Share Determinants

Statistical analysis reveals four factors as important determinants of share: relative prices, backlogs, manufacturing capacity shares, and "buffering" (see Appendix 15).

(1) Relative Prices and Market Share

Relative price is one market share determinant most subject to managing. It is the statistic which captures the autonomous pricing decision of one firm, relative to the price of its rival.[5]

---

[4] Testimony of George Cox, marketing manager, General Electric Large Steam Turbine Generator Division, stenographer's minutes, *Ohio Valley Electric v. General Electric et al.*, 62 Civ. 695, S.D.N.Y., p. 1,440.

[5] This analysis is based upon actual transactions prices, and not on the basis of book or list prices. Book prices served merely as the signal flags to rivals and as a convenience to customers when crudely estimating their own investment costs—but were virtually meaningless as indi-

Over the period 1948–1963, General Electric's relative price ranged from 1.03 (indicating General Electric was 3 percent higher in price than the industry average) to approximately .98 (General Electric 2 percent under the industry average). The maximum value of 1.03 attained in 1960–1961, implies that Westinghouse and Allis-Chalmers were jointly undercutting General Electric by approximately 8 percent. At the minimum value of .98, on the other hand (in 1957–1958), General Electric was undercutting its two rivals by approximately 5 percent. Normally, the price sensitivity of utility choice guaranteed that price differentials among competitors would be much less (Chart 13.2). Otherwise, large and rapid shifts in market share would wipe out one competitor or the other.

CHART 13.2.   Actual Order Price of General Electric Relative to Industry Average Price, 1948–1963.

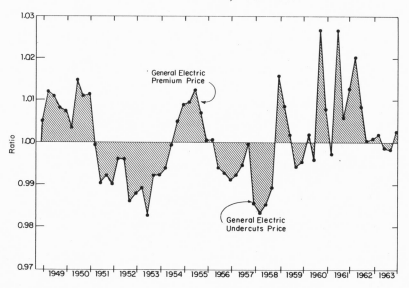

The statistical results indicate that, all other things equal, if General Electric was 8 percent above the average price of its two competitors, neutrality prevailed; there would be no expected change in market share. Because of its product technology and marketing strength, General Electric could charge a premium price without losing share.

On the other hand, if General Electric priced *level* with its competitors, its market share would tend to creep upward. And if General Electric could succeed in undercutting its competitors' prices, there was a sharp increase in its market share. For example, if General Electric underpriced its competitors by 5 percent and sustained this relative price cut, on the average, for three months, then on the average it would gain almost 11 share points. This might seem to be

cators of the final price. Furthermore, since book prices were usually identical for all competitors, their impact upon market shares would be negligible.

formidable market share "clout" but it says nothing about feasibility—whether or not competitors would actually sit still and tolerate General Electric's underpricing them. Normally, they were *not* so tolerant of being underpriced.

The statistical results also indicate that if General Electric moved its relative price to below the industry average, it was Allis-Chalmers' market share which was particularly affected. Allis-Chalmers stressed price in its marketing mix and could scarcely afford to allow General Electric to underprice it; the loss of market share would be disastrous—for example, a loss of 15 share points in three months, given a 13 percentage point reduction in General Electric's relative price, according to our elasticity estimates.

Thus, over 1948–1963, it was General Electric and Allis-Chalmers which traded share points, depending upon the relative price of each. Westinghouse maintained its market share, probably offsetting competitive pricing movements with shifts in its own nonprice marketing variables.

(2) *Backlogs and Market Share*

Backlogs also had a measurable impact on market share. Some utility customers on the margin were always shopping for speedy delivery. If one manufacturer loaded its factories, some regular customers would be diverted to competitors—assuming those competitors' shops were less tightly plugged with work. Market shares would, accordingly, be influenced by relative backlogs standing. Backlogs are here measured by the years of delivery time (years of backlog) which each competitor offered.

Statistical analysis suggests that, in a three-month period, General Electric would tend to lose 2.5 percentage points of market share for every year of backlog it had at the factory. The downward drift in market share would be maintained, quarter-by-quarter, until backlogs diminished and market equilibrium was restored. (Other factors implicit in the model would prevent a long-term secular decline in General Electric's market share.)

For Allis-Chalmers, the backlogs effects were seemingly reversed. There is some hint that high backlogs stimulated market share! For each year of prior increase in backlogs, Allis-Chalmers' market share increased by another 3.8 percentage points. These results may derive from Allis-Chalmers' problem of establishing credibility in turbine generator manufacturing and design. Customers were assured that Allis-Chalmers was indeed a reliable source when other customers were purchasing too and when Allis-Chalmers' backlogs were high. It was a bandwagon situation. But when Allis-Chalmers' backlog declined, customers lost confidence and leaped off the bandwagon. Thus, in order to win orders, Allis-Chalmers had to have a large backlog of orders. In a downturn, as backlogs for all began to shrink, Allis-Chalmers suffered a disproportionately large reduction in market share.[6]

---

[6] One is tempted to conclude that the finding is tautological: that when Allis-Chalmers' orders

(3) Manufacturing Capacity and Market Share

Market shares also tended to follow shifts in the shares of industry manufacturing capacity held by individual competitors. The reasons for this were twofold: First, a shift in capacity shares would mean a shift in the competitors' relative capability to serve (rapid delivery, good service, and so on), and on this score some utility organizations were always comparison shopping. Second, the oligopolists themselves would feel pressured to permit competitors' new manufacturing capacity to receive, *pro rata*, their share of the available market demand. The motivation for such backlogs balancing would be completely selfish: to avoid any more price depression than could be helped, given a competitor's aggressive—perhaps imprudent—expansion of manufacturing capacity. The statistical results tend to support these propositions.

In this respect, it appears once more that Allis-Chalmers was subject to unique acceleration forces. Our statistical measures imply that when Allis-Chalmers *increased* its share of industry manufacturing capacity by 2 percentage points, it *raised* its market share by over 6 percentage points. But we are dealing here with *changes* in capacity and, merely to stay even, it seems that Allis-Chalmers would have to increase its share of manufacturing capacity *another* 2 percentage points in the next three-month period as well—an implausible suggestion. Allis-Chalmers in fact increased its share of capacity significantly, in several stages. With each increment there was a corresponding rise in its share of orders. *However, Allis-Chalmers could not hold on to that increment in market share.* Allis-Chalmers could therefore play the game of bluff as well as anyone, buying market share by investing in plant capacity, thereby threatening its competitors and preparing to serve its customers. But its beachhead would be temporary, never consolidated, and eventually it would be worn away by competition.

(4) Buffering

A fourth phenomenon was present: "buffering." Buffering refers to the larger firm's conscious decision to disinvest in market share when backlogs and prices are falling.[7]

The apparent purpose of buffering is to ease the shock of a business downturn upon the less-resilient follower firms. The leader firm does this by absorbing more than its "share" of the volume adjustment to a fluctuating market. Thus, the leader firm is deliberately less aggressive during a market downturn, a policy

---

climbed, so too did its backlogs. But as a general rule, Allis-Chalmers' market share climbed when the level of industry orders was at an ebb. Thus, the tautology does not apply.

[7] The buffering strategy was first analyzed by Derek Abell with reference to the power capacitor industry, as part of this research project. See: Derek Abell, "Pricing in Oligopoly," unpublished doctoral dissertation, Harvard University, Graduate School of Business Administration, 1969.

which is translated into some loss of its market share. Its motives may be completely selfish: to discourage the worst of price competition.

The corollary strategy is share recoupment during a market upturn. The leader firm, if it is not to be ratcheted over time to a lower and lower market share, must regain its lost share points at some time. Obviously the propitious time to do it is when backlogs are waxing strong, and when overall industry price levels are climbing. We call such cyclical behavior "buffering."

In summary, our statistical model reveals the determinants of the change in General Electric's market share as being: relative price, backlog loading condition, and changes in capacity. The determinants of Allis-Chalmers' share are similar: relative price and backlog loading at the factory, as well as change in share of manufacturing capacity, and—due to the price umbrella effect of buffering—the average industry price level. Changes in Westinghouse market share are the mirror image of changes in the share of its two competitors and, by definition, are subject to the same determinants as those of the other two firms.

The Integration of Strategy with Corporate Goals

Operating managers must link their strategies—their market share strategy, manufacturing capacity strategy, and technological strategy—to the larger goals of the enterprise. We now examine these discretionary rules of conduct, as witnessed in the actual General Electric behavior over 1948–1962.

While the following discussion is based upon management procedures within General Electric, available evidence suggests that similar internal management processes were also at work for its competitors.

Goal Setting and Feedback of Results

In these large corporate enterprises, goals are set at the top. For example, within General Electric general objectives emanated from corporate head-quarters in New York. Each year, via the budgeting and planning process, specific targets were negotiated for each operating division of the corporation, in terms of market share, earnings, and return on investment. The design and implementation of business strategies to achieve these general targeted results then became the responsibility of management at the operating division level. Strategies and plans thus developed were expected to be consistent with the specified targets.

Feedback of actual operating results would often lead to a modification of corporate targets, and to a change in business strategy. In addition, it would often result in the appearance of new faces within operating management. Job security was a powerful motivating force, driving managers at the operating level to fulfill the objectives defined at the top by the corporate level. One

General Electric manager, when asked what incentives there were to achieve profit goals, replied simply, "To keep the job."[8]

Corporate Goals

Clues as to the nature of the goals imposed upon managers in the General Electric turbine generator business may be gained from the "Operating Division General Manager Position Guide," promulgated under the authority of the chairman of the board. According to this directive, General Electric division managers were expected to maximize long-run profits and sales volume, *as measured by return on investment, total profits, and market share.* There were supplementary exhortations concerning the need also to enhance product leadership, develop division resources, build constructive human relations, earn the respect of employees, customers, shareholders, and so on.[9]

One may safely assume that this position guideline, insofar as the turbine generator business is concerned, would motivate managers to maintain General Electric's market share at the historical 60 percent level, and to take maximum earnings flow from the business, all the while investing to insure General Electric's long-term technical and marketing leadership.

Profits

Interestingly, explicit profit goals seem to have been only hazily established. According to one General Electric manager, profit goals were determined through "philosophical discussions" between the division manager and the

---

[8] Question: "What incentives were there in the department relating to the attainment of profit goals in 1957?" Answer: "To keep the job." (Deposition of General Electric marketing manager Clyde A. Lilly, Jr., March 4, 1963, Electrical Equipment Antitrust Actions, in all U.S. district courts.) See also the following General Electric memorandum (excerpts): ". . . our earnings will be below 1954 and 1955 results in both 1957 and 1958 and . . . confidence in our performance could be restored at the next Business Review if we show radical improvement for 1959. . . ." (Letter of C. F. Buehler, manager of finance, General Electric Large Steam Turbine Generator Department, to G. W. Marsh, New York office, March 15, 1957, p. 2, electrical litigation exhibit NX 1126, in all U.S. district courts.) And also: ". . . when I made up the budget for my first year, I was scared to death . . . [my superiors] raised hell with us if they were in red ink. . . . I don't recall that they ever changed any budget figures, but there were caustic comments. . . ." (Deposition of J. W. McMullen, vice president and general manager, Allis-Chalmers Power Equipment Division, January 21, 1963, in Electrical Equipment Antitrust Actions, all U.S. district courts.)

[9] The operative paragraphs were: "Teach, advise, counsel, review, and appraise, in channels, the performance of Department General Managers and Managers as to the successful and profitable conduct of the businesses of each of the components of the Division; and hold subordinates accountable for results in order to: Earn maximum long-range profits and sales volume from the businesses of Division components and from each of their products lines, *as measured by the return earned on investment, the total profits earned, and the percent of available business obtained,* by providing valuable service to their customers." (Italics in original.) SOURCE: Operating Division General Manager Position Guide, as issued by the chairman of the board, General Electric Company, 1955. National Exhibit NX 332, Electrical Equipment Antitrust Actions, as filed in all U.S. district courts.

group executive above him in the General Electric organization.[10] Haziness as to profit *goals* was not translated into *budgetary* vagueness, however. There was an important distinction between goals and the explicit profit results defined each year in the budget. As one General Electric manager put it, "There is a lot of difference between budget and goals. If I could have ever broken even on gas turbines I would have considered that a wonderful situation from a budget standpoint, but certainly not from a goal."[11] It seems, in fact, that the only long-run earnings guideline was that more profits were better than less, and that a regular year-to-year *improvement* in earnings was expected. When asked what profit rate would suffice, Cordiner, former chairman of the board of General Electric, asserted "I would be happy with whatever the market developed [in profit rates]."[12]

Such a happy state of mind could not be enjoyed by General Electric's higher cost competitors in the turbine business. For Westinghouse and Allis-Chalmers to achieve some minimum return on investment must have been a principal objective. What is suggested is a hierarchical set of goals and objectives, depending upon the profit margins being achieved.

"Norms" in Market Share

Another important goal was market share. It is obvious that 60 percent was regarded by General Electric managers as their appropriate long-run share in turbine generators.[13] However, the short-run strategy of "buffering" would permit short-run departures from the long-run market share goal. This was aided by the fact that managers had some latitude in the profits and market share results which they reported up the line each year. Let us discuss this "managing" of annual results in detail, because it is an important determinant of competitive behavior from year to year.

"Managed" Operating Results

To a degree, the reported *market shares* could be managed up or down. There could be a genuine shift of market shares, or managers could create the tempo-

---

[10] Deposition of William S. Ginn, vice president of General Electric Turbine Generator Department, January 14, 1963, in Electrical Equipment Antitrust Actions, all U.S. district courts, p. 78.

[11] Ibid.

[12] Deposition of Ralph J. Cordiner, March 12, 1964, in Electrical Equipment Antitrust Actions, all U.S. district courts. Cordiner added: "I wouldn't be at all concerned about 80 percent [return on average investment] because that isn't our determination; [it] is the determination of the customer. He will buy from somebody else if he doesn't think this is good value." Ibid.

[13] During the electrical litigation, the president of I-T-E Circuit Breaker Company related his conviction that there was a "60-40" tradition in the industry, tracing back to the well-known patent pooling agreement which existed between General Electric and Westinghouse for approximately 15 years commencing in 1896. (Testimony of Maxwell Scott, United States Congress, Senate, Committee on the Judiciary, Subcommittee on Antitrust and Monopoly, *Administered Prices*, Hearings Pursuant to S. Res. 52, 87th Cong., May 11, 1961 (known as the Kefauver Hearings).

rary illusion of gains and losses by shifting the timing of their reported orders. This could be useful when preparing statistics for internal corporate consumption. The moment when an order was finally "booked" was often a matter of judgment. During periods of great organizational pressure for an increase in market share, operating managers had great incentive to report vague (and cancellable) commitments on the part of their utility customers, as if they were firm orders. By the same token, orders could be secretly hidden away, to be reported on a rainy day.

Statistical analysis, order by order, reveals that there was in fact a tendency for General Electric managers to overreport their incoming turbine orders when orders were slowing down, and a corresponding tendency to underreport their orders when the volume of total orders was rising. In other words, there was a systematic smoothing of the reported orders flow, for internal management consumption.[14]

Within certain limits, reported *profit* results were also amenable to short-run management. This was feasible because managers of the turbine generator business had a clear picture of what the earnings picture would in fact be, for about two years into the future. (The orders backlog was already priced, and the backlog typically amounted to about two years of work. Costs were the greatest unknown, plus possible fabrication or assembly delays.) William Ginn, former vice president of the General Electric Turbine Division, explained:

> You have got your backlog. You try to price your backlog, then budget what your expenses are going to be for the year and from that try to determine what is your income going to be per month.
>
> You would sit down and figure out what kind of a mix you had in the shop, what capacity you were going to have in the shop, what your costs looked like, how much money you were going to spend for research and development, how much money you were going to spend for commercial expense, advertising, everything else. The same way you make out a budget in anything.[15]

---

[14] The results of this analysis may be summarized as follows: Manufacturers and utilities submitted, independently of one another, order dates on 523 turbine generators purchased in the 1948–1961 period. Matching and comparison revealed how the operating managers shifted their reported order dates. There is fair agreement; the particular year of the order was identical in 85 percent of cases. But, on balance, the utilities were prone to claim a *later* year than did the manufacturers (8.4 percent of transactions) more often than they claimed an *earlier* year than did the manufacturers (5.7 percent of transactions), which is indicative of manufacturer bias to borrow prospective orders from the future, on average. However, the manufacturers tended to be tardy in reporting orders in years of rapidly accelerating order volume, while overreporting their orders during periods of declining orders. (Sources: *Plaintiffs Request to Admit Facts in the Turbine Generators Actions*, Atlantic City Electric et al., v. General Electric et al., Civil Action 4258, S.D.N.Y.; and *Turbine Generator Transactions 1948 Through 1962*, submitted by the manufacturers in the same action. On file at U.S. Court House, S.D.N.Y.)

[15] Deposition of William S. Ginn, January 14, 1963, in Electrical Equipment Antitrust Actions, all U.S. district courts. While it is the thesis of this chapter that earnings were primarily managed

Thus, in the immediate future, there was little reason for earnings surprises; the profit projections were relatively certain. This factor gave management time to think, lay plans, and make adjustments if appropriate. Expenses, and therefore earnings, could be managed upward or downward, depending upon managerial objectives.

The upward or downward adjusting of earnings was more than a mere bookkeeping maneuver; it could often be achieved by the tradeoff which exists between short-run earnings and changes in market share, such changes in share arising through shifts in expenditure or pricing. Market share can be acquired through investing in greater marketing effort, at the expense of the forthcoming reported earnings. In contrary fashion, the earnings level to be reported could be raised through expense-reducing relaxation of marketing effort. Thus, through investing or disinvesting in market share on incoming new orders, reported earnings on the invoiced outgoing shipments, that is, on reported earnings for the firm next year, could be reduced or raised. Consider now how this flexibility was actually exploited by managers of the turbine business at General Electric.

"Balance" in Reported Operating Results

The mix of profit and market share results to be reported each year was heavily influenced by considerations of "balance." Strong organizational norms existed as to the mix of long-run versus short-run accomplishments which represented good management.

Within General Electric, for example, there was a great sensitivity to the need for balance between long-range strength as measured by market position (market share), and short-range results as measured by current accounting rate of profit. For example, the former general manager of General Electric's Turbine Division, William Ginn, was queried concerning his interpretation of the "position guide" under which he had lived. Note his stress upon the balance to be achieved among the various managed factors in the business:

> Percentage of available [i.e., market share] has got [a] connection with profits. You can't just treat each one of these as independent things. They are all correlated. You are trying to do the right balance. If you want to give up some percentage of the available, it may be possible you could increase your profits. You had a historical position, earned position in the market place, that was earned by your product, your facilities, your sales organiza-

---

by expense control, the litigation also uncovered evidence of managers hoping to achieve profit targets through direct management of selling prices: "We have, in accordance with your request, analyzed the anticipated profit levels of the Department through 1962 and conclude that it will be necessary to make certain adjustments in price levels if the Department is to obtain the desired profit goal." (Letter from J. T. Peters, pricing specialist, General Electric, to Clyde Lilly, marketing manager, dated October 4, 1957. City of San Antonio v. Westinghouse et al., Civil Action 3064, W. D. Texas, p. 1,114.)

tion, your reputation, and everything else, [and] you certainly wanted to maintain that position unless there was a good reason for giving it up in order to achieve more profitability. Now in certain cases it might be to [your] advantage to let your marketplace go down in order to get your profits up. You might raise prices, you might turn down jobs that didn't have good margins in them, not spend any money for new equipment, not spend any money for facilities, quit spending money for engineering and development, quit trying to sell so hard, have sales expense. If your market share was going up chances are you might be quoting prices too low, [or] maybe you are spending too much money for research and development.[16]

Cordiner, former General Electric chairman of the board, was equally sensitive to the need for balance in operating results:

> If you try to go for the maximum profit that you can have, either net to sales or return on investment, you liquidate the future of the company, so somewhere in there you have to hit a balance.[17]

Thus, under normal circumstances, market share points could be traded away in return for immediate profits. Share points were often deliberately yielded as a matter of strategy through raising prices relative to the competition, or through less aggressive marketing effort. But all the while "balance" had to be maintained.

STATISTICAL ANALYSIS OF GENERAL ELECTRIC STRATEGY

The validity of this discussion can be demonstrated by a time-series analysis of the behavior of General Electric's market share, earnings, and relative pricing behavior in the turbine generator market over 1948–1963. Three factors (profit levels, deviations from long-term share goals, and buffering) were statistically tested to ascertain whether they were related to the relative price ratio of General Electric (see Appendix 16). General Electric's discretionary strategy is thereby revealed.

(1) *Profit Rate v. Market Share*

As expected, the current rate of General Electric operating profits (as a percent of sales) in the turbine generator business over 1951–1963 was closely related to the relative price ratio. The direction of influence was positive; that is, when General Electric profit rates on current shipments were high, the ratio of General Electric-to-industry prices was high and General Electric would tend to lose in share of incoming orders. Some readers may reason that this relationship merely demonstrates that low prices mean low

---

[16] Ginn, ibid.

[17] Testimony of Ralph J. Cordiner, United States Congress, Senate, Committee on the Judiciary, Subcommittee on Antitrust and Monopoly, *Administered Prices*, June 15, 1961.

profits. Others may sense that current profits affect relative price, which affects current market share, which then affects the current volume of incoming orders and therefore profits—hardly a novel statistical correlation. However, the evidence is *not* circular. Market share of orders will indeed influence sales volume and profits—but only at some distant date, years in the future, when those orders have been processed. We are not, therefore, dealing with contemporaneous phenomena.

It might seem more reasonable to have discovered General Electric investing in share points when earnings were high and when funds were therefore readily available and, conversely, divesting share points to bolster earnings when such an improvement in earnings was badly needed. Did not General Electric's actual market share strategy needlessly accentuate its swings in reported results? Not necessarily. We shall see that it actually dampened such oscillations, consistent with a balanced reporting of overall operating results.

(2) Long-Term Market Share Goals

Statistically, General Electric's average market share of the *past* 12 months was highly correlated with its relative price ratio of the *next* 12 months. This means that if General Electric's average market share had been low, then it would react by keeping its prices low relative to the competition, thereby regaining market share. Conversely, if General Electric's market share had been high, its relative price ratio would be raised and eventually General Electric's market share would decline. In this manner, General Electric managers strived to maintain a stable long-term market position.[18]

(3) Buffering of Market Share

The third explanatory variable which was statistically tested was "buffering": the deliberate yielding of market share when backlogs and prices were declining, and its recoupment when backlogs and prices were being restored. It was also a significant influence upon General Electric's discretionary behavior.

The conclusion is: General Electric's discretionary pricing strategy in the turbine generator market, over the period 1948–1962, was influenced by the profitability of the turbine generator division, by the desire to maintain a long-term market share norm of 60 percent, and—to a much lesser degree—by the desire to buffer its competitors over the business cycle.

Interpretation

In order to understand this profit-share strategy, it is helpful to ponder another striking fact: when viewed on an annual basis, the *change* in General

---

[18] Note that the model implies a "hunting" or wandering market share strategy which moved share points up if they were below target, and vice versa, but which never explicitly "homed in" upon the specified long-term market share objective. This gave ample flexibility for other short-term market share maneuvers.

Electric's turbine generator profit rate shows an extremely high correlation with its *change* in percentage market share. On the average, an 8.0 percentage point increase in the market share was associated with a 5.0 percentage point increase in the earnings rate, the specific relationship being:

$$\begin{bmatrix} \text{Change in} \\ \text{General Electric} \\ \text{market share of} \\ \text{orders} \\ \text{(percentage points)} \end{bmatrix} = 1.6 \times \begin{bmatrix} \text{Change in} \\ \text{General Electric} \\ \text{earnings rate} \\ \text{(percentage points)} \end{bmatrix}$$

One cannot explain this correlation on the simple-minded grounds that greater market share means a busier factory which means greater earnings. The earnings which were experienced this particular year were the consequence of marketing efforts (and market share accomplishments) of two or more years ago. The correlation probably resulted from managers managing their earnings and market share.

If the profit rate on sales was low, General Electric sought to acquire market share. That gain in market share was accompanied by (but was not directly the cause of) an increase in the profit rate. Contrariwise, if the profit rate on sales was high, General Electric seemed deliberately to yield a few percentage points of market share.

The typical historical pattern is sketched in Chart 13.3. If market share of

CHART 13.3.   Typical Profit Rate-Market Share Relationship for General Electric Turbine Generator Division, 1948–1962.

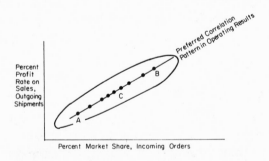

incoming orders was high (at point B) there was a tendency to move it down next year (toward point C), with a corresponding reduction in the earnings rate on outgoing shipments. If market share was low (at point A), there was a tendency to move it up next year (toward C), with an associated increase in the earnings rate on shipments. The line ABC depicts the managers' revealed preference in earnings-share combinations, their preferred correlation pattern of operating results.

Why were profits and share managed to yield this particular result? In any market environment, a manager may trade his market share points for current

CHART 13.4.   Typical Tradeoffs Which Can Be Achieved Between Reported Profit
Rate on This Year's Business, v. Market Share of Orders,
Under Varying Market Environments.
(*Example: Discretionary Shift of Business From X to Y.*)

earnings, along a set of tradeoff curves, as depicted in Chart 13.4. Since the
tradeoffs would seemingly be made in competitive fashion against determined
rivals, these share points may be priced at their expected economic value. Thus,
the tradeoff curves could approximate "iso-present value" contours or curves
of equal present value.[19]

The following strategy thinking probably prevailed: If General Electric
turbine managers were entering a year in which they knew the profit rate on sales
was going to increase, they deliberately chose to take *part* of that earnings
increase in the form of increased market share. Assume they were operating in
1965 at point A in Chart 13.5. For 1966 the earnings rate is projected to be

CHART 13.5.   Investing a Portion of an Expected Earnings Gain in Increased
Market Share.

much greater (point B) if they just maintained their current share of new
orders. The managers could decide to invest in an enlarged share of orders
during 1966, to draw down the projected earnings (to end up at point C).

Confronted with an earnings decline, the opposite choice would be made.

---

[19] The argument is based on the assumption that present value is a function of market share
and the earnings rate. This will tend to be true, as a first approximation, if one disregards year-to-
year changes in the size of the market. One reviewer observes that the argument could be alternatively phrased in terms of the profit versus share tradeoff *permitting* point C to be on a higher
iso-PV curve than point B, thereby giving an incentive in present value terms to make the
tradeoff. However, it is not clear that the systematic behavior which was observed would thereby
emerge.

If at point C, with a prospective decline in earnings to point D, managers would tend to soften the blow by selling some of their market share, to gain position A.

Note that from one year to the next, the businesses broach varying levels of "present value" (according to the exogenously determined price and demand environment). But, in a given year, it is likely the "present value" of operating results for the current year need be reduced only through mismanagement. Nevertheless, managers could still alter the share-profits mix to be reported.

If competitive forces did not generate a true economic valuation of market share points—that is, if competitors were sleepy and permitted share points to be bought from them at less than their intrinsic economic worth, then other firms in the marketplace could improve the present value of their business by adjusting their mix of profit and market share results in any particular year.

Other considerations influence market share strategy, as has been noted. There is clearly a zone within which market shares are expected to lie in the long run. In the case of General Electric, for example, 60 percent plus or minus 10 percent, might describe the long-run share goal. Furthermore, if year after year the percentage return on sales (closely correlated with the percentage return on investment) fell below some minimum expectation level, top management would be compelled to consider liquidating the business—as did happen to Allis-Chalmers in the early 1960s.

We can therefore complete the graphical analysis by noting the existence of two other constraints operating on managers: a long-term market share goal or "norm," and a long-run minimum profit rate. These can be sketched as shown in Chart 13.6. Now the constrained nature of decentralized decision making is apparent. Operating managers were given a narrow target area (designated ABCD) within which to maneuver their business.

The motivation of managers to stay on the path of "preferred operating

CHART 13.6.   Fully Constrained Zone of Preferred Operating Results Which Guide
the Tactics of Operating Managers.

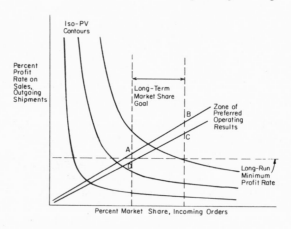

results" was probably a consequence of performance appraisal measures. In General Electric, these criteria emphasized total profits, market share, and return on investment. The investment base changes slowly, so return on investment performance is tantamount to total profits performance, over the career span of most managers. Total dollar profits were, in turn, a function of total dollar sales and the percentage profit rate on sales. Total dollar sales depend upon the exogenous total industry demand experienced in any one year, and percent market share. Thus, what the three performance measures boiled down to, *in terms of performance criteria the manager could be held accountable for in the short run*, were: *percentage earnings on sales, and the percentage market share.*

Top management held strong views as to the proper "balance" to be maintained between earnings and market share and communicated the preferred pattern of operating results to the operating management. Top management did not appreciate wild swings in market share nor in profit results. They much preferred steady, middle-of-the-road performance. They were wary of the operating manager who reported low share and high earnings: that manager could be accused of "milking the business." And they were seldom impressed by the operating manager reporting large gains in market share and very low earnings: he could be accused of neglecting the shareholders.

In the period 1951–1963, there was one occasion when General Electric's preferred change-of-share-change-of-earnings strategy was tested to the limit. This was prior to the White Sale of January 1955. During 1954, General Electric lost market share and simultaneously *gained* in earnings rate. This would be represented as a 90-degree tangent to the path of "preferred operating results"—and could be interpreted as selling market share to gain short-run profits. But after the White Sale, during 1955, General Electric *returned* to the long-term path of "preferred operating results," by simultaneously sacrificing profits and buying back market share. The reason for the White Sale, therefore, was that General Electric operating managers strayed from their normal share-earnings path during 1954, which necessitated a massive correction effort during 1955.

One final point of interest: there is evidence that the accounting systems of General Electric and Westinghouse were uniquely suited to the strategies of these respective competitors. In the turbine generator business, General Electric managed the timing of the reporting of its costs—and therefore of its earnings—in part through its accounting conventions, while Westinghouse did likewise. It seems that the General Electric system would tend to smooth over the year-to-year fluctuations in reported earnings, relieving some of the performance pressures which otherwise might force managers into short-sighted, short-term market behavior (see Appendix 17).

CHAPTER Fourteen The Simulation of Alternative Strategies in Oligopoly

THE PRECEDING CHAPTERS HAVE OUTLINED A MODEL of the turbine generator oligopoly in the United States and its relationship with the consumers of electrical energy and the middleman purveyors of electrical energy, the utility organizations. One may now explore the effect of *changes in strategies* by individual firms within the oligopoly. For example, we have observed an historical tendency for General Electric to "buffer" its smaller competitors, but what would happen to prices, profits, market shares, and utility reserve margins if General Electric implemented a *less* benevolent strategy? Or what would happen if General Electric directly sought to maximize its own short-run profits in this business? Or the joint profits of *all* competitors? To consider other possibilities, what would occur if the oligopolists behaved according to the theoretical assumptions of such students of oligopoly as Cournot, Bertrand, Fellner, or Baumol? The ramifications of alternative strategies in oligopoly are explored in this chapter, through mathematical simulation on the model.

By design, we have the building blocks for a complete system model, which is defined in Appendix 18. There are three major blocs: a sector in which turbine generator demand is created; a sector which explains the various elements of discretionary management behavior—or "strategy"—; and a sector in which turbine generator orders are processed into shipments.

"Strategy" is here used in the sense of the management decision rule which defines the market response of the oligopolist under all future circumstances. The interpretation of strategy as a recipe book for future actions was proposed by John von Neumann and Oskar Morgenstern: "A complete plan: a plan which specifies what choice the player will make in every possible situation, for every possible actual information which he may possess at that moment."[1] In the model, a strategy is defined by a system of equations which specifies management response for given values of other variables in the system. If demand is falling, for example, management may invariably reduce its manufacturing capacity.

In the present context, the specific strategic plans to be examined through simulation are those decision rules by which the oligopolist changes his *relative price*, in order to adjust his *market share*, and thence his flow of *orders* and its *output*. Other elements of the oligopolist's strategic plan remain unvarying in the analysis. Relative price is a strategy variable which management can control, but average market prices are exogenous to him, beyond direct control.

Relative price enters the simulation model in two places, first as an influence on customer behavior, second as an element of management strategy. First, it is an *explanatory* variable, one of several determinants of market share. Second, it is a *dependent* variable, established according to management decision rules which are changed in each simulation experiment. Changing the management decision rules which establish relative price will tend to change market shares, and thus the order flows to each competitor, factory loads, average market prices, and the financial results of each competitor. And via the feedback effect which backlogs have upon demand, alterations in the relative price decision rule will also alter utility ordering behavior, and, ultimately, electric power generating reserves. These are some of the indirect consequences of changes in business strategy which are measured in the simulation.

In the model, competitors are assumed to adjust both prices and output almost simultaneously. They adjust their relative prices in order to defend, yield, or increase their market share, in order to influence their volume of orders, and eventually their output. These assumptions, developed from the experience of the electrical industry, contrast with the curiously unreal dichotomy which prevails in many theoretical models of oligopoly and duopoly: the distinction which is made between "quantity-adjuster" decision rules, and "price-adjuster" decision rules.[2]

GOALS, OPERATING DECISIONS, AND RESULTS

The purpose of this simulation is to appraise the long-run consequences which are implied when management adopts any particular strategy or "game plan." It is necessary to distinguish among (1) goals, (2) operating decision

[1] John von Neumann and Oskar Morgenstern, *Theory of Games and Economic Behavior*, third edition (Princeton, N.J.: Princeton University Press, 1953), p. 79. Cited in D. K. Osborne, "The Duopoly Game: Output Variations," *American Economic Review*, December 1971, p. 539.

[2] For a discussion and experimental analysis of "price-adjuster" versus "quantity-adjuster" models of oligopoly see: Lawrence E. Fouraker and Sidney Siegel, *Bargaining Behavior* (New York: McGraw-Hill, 1963), Part Three.

rules, and (3) actual business results, because they will not always coincide. The freshman economics lecturer can maximize profits for the hypothetical firm with a stroke of chalk, but for the business manager the appropriate actions are seldom so obvious. There is an obvious practical distinction in business between the aspirations or goals of management (such as "maximize long-run profitability") and the operating decision rules which are adopted by management in the expectation of achieving that goal (such as "cut prices if we are losing market share"). In most of the computer simulations, we asserted some general goal, such as "maximize earnings," and then, exercising judgment (just as management must exercise judgment), we formulated a decision rule which might reasonably be expected to achieve that goal. Whether the goal will actually be achieved remains to be seen. In the jargon of economics, there is a distinction here between "subjective expectations" and "objective realizations"; between ex *ante* and ex *post*.[3]

As in real life, therefore, the bulk of our analysis proceeds from (1) the formulation of subjective expectations (goals) for the business, to (2) the judgmental specifications of concrete decision rules for the business (mathematical equations which define relative price in the simulation), to (3) the assessment of the actual operating results attained by the business when it was operated according to those decision rules. It will be interesting to contrast actual operating results with the original goals which were specified.

There are nine such "judgmental simulations." These simulations incorporate decision rules derived from goals, via a process of management judgment, in the hope of achieving some specified result.

There is an alternative mode of simulation analysis. We may specify some goal, such as "maximize total ten-year profits," and then search for the operating decision rule which actually achieves that result in the model. Here there is no distinction between goals and results; we force actual results to comply with our goals. For example, we may specify a decision rule for relative prices, based upon industry backlogs and market shares, and then search for the optimal set of coefficients relating relative prices to backlogs and to market share which will maximize total ten-year profits. Just how maximum is "maximum" will depend upon our cleverness in specifying variables to take into account in the decision rule which is to be optimized. Since in this mode of analysis we first specify the answer and then work backwards to the game plan which produces that result, it is not typically a decision-making approach which is feasible for management. Nevertheless, the results may be suggestive of appropriate strategies to achieve specified end results. The results of four such "optimizing" simulations are reported.

---

[3] For a discussion of this distinction, see: Howard W. Pifer, III, "A Comparison of Alternative Decision-Making Strategies Within a Simulated Oligopolistic Market," unpublished dissertation presented in partial fulfillment of the requirements for the degree of doctor of philosophy, Carnegie-Mellon University, Graduate School of Industrial Administration, 1969, Chapter 1.

Therefore, there are 13 different simulations in all, 9 "judgmental" and 4 "optimizing." The strategic thinking underlying each simulation is summarized in Table 14.1.

Results were simulated for 68 quarters encompassing the 17 years 1956–1972, under each of the 13 different decision rules. As noted earlier, the results assume that technological and manufacturing capacity strategies remained unchanged from those which were historically observed for 1948–1962. Only the decision rule concerning relative price was changed during the analysis.

The Judgmental Simulations

(1) *Actual Historical Behavior*

The first of the judgmental simulations was an extrapolation of actual historical 1951–1963 relative pricing behavior, over the full 1956–1972 simulation period. This would provide a benchmark, against which to compare other strategies. According to the analysis in Appendix 16, General Electric and its two competitors altered their relative price ratio so that General Electric tended to move upward in relative price (to an even higher premium price versus Westinghouse and Allis-Chalmers) when: (1) General Electric's earnings rate on sales had been high—motivated by the "balance" phenomenon in management reporting of share and profits operating results—; when (2) its historical market share had been high—the feedback mechanism which tends to hold the long-term market share within a narrow range—; and when (3) the average industry price level had been declining—the "buffering" phenomenon which implies that General Electric tends to undercut its competition in price only when industry price levels are rising, whereas it tends to hold a price umbrella over its competitors when average industry prices are falling. This rule was maintained without change over 1956–1972 in the first "judgmental" simulation.

(2) *Hold Long-Term Share and Buffer*

In the second simulation, actual historical behavior was modified to eliminate one of the three historical inputs to relative price: management's attempt to achieve a "balanced" reporting of profit and market share results. Under the historical 1948–1962 decision rule, managers of General Electric were assumed to yield market share when the profit rate on current shipments was high, as a matter of internal organizational tactics. And they would attempt to "buy back" market share when the profit rate was low. The presumed aim was to present a balanced operating picture to top management. In the second simulation, General Electric management was assumed to drop this objective, but to adhere still to the other goals of

TABLE 14.1.
SUMMARY OF ALTERNATIVE GOALS, ANTECEDENT THEORISTS, AND OPERATING DECISION RULES.

Goal	Antecedents
A. JUDGMENTAL SIMULATIONS	
(1) Hold long-term share, buffer, and invest profits in market share (actual historical behavior)	Actual historical GE behavior, by inference
(2) Hold long-term market share and buffer	Simplified version of actual historical behavior
(3) Hold long-term market share	Still more simplified version of actual historical behavior
(4) Harvest share, subject to minimum share constraint	Classical "milking" of a business
(5) Maximize profits, assuming competitors' output will not change	Augustin Cournot
(6) Maximize profits, assuming competitors' price will not change	Joseph Bertrand
(7) Maximize sales subject to minimum profit rate constraint	William Baumol
(8) Maximize short-term profits subject to no loss of market share	Franklin Fisher
(9) Achieve maximum growth in sales, subject to maximum market share constraint	Marris, Williamson
B. OPTIMIZING SIMULATIONS	
(10) Maximize total cumulative industry profits	William Fellner
(11) Maximize present value of the firm	Irving Fisher
(12) Maximize present value of the industry	Fellner modified
(13) Maximize ratio of profits to sales for firm	Maximize return on investment

TABLE 14.1. (*Continued*)

Operating Decision Rule in the Simulation

RELATIVE PRICE = 0.95 + 0.25 GE PROFIT RATE
  + .039 AVERAGE GE SHARE OF ORDERS (−4)
  − .024 DELTA INDUSTRY PRICE LEVEL

RELATIVE PRICE = .99 + .039 AVERAGE GE SHARE OF ORDERS (−4)
  −.024 DELTA INDUSTRY PRICE LEVEL

RELATIVE PRICE = 1.0 + 1/4 [AVG. GE SHARE (−4) − .60]

RELATIVE PRICE = 1.03

PERIOD 1, 3, 5 etc:

$$\text{RELATIVE PRICE} = \begin{cases} .90 \text{ IF WESHIPMENTS + ACSHIPMENTS RISING} \\ \quad \text{ABOVE PRIOR MAX.} \\ 1.10 \text{ IF WESHIPMENTS + ACSHIPMENTS} \\ \quad \text{FALLING BELOW PRIOR MIN.} \end{cases}$$

PERIOD 2, 4, 6 etc:

$$\text{RELATIVE PRICE} = \begin{cases} 1.10 \text{ IF GESHIPMENTS RISING ABOVE PRIOR} \\ \quad \text{MAX.} \\ .90 \text{ IF GESHIPMENTS FALLING BELOW PRIOR} \\ \quad \text{MIN.} \end{cases}$$

RELATIVE PRICE = .90 and 1.10 in successive periods

RELATIVE PRICE = .97 IF PROFIT RATE ⩾ .75 (10-YEAR PROFIT RATE)
  1.00 IF PROFIT RATE < .75 (10-YEAR PROFIT RATE)

RELATIVE PRICE = .98 + .04 AVERAGE GE SHARE OF ORDERS (−4)
  − .05 IF PROFIT RATE < .75 (10-YR. PROFIT RATE)

RELATIVE PRICE = 1.00 + .06 [GE Backlog in Years − 2.0]

RELATIVE PRICE = $a + b_1$ (HERF) + b_2 (DELTAPRICE)

RELATIVE PRICE = $a + b_1$ (HERF) + b_2 (DELTAPRICE)

RELATIVE PRICE = $a + b_1$ (HERF) + b_2 (DELTAPRICE)

RELATIVE PRICE = $a + b_1$ (HERF) + b_2 (DELTAPRICE)

maintaining in the long run its historical market share, and in the short run continuing to "buffer" competitors over the business cycle.

(3) Hold Long-Term Market Share

The third judgmental simulation was a further simplification of observed actual 1948–1962 strategic behavior. It is now assumed that the oligopolists have adjusted their individual prices, so that their relative prices tend to maintain the status quo in market shares. Thus, if the market share of General Electric is below 60 percent (perhaps because of the random assortment of buyers in the marketplace who have strong Westinghouse loyalties), General Electric will tend to become more aggressive in price and undercut Allis-Chalmers and Westinghouse. These actions to maintain the status quo in market shares are not ameliorated by buffering considerations, nor are they modified according to the tactics of a balanced internal reporting of results, such as characterized the decision rules of the first and second simulations.

The objective of maintaining 60 percent share of orders, regardless of conditions in the industry, is based upon the long-term market share actually achieved by General Electric. Under this decision rule, the leader establishes its relative price policy each quarter based upon the actually realized market shares for the twelve-month period just ended. The assumed pricing sensitivity is judgmentally determined. If General Electric's market share declines to 50 percent then it will lower its relative price to 2.5 percent beneath the industry average. On the other hand, if General Electric market share climbs to 70 percent, it will establish its relative price 2.5 percent greater than the industry average. This decision rule may be viewed as the most stolid, least provocative of the simulated decision rules for the leader firm. General Electric merely strives to hold its historical "fair share" of the business, disregarding other factors in the situation.

(4) Harvest Market Share

The fourth simulation is based upon the assumption that the management of the leader firm seeks short-term profit results. This leads to a "milking" or "harvesting" price policy. The operating decision rule is very simple: the leader's relative price is held at a constant, unvarying, 3 percent premium over the competition. The expectation is that General Electric will gradually divest its market share, while Westinghouse and Allis-Chalmers will gain.

However, in this simulation *as in all of the others*, each competitor is constrained by an upper bound and a lower bound upon market share. Because of the utility customers' desire for maintaining alternative sources of supply, and for reasons of antitrust, it is assumed that in the short run General Electric cannot drop below 20 percent market share under any circumstance, nor can it exceed 75 percent market share. The corresponding figures for Westinghouse, given its slightly weaker market position, are assumed to be 5 percent and 75 percent. Allis-Chalmers, even under the most optimistic assumptions, is not permitted to acquire more than 20 percent market share, in keeping with its historically lower customer acceptance in the industry. Also in line with historical experience, Allis-Chalmers is permitted to drop to as low as one half of one percent—but no lower.

Thus, these simulations rule out the exit of Allis-Chalmers or any other competitor from the turbine generator industry, regardless of how bleak their operating experience. In this respect, the simulations will fail to predict Allis-Chalmers' actual 1963 withdrawal from the industry, although it may accumulate such large losses in the simulation experiment that this decision could be predicted. The simulated results will depict the consequences of triopoly, not of the virtual duopoly which actually prevailed for part of the simulation period: 1964–1969. This fact aside, the constraints upon market share which are imposed during the simulation are quite loose, permitting a range of market share results which exceeds the actual range of market shares experienced over the 1948–1963 period.

(5) Maximize Profits—Output (Cournot)

This simulation incorporates the duopoly logic expounded by Augustin Cournot.[4] According to this famous model, each firm in a duopoly assesses the industry demand curve and his own costs, and then assumes that his rival's output will not change from its present rate, regardless of his own behavior. The duopolist establishes his own output rate accordingly, to maximize profits. In mirror-image fashion, the opposing duopolist reasons likewise. For Cournot's duopolists, output spirals upward and prices spiral downward to an eventual equilibrium. In this simulation we first adopt Cournot's assumptions *for the leader firm only*: General Electric's assumption is that the other two firms in the industry are not so naive as Cournot might suppose, but that they nevertheless may be persuaded to accept General Electric's market leadership if they can be assured of maintaining a constant rate of output. This means the leader (General Electric) will move forcefully to offset any cyclical *slack* in demand, and that (as an implicit reward) the leader (General Electric) will hope to be permitted, with not much resistance, to capture the bulk of any cyclical *growth* in demand. This may be viewed as an extreme version of the buffering strategy described earlier, but now applied to output and not to orders. This describes the strategy rule for one period (three months) of play in the simulation.

In the following period, the tables turn. Now it is Allis-Chalmers and

---

[4] Augustin Cournot, *Researches into the Mathematical Principles of the Theory of Wealth* (Homewood, Illinois: Richard D. Irwin, 1963).

Westinghouse who reason that General Electric should be content to hold its output constant. They will set their prices accordingly.

In the mechanics of this simulation to replicate Cournot-type thinking, the leader firm (General Electric) is assumed first to *cut* its prices 10 percent below the industry average, in order to increase market share, whenever the sum of its two rivals' shipments climbs above its previous historical maximum rate. Similarly, General Electric will *raise* its prices 10 percent above the industry average whenever its rivals' collective shipments drop below their previous historical minimum rate. The goal is to maintain an even flow of Allis-Chalmers plus Westinghouse collective shipments. In the long run, as total demand grows, General Electric intends to capture all of the growth in industry sales. General Electric's greater pricing flexibility in the face of any cyclical increase in demand is expected to produce this result.

But this goal may not be achieved because, in the very next period, the identical decision rule is applied by Allis-Chalmers and Westinghouse, against General Electric.

In this simulation, as "leadership" roles switch back and forth, there is a running tally of the maximum output in any quarter of each competitor, and the decision rules are revised or recalibrated each quarter as necessary.

It may be noted that our triopolists are playing a duopoly game, a feat which is facilitated by the staged structure of our model. The pivotal decision rule determines the relative price (and market shares) of General Electric versus Westinghouse-plus-Allis-Chalmers-together. Once the Westinghouse-plus-Allis-Chalmers-together market share has been determined in the simulation, the Allis-Chalmers market share alone is determined according to its historical 1948–1962 behavioral rule. Westinghouse acquires the residual market share. Market shares in the triopoly are thus established in two steps, first as a duopoly, then as a duopoly again.

(6) Maximize Profits—Price (Bertrand)

A rather similar set of assumptions is incorporated in the duopoly model of Bertrand. According to Bertrand, a duopolist would probably assume that his rival would not change his price, and, under this (mistaken) assumption, the duopolist would proceed, in Cournot-like fashion, to maximize his own profits by cutting prices despite repeated evidence of parallel, disrupting price-cutting inclinations on the opposing side. (Like Cournot, Bertrand apparently had little faith in the perspicacity of businessmen.) There would be no limit to the fall in Bertrand's price, since each producer would always believe he could double his output by underbidding the other and taking over the entire market.[5]

---

[5] Review by Joseph Bertrand of Cournot's *Researches into the Mathematical Principles of the Theory of Wealth*, in *Journal des Savants*, September 1883; see also discussion in Edward Hastings

We approximate the assumptions of Bertrand by permitting first the leader firm and then the two follower firms to undercut one another in price in turnabout fashion. In the very first quarter (three months) of the simulation, the leader firm of the moment is defined as being 10 percent *over* the average industry price level. In the very next quarter, he is a follower and 10 percent *under* the average industry price level. In the third quarter he is 10 percent *over* once more, and so the turnabout is repeated over the years. The taking of turns in price-cutting proceeds without end.

(7) Maximize Sales (Baumol)

William Baumol suggests that, "sales volume ranks ahead of profits as the main object of the oligopolist's concern."[6] But while sales may be the ultimate objective, Baumol observes also that the business must earn some minimum profit. Citing authorities such as John Lintner in addition to his own impressionistic judgments, Baumol concludes that the most realistic objective which describes the behavior of the oligopolistic firm is "sales maximization subject to a minimum profit constraint."[7]

Simulation #7 was an attempt to implement Baumol's objectives, from the perspective of the leader firm (General Electric). But how to maximize General Electric's revenues is not immediately obvious. The leader firm is torn between the option of increasing its market share—which will surely tend to drag down the average industry price level and damage sales revenues —and the alternative option of adopting a more passive stance in the marketplace—which may help to firm prices and revenues, but which may also lead to a loss of market share and physical sales volume.

It seems likely that management would judge the long-run sales volume benefits of acquiring market share as more than offsetting any short-run penalties incurred by reason of depressing the industry price level in the quest for market share. In other words, management may judge that it usually pays to buy market share. The decision rule which is implemented in this simulation is therefore the following: the relative price of the leader firm will be cut 3 percentage points below the industry average price so that it may acquire market share and long-run sales volume, subject to a minimum profit constraint. The constraint is the condition that the percentage profit rate on sales is not more than one quarter below the ten-year average for that firm. If this profit constraint is not met, the leader firm will alternatively adopt a "neutral" pricing stance, which means a price which is equal to the industry average.

Chamberlin, *The Theory of Monopolistic Competition*, 7th ed. (Cambridge, Mass.: Harvard University Press, 1960), pp. 35–37.

[6] William J. Baumol, *Business Behavior, Value and Growth*, rev. ed. (New York: Harcourt, Brace & World, 1967), Chapter Six.

[7] William J. Baumol, ibid., p. 49; and John Lintner, "Effect of Corporate Taxation on Real Investment," *American Economic Review*, Vol. XLIV, May 1954, p. 522.

We set the target operating profit equal to 20 percent of sales revenues (before tax).

(8) *Maximize Profits Subject to a Share Constraint (Franklin Fisher)*

Franklin Fisher and others have suggested that the oligopolistic firm may wish to maximize profits subject to a constraint upon sales or market share.[8] Once more, such a goal is easier to state than it is to implement, from a management viewpoint. In simulating the consequence of such a decision rule, the constraint upon market share may be borrowed from that which applied to the historical decision rule for General Electric over 1948–1962 (simulation #1). When market share slips, the leader will tend to cut prices. When his market share rises, he will move to a premium price. Beyond that, how are profits to be maximized? Unfortunately, Fisher's proposed objective function tends to have a built-in contradiction. The natural, controllable way to increase profits is to "sell off" some market share, by cutting marketing expenses, cutting product quality, and the like. But in the long run this will violate the market share constraint. In this simulation, we reason that the best which the manager can be instructed to do, in order to fulfill Fisher's objectives, is to do nothing as long as profits are rising *above* their historical maximum percentage of sales. However, when the profit rate is far below the 10-year average of 20 percent, the firm is assumed to cut prices rather sharply in order to increase market share, sales, and, hopefully, the future flow of profit dollars.

(9) *Maximize Growth (Marris, Williamson)*

The final simulation, of the nine which incorporated "judgmental" decision rules, considers the objective of growth for its own sake. Robin Marris and others have suggested that managers strive to maximize "prudent" growth for personal sociological reasons, and to forestall corporate raiders. According to Marris, managers "may influence the growth rate of required capacity (demand) by various policy decisions relating to diversification, prices and marketing expenditures, all of which, given the production techniques employed and the general level of internal efficiency, have contingent effects upon profitability. [Furthermore] the rate of efficient managerial expansion is limited. [And] profitability is a vital element in the final solution because if management is to feel reasonably secure and be reasonably fair to shareholders, there is a close relation between the rate of return and the maximum sustainable growth rate of capacity. Thus . . . the set of possible growth

---

8 Review of Baumol's *Business Behavior, Value and Growth*, in *Journal of Political Economy*, Vol. LXVIII, June 1960; also D. K. Osborne, "On the Goals of the Firm," *Quarterly Journal of Economics*, Vol. LXXVIII, November 1964; and D. K. Osborne, "The Duopoly Game: Output Variations," p. 544.

rates of demand is confronted with a set of safe growth rates of capacity."[9] The prudent growth objectives perceived by Marris have a counterpart in the personalized, complex utility functions of managers (incorporating, among other variables, the size of staff) which Williamson suggests may govern decisions within the firm.[10] Growth in staff and emoluments may be most easily justified by a growth in sales.

In the context of this research, Marris-type objectives of stimulating growth in industry demand through progressive price cuts and technological innovation are consistent with the long-run equilibrium model outlined in Chapter Two. In the short run, a manager operating according to this philosophy may be persuaded to be relatively neutral in price, so long as his sales revenues are growing at their average historical rate. However, when his sales revenues decline, he may attempt to increase his market share, so as to maintain the historical annual sales increase. This is the exact opposite of the "buffering" philosophy which apparently prevailed for the market leader over 1948–1962 in this industry. It recognizes the fact that total industry demand cannot be inflated through price cuts in the short run.

To implement the growth plan, it would be foolish indeed for managers to establish their decision rules based upon realized sales revenues. In this industry, by the time sales revenues decline it is too late for management to take any action which will alter the revenue situation at least for several years. This is because of the long lead time between orders and delivery in the turbine generator industry. It is more practical, if management is to operate under a constant growth philosophy, to maintain a steady *backlog* of orders, so as to be able to maintain the historical rate of billings increases even when the flow of total industry orders declines. In this simulation, therefore, General Electric is assumed to set its price relative to that of Westinghouse and Allis-Chalmers with the goal of maintaining two years of backlog in its own factories. If General Electric discovers its backlog to be less than two years, it will cut prices and gain in market share. If, on the other hand, General Electric has more than two years of backlog, it will premium price its turbines and lose market share in order not to disrupt the market price more than is necessary.

The sensitivity of General Electric's relative price behavior to its own backlog condition was set judgmentally: if backlogs are just equal to two years, then General Electric is assumed to premium price by one percentage point, which should just about maintain its current market share position. If General Electric backlogs rise to three years, then its relative price will be almost 7 percentage points over the industry average, which will lead to a

9 Robin Marris, *The Economic Theory of Managerial Capitalism* (New York: Basic Books, 1968), Chapter Six.

10 Oliver E. Williamson, *The Economics of Discretionary Behavior* (Englewood Cliffs, N.J.: Prentice-Hall, 1964), pp. 40–54.

rapid loss of share. On the other hand, if General Electric backlogs drop as low as one year, then General Electric prices will be less than 95 percent of the industry average, which will lead to a large gain in General Electric market share, all other market share factors being equal.

This maximum growth policy is the most "inward-looking" of the simulated strategies. It describes a market leader attempting to keep his own backlogs heavy, regardless of conditions in the marketplace, and regardless of the impact of this policy upon his other competitors. One may expect this policy to provoke maximum retaliation by the competitors, during any slowdown of demand.

OPTIMIZING SIMULATIONS

The next four simulations involved the optimization of the management decision rule, to achieve some maximum goal. The analytical procedure was the following: Assume the goal is to maximize total industry profits. First, a decision rule for the leader firm must be *specified*, as to the variables to which management will respond. For example, perhaps relative price is to be managed as a function of the current rate of inflation in industry selling prices. Next, the parameters of the decision rule must be assigned values in order to complete its mathematical definition (e.g., the coefficients which define the responsiveness of relative price to the rate of inflation in industry prices). The best possible set of parameters is then to be found through a search procedure; this will be the set of parameters which maximizes the sum of the operating profits of the three turbine generator competitors over the simulated 1956–1972 period.[11]

The critical issue is the specification of decision rule structure: what variables are to be included in the decision rule which governs relative price? Once that question has been decided, the computation of optimal coefficients

---

[11] The maximization procedure was the following: Values of the objective function (e.g., General Electric cumulative sales) were printed out for successive runs with the simulation model over 1956–1972, for all combinations of assigned values for the coefficients b_1 and b_2 in the decision rule:

$$\text{Relative price}_t = 1.00 + b_1 \, (\text{Herfindahl index}_{t-1})$$
$$+ \, b_2 \, (\text{price}_{t-1} - \text{price}_{t-5})$$

and the highest value of the objective function was selected by visual inspection. The search of possible combinations of b_1 and b_2 proceeded in two stages. First, b_1 was varied in ten steps from .4 to −.4, while b_2 was varied from .00075 to −.00075 in 10 steps. The results hinted that perhaps the range of search over values of b_2 was too narrow. Therefore, there was a wider search, in which b_1 was varied in 17 steps from .8 to −.8, and b_2 was varied in 17 steps from .0008 to −.0008, with a search for maxima among the resulting 289 values of the objective function. It is possible—but it seems unlikely—that local maxima were bypassed in this search. The risk seems low. The response surfaces were rather uniform over wide ranges of b_1 and b_2 coefficient values. The probability of overlooking some maximum would seem to be greatest in the vicinity of zero values of b_1 and b_2, where the search procedure was somewhat coarse.

for the decision rule is relatively straightforward. The specification of the decision rule must be judgmental, because to deduce an optimal specification for the structure of the decision rule itself appears to be computationally too great a burden. (Remember, we must assess optimality in the context of a quarterly 1956–1972 simulation of results, using a moderately complex model.)

Our best possible clues as to the most potent variables to consider are those factors which the electrical equipment conspirators concentrated upon in their illegal endeavor to rig the market in the 1950s. The conspiratorial meetings dwelt upon their respective market shares, and the trend in actual market prices.[12]

To accommodate the market share factor, we hypothesize that it would be useful to incorporate in the decision rule a measure of the current *disparity* in market shares. One such convenient measure is the Herfindahl index, given by the formula:

$$H = \sum_{i=1}^{3} S_i^2$$

where S_i is the market share of the ith firm.[13] The value of the Herfindahl index (denoted hereafter as HERF), will increase with rising inequality in market shares among the three firms. This index of market share disparity will be one input into the relative pricing decision. It is computed during each period of the simulation, in the repeated simulation trials to find the optimal decision coefficients.

For the second management decision input, we take a form of the pricing variable which was, it appears, historically important in pricing decisions over 1948–1962: the *change* in the industry price level as measured in each quarter over the preceding twelve months (denoted hereafter as DELTA-PRICE).

The two inputs will be related linearly to relative price, a specification adopted for ease of interpretation. Thus, the specified form of the management decision rule for relative price is:

RELATIVE PRICE$_t$ = a + b$_1$ (HERF$_t$) + b$_2$ (DELTAPRICE$_t$).

Optimal values of the coefficients a, b$_1$ and b$_2$ are now to be computed, so as to maximize, for example, the combined 17-year sum of operating profits for Allis-Chalmers, Westinghouse, and General Electric in the turbine generator business. The actual objectives which were maximized in each of these four simulations, will now be described:

---

[12] See Ralph G. M. Sultan, *Pricing in the Electrical Oligopoly*, Vol. I (Boston, Mass.: Harvard Business School, Division of Research, 1974).

[13] For a discussion of the origins of the Herfindahl index see: Frederic M. Scherer, *Industrial Market Structure and Economic Performance* (Chicago: Rand McNally, 1970), p. 51.

(10) *Maximize Sales: Leader Firm* (*Fellner*)

In the first of the "optimizing" simulations, we search for the optimum decision rule in order to maximize *sales revenue* for the leader firm, General Electric. The only constraint is that the market share of the leader firm cannot exceed 75 percent.

We maximize sales revenue directly. There is no attempt to constrain the leader's actions according to his profit situation, unlike the Baumol-type simulation (#7). Nor is there any indirect attempt to maximize sales by maintaining constant backlogs (simulation #9). The procedure we follow is to run the model to discover the maximum sales result over a broad range of values for the coefficients of a predetermined decision rule: that decision rule which relates the competitors' relative prices to the index of the market share disparities, and to the trend in the market price.

(11) *Maximize Present Value of the Leader Firm* (*Irving Fisher*)

For the next simulation we discard such narrow measures of success as current sales and profits, to consider instead the long-run value of the enterprise.

This seems important because in such a long-cycle business as turbine generators, to maximize the flow of *current* earnings may rape the enterprise, while a single-minded building of market share may be equally unsound: A Pyrrhic victory with no economic return. Any balanced measure of success must therefore consider both the current stream of earnings and the value of the market position which is finally achieved. Therefore, our goal is assumed to be to maximize the "present value" or "present worth" of the enterprise, taking into account the time value of money. We seek the decision rule which will maximize the leader firm's future stream of operating earnings, plus the ending value of his business, all discounted at an 8 percent interest rate. The theoretical tradition being exploited here is that of Irving Fisher.[14] The end position of the business is valued at its potential selling price, which is assumed to be 10 times its 1972 earnings.

If the leader firm is to maximize its present value, it must move cautiously. The firm cannot yield too much in market share. The earnings stream may be depressed over the 1956–1972 period but the end result could be to build a business with a very high 1972 earnings flow. Neither can it move so aggressively as to damage its competitors unduly and force them into desperation acts which will depress the market price and short-term earnings for all. As in the other simulations, the leader firm is constrained in market share by antitrust considerations, and by the customers' desire to maintain dual or triple sources of supply. And it must consider the time value of money, a

---

[14] Irving Fisher, *The Theory of Interest* (New York: Augustus M. Kelley, 1961).

factor which discourages simple "building" strategies which forsake profits of the moment for success in the very long run. The coefficients a, b_1, and b_2 are assigned values through heuristic search, in order to accomplish all of this in the best possible way.

(12) *Maximize Total Industry Profits (Fellner)*

Many economists are drawn to the conclusion that the result of oligopolistic competition will be cooperative action to exploit maximum *joint* gain at the expense of customers. The electrical equipment industry is often cited as an excellent case history illustrating this tendency.[15]

Fellner, on strictly theoretical grounds, concluded that oligopolists would tend to arrive at decisions which yielded "qualified" *joint-profit maximization*. Qualifications would arise in part because of (1) an unwillingness on the part of the participants in the oligopoly to pool all of their resources and all of their earnings, (2) differences in their costs, which would lead to differences in desired prices and outputs, (3) incompleteness of coordination, and (4) long-run considerations which prompted them to consider the present value of the enterprise, rather than today's joint profits alone.[16]

We may use the turbine generator industry model to ascertain what behavior on the part of the leader firm would lead to maximum joint profits for all of the oligopolists in the industry over the 17 years of the simulation. By joint profits we refer to the cumulative operating profits in the turbine generator business of Westinghouse, Allis-Chalmers, and General Electric combined. It is the sum which counts; we sweep under the rug the interesting second-order question of how those profits are to be divided up among the three firms. That is a "side payments" issue, the bargaining and legality of which are not at issue here.

(13) *Maximize Total Industry Present Value*

The final simulation combines elements of the thinking of William Fellner and Irving Fisher. Once more we assume collective action, or perfect collusion, and we establish as the objective of the oligopoly the maximization of total industry present value. This is the sum of the present values of Allis-Chalmers, of Westinghouse, and of General Electric. The division of the spoils is once more ignored. The computation of the present worth in 1956 of the earnings stream of each business over 1956–1972, and the assessment of the terminal value in 1972 of each business, follow the procedures outlined in the previous sections.

---

15 See, for example, Frederic M. Scherer, *Industrial Market Structure and Economic Performance*, Chapter Six.

16 William Fellner, *Competition Among the Few, Oligopoly and Market Structures* (New York: Augustus M. Kelley, 1960), Chapter Seven.

Maximizing total industry present value, instead of the present value of the leader firm alone (simulation #11) may be predicted to yield a more extreme market behavior. It seems possible, for example, that the highest present value for the industry would result if production was concentrated at the (antitrust defined) upper limit of market share for the leader firm, and with the market share of the high-cost number three competitor hovering at its lowest possible constrained level. This result could arise because of the lower costs and greater earning capacity of the leader firm. It would seem to pay the industry to concentrate its production with the lowest cost supplier. Remember, however, that the other strategic rules, particularly those which attribute an arms' race factory expansion mentality to the oligopolists, remain unaltered even in this cooperative world, so the obvious conclusions may not apply.

CRITERIA

Space obviously does not permit a full reporting of results for every competitor, every period, and every variable in the simulations. Results are reported for market shares, operating profits, sales, factory utilization, backlogs and overhead spending, for the individual competitors, and for the industry as a whole. The present values as of late 1955 for each competitor and for the total industry, are reported for each strategy. These are all important criteria of business success.

Standard deviations on each firm's earnings, sales, percentage earnings, and backlogs are also reported. These provide a measure of risk, or the degree of the "peaceful life" which each oligopolist can enjoy under each strategy.

WELFARE EFFECTS

The welfare effects of each strategy are also important. A key measure of performance is the ability of the industry to maintain an adequate, but not excessive, reserve of generating capacity in the utility sector. This model was not constrained so that utility electric power peak loads could not exceed the available generating capacity. Negative reserves would therefore be one obvious indication of inadequate load forecasting and inadequate manufacturer response. Very high utility reserves margins, on the other hand, would indicate an excess investment in generating capacity. Any indication of negative reserves could be assumed to force the utilities to purchase short-term "peaking" capacity, such as gas turbine plants, a phenomenon which was not directly accommodated within the model, and which was fortunately not necessary, given the simulation results.

Also reported are two other indicators of general welfare consequences: the percentage utilization of manufacturing capacity, and the average (and standard deviation) of the industry price level. It is conventional to describe as deleterious to consumer welfare, any condition of consistently elevated and inflexible prices and chronic idle manufacturing capacity. When very high profit rates are obtained as well, the denunciations ·can be loud and clear.

Such short-run criteria must be tempered by the model of long-term equilibrium outlined in Chapter Two, describing the relationship between prices and the funding of overhead and the rate of technological progress. The analysis of Chapter Two suggests that short-term results which appear deleterious to welfare under the conventional standards, could be highly beneficial in the long run, through accelerated funding of technology.

It will also be interesting to assess the simulation results to the degree "good performance" is correlated with changing market shares. Conventional wisdom holds that "deconcentration" is a good thing.[17] But recent developments in game theory suggest that a high degree of *disparity* in market shares may indeed be preferable from a welfare perspective, if there is to be concentration at all.[18] The results of the simulation may cast some light upon the relationship between the "bust up" of the oligopoly, the equalization of market shares, and industry performance.

OTHER KEY ASSUMPTIONS

The market share constraints prohibited any single firm from taking 100 percent of industry orders, and they permitted no firm to be driven out of the industry completely. These were the only constraints applied. For example, it was conceivable that kilowatts shipments for a firm could exceed its manufacturing capacity, through operation of facilities beyond their standard rated capacity, and through heavy use of subcontracting, such as actually occurred in this industry during the late 1950s and again during the late 1960s. Operation beyond 100 percent of capacity was indeed common in the simulations.

The economic environment of the simulation is that which actually prevailed over 1956–1972. In other words, the key exogenous driving variable was the Federal Reserve Board index of industrial production and it was assigned the actual values which it experienced for 1956–1972. The simulation therefore encompasses two boom periods in the economy (1956–1958 and 1960–1969) and two recessions (1958–1959 and 1970–1971).

Some potential simulation problems which did *not* arise, should be noted. In large measure, the predetermined variables of each time period were

---

[17] For the most recent deconcentration thrust in terms of federal legislation, see Senator Hart: S.3832, a bill to supplement the antitrust laws, and to protect trade and monopoly power, and for other purposes, called the "Industrial Reorganization Act." *Congressional Record*, Vol. 118, No. 115, Washington, D.C., July 24, 1972.

[18] For a provocative analysis of this point, see: D. K. Osborne, "The Duopoly Game: Output Variations," p. 557.

endogenous variables from the previous period. The simulation was run over 68 time periods, accumulating the errors and biases of the model and feeding them back into the next period's solution. Despite the obvious potential for an accumulation or explosion of errors, the actual simulation results were stable, believable, and revealing.

RESULTS

A comparison of the 13 simulated strategies is presented in Tables 14.2 through 14.10.

TABLE 14.2.
AVERAGE MARKET SHARES, 1956–1972.[a]

Simulated Strategy	Allis-Chalmers	Westinghouse	General Electric
(1) Historical behavior	15.7%	32.4%	51.9%
(2) GE hold share, buffer	16.3	42.1	41.6
(3) GE hold share	13.4	28.9	57.7
(4) GE harvest	18.9	60.7	20.4
(5) Cournot	8.1	28.4	63.5
(6) Bertrand	10.2	39.1	50.6
(7) Baumol	9.3	39.7	50.9
(8) F. Fisher	8.3	23.8	67.9
(9) Marris	16.7	38.9	44.3
(10) Max. sales: GE	2.1	22.9	75.0
(11) Max. PV: GE	14.9	25.5	59.6
{(12) Max. profits: industry	16.3	41.2	42.5
{(13) Max. PV: industry			

[a] Average of percent market share reported for each quarter; thus not weighted according to volume of business in each quarter.

(1) Extrapolation of Historical Behavior: the Benchmark Run

The first or benchmark simulation was based upon an extrapolation through 1972 of observed historical behavior. The resulting average market shares for Allis-Chalmers, Westinghouse, and General Electric were respectively 16 percent, 32 percent and 52 percent, virtually no violation of the status quo of earlier years. It will be recalled that competitors' relative prices were adjusted with the goal, among others, of maintaining the historical market shares; in this respect the intended results were actually achieved.

It is more difficult to compare intended versus actual results for the other two goals: profit balancing and buffering. However, all of the competitors had simulated 1956–1972 profits which were reasonably consistent with their historical experience. None of the competitors was driven "to the wall," nor was any competitor more successful than an extrapolation of history would have indicated it to be. Thus the profit trade-offs and the buffering which

TABLE 14.3.
AVERAGE SALES REVENUE, 1956–1972.
(*Millions of Dollars Per Quarter*)[a]

Simulated Strategies	Allis-Chalmers	Westinghouse	General Electric	Total Industry
	$	$	$	$
(1) Historical behavior	18.1 ± 12.9	22.1 ± 11.5	71.3 ± 37.4	111.5 ± 54.7
(2) GE hold share and buffer	19.3 ± 13.7	30.0 ± 16.3	62.6 ± 31.5	111.9 ± 55.7
(3) GE hold share	16.3 ± 12.9	23.7 ± 12.4	70.8 ± 34.7	110.8 ± 54.2
(4) GE harvest	22.3 ± 13.7	45.9 ± 27.9	41.1 ± 14.2	109.2 ± 52.4
(5) Cournot	11.2 ± 9.2	23.4 ± 12.9	73.3 ± 37.0	107.8 ± 53.8
(6) Bertrand	11.7 ± 6.5	30.0 ± 22.4	64.3 ± 29.3	106.0 ± 51.5
(7) Baumol	11.6 ± 9.7	32.3 ± 22.0	61.9 ± 32.7	106.0 ± 57.0
(8) F. Fisher	9.9 ± 8.2	20.0 ± 8.5	78.4 ± 40.5	108.0 ± 51.9
(9) Marris	20.3 ± 12.9	27.5 ± 14.2	62.5 ± 35.4	110.0 ± 53.7
(10) Max. sales: GE	4.7 ± 3.9	19.8 ± 8.0	80.2 ± 41.0	105.0 ± 50.0
(11) Max. PV: GE	17.7 ± 12.6	17.2 ± 8.9	76.8 ± 40.0	112.0 ± 54.5
(12) Max. profits: industry (13) Max. PV: industry	18.6 ± 13.5	32.9 ± 21.3	60.2 ± 28.8	111.7 ± 52.0

[a] Figures shown are the 1956–1972 average of sales per quarter, and the 1956–1972 standard deviation, computed on a quarterly basis.

TABLE 14.4.
AVERAGE OPERATING PROFITS, 1956–1972.
(*Millions of Dollars Per Quarter*)[a]

Simulated Strategy	Allis-Chalmers	Westinghouse	General Electric	Industry
	$	$	$	$
(1) Historical behavior	0.8 ± 2.8	3.0 ± 5.2	14.3 ± 8.9	18.1 ± 11.3
(2) GE hold share and buffer	1.3 ± 3.4	3.6 ± 6.2	15.3 ± 7.9	20.2 ± 12.3
(3) GE hold share	0.8 ± 2.8	3.3 ± 4.9	15.0 ± 10.7	19.2 ± 12.9
(4) GE harvest	2.1 ± 4.7	6.0 ± 9.9	15.9 ± 5.3	24.0 ± 14.0
(5) Cournot	0.7 ± 1.9	3.2 ± 4.1	13.8 ± 13.3	17.7 ± 12.9
(6) Bertrand	0.17 ± 2.0	3.6 ± 8.0	12.8 ± 7.6	16.6 ± 12.7
(7) Baumol	−0.35 ± 3.4	3.7 ± 6.5	14.2 ± 13.9	17.6 ± 13.5
(8) F. Fisher	0.88 ± 1.9	3.2 ± 3.5	13.8 ± 12.8	17.9 ± 12.9
(9) Marris	1.4 ± 4.4	3.4 ± 6.4	14.3 ± 7.8	19.1 ± 11.2
(10) Max. sales: GE	1.2 ± 0.9	3.1 ± 2.4	11.8 ± 12.9	16.1 ± 13.6
(11) Max. PV: GE	0.89 ± 2.6	3.2 ± 4.3	14.4 ± 10.9	18.2 ± 11.1
(12) Max. profits: industry (13) Max. PV: industry	0.70 ± 3.7	4.7 ± 6.0	14.0 ± 6.4	19.4 ± 12.4

[a] Figures shown are the 1956–1972 average of pretax profits per quarter and the 1956–1972 standard deviations, computed on a quarterly basis.

TABLE 14.5.
AVERAGE OPERATING PROFIT RATE, 1956–1972.[a]

Simulated Strategy	Allis-Chalmers	Westinghouse	General Electric	Industry
	%	%	%	%
(1) Historical behavior	4.4	13.6	20.0	16.2
(2) GE hold share, buffer	6.9	12.0	24.4	18.1
(3) GE hold share	5.3	14.2	21.1	17.4
(4) GE harvest	9.2	13.2	38.7	22.0
(5) Cournot	6.3	13.6	18.8	16.4
(6) Bertrand	1.5	12.0	19.9	15.6
(7) Baumol	−3.0	11.5	23.0	16.6
(8) F. Fisher	8.9	16.2	17.6	16.5
(9) Marris	7.1	12.2	22.8	17.3
(10) Max. sales: GE	26.0	15.5	14.7	15.4
(11) Max. PV: GE	5.0	18.7	18.7	16.6
{ (12) Max. profits: industry (13) Max. PV: industry	3.7	14.3	23.3	17.4

[a] Average 1956–1972 profits before income tax divided by average 1956–1972 sales.

TABLE 14.6.
PRESENT VALUE: MILLIONS OF DOLLARS, 1956.[a]

Simulated Strategy	Allis-Chalmers	Westinghouse	General Electric	Total
	$	$	$	$
(1) Historical behavior	51	158	791	1000
(2) GE hold share, buffer	85	228	799	1112
(3) GE hold share	78	171	794	1043
(4) GE harvest	132	392	755	1279
(5) Cournot	24	172	790	986
(6) Bertrand	16	215	683	914
(7) Baumol	−23	264	743	984
(8) F. Fisher	29	166	782	977
(9) Marris	80	160	738	978
(10) Max. sales: GE	34	172	715	921
(11) Max. PV: GE	54	150	786	990
{ (12) Max. profits: industry (13) Max. PV: industry	55	306	682	1043

[a] Operating profits plus ten times final period earnings, all discounted at 8 percent.

TABLE 14.7.
AVERAGE RATE OF OVERHEAD SPENDING.
(Millions of Dollars Per Quarter, 1956–1972)

Simulated Strategy	Allis-Chalmers	Westinghouse	General Electric	Total
	$	$	$	$
(1) Historical behavior	2.9	4.5	8.4	15.8
(2) GE hold share, buffer	3.1	6.1	7.6	16.8
(3) GE hold share	2.7	4.8	8.4	15.9
(4) GE harvest	3.6	9.2	5.8	18.6
(5) Cournot	1.9	4.7	8.6	15.3
(6) Bertrand	2.1	6.0	7.8	15.9
(7) Baumol	2.1	6.5	7.6	16.3
(8) F. Fisher	1.8	4.1	9.1	14.9
(9) Marris	3.3	5.5	7.4	16.3
(10) Max. sales: GE	1.0	4.0	9.3	14.4
(11) Max. PV: GE	2.9	3.5	8.9	15.3
{ (12) Max. profits: industry (13) Max. PV: industry	3.0	6.7	7.5	17.2

TABLE 14.8.
AVERAGE INDUSTRY ORDER PRICE INDEX, 1956–1972.

Simulated Strategy	Price Index (1961 = 100)	Standard Deviation
(1) Historical behavior	97	35
(2) GE hold share, buffer	100	38
(3) GE hold share	96	37
(4) GE harvest	106	40
(5) Cournot	93	39
(6) Bertrand	94	32
(7) Baumol	96	43
(8) F. Fisher	92	38
(9) Marris	102	38
(10) Max. sales: GE	86	33
(11) Max. PV: GE	95	38
{ (12) Max. profits: industry (13) Max. PV: industry	100	33

TABLE 14.9.
AVERAGE INDUSTRY MANUFACTURING CAPACITY UTILIZATION,
1956–1972.[a]

Simulated Strategy	% Utilization
(1) Historical behavior	120
(2) GE hold share, buffer	122
(3) GE hold share	118
(4) GE harvest	128
(5) Cournot	117
(6) Bertrand	115
(7) Baumol	119
(8) F. Fisher	115
(9) Marris	124
(10) Max. sales: GE	112
(11) Max. PV: GE	117
(12) Max. profits: industry (13) Max. PV: industry	122

[a] Average of the percent capacity utilization reported in each quarter.

TABLE 14.10.
UTILITY RESERVES OF GENERATING CAPACITY.

Simulated Strategy	Ending Value 1972	Standard Deviation 1956–1972
	%	
(1) Historical behavior	22.0	2.9
(2) GE hold share, buffer	22.0	2.8
(3) GE hold share	21.8	3.1
(4) GE harvest	22.1	2.8
(5) Cournot	21.6	3.0
(6) Bertrand	21.9	2.8
(7) Baumol	21.5	3.3
(8) F. Fisher	21.9	3.1
(9) Marris	21.8	2.7
(10) Max. sales: GE	21.8	3.2
(11) Max. PV: GE	21.9	3.1
(12) Max. profits: industry (13) Max. PV: industry	22.4	2.6

we embodied in the decision rule seem to have been accomplished as well over the 1956–1972 period.

In this benchmark simulation, sales and profit results were as follows:

	1956–1972 average dollars per quarter
Allis-Chalmers	$18.1 ± $12.9 million
Westinghouse	$22.1 ± $11.5 million
General Electric	$71.3 ± $37.4 million
Total Industry	$111.5 ± $54.7 million

These simulation results are in accord with the historical 1948–1962 variance in sales revenues for these three competitors.

A word on scaling. The cumulative sales revenue for the industry, over the full 17-year simulated history, was $7.58 billion (17 years × 4 quarters × $111.5 million average). These amounts are approximately "in the ballpark" with official U.S. government statistics on the industry. But the dollar amounts in these simulations should be interpreted as indicating only the *relative* situation of the industry under alternative strategies. It is not prudent to accept, as real-world data, the literal dollar results.[19] This is because of the incomplete coverage of the industry which was inherent in the original historical figures derived from the electrical litigation.

The reported market share statistic for 1956–1972 is the average of the individual (quarter-by-quarter) figures, calculated on a *physical* kilowatts *orders* basis. These market shares obviously do not coincide with market shares which could be computed on the alternative basis of the quarterly *dollar* amounts of revenue from *shipments*. Market shares on an aggregate dollars-of-revenue-basis were 16 percent, 20 percent and 64 percent over the simulated period, as contrasted with 16 percent, 32 percent, and 52 percent when based upon physical orders.

Average operating profits in this benchmark simulation were:

	Average 1956–1972 operating profits per quarter
Allis-Chalmers	$ 0.8 ± $2.8 million
Westinghouse	$ 3.0 ± $5.2 million
General Electric	$14.3 ± $8.9 million
Total Industry	$18.1 ± $11.3 million

The standard deviations shown above hint at what actually did occur: a frequent dipping "into the red" for Allis-Chalmers in this benchmark simulation, and a tendency for Westinghouse to operate at a loss from time to time as well. General Electric, on the other hand, operated at a loss in only one quarter of the full 68-quarter simulation period, and its fluctuation in profits, while largest of all firms, was still smaller in comparison with its average profits. These results again coincide with the actual historical behavior of the profits in this industry.

---

[19] In 1963, the approximate mid-year of the simulation, the steam engine and turbine generator industry actually shipped $475 million, according to Department of Commerce census figures. This is equivalent to a rate of shipments of $118.8 million per quarter. Thus, the magnitude of the dollar data in the simulation may be "in the ballpark," in terms of the actual industry. However, to be safe, it is best to view the numbers as representative of the *relative* situation in the industry, and not as a precise forecast of actual dollar amounts. See: U.S. Department of Commerce, Bureau of the Census, *1963 Census of Manufactures*, Report MC63(2)-35A, *Engines and Turbines and Farm Machinery* Equipment, Major Group 35 (Washington: U.S. Government Printing Office, 1966), page 35A-46, referring to industry or product class 3511, for value of shipments of 13 establishments in 1963.

The profit rate (calculated as cumulative 1956–1972 pretax operating profits divided by cumulative 1956–1972 sales revenues[20]) displayed a familiar hierarchy of results in the first simulation.

	Average 1956–1972 operating profits
Allis-Chalmers	4.4% of sales
Westinghouse	13.6% of sales
General Electric	20.0% of sales

The present value of the Allis-Chalmers, Westinghouse, and General Electric turbine generator businesses, computed by discounting their profit flows and their end (1972) values to 1956, were $51 million, $158 million, and $791 million respectively, giving a total industry present worth of $1 billion as of 1956.

Average overhead expenditures, an indicator of the capability of the industry to fund advanced technologies, were $2.9 million, $4.5 million, and $8.4 million per quarter, respectively, giving a total industry average of $15.8 million per quarter. The industry is spending about 14 percent of sales on overhead activities of all types, including technology.

Backlogs of unfilled orders were of a magnitude which was consistent with historical experience, when appraised in terms of years of manufacturing capacity.

In the first benchmark simulation, the average order price index was 97, computed according to a base of the 1961 book price equal to 100. A measure of the flexibility (or lack of "rigidity") in pricing, is given by the standard deviation of the price index. In the first simulation, the standard deviation was 35, indicating considerable cyclical movement in prices.

Two other measures of industry performance, under the first simulation, are the average percentage utilization of industry manufacturing capacity (which was 120 percent) and the average utility reserve of generating capacity, which was an ample 22 percent at the end of the simulation period. It was clear in all of the simulations that the average utilization of factory capacity tended to be very high by actual historical standards, because of the conservatism of the manufacturing capacity decision built into the model.

While there was some change in the standard deviation of the percent reserves statistic from one simulation to the next, the *average* reserves position of the utilities over 1956–1972 did not vary from one strategy to the next. In

---

[20] In the reported results, the average 1956–1972 profit rate (profits as a percent of sales) was based upon the cumulative 1956–1972 profits divided by the cumulative 1956–1972 sales, for each competitor and for the industry as a whole. The standard deviation of the profit rate, however, was computed on the basis of the time series of the percentage profit rate experienced by each firm in each quarter. The mean of this time series was not, therefore, identical to the average profit rate which was reported. In assessing economic results, it is the cumulative average which seems more relevant.

other words, there was but modest feedback from the alternative manufacturer strategies to utility reserves.

(2) *Hold Market Share and Buffer*

By dropping the goal of managing its profit-market share balance, General Electric unexpectedly loses about 10 percentage points in market share, share points which are largely gained by Westinghouse. The change in Allis-Chalmers' market position is essentially zero. The result is that Westinghouse now has a slightly higher average market share (42.1 percent) than does General Electric (41.6 percent). This simulation is our best example of the restructuring of market positions to obtain two evenly matched competitors in the oligopoly.

Clearly, the General Electric goal of maintaining market share has now been outweighed by its goal of buffering the competition, and Westinghouse is the gainer. General Electric declines in average sales volume, but the strategy also decreases the volatility of its sales revenues; for Westinghouse the opposite is true: sales volume increases but so does the variance of sales over time. General Electric has gained some stability of sales and profit results by surrendering its goal of balancing the reported mix of profit and market share in each period.

For all three competitors, reported average profits are considerably higher under this strategy. General Electric and Allis-Chalmers also enjoy an increase in their profit *rate*. Indeed, this simulation yields one of the highest average *industry* profit rates of any simulation (18.1 percent), and one of the highest average industry dollar profits. The equalization of market shares, and General Electric's dropping of its endeavor to "manage" its annual profit and share reports, has, if anything, increased the ability of the industry to earn long-run profits.

Given the increases in long-run earnings, it is not surprising that the present worth of the industry has also climbed by about 11 percent, by comparison with the benchmark strategy. This is one of the very highest present worth results of any strategy. The gains in present worth are not, however, evenly distributed: the present worth of Allis-Chalmers climbs by 66 percent, that of Westinghouse by 44 percent, and that of General Electric by only 1 percent—tantamount to no change.

It is noteworthy that throughout the many diverse permutations of strategy which were explored via this model, virtually *none* yielded a higher present value to General Electric than that of the benchmark run, which was simulating the historical policy that General Electric was observed to be already following. The historical 1948–1962 behavioral rules of General Electric resulted in the very "best" economic performance for that firm, if one accepts the philosophy that the maximizing of present value is the most rational economic goal for the profit-seeking enterprise. Through accident or wisdom, General Electric managers had adopted a strategy which we could not improve upon.

What is the impact of strategy #2 upon technology? We offer some speculations: overhead spending, in the industry aggregate, rises, but the individual firms show a mixed response. General Electric cuts its overhead spending, while Allis-Chalmers and Westinghouse increase theirs significantly by comparison with the benchmark run. The overhead spending rate is a useful indicator of the *feasibility* of spending but not necessarily of *actual* spending on advanced technology.

Unfortunately, it is not possible to draw a firm conclusion. Certainly the redistribution of market shares means that the industry is now spending more on overhead in the aggregate, by reason of the accelerated overhead spending of Westinghouse and Allis-Chalmers. But some portion of their increase in overhead spending, according to our previous theorizing, is required just to support their increase in sales volume, and the ability of General Electric to fund advanced technology from discretionary overhead funds has certainly been reduced.

Overall, the results of strategy #2 must be viewed as unfavorable to General Electric. Its once commanding market position is eroded. It is more susceptible to a bold attack by Westinghouse, which indeed creeps ahead of General Electric in average market share. This greater risk of attack might have been compensated by a dramatic gain in the net worth of General Electric's business, but along this dimension there has in fact been virtually no gain.

For Westinghouse and Allis-Chalmers the results of this strategy are clearly favorable. Sales and market shares are increased, and profits climb. Westinghouse has moved into an excellent position from which to launch an attempt to seize the front-runner position.

The consumer may not have benefited much under strategy #2. Prices are about 3 percent higher, on the average. Utility reserves of generating capacity are about average.

(3) Hold Market Share

The aim of the third strategy is to hold the market share of General Electric in the vicinity of 60 percent. The objectives of managing the profit-share balance, and of buffering competitors, are gone.

On average, the hoped-for objective was actually achieved. Market shares were in the proportions of 13 percent, 29 percent and 58 percent for Allis-Chalmers, Westinghouse, and General Electric, respectively. Compared with the benchmark situation, General Electric's share has increased slightly, whereas that of Westinghouse and Allis-Chalmers has declined. The sales and profits results, however, are similar to those under the benchmark strategy. Profit rates are only slightly higher, present values are somewhat higher, and so is overhead spending. The average industry price index has been pushed down an average of 1 percentage point below the benchmark, and ending utility reserves have declined a very modest amount (21.8 percent).

On balance, the average 1956–1972 results under this strategy do not display much interesting variation from the benchmark run. In terms of the *ending* position of the players, however, it is noteworthy that General Electric's strategy of holding market share ultimately fails. Westinghouse emerges from the contest holding 41 percent of the orders in 1972, while General Electric has been driven down to 39 percent. Allis-Chalmers completes the run at its constrained upper limit of 20 percent market share.

(4) Harvest

The fourth simulation produced unique and interesting results: this was the "harvest" strategy, under which General Electric moved to hold a constant 3 percent premium over the market price, whatever that market price happened to be. (This was the ultimate in holding a price umbrella over one's competitors.)

There was a drastic reduction in the General Electric market position. It averaged only 20.4 percent share of orders, barely above its constrained bottom limit. Westinghouse picked up the lion's share of the business (60.7 percent). Allis-Chalmers also expanded (18.9 percent). For the latter two competitors these were the highest average market shares recorded under any simulation. This "harvest" simulation represents the extreme in switching of ranks in the marketplace. General Electric is in full retreat.

Because it divested the bulk of its market share, General Electric received the very lowest sales volume under the harvest strategy by comparison with all of the other simulation results. But, in contrast, *it also achieved the very highest profit results.* Dollar profits were at their peak, as was the profit rate (39 percent). No other strategy could beat "harvest" in generating short-term profits.

It would be reasonable to suspect that the cost of such a rich profit flow would be a very low-end value of the business, which would in turn be reflected in its present worth. However, in terms of present value, there was but a modest penalty accruing to the market leader through adopting this strategy. Present worth for General Electric was reduced only 5 percent from what it was under the benchmark strategy. This is a tribute to the 8 percent discount rate which assigns a premium value to the early inflow of enhanced profits as contrasted with a shrunken terminal value of the business. The temptation to "milk" a business, by eliminating investment-type expenditures and by permitting a gradual slippage of market share is obvious: it is very profitable in the short run, and frequently justifiable according to present value criteria. One is tempted to observe that only managers with noneconomic objectives in sight (e.g., service to the community or engineering pride) would resist the temptation to milk this business for short-term gains even though this may be a very bad choice from a welfare point of view.

The harvest strategy also raised the profits of Westinghouse and Allis-Chalmers significantly. Thus, everybody had maximum earnings under this strategy.

While the impact of the harvest strategy was favorable to short-run profits, it would probably be unfavorable to technological progress, at least in the short run. The results demonstrate that with General Electric operating in this mode, its overhead spending was sharply reduced. However, overhead spending was accelerated for the other two firms, and for the industry as a whole. Indeed, overhead spending was now higher than under any other simulation, which might seem to augur favorably for technological spending. Once again, how much of the increase in overhead funds would be devoted to advanced technology is difficult to judge. Under the harvest philosophy it would be most natural for General Electric to eliminate the bulk of its long-term investment spending, and this would certainly be unfavorable for technological change. Furthermore, there would probably be a delay before the technological spending of Westinghouse and Allis-Chalmers picked up the slack. Also, while General Electric was executing its maneuver, there would be less competitive pressure forcing the introduction of new technology to the marketplace; General Electric would be simply cashing in its chips. Thus, the short-term result could well be a slackening in technological effort and output.

In the long run, the amount of technological spending would probably hinge upon how fast Westinghouse, the new market leader, could acquire a marked advantage in direct costs, vis-à-vis General Electric and Allis-Chalmers.

From a consumer perspective, the harvest strategy has another questionable byproduct: under this strategy, average order prices are inflated more than they are under any other strategy. The reason is plain: General Electric withdraws from the market, premium-prices its products, and ceases to fight for market share. The other two firms acquire it without a fight. The result is a decline in competition, which shows up in the simulation as a sharp increase in average selling prices; and also in profits.

It is worth emphasizing this policy conclusion: forcing General Electric into a voluntary retreat from its established strong market position would surely reduce competitive pressure in the market and raise prices.

There is yet another startling implication. If the managers of this oligopoly are to collude for maximum gain, they should play a game of turnabout in leading the industry. First, A will yield its market share to B; then B will yield its market share to A. The friendly see-saw provides maximum profits for everyone; far more than a dogged defense of the status quo in market shares.

(5) and (6) *Cournot and Bertrand*

Simulations #5 and #6 were based upon the Cournot and Bertrand theoretical models of oligopoly. The key assumption of Cournot was that the individual firms would maximize their profits, assuming their rivals' *output* would not change. The key assumption of Bertrand was that individual firms would maximize their profits assuming their rivals' *prices* would not change.

Oligopolists behaving according to Cournot logic are predicted in the theory to reach an equilibrium level of prices and output. This equilibrium would be more "competitive" in nature than any solution based upon monopoly behavior or a maximization of joint profits. But it would, on the other hand, not reach the very low price and profit levels which obtain under the theoretical conditions of perfect competition.[21] As the number of sellers increases, Cournot asserted that the equilibrium price would be continually lowered, from what it would be under monopoly, to what it would be under purely competitive conditions.[22]

Bertrand, on the other hand, reasoned that there would be no limit to the fall in price, since each producer always believed he could capture the entire market by underbidding his rival. In the context of this simulation, Bertrand-type behavior may be expected to lead to the lowest average industry prices. The hierarchy of price and profit results is therefore hypothesized to be:

(1) Highest price and profits: joint profit maximizing solution (simulation #12)
(2) Lower prices and profits: Cournot (simulation #5)
(3) Still lower prices and profits: Bertrand (simulation #6)
(4) Lowest prices and profits: "competitive" market structure (not simulated)

The simulation results permit us to check the assumptions of the theory. Cournot and Bertrand apparently believed that market shares would tend to equalize among the oligopolists. However, it is demonstrated that Allis-Chalmers tends to be forced down in market share in these two simulations, while Westinghouse and General Electric tend to preserve the large differential in their respective market shares. This is contrary to the theory.

The Cournot decision rule was not as successful in generating high profits

---

[21] Lawrence E. Fouraker and Sidney Siegel, *Bargaining Behavior* (New York: McGraw-Hill, 1963), pp. 126–127.

[22] For a clear exposition of Cournot versus Bertrand, see Edward Hastings Chamberlin, *The Theory of Monopolistic Competition* (Cambridge, Mass.: Harvard University Press, 1960), 7th ed., pp. 32–35.

for the oligopolists, as were some of the historical "behavioral" rules which were applied in simulations #1 through #3. Since under triopoly Cournot seemed confident that rather high prices and profits would be generated, in this respect also the simulation results are probably not consistent with his theory.

On the other hand, a comparison of the Cournot simulation result with the Bertrand simulation result produces some support for the theories. Bertrand profit levels were *below* the Cournot profit levels for two of the three competitors and for the industry as a whole. This is in accord with theoretical predictions. The Bertrand simulation also produced the very lowest present worth for the industry as a whole. This result seems to be in the spirit of Bertrand's original theoretical prediction. However, another result is *not* in accord with theory: the Cournot average price level for the industry is *below* the Bertrand average price level by a slim margin.

Neither Cournot nor Bertrand have much practical advice to offer the manager. In the simulation, profit-seeking managers could devise more profitable historical rules to guide their pricing actions. And even from the perspective of the consumer, seeking low prices and maximum technological change, other simulated strategies performed better.

"Judgmental" Maximizing

Simulations #7, #8, and #9 are all of a similar genre: the maximizing, through judgmental decision rules, of some operating result, subject to constraints. In #7 (Baumol) we are attempting to maximize the leader's sales subject to maintaining a minimum 20 percent operating profit. In #8 (Franklin Fisher) we are attempting to maximize his profits while holding his market share constant. In #9 we are endeavoring to maximize his growth, subject to the market share constraints imposed by customer loyalties and by antitrust. *Ex post facto*, how successful are the judgmental decision rules in achieving these goals?

(7) Baumol

The Baumol results are fascinating and quite unexpected. Simulation #7 does not maximize the leader's sales as intended, but it comes close. Only the harvest strategy and one other strategy (#12) produced a higher average sales result for General Electric. Furthermore, as intended, this simulation was also successful in maintaining General Electric's operating profit rate above the 20 percent minimum which was targeted. We conclude that the decision rule performs about as planned, to achieve Baumol-type goals.

The problem is that Baumol strategies are too devastating to the competition. One may question the wisdom of adopting a Baumol-type decision rule if you are a dominant firm, because it decimates competitors. Baumol-type behavior on the part of General Electric is quite disastrous to the profits of the other two firms, Westinghouse and Allis-Chalmers. In this simulation, their profit rate was the lowest of any simulation. Furthermore, this is the one simulation where Allis-Chalmers experiences a *negative* cumulative earnings flow, over the entire 1956–1972 period. Such an adverse earnings performance by competitors is not a result which a market leader is likely to enjoy. The risks of extremely sharpened competition, antitrust action, or damage to customer goodwill, are all too great if competitors are unduly weakened, as they are in these results.

The low profit results under Baumol behavior are not the consequence of particularly depressed industry price levels. Average order prices were not much lower than the average prices of the benchmark simulation. Rather, the competition seems to have been quite demoralized in a fashion which could not be foreseen.

Another negative feature of Baumol-type strategic behavior was its impact upon utility supply. In this simulation, utility reserves were at their lowest at the end of the simulation run, and the variance of percentage utility reserves was the highest—by a modest amount. All in all, Baumol cannot be recommended to management.

(8) *Franklin Fisher*

In simulation #8 the leader endeavors to hold his market share and to maximize his profits, pursuing the goals suggested by Franklin Fisher. The first goal was not actually achieved; the market share of General Electric dropped to less than 24 percent. However, the second objective was accomplished: profits for General Electric in this simulation were almost at their peak dollar amount.

Strategic behavior of the Franklin Fisher sort also depressed industry prices but, despite this fact, the impact on the operating profits of Allis-Chalmers and Westinghouse was not as severe as in the preceding simulation under Baumol-type rules. The key distinction seems to be the following: decision rules for the leader firm which are essentially self-centered, concentrating solely upon such *inner-directed* variables as absolute sales dollars, or profits, will tend to produce less prosperous results for competitors. The Baumol-type decision rule is an example of an inner-directed rule which hurts competitors badly. In contrast, decision rules such as the present one, which incorporate some *outward-directed* assessment of the competitive situation for *all* firms (for example, a decision rule which incorporates market share), will tend to produce more prosperous operating results for competitors. The strategic rules suggested by Franklin Fisher are of this more beneficent, outer-directed type.

(9) Marris, Williamson

In simulation #9, the leader firm is trying to maximize his own sales growth, the competitors' situation notwithstanding, and to reduce the variance of his earnings over time. He does this by endeavoring to maintain a constant two years backlog. The objective of maximizing sales, or growth for its own sake, has a counterpart in the theoretical reasoning of such economists as Marris or Williamson. The implementing strategy we propose, to maintain two years of backlog regardless of the circumstance of the total industry, is extremely inner-directed.

Marris has also stressed managements' need to manage the risks which are attendant in profit flows. We judge that the business may be operated in the most stable manner, with a minimum variance of sales and profit results over time, if backlogs are maintained. The goal of the simulation is to maintain smoothly growing operations from year to year, and to maintain backlogs, at the expense of competitors if necessary, to sustain the growth of the firm across any business cycle.

In large measure, the leader firm is frustrated in his objective of maximizing and stabilizing growth through this decision rule. Average backlogs are indeed maintained in excess of two years, but the resulting sales volume is very small and quite variable by the standard of the other simulations. And profit flows are only about average. As an instrument to maximize and stabilize growth, the maintenance of backlogs is poor strategy. Because the variance in sales and profit flows is not reduced, the goal of reducing risk and instability is not achieved.

Surprisingly, average order prices are rather high. Therefore, whether from the viewpoint of the firm or from the viewpoint of the consumer, this decision rule is not a success. It was one of the most "inward-looking" of all the decision rules. Optimal decision rules either from the perspective of the firm, or from the perspective of general welfare, should probably incorporate data on the competitors' circumstance and the industry situation, in addition to operating variables for the oligopolist himself.

Next, we report the results of simulations which were run on "optimal" decision rules. These were the decision rules which were "tuned" through heuristic search in order to maximize some specified objective, such as sales or profits.

(10) Maximizing Sales (Fellner)

Simulation #10 was run on the basis of a decision rule which maximized the cumulative 1956–1972 sales volume of General Electric. The search for an optimal set of coefficients for the decision rule produced interesting results. Sales were maximized for negative values of the coefficient of "delta price" and for negative values of the coefficient of market share disparity (the Herfindahl index). In other words, sales were maximized if General Electric deliberately yielded market share during a pricing downturn (buffering behavior), but also if General Electric increased its market share further whenever the disparity in market shares increased. Such a decision rule would encourage the leader firm to take over the marketplace to the maximum limit. And this is what actually occurred. General Electric acquired 75 percent share, Westinghouse 23 percent, and Allis-Chalmers slightly over 2 percent in this simulation. General Electric attained its specified goal of maximum sales volume by increasing its market share to the upper limit and holding it there. This simulation was the ultimate in aggressive behavior by the market leader. It was also the simulation which produced the lowest market share for Allis-Chalmers.

Given the squeeze exerted on smaller competitors under this strategy, it is not surprising that this simulation also produced the lowest· industry price level. Competitors' factories were unloaded with a vengeance. This created a severe backlogs imbalance, and a quite low utilization of manufacturing capacity, all of which tended to knock down the industry price level—particularly in view of the fact that Allis-Chalmers and Westinghouse continued to add to their manufacturing capacity, to match General Electric's expansion.

Despite the fact that General Electric seized three quarters of available industry volume, this strategy was not particularly self-serving for General Electric. The present worth of General Electric was quite low, as it was for the two other competitors. The industry price level was so badly disturbed, it adversely affected the earnings of everyone. The most characteristic result of this strategy, therefore, was the "ruining" of the industry price. It is also important to note that this strategy which yielded the *lowest* industry price also produced the *highest* degree of supplier concentration. If the welfare goal is very low prices, then the leader firm should be encouraged to take over the market, thereby *increasing* industry concentration.

(11) *Maximizing Present Value of the Leader Firm (Irving Fisher)*

In simulation #11, the optimum decision rule was derived in order to reach the highest present worth for General Electric. This goal would tend to eliminate extreme strategies which either lead to Pyrrhic victories in acquiring market share, or to a short-sighted divestment of market share, in temporary pursuit of profits.

Interestingly, the "maximum" present worth achieved under this optimizing approach, was not as great as the present worth achieved by General

Electric under a much simpler, earlier strategy: harvest. This may be attributed to a flawed specification of our optimizing decision rule.

The optimum strategy rule was well worth pursuing nonetheless: in the optimum decision rule which was derived, relating relative price to the trend in industry price and to the (Herfindahl) index of market share disparity, both coefficients had a zero value. In other words, relative price should equal 1.00. The present value of the leader firm declines as the values of the coefficients assume either positive or negative (nonzero) values. The results are illuminating. They imply that the best pricing strategy for the leader firm, if it seeks to maximize its present worth, is merely to follow the competition; in other words, to set its price ratio equal to one. The oligopolist should merely match his competitors' prices, immediately and exactly. His own average price should neither lead nor lag any movement in the industry average price. He should ignore any short-term shifts in market share which might be signaled by movements in the Herfindahl index; market shares will be determined by backlogs and manufacturing capacity, not by price.

The resulting pricing decision making may indeed resemble the "quiet life" which theorists sometimes ascribe to the highly concentrated industries. However, market prices would not be stable under this scheme. What is required, therefore, is some barometric price leader who calls the supply and demand turns, with the others following immediately.

It should be noted, however, that follow-the-barometric-leader is not the very best of pricing strategies. Less passive pricing strategies, incorporating other combinations of decision variables, have yielded an even higher present worth for the market leader in these simulation experiments. In particular, the frequent price adjustments which are implied under the strategy derivatives of actual historical behavior (simulations #1, #2, and #3), and the harvest strategy (simulation #4), all yielded a higher present value for the leader.

(12) and (13) *Maximizing Industry Profits and Present Value*

In these final two simulations there was a search for the decision rule coefficients which would maximize total industry profits (simulation #12) and total industry present value (simulation #13). In terms of economic theory, this is a search for Pareto-optimal solutions, so that aggregate profits and values cannot be increased by moving any single oligopolist in any different manner. Joint profits (or values) will be maximized. This is the monopoly solution. It is also the solution which, with limitations, Fellner predicted for oligopoly.

The optimal decision rule was discovered to be identical for both strategy #12 and strategy #13. The set of coefficients which maximized total industry profits was also the set of coefficients which maximized total industry present value. (Thus, only one set of results is reported in the accompanying tables, since the results for #12 and #13 were identical.)

The behavior of total industry profits and total industry present value, as the decision rule was altered, is illuminating. Highest industry profits and highest industry present values were achieved over the negative range of coefficients for the delta industry price variable. However, the results did not discriminate among different-valued coefficients for the current Herfindahl index variable. The thrust of the optimal decision rule, therefore, was to have the market leader buffer industry market shares depending upon the trend in price, but to ignore the degree of concentration which resulted. The results of this behavior are a virtual equality of average market positions between Westinghouse and General Electric (about 42 percent share each) and a 16 percent share for Allis-Chalmers. Industry profits and present values are maximized through decreasing the industry concentration, but in a carefully paced fashion which is dictated by the trend in industry price.

It again must be noted that other strategies, incorporating structurally different decision rules, outperformed even this "optimal" rule. For example, the harvest strategy yielded higher total industry profits and a higher present value. Our optimized decision rule could not achieve the profit results which were characteristic of the constant and unwavering premium price—the harvest strategy.[23] Paradoxically, our "optimum" is not really the optimum.

In oligopoly theory, oligopolists who are maximizing their joint profits are assumed to charge the monopoly price. In the context of this model, given the inelasticity of short-run turbine generator demand, this would be a very high price indeed. Simulation #12, in which the joint profits of the oligopolists were maximized, did yield a fairly high profit rate for the industry (17.4 percent) and rather high prices. Within limits, the theoretical predictions are demonstrated to hold.

CONFLICT AND COOPERATION IN OLIGOPOLY

To what degree are the objectives of the competing oligopolists served by joint pursuit of a single strategy? For example, is the strategy which yields maximum profits for the market leader also the strategy which yields maximum profits for the other competitors in the industry? If strategies produce similar long-run results for all of the oligopolists, we may anticipate maximum mutual support for such a strategy. On the other hand, if a strategy which produces maximum profits for one firm is the strategy which produces minimum profits for another, then we may anticipate maximum strategic conflict, or a "prisoner's dilemma" in game theory terms. The results of the

---

[23] In the search for optimal coefficients, the decision rule being optimized was relative price = $a + b_1$ (delta price) + b_2 (Herfindahl). The intercept value "a" was assigned a value of 1.00. Only b_1 and b_2 were systematically modified, and the resulting simulation checked for a maximum.

12 simulations will enable us to assess the likely degree of conflict or co-operation among the oligopolists, in their selection of strategies.

Table 14.11 is a summary of the "best" strategy for each competitor, according to various criteria of "success." For example, the strategy which produces the highest market. share for Allis-Chalmers is #4; the harvest strategy for General Electric. However, the strategy which produces the highest market share for General Electric is #10: the sales maximizing strategy.

There is only one criterion of success upon which the competitors could easily reach strategy agreement: this is the aim of producing highest short-run profits. For all three competitors, this result is obtained under the harvest strategy for General Electric. Considering the many diverse criteria of success which oligopolists may choose for themselves, we judge this single case of agreement to reflect a rather low probability of agreement among the oligopolists. Strategic conflict seems much more likely than strategic cooperation.

THE CAUSE OF VARIATIONS IN PROFIT RESULTS

The simulations yielded an enormous diversity of profit and market share results for each firm. Are there any underlying principles? We seek simple generalizations which can be used to predict the profit outcome of any oligopolist strategy.

The expected profit of the oligopolist is determined by the *competitive position* of the firm, and the *strategy* which the firm is pursuing. Consider first the competitive position of the firm. There is strong evidence in this study that the operating profit of the firm is related to its costs, which are in turn a function of its market share. Consider next the strategy which the firm is pursuing. It seems from these simulation results that profits could be given a short-term boost through the maneuver of yielding market share, such as in the harvest strategy. Other strategies, such as the move by General Electric to take over market share, were costly in terms of depressed profits in the short run.

We state three general propositions: market share is (1) profitable to have, (2) costly to acquire, and (3) an asset which can be sold. These general propositions may be quantified, using the simulation results. Perhaps the entire variation in average profit results for Allis-Chalmers, Westinghouse, and General Electric, in each of the simulation trials, may be explainable in terms of their average market positions, and the market share *changes* which they were pursuing.

Table 14.12 presents regression analysis results based upon average 1956–1972 profits and market shares from the simulation. These results are based upon data for the 3 firms, under 13 strategies, yielding a total of 39 strategy trials or observation points. Two variables, market share and the deviation in

TABLE 14.11.
"BEST" STRATEGY ACCORDING TO VARIOUS CRITERIA.

Criteria of "Success"	Allis-Chalmers	Westinghouse	General Electric	Industry
Highest average market share (%)	4: GE harvest	4: GE harvest	10: Max. sales: GE	—
Highest average sales revenue ($)	4: GE harvest	4: GE harvest	10: Max. sales: GE	11: Max. PV: GE
Highest average operating profits ($)	4: GE harvest	4: GE harvest	4: GE harvest	4: GE harvest
Highest average profit rate (%)	10: Max. sales: GE	11: Max. PV: GE	4: GE harvest	4: GE harvest
Highest present value in 1956 ($)	4: GE harvest	4: GE harvest	2: GE hold share and buffer	4: GE harvest
Highest imputed ending value 1972 ($)	4: GE harvest	4: GE harvest	8: F. Fisher	4: GE harvest
Highest overhead spending ($)	4: GE harvest	4: GE harvest	10: Max. sales: GE	4: GE harvest
Lowest industry prices (index)	—	—	—	10: Max. sales: GE
Highest industry manufacturing capacity utilization (%)	—	—	—	4: GE harvest
Lowest variance in utility reserves (%)	—	—	—	9: Marris

TABLE 14.12.
ANALYSIS OF PROFIT RESULTS.

Description of Variables	
$I = 1, \ldots, 3$ firms	
$J = 1, \ldots, 12$ strategies	
PROFIT $(I, J) =$	Average percent profit rate of ith firm when following jth strategy, over 68 quarters 1956–1972
SHARE $(I, J) =$	Average percent market share of ith firm when following jth strategy, over 68 quarters 1956–1972
DELTASHARE $(I, J) =$	Deviation of average 1956–1972 market share of ith firm, when following jth strategy, from mean share of ith firm under all of the strategies

$$= \text{SHARE } (I, J) - \overline{\text{SHARE}} \ (I)$$

$$\text{where } \overline{\text{SHARE}} \ (I) = \frac{1}{12} \sum_{J=1}^{12} \text{SHARE } (I, J)$$

Dummy $(1) =$	dummy variable equal to one if Allis-Chalmers
Dummy $(2) =$	dummy variable equal to one if Westinghouse
STRATEGY $(J) =$	dummy variable for strategy pursued in industry. $J = 1, \ldots, 12$

Data (36 observations)

	Mean Value	S.D.	Pearsonian Correlation with Profit (I, J)
PROFIT (I, J)	14.2	8.18	1.00
SHARE (I, J)	33.3	19.5	.43
DELTASHARE (I, J)	.025	10.4	−.40
Dummy (1)	.33	.48	−.65
Dummy (2)	.33	.48	−.025
STRATEGY (4)	.083	.28	.23
STRATEGY (10)	.083	.28	.17

Regression Results

(1) $R^2 = .74$ SEE $= 4.29$ F $= 46.9$

PROFIT $(I, J) = 1.60 + .379$ SHARE $(I, J) - .693$ DELTASHARE (I, J)
                          (F $= 73.7$)   (F $= 70.3$)

(2) $R^2 = .83$ SEE $= 3.6$ F $= 37.7$

PROFIT $(I, J) = .53 + .379$ SHARE $(I, J) - .693$ DELTASHARE (I, J)
                          (F $= 105.$)   (F $= 101.$)
                    $+ 7.2$ IF STRATEGY (4)
                          (F $= 11.1$)
                    $+ 5.6$ IF STRATEGY (10)
                          (F $= 6.7$)

(3)   Adding Dummy (1) and Dummy (2): NOT SIGNIFICANT,

F's less than 0.5

market share from its long-run historical average, "explain" three quarters of the variation in profit results in these cross-sectional data. The resulting model of operating profits is:

$$\text{percent operating profit} = 1.6\% + .379 \text{ (percent share)} - .693 \text{ (Δ percent share)}$$

In other words, for every 10.0 points of market share held, the oligopolist's operating profit was about 3.8 percent. But for every 10.0 percentage points of market share the oligopolist *acquired* above his historical average, he paid about 6.9 percent of operating profit. On the other hand, for every 10.0 percentage points of market share which the oligopolist *yielded*, his operating profit was enhanced by 6.9 percent. These general propositions hold very strongly in the data.

In general, it appears to be profitable to invest in market share in this industry, the transitory cost of acquiring share being 69 cents, for market share which has a permanent value of 38 cents.

This simple rule of thumb explains most of the variation in profit results for the 3 competitors in the 13 simulations. But a residual 25 percent of variance is not explained. We therefore explore two additional profit factors: the company itself, and the way in which its strategy is implemented.

Are some *companies* inherently more profitable than others, market share and change-in-market share factors considered? This proposition was tested statistically using dummy variables, with negative results. Allis-Chalmers, for example, was *not* less profitable than Westinghouse or General Electric, to a degree which could not be explained by its average market share and the change in market share strategy which it was pursuing.

The next question is: Is there a "strategy effect" in profitability? Are some *strategies* more profitable than others, even taking the preceding market share and change-of-market share factors into account? We tested each of the 13 strategies for its unique profit impact, using regression analysis once more (see Table 14.11). Only two strategies produced profit results which were significantly different, once the amount of shift in market share which was embodied in the strategy had been considered. These were strategies #4 and #10, the harvest strategy and the strategy in which General Electric achieves 75 percent market share.

The other ten strategies did not exhibit a statistically significant difference in profitability, once the market share and change in market share factors had been taken into account.

Both of the "nonconforming" strategies, #4 and #10, represent extreme movements by the market leader. In one the leader retreats suddenly. In the other, it advances suddenly. In both, profits are enhanced for everybody. We interpret this unusual finding as follows:

Market share brings its rather predictable profit rewards in most market situations. Furthermore, the *changing* of market share also has its rather predictable investment cost or profit reward.

However, in two special cases, the cost of changing market shares *is* dramatically different: if the market leader suddenly and dramatically relinquishes its market position, or if the market leader suddenly and dramatically seizes maximum market share. Sudden and abrupt thrusts in market share seem to produce an extra benefit for winner and loser alike.

Perhaps a suitable analogy would be trench warfare versus the blitzkrieg. The cost of a prolonged conflict in the trenches is rather predictable for both sides: much blood spilled by winner and loser alike. Successful blitzkriegs, on the other hand, seem remarkably inexpensive, both for attacker and defenders alike. Battles for market share follow similar rules of cost and payoff.[24]

There is another important conclusion, quite unanticipated: In oligopoly, *what* is accomplished is much more important than *how* it is accomplished. The "how," in this context, was the multitude of relative pricing rules we implemented, each one designed to accomplish some unique and specific objective. Thus, the strategies of Cournot and of Bertrand, of Baumol and of Fisher, produced a uniformity in results. Only blitzkrieg tactics could break the underlying rules of profit.

Profit versus Risk

Finally, consider the *variability* of the profit results. The period-to-period variance in profit rate is an excellent indicator of the riskiness or uncertainty of profit flows. Another basic principle emerges from the simulation results: businesses with high profit rates tend to have also steady, consistent period-to-period profit flows. On the other hand, businesses with a low profit rate tend to have a highly variable profit rate. (See Chart 14.1.) In oligopoly, the weak firms lose two ways: their profits are lower and their risks are higher.

These simulation results are merely suggestive evidence, not conclusive proof, of the market share, profit and risk tradeoffs in this oligopoly. However, the results seem credible to practicing experienced managers in the industry, and they also jibe with the history of events in this industry.

Welfare Implications

We conclude by asking what these results portend for a key public policy question: Would the public interest be better served by a strategy of volun-

---

[24] The economics of buying and selling market share have been studied intensively under the aegis of the "PIMS Project" (Profit Impact of Market Strategy) which the author directed in 1971–1972. The profit, cost, and market share experiences of 350 businesses tended to support the propositions outlined in the concluding section of this chapter. I am indebted to Dr. Sidney Schoeffler, General Electric Company manager of plans evaluation, and co-researcher on the PIMS Project, for these insights. See Robert D. Buzzell, Bradley T. Gale, and Ralph G. M. Sultan, "Market Share—A Key to Profitability," *Harvard Business Review*, January-February 1975, pp. 97–106.

CHART 14.1.   Seventeen-Year Average Profit Rate and Variability of the Annual Profit Rate (Simulation Results).

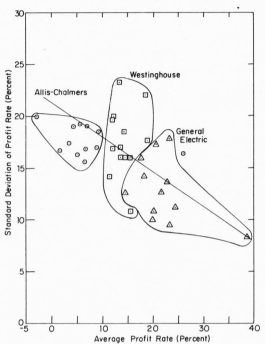

tary *deconcentration* of the industry (i.e., through forcing General Electric to yield its dominant market position, thereby increasing the market share of Westinghouse and, particularly, of Allis-Chalmers); or, would the public interest be better served by the status quo in market shares? And if it is to be the status quo in market shares, what form of rivalry best serves the public interest? There is yet another possibility to ponder: What would be the welfare consequence of *increasing* concentration still further, in this already highly concentrated oligopoly.

The following seem to be reasonable criteria for assessing the public benefit:

(a) Are average selling prices low, disregarding any change in product mix or technology?

(b) Are industry conditions conducive to the funding of rapid technological change? This will be measured by the rate of overhead accumulation. Is the accumulated spending at a maximum, particularly for the leader firm which must set the pace of R&D funding for the industry?

(c) Are *industry* average profits not so high as to suggest—in today's colorful jargon—a corporate "rip off?"

(d) But are the profits of *each* of the individual firms sufficiently high, so that all of the oligopolists may be expected to survive? Here, the profit experience of the marginal firm, Allis-Chalmers, is most relevant.

(e) Again with respect to the marginal firm, is the variability of the profit rate minimized, so as not to encourage exit for reasons of risk?

(f) Is industry supply sufficiently responsive to utility demand, so that utility reserves are maintained? Since the *average level* of utility reserves was adequate under all of the strategy simulations, we adopt as our criteria the *variability* of utility reserves.

The market share results of the various strategy simulations can be grouped, arbitrarily, into three categories for the purpose of this welfare analysis:

I. *Strategies Which Tend to Increase Concentration:*

(5) Cournot
(8) Franklin Fisher
(10) Maximize sales of General Electric

II. *Strategies Which Maintain the Status Quo in Market Shares*

(1) Historical behavior
(3) General Electric hold share
(6) Bertrand
(7) Baumol
(11) Maximize present value of General Electric

III. *Strategies Which Tend to Deconcentrate*

(2) General Electric hold share and buffer
(4) General Electric harvest
(9) Marris
(12) and (13) Maximize profits and maximize PV for industry

The welfare statistics, according to each strategy, are shown in Table 14.13, and are summarized in Table 14.14.

Our results contradict the generally accepted theory of antitrust, which holds that a *less* concentrated (or more atomistic) industry structure will lead to a more competitive (i.e., "better") industry performance. Our contrasting conclusion: strategies which *increase* supplier concentration tend also to result in the *lowest* industry price, the highest overhead funding rate, the lowest average industry profit rate, the highest profit rate for the marginal firm, and the lowest variance in profit rate for the marginal firm. All of these are "good things" according to the suggested performance standards. The only bad result is the effect which increasing concentration tends to have upon supply: the variability of utility reserves is increased slightly.

Obviously, the results of any computer simulation must be viewed with a

TABLE 14.13.
WELFARE IMPLICATIONS OF STRATEGIES.

	(a) Average Industry Price (Index)	(b) Leader's Average Overhead (Millions of Dollars)	(c) Industry Profit Rate (Percent)	(d) Allis-Chalmers Profit Rate (Percent)	(e) SD of Profit Rate (Percent)	(f) SD of Utility Reserves (Percent)
Strategy Result						
I. Increase Concentration						
Strategy 5	93	8.6	16.4	6.3	15.7	3.0
8	92	9.1	16.5	8.9	17.0	3.1
10	86	9.3	15.4	26.0	16.4	3.2
Average	90.3	9.0	16.1	13.7	16.4	3.1
II. Status Quo						
Strategy 1	97	8.4	16.2	4.4	19.0	2.9
3	96	8.4	17.4	5.3	19.3	3.1
6	94	7.8	15.6	1.5	16.8	2.8
7	96	7.6	16.6	−3.0	20.0	3.3
11	95	8.9	16.6	5.0	16.4	3.1
Average	95.6	8.2	16.5	2.6	18.3	3.1
III. Deconcentrate						
Strategy 2	100	7.6	18.1	6.9	16.9	2.8
4	106	5.8	22.0	9.2	18.6	2.8
9	102	7.4	17.3	7.1	19.0	2.7
12 and 13	100	7.5	17.4	3.7	17.4	2.6
Average	102	7.1	18.7	6.7	18.0	2.7

TABLE 14.14.
WELFARE CONSEQUENCES: SUMMARY.

| | Strategy | | |
Welfare Objective	Increase Concentration	Status Quo	Deconcentrate
(a) Low industry price	best	middle	worst
(b) High OH funding $	best	middle	worst
(c) Low industry profit %	best	middle	worst
(d) High Allis-Chalmers profit %	best	worst	middle
(e) Low variance of Allis' profit %	best	worst	middle
(f) Low variance utility reserves %	worst	worst	best

healthy skepticism. But these results coincide with our original hypothesis; that is, *increasing* the disparity of market shares in an oligopoly tends to be of benefit to the general public welfare. On the other hand, strategies of deconcentration, which are equivalent to forcing a greater equality of market shares, will tend to harm the public welfare.

CHAPTER Fifteen   Conclusions for Public Policy

TWELVE YEARS AFTER CYERT AND MARCH PUBLISHED their path-breaking *A Behavioral Theory of the Firm*,[1] some economists still find it difficult to accept nonoptimizing theories of management behavior. The reaction of some economists to the foregoing model of oligopoly has been, in effect, "Well, that cannot be how these businessmen behave, because they are not maximizing profits." To restate the obvious, this model is a statement of how the turbine generator oligopolists have behaved historically. Whether they behaved wisely or foolishly is for others to judge—that would require a complex dynamic programming analysis.

Clearly, the strategy puzzle is not easy for managers to solve. The puzzle is based upon numerous interacting links of industry behavior. Any single competitor, regardless of leadership position, is rather powerless to levitate prices upward directly, if supply and demand conditions do not warrant this. However, there are numerous indirect ways in which the industry level of prices may be changed: by starving one's competitors for orders, or by giving them orders, by encouraging backlog buildups or by slimming them down, by expanding capacity or by contracting it, by investing rapidly in new technology, or by slowing down the pace of change. In all of these matters, managers must apply their best judgment. The resulting behavior of prices may not necessarily be "optimal" in the sense that, given the same structural model, hindsight, and a computer, one may not trace a more profitable set of decisions for any one firm. It is not immediately apparent, however, that the behavior of managers, which led to the pricing actions described, was nonoptimal in the sense of not meeting to the fullest extent possible whatever ephemeral long-run goals some economists proclaim that businessmen should (or must) be seeking. Indeed, in our own elaborate computer simulations, we could not improve upon General Electric's actual historical strategy for the business.

---

[1] Richard M. Cyert, and J. G. March, *A Behavioral Theory of the Firm* (Englewood Cliffs, N.J.: Prentice-Hall, 1963).

In the United States, a vigorous antitrust policy has been inspired, in part, by the precepts of classical microeconomic theory—a theory which was originally developed from empirical observation of economic units in the nineteenth century. Unfortunately, that intellectual base has become increasingly obsolescent in the late twentieth century, as the economy has shifted to the high-technology industries epitomized by turbine generators, computers, electronics, chemicals, nonpolluting automobiles, and nuclear energy. In a high-technology industrial society, the thrust of public policy should enforce those conditions of industry structure which will encourage rapid and low-risk technological development, and the introduction of new, lower cost technologies. Policies which are aimed instead at the encouragement of maximum price competition for today's products, can actually hinder the pursuit of low-risk, rapid, technological change for tomorrow's products. Nevertheless, examples of thinking which are essentially rooted in the nineteenth century industrial structure are commonplace.

For example, one Clayton Act action during the electrical antitrust cases charged that "by preventing price competition, the alleged conspirators may have reduced the inventive cost reductions which have historically marked free competition."[2] We see here the classical suspicion of the tightly knit cartel, allegedly withholding technological progress for private profit—surely not a proposition which is valid for the industry studied here—and probably seldom valid anywhere else.

Nevertheless, chronic suspicions of cartels tend to generate frequent proposals to break up the highly concentrated industries. For example, in 1968, the Task Force on Antitrust Policy, headed by Philip C. Neal of the University of Chicago, and commissioned by President Lyndon Johnson to review the existing antitrust statutes, submitted its report to the White House.[3] The recommendations, if ever implemented, might have interesting consequences for the turbine generator builders, i.e., they might be minced into little pieces, or euphemistically, "deconcentrated." Reiterating the theme that the interdependent mode of decision making in oligopoly "may approximate the profit-maximizing decisions of a monopolist," the Neal

---

[2] Commonwealth Edison Company, et al. v. Allis-Chalmers Manufacturing Company, et al. in the U.S. District Court, Northern District of Illinois, Eastern Division, Clayton Act, Private Suits—Damages from Price Fixing—Defendant's Actual Costs, Profits, or Losses—In an action by a purchaser to recover treble damages for injuries allegedly resulting from a price-fixing conspiracy, evidence of defendants' and other alleged conspirators' actual costs, profits, or losses, for the purpose of showing that prices paid by the purchaser would not have differed without the alleged conspiracy, are relevant only if the defendant (1) establishes that actual costs, profits, or losses were unaffected by the alleged collusion and (2) offers such evidence for all significant market factors. The insulation from competition occasioned by an alleged collusive oligopoly may and probably does increase costs. (1966 Trade Cases, © 1966, Commerce Clearing House, Inc., Paragraph 71,756.)

[3] White House Task Force on Antitrust Policy, Report Number 1, Trade Regulation Reports, May 26, 1969.

report observed that concentrated industries generally have above-average rates of return on capital, and that the persistence of high rates of profit, at the industry level, over long periods of time, would suggest "artificial restraints on output and the absence of fully effective competition."[4] The recommended solution was "deconcentration"; that is, proceedings to reduce the market share of any firm with over 15 percent market share, in any industry wherein the largest four firms collectively had more than 70 percent share. The market share to which the truncated oligopolist would be banished, presumably forever, would be 12 percent.

In 1969, a counter task force, headed by George Stigler of the University of Chicago, refused to endorse the "deconcentration" aspects of the Neal report, given the present state of knowledge of the likely impact on efficiency of such drastic surgery.[5]

Even in the Neal report, there were apparently a few saving qualifications, permitting dominant firms to survive intact, if it could be demonstrated that sufficient economies of scale existed which would disappear under the decree. Thus, if the Neal report (*including footnotes*) was implemented as antitrust policy, the economies of scale in turbine generator manufacturing could presumably leave the industry intact, in its present structure.

Yet another example of public policy thinking was the Concentrated Industries Project of the Federal Trade Commission. In 1971, the Commission approved broad-scale economic studies of certain concentrated industries: energy, automobiles, ethical drugs, and electrical machinery. Director Michael Mann explained:

> Economic theory predicts that firms operating in concentrated markets will earn rates of return persistently above the opportunity cost of capital —that rate of return which is necessary to attract and to maintain investment in the industry. The suggested reason is that the concentration of output among a few firms permits them to pursue a common price policy, aimed at obtaining the profit levels coincident with what a single-firm monopolist would earn.
>
> The same economic theory predicts that firms in unconcentrated markets will tend to earn rates of return close to the opportunity cost of capital. The reasons given are that large numbers make it difficult to establish an agreement[6] to seek monopoly profits and that entry is easy enough to erode any profits which confer a higher rate of return than the opportunity cost of capital. The studies of some economists confirm these predictions of economic theory.

---

[4] Task Force Report, I-8-9, cited in Yale *Brozen*, "The Antitrust Task Force De-concentration Recommendation," *The Journal of Law and Economics*, Vol. XIII (2), October 1970, p. 280.

[5] Congressional Record, U.S. Senate, Vol. 115, No. 98, June 16, 1969, pp. 6,472–6,858.

[6] By "agreement," I do not mean to suggest a violation of Section I of the Sherman Act. The agreement can be tacit, e.g., price leadership. (Mann's footnote.)

Mann listed the following ills as probably attributable to excessive concentration in an industry:

(1) Costs may be higher, and thus reported profits lower, in a monopoly because of expenditures on executives' fringes in the form of fancier suites, thicker rugs, and such. In other words, monopolists do not minimize costs, and thus score badly with regard to what economists call x-efficiency.

(2) The higher costs of production which arguably arise from monopolistic protection of excess capacity.

(3) The excessive selling costs which seem to characterize certain highly concentrated industries.

(4) The effect of monopolistic pricing in producers' goods, which may influence the choice of production progress by purchasing industries. If, for instance, the monopoly price for electrical machinery leads purchasers to economize in electrical machinery, a less efficient production process may be used by the purchasers of electrical machinery thereby raising the price of their product, forcing changes in production processes, further up the line. In short, monopolistic pricing in producers' goods may have a widespread influence on efficiency through the economy. The sum of all these could amount to about 6 percent of GNP, or $60 billion.

Mann was particularly interested in the performance of the electrical industry, observing that his FTC study of the electrical machinery industry would involve a determination of the effectiveness of the antitrust action against the price-fixing conspiracy in 1960. He stated, "There exists doubt among many students of antitrust about whether firms in highly concentrated markets, when found guilty of price-fixing, really change their price behavior in a substantive way. Rather, it is argued, they turn to legal means, e.g., price leadership, to accomplish the same result."[7]

As a final example of the spirit of public policy measures, we have Senator Philip Hart's proposals in Congress, to "deconcentrate."[8] Senator Hart ex-

---

[7] "The Concentrated Industries Project," speech by Dr. H. Michael Mann, Director, Bureau of Economics, Federal Trade Commission, before the Marketing Committee Meeting, National Association of Manufacturers, November 11, 1971, Washington Hilton Hotel, Washington, D.C.

[8] Congressional Record, Proceedings and Debates of the 92d Cong., 2d Sess., July 24, 1972, Washington, D.C., Vol. 118, No. 115. The Hart bill contains these formidable prescriptions:

Sec. 101.

(a) It is hereby declared to be unlawful for any corporation or two or more corporations, whether by agreement or not, to possess monopoly power in any line of commerce in any section of the country or with foreign nations.

(b) There shall be a rebuttable presumption that monopoly power is possessed—(1) by any corporation if the average rate of return on net worth after taxes is in excess of 15 per centum over a period of five consecutive years out of the most recent seven years preceding the filing of the complaint, or (2) if there has been no substantial price competition among two or more corporations in any line of commerce in any section of the country for a period of three consecutive years out of the most recent five years preceding the filing of the complaint, or (3) if

plained his bill as follows: "I shall resist a flowery and overdone introduction for the bill which I offer today. It is called the Industrial Reorganization Act. It seeks to bring closer to reality what this country has pretended to have for years: a competitive economy. It grew out of years of study by the Antitrust and Monopoly Subcommittee, partly under the chairmanship of Senator Kefauver, and partly during my tenure. It is not a perfect bill. But it does represent perhaps the greatest effort which has been put to finding a solution for economic concentration. And it may bear the seeds for producing an economy in which inflation and high unemployment are not a way of life."

In Hart's bill, top priority was given to reorganizing seven industries: (1) chemical and drugs; (2) electronic computing and communication equipment; (3) electrical machinery and equipment; (4) energy; (5) iron and steel; (6) motor vehicles; and (7) nonferrous metals. Hart claimed that these industries were selected because available research suggested that these industries had the greatest impact on "the persistent inflation eating away at the Nation" and that they "contribute most to the unemployment problems." Hart made the further interesting observation—contradicted by this present study—that concentrated industries not only display little price competition but tend to maintain or increase prices as demand falls—in order not to erode profits. Thus, Hart concluded, "Government steps to halt inflation by cutting demand tends in these industries to backfire. Cuts in demand too frequently result in higher prices—and more layoffs—as the companies seek to make the target profits."

The Neal report, the Mann-FPC project, and the Senator Hart bill, share one common flaw: a less than complete understanding of how economies of scale, concentration, product rivalry, and pricing interact in modern oligopoly. Their policy prescriptions would dilute the very economies of scale, and the disparities of market share, which are the mainsprings of rapid innovation in high-growth, highly concentrated industries.

Scale Economies: An Ubiquitous Force

Scale economies are noted as one saving grace in the Neal report, but since they are relegated to footnote status, one suspects that only minor significance is attached to them. But there is worldwide evidence concerning the available scale economies in this industry. Allis-Chalmers, with about 10 percent market share, and despite some deliberate assistance by its larger competitors (i.e., buffering strategies), had costs which were too high for

---

any four or fewer corporations account for 50 per centum (or more) of sales in any line of commerce in any section of the country in any year out of the most recent three years preceding the filing of the complaint.

In all other instances the burden shall lie on the Industrial Reorganization Commission established under Title II of this Act to prove the possession of monopoly power.

the price collapse of the early 1960s. British turbine builders were forcefully led into merger by government decree, and even as a single entity had difficulty in maintaining their competitive edge. Perhaps the United Kingdom was too small to support even one manufacturer. In Germany, Siemens and AEG joined forces in the Kraftwerk Union enterprise. The pattern in Japan is unclear, with much technological transfer from Westinghouse and General Electric still occurring. It appears that the United States market will not support, economically, more than two producers (i.e., producers that are not relying upon the licensed technology of others), and even with this industry structure, the number two competitor appears to operate at a cost disadvantage, throwing a disproportionate responsibility upon the number one firm.

The United States and Canada, combined, constitute approximately 40 percent of the world electric power industry. This share has been shrinking, since growth in electric power demand has been only about 7 percent annually in North America, but over 8 percent annually in Western Europe, and almost 13 percent annually in Japan and Asia.[9] North America will eventually represent one third of the world electric power market. If the United States can support two viable competitors, one would therefore judge that the world can economically support about six: two in the United States, one in Russia, two in Western Europe, and one or two in Japan. One factor can disrupt this competitive outcome: economic nationalism, by which suboptimal producers can garner the necessary protection to survive.

In the energy producing industries, the need for rapid, low-risk technological innovation is so imperative, that governments would not seem to be able to afford the luxury of a less-than-optimal industry structure. Economies of scale overwhelmingly discourage the small producer. Duopoly or triopoly will therefore tend to be the natural order.

The Funding of Technology

This research has addressed, at length, how technology can be privately funded. For a time, during the splurge of government-financed research which characterized the post-Sputnik decade, it appeared that the *private* financing of new technology was waning in the United States and that the government would gradually emerge as the major source of R&D funds. This belief was laid to rest by the budget cutbacks of the 1970s, and the resulting high unemployment rates among scientists, engineers, and technologists along the Route 128 "golden circle" of Boston, and in other high-technology centers. High-technology firms were forced to re-think how to fund their advanced technology through dollars earned in the current marketplace—

---

[9] N. B. Guyol, *The World Electric Power Industry* (Berkeley, Cal.: University of California Press, 1969), Chapter 6.

the model hypothesized in this research. In the electrical machinery industry, such financing was the rule.

We have seen how the rate of introduction of new technology was controlled. The relative price to be charged for products of varying technologies was a key management tool in controlling the rate of adoption of new technology. A closely related issue, we discovered, was the maintenance of smaller, weaker competitors (preserving the disparity of market shares), which was important in maintaining an average price level which permitted the capture and accumulation of technological funds. Similar technological funding and new product pricing principles seem to apply in computers (with IBM playing the leader role, obviously); in automobiles (with General Motors forcing the play); and even in strategic weaponry worldwide.

It is clear that in the typical oligopoly struggle, the market leader must simultaneously preserve his leadership, co-exist with powerful competitors, maintain outward calm on the pricing front, and push for maximum advantage through technology, all the while preserving some stability of market structure for reasons of antitrust. However, not all oligopolies operate in this fashion. Many high-technology businesses of the 1960s, which flourished under the umbrella of government funding, failed during the 1970s, when it became necessary to fund from the marketplace. At the same time, technological risk, as measured by the incidence of high-technology failures, seemed to increase.

When technological progress suffers at a critical time, such as when the need is great for high-technology solutions to our energy supply problem, one option is renewed government funding of the quest for new and advanced technologies. However, another alternative is increased private funding of research and development through the market mechanism. The turbine generator industry has provided one case history of how it can be done, while maintaining profit margins and while preventing an accelerating rise in technological risk. Unfortunately, the dilemma is that the resulting industry structure is anathema to the antitrust tradition.

The Need for Performance Standards

The electrical antitrust cases illustrated the treble-damage penalties which could be obtained when conventional microeconomic theory was applied to the analysis of a high-growth, high-technology industry. The "performance" of this industry, under such criteria as progressiveness, technological innovation, productivity growth, export performance, cost reduction, and the like, seemed impeccably sound. The problem was the industry's blatantly illegal conduct which, by standards of the Sherman Antitrust Act, was anticompetitive, and therefore, according to the theory, likely to lead to poor performance. This illustrates our unfortunate preoccupation with the symbols of competition, rather than with the realities of performance.

An alternative approach to antitrust policy is suggested, only slightly with tongue-in-cheek: ignore the symbols of competition, and get to the heart of the matter: performance. It would not be impossible, at least in those technology based industries which have a strong engineering or physical output orientation, to establish norms of economic performance, in objective terms of cost and real price reduction, innovation, productivity gains, real wage gains, discrimination removal, increase in total employment, pollution control, and the like. Public policy could then move vigorously against the sleepy oligopolists: those which consistently failed to achieve targeted performance. The antitrust statute book, defining permissible conduct on how those objectives were to be achieved, could be discarded. This might achieve better results than our continuing focus upon vague correlates of "competitive" conduct.

Appendixes

Index

APPENDIX 1.
Utilities' Turbine Generator Orders.

Data:

Edison Electric Institute time series of total kilowatts ordered by utilities, from *Manufacture of Heavy Electric Power Equipment in the United States, 1948–1966,* EEI Publication Number 67–63, and various *Year-End Summary of the Electric Power Situation in the United States,* for years 1967–1970, published by EEI.

Quarterly data, 1951–1969 inclusive, 71 observations.

Steam turbine generators 10,000 kilowatts and larger, excluding nuclear units, excluding exports, excluding nonutility orders.

Description of variables

KWORDERS (T) = total kilowatts ordered in quarter T, by utilities, at annual rates, moving 4-quarter average, thousands of kilowatts.

FCSTPK (T + 12) = forecast of peak loads for total United States, in thousands of kilowatts, three years (or 12 quarters) into the future.

YRSBACKLOG (T) = years of backlog of unshipped orders for total turbine generator manufacturers as of quarter T.

$$= \frac{\text{total kilowatts backlog of unshipped orders, industry}}{\text{total kilowatts manufacturing capacity, industry}}$$

DELTAFCST (T) = change in forecast made in period corresponding to quarter T, of peak loads three years hence, as that particular forecasted year becomes two years hence.

OLS Regression Results: $R^2 = 0.66$ Durbin-Watson = 0.6*

$$
\begin{aligned}
\text{KWORDERS (T)} = {}& -1931 & + & \ \ .050 \ \text{FCSTPK (T + 12)} \\
& (t = 0.9) & & \ \ (t = 4.3) \\
& & + & \ \ 1919 \ \text{YRSBACKLOG (T)} \\
& & & \ \ (t = 1.8) \\
& & + & \ \ .864 \ \text{DELTAFCST (T)} \\
& & & \ \ (t = 5.0)
\end{aligned}
$$

2SLS Regression Results: $R^2 = 0.63$ Durbin-Watson = 0.6*

$$
\begin{aligned}
\text{KWORDERS (T)} = {}& -1212 & + & \ \ .038 \ \text{FCSTPK (T + 12)} \\
& (t = 0.3) & & \ \ (t = 3.3) \\
& & + & \ \ 524 \ \ \ \text{YRSBACKLOG (T)} \\
& & & \ \ (t = 0.3) \\
& & + & \ \ .612 \ \text{DELTAFCST (T)} \\
& & & \ \ (t = 1.0)
\end{aligned}
$$

*Hildreth-Lu Regression Estimates: $R^2 = .20$ Durbin-Watson = 1.8

$$
\begin{aligned}
\text{KWORDERS (T)} = {}& -2782 & + & \ \ .070 \ \text{FCSTPK (T + 12)} \\
& (t = 0.4) & & \ \ (t = 2.0) \\
& & + & \ \ 466 \ \ \ \text{YRSBACKLOG (T)} \\
& & & \ \ (t = 0.3) \\
& & + & \ \ .932 \ \text{DELTAFCST (T)} \\
& & & \ \ (t = 3.2)
\end{aligned}
$$

NOTE: This is equation defining Variable VAR 90 in the simulation.

APPENDIX 2.
THE LONG-RANGE LOAD FORECASTING BIAS.

The following data illustrate the tendency of the electric power industry to under-forecast the growth in electrical energy output and peak loads in the long run. One important consequence of this behavior is the "tautness" of the generating equipment market: the chronic tendency for demand to outrun supply, and the impact which this has upon pricing and strategic behavior, as outlined in the main text. The data below show long-range forecasts, compared with actual results. In the case of forecasts for 1975, the comparison is made with the most recent forecast for 1975.

Forecaster and Year Forecast Made		Forecast Year, and Forecast Quantity			Forecasting Error	
		Year	Gigawatts	Billions KWH	Gigawatts	Billions KWH
FEDERAL POWER COMMISSION						
1949[1]	11 years	1960	115	525	38% low	30% low
1954[2]	11 years	1965	117	957	4.8% low	9.7% low
	16 years	1970	217	1173	29.0% low	24.3% low
	21 years	1975	262	1420	36.4% low	37.6% low
1959[3]	6 years	1965	194	1064	4.3% high	0.4% high
	11 years	1970	246	1349	12.1% low	13.0% low
	16 years	1975	304	1668	26.2% low	26.8% low
1962[4]	8 years	1970	—	1559	—	0.6% high
	13 years	1975	—	2132	—	6.4% low
1964[5]	6 years	1970	271	1484	3.2% low	4.3% low
	11 years	1975	370	2024	10.2% low	11.1% low
1968[6]	7 years	1975	370	2024	10.2% low	11.1% low
EDISON ELECTRIC INSTITUTE (PRIVATE UTILITY ASSOCIATION)						
1954[7]	11 years	1965	150 to 190	—	actual peak was at upper limit of range	
	21 years	1975	262 to 367	—	upper limit was forecasted 11% low	
1955[8]	10 years	1965	—	850	—	19.8% low
1959[9]	11 years	1970	—	"2.09 times"	—	KWH 2.8% low

Forecaster and Year Forecast Made		Forecast Year, and Forecast Quantity			Forecasting Error	
		Year	Gigawatts	Billions KWH	Gigawatts	Billions KWH

PHILIP SPORN (PRESIDENT, AMERICAN ELECTRIC POWER)

Forecaster and Year Forecast Made		Year	Gigawatts	Billions KWH	Gigawatts	Billions KWH
1948[10]	4 years	1952	66	—	12.3% low	—
	9 years	1957	86.7	—	21.2% low	—
	11 years	1959	96.8	—	22.8% low	—
1954[11]	11 years	1965	200	—	7.4% high	—
	16 years	1970	275	—	1.8% low	—
1955[12]	10 years	1965	—	"over 1,000"	—	actual was 1060
	20 years	1975	—	2000	—	12.2% low
1962[13]	13 years	1975	—	2000	—	12.2% low
1963[14]	12 years	1975	—	2000	—	12.2% low
1964[15]	11 years	1975	—	2000	—	12.2% low
1968[16]	7 years	1975	—	2150	—	5.6% low

GENERAL PUBLIC UTILITIES CO.

		Year	Gigawatts	Billions KWH	Gigawatts	Billions KWH
1951[17]	9 years	1960	112	500	39% low	34% low
1951[18]	9 years	1960	125	526 to 550	32% low	27 to 30% low

EBASCO (ENGINEERING CONSULTANT TO UTILITIES)

		Year	Gigawatts	Billions KWH	Gigawatts	Billions KWH
1950[19]	10 years	1960	96–104	—	43 to 48% low	—

GENERAL ELECTRIC COMPANY

		Year	Gigawatts	Billions KWH	Gigawatts	Billions KWH
1950[20]	10 years	1960	123–139	540–605	19 to 33% low	31 to 39% low
1954[21]	10 years	1964	187	—	7% high	—
1955[22]	9 years	1964	230	—	31% high	—

WESTINGHOUSE ELECTRIC CORPORATION

		Year	Gigawatts	Billions KWH	Gigawatts	Billions KWH
1947[23]	10 years	1957	—	375	—	41% low
1950[24]	10 years	1960	—	532	—	29% low
1954[25]	9 years	1963	—	735	—	41% low
1959[26]	5 years	1963	—	"could pass 1000"	—	actual was 1010
1959[27]	9 years	1968	—	"5.6 annual growth"	—	7% low

Forecaster and Year Forecast Made		Forecast Year, and Forecast Quantity			Forecasting Error	
		Year	Gigawatts	Billions KWH	Gigawatts	Billions KWH
ELECTRICAL WORLD MAGAZINE						
1954[28]	16 years	1970	250	1200	10.7% low	22.5% low
1955[29]	15 years	1970	320	1451	14.3% high	6.4% low
1956[30]	14 years	1970	295	—	5.4% high	—
1959[31]	11 years	1970	276	1682	1.4% low	8.5% high
	16 years	1975	393	2423	4.6% low	6.4% high
1960[32]	10 years	1970	276	1672	1.4% low	7.9% high
	15 years	1975	392	2423	4.9% low	6.4% high
1962[33]	8 years	1970	256	1615	8.6% low	4.2% high
	13 years	1975	349	2311	15.3% low	1.5% high
1963[34]	7 years	1970	260	1544	7.1% low	0.4% low
	12 years	1975	364	2195	11.7% low	3.6% low
NATIONAL INDUSTRIAL CONFERENCE BOARD						
1952[35]	8 years	1950–1960	—	2.3%		(low) actual was 8.6%
	18 years	1960–1970	—	.5%	—	(low) actual was 7.2%
	28 years	1970–1990	—	(1.9%)		(low) probably
NATIONAL BUREAU OF ECONOMIC RESEARCH						
1946[36]	9 years	1955 (hypothetical)	—	zero growth	—	(low) actual growth in 1955 was 15%+

[1] Cited in Edward W. Morehouse, "Regularization of Business Investment in the Electric Utility Industry," in National Bureau of Economic Research, *Regularization of Business Investment* (Princeton University Press, 1954). Kilowatts refers to total generating capacity in place, rather than kilowatts actual load, in Morehouse references.

[2] Federal Power Commission, *Annual Report*, Fiscal Year 1954 (Washington, D.C., 1955).

[3] Cited in *Electrical World*, September 14, 1959, 110.

[4] United States Atomic Energy Commission, *Civilian Nuclear Power, A Report to the President*, 1962, Federal Power Commission projections of annual utility generation reported in Table 15, Appendix, 64.

[5] Federal Power Commission, Power Requirements Special Technical Committee, "Forecast of Electric Utility Power Requirements to the Year 1980," in Part II, *National Power Survey* (Washington, D.C., 1964).

[6] Federal Power Commission, *Annual Report*, Fiscal Year 1967, (Washington, D.C., 1968).

[7] Walker Cisler, president, Detroit Edison Company, and chairman, EEI Electric Power Survey Committee, "Looking Ahead to the Last Quarter of the First Century of Electric Power in the United States," address before 22nd Annual EEI Convention, Atlantic City, N.J., June 2, 1954, cited in *EEI Bulletin*, June 1954.

8 Harllee Branch, Jr., president, EEI, and president, Georgia Power Co., "The Electric Utilities—Opportunity and Challenge," *Edison Electric Institute Bulletin*, December 1955.

9 A. S. King, president, Northern States Power Co., "Prospects for the Sixties," address to the National Coal Association, Washington, D.C., June 7, 1961, cited in *EEI Bulletin*, July–August 1961.

10 Philip Sporn, "Opportunities in Shaping Destiny of America," 21st Steinmetz Memorial Lecture, Schenectady, New York, May 20, 1948, reprinted in P. Sporn, *Vistas in Electric Power* (London: Pergamon Press, 1968).

11 Philip Sporn, "The Development of Competitive Atomic Power," talk before Public Utilities Advertising Association, delivered in New York, December 2, 1954.

12 Philip Sporn, "The Engineer's Responsibility," Response of the Medalist to John Fritz Award, ASME, AIEE, ASCE, and AIMME, Chicago, Illinois, November 17, 1955.

13 Philip Sporn, "Economic Evaluation of Primary Energy Supplies and Conversion," 6th World Power Conference, Melbourne, Australia, October 1962, reprinted in Sporn, *Vistas in Electric Power* (London: Pergamon Press, 1968).

14 Philip Sporn, chairman, System Development Committee, American Electric Power Company, "Research on the Foundations of the Electrical Supply Industry: Load and Load Growth," The Citrine Lecture, presented to the Fifteenth British Electrical Power Convention, at Torquay, June 18, 1963.

15 Philip Sporn, "Engineering in Energy," Cornell College of Engineering Lectures, Spring 1963, in P. Sporn, *Foundations of Engineering* (London: Pergamon Press, 1964).

16 Philip Sporn, "The Power Industry looks Ahead," Cornell University, *Engineering Quarterly*, Volume 3, Number 1, 1968–1969.

17 Forecast by Hooper of General Public Utilities Co., cited in Morehouse, *Regularization of Business Investment*.

18 Forecast by Morehouse of General Public Utilities Co., cited in Morehouse, *Regularization of Business Investment*.

19 Forecast by Ebasco cited by Morehouse, *Regularization of Business Investment*.

20 Forecast by Lang of General Electric cited by Morehouse, *Regularization of Business Investment*.

21 R. S. Neblett, "The Steam Turbine of Tomorrow," 16th Annual Meeting of American Power Conference, Chicago, March 24, 1954.

22 Glenn B. Warren, "Research and Development in the Field of Turbine-Generator Prime Movers in the General Electric Company," 17th Annual Meeting of American Power Conference, Chicago, April 1, 1955.

23 Cited in Morehouse, *Regularization of Business Investment*.

24 Ibid.

25 Westinghouse Electric Corporation, *The Third Future Power Market Forum, A Record of Proceedings* (Pittsburgh, February 1954).

26 J. H. Jewell, vice president, marketing, Westinghouse Electric Corporation, "The Electric Power Market and a Growing America," talk at the *Fourth Future Power Market Forum*, Westinghouse Electric Corporation, January 13, 1959.

27 A. C. Monteith, senior vice president, Westinghouse Electric Corporation, "Innovation: A Broad Base for New Growth," talk at the *Fifth Future Power Market Forum, 1964*.

28 "Electrical Industry Forecast for 1954–1970," *Electrical World* September 20, 1954.

29 "Electrical World Annual Electrical Industry Forecast 1955 to 1970," reprinted from *Electrical World*, September 19, 1955.

30 "7th Annual Electrical Industry Forecast," reprinted from *Electrical World*, September 17, 1956.

31 "10th Annual Electrical Industry Forecast," *Electrical World*, September 14, 1959.

32 "11th Annual Electrical Industry Forecast," *Electrical World*, September 19, 1960.

33 "13th Annual Electrical Industry Forecast," *Electrical World*, September 17, 1962.

34 "14th Annual Electrical Industry Forecast," *Electrical World*, September 23, 1963.

35 National Industrial Conference Board, *Studies in Growth Patterns* (New York: 1952).

36 J. M. Gould, *Output and Productivity in the Electric and Gas Utilities, 1899–1942* (National Bureau of Economic Research, New York: 1946).

APPENDIX 3.
How Utilities Forecast Peak Loads.

Data: Edison Electric Institute, *Semi-Annual Electric Power Survey,* 1949 to 1969. Total of 40 observations.

Description of Variables:

FCSTPK(T) = forecast peak load, in thousands of kilowatts, for total United States, in year T (summer or winter peak, whichever is higher).

PEAK(T) = actual peak load, in thousands of kilowatts, for total United States, in year T (summer or winter peak, whichever is higher).

T = year: 49, 50, 51, etc. Note that we have two observations for each year.

Results: Regression Model: Extrapolation Growth Rates

$$(\log \text{FCSTPK}(T + 3) - \log \text{PEAK}(T))$$
$$= A + B (\log \text{PEAK}(T) - \log \text{PEAK}(T - N))$$

	N	Coefficient A	Coefficient B	R²	Durbin-Watson
OLS:	5 years	.198 (t = 8.9)	.046 (t = 0.8)	.02	1.1

Results: Regression Model: Extrapolation Change in Absolute Peak Loads

$$(\text{FCSTPK}(T + 3) - \text{PEAK}(T)) = A + B (\text{PEAK}(T) - \text{PEAK}(T - N))$$

	N	Coefficient A	Coefficient B	R²	Durbin-Watson
OLS:	5 years	−4638 (t = 3.0)	0.877 (t = 26.)	.95	1.6
2SLS:	5 years	−5441 (t = 3.4)	0.896 (t = 25.)	.95	1.7

Note: This is equation defining Variable VAR 5 in the simulation.

How Utilities Adjust Their Forecasts of Peak Loads.

Data: Edison Electric Institute, *Semi-Annual Electric Power Survey*, Numbers 6 through 47.

Semi-annual data for years 1949 through 1969.

Total of 34 observations.

All data in thousands of kilowatts.

Description of Variables:

$FORECAST(T,T-N)$ = forecast of kilowatts peak load for total utility industry in the United States in year T, made N years earlier.

$ESTIMATE(T)$ = estimate of kilowatts peak load for total utility industry in the United States in the current year T.

$ERROR(T)$ = error perceived in year T, between estimate of peak loads for the current year, and the original forecast made three years earlier for the current year.

= $FORECAST(T,T-3) - ESTIMATE(T)$.

$DELTAFCST(T)$ = change in forecasts which is made in year T of peak loads three years hence, as that particular forecasted year becomes two years hence.

= $FORECAST(T+2,T) - FORECAST(T+3, T-1)$.

OLS Regression Results: $R^2 = .14$ Durbin-Watson = 0.5*

$DELTAFCST(T)$	= 559.4 − 0.224 $ERROR(T)$
	(t = 1.1) (t = 2.3)

2SLS Regression Results: $R^2 = .14$ Durbin-Watson = 0.5*

$DELTAFCST(T)$	= 577.0 − 0.198 $ERROR(T)$
	(t = 1.1) (t= 1.1)

*Hildreth-Lu Regression Estimates: $R^2 = .13$ Durbin-Watson = 1.0

$DELTAFCST(T)$	= 501.0 − 0.280 $ERROR(T)$
	(t = 0.9) (t = 2.5)

Note: This is equation defining Variable VAR 18 in the simulation.

APPENDIX 5.
Utilities' Increase in Generating Capability.

Data:

Total shipments data from Edison Electric Institute and private sources for years 1951–1968, quarterly data, kilowatts shipped to United States utility organizations.

Additions to generating capacity, taken from *Historical Statistics of the Electric Utility Industry*, and from *Year-End Summaries of Power Situation*, Edison Electric Institute, for new steam turbine generator capacity added, annual data converted into equivalent "quarterly" time series, 1951–1968. 48 observations.

Description of Variables:

KWSHIP(T) = shipments from manufacturers to United States utility organizations, in quarter T, in thousands of kilowatts.

KWADD(T) = new additions of steam turbine generating capacity, by United States utilities in "quarter" T, in thousands of kilowatts.

OLS Regression Results:

KWADD(T) = 995 + 0.404 KWSHIP(T − 2)
             (T = 4.9) (T = 6.0) R^2 = .45 Durbin-Watson = 1.2

NOTE: This is equation defining Variable VAR 60 in the simulation.

APPENDIX 6.
Utilities' Generating Reserves.

Data:

Information on reserves in current period, forecasted generating capability, and forecasted peak loads, all taken from Edison Electric Institute *Semi-Annual Power Survey*, 1949–1970. Peaks refer to noncoincident peak loads for United States utility organizations.

Semi-annual data, 34 observations.

Description of Variables:

PCMARGIN(T) = percent margin of generating reserve, United States utilities, in period T; expressed as percent of total capability.

PERRORPK(T) = percent error in forecast of peak load in period T; forecast made three years earlier.

$$= \frac{ERRORPK(T)}{PEAK(T)}$$

Where ERRORPK(T) is kilowatts error in forecasting peak load, and PEAK(T) is current peak load in kilowatts, in period T.

PERRORCAP(T) = percent error in forecast of generating capability in period T; forecast made three years earlier.

$$= \frac{ERRORCAP(T)}{CAPABILITY(T)}$$

where ERRORCAP(T) is kilowatts error in forecasting generating capability, and CAPABILITY(T) is generating capability in kilowatts in period T.

OLS Regression Results: $R^2 = .80$ Durbin-Watson = 0.6*

PCMARGIN(T) = 6.89 + 0.21 T + .989 PERRORPK(T)
     (t = 1.4) (t = 2.7)   (t = 10.)

                        − .798 PERRORCAP(T)
                           (t = 5.4)

2SLS Regression Results: $R^2 = .70$ Durbin-Watson = 0.6*

PCMARGIN(T) = 14.9 + 0.095 T + 1.11 PERRORPK(T)
     (t = 0.5) (t = 0.3)   (t = 1.2)

                        − .350 PERRORCAP(T)
                           (t = 1.5)

*Hildreth-Lu Regression Estimates: $R^2 = .47$ Durbin-Watson = 1.7

PCMARGIN(T) = 3.96 + 0.056 T + .538 PERRORPK(T)
     (t = 2.9) (t = 0.12)   (t = 5.4)

                        − .517 PERRORCAP(T)
                           (t = 6.0)

NOTE: This is equation defining Variable VAR 16 in the simulation.

APPENDIX 7.
Utilities' Forecasts of Generating Capability.

Data:

Forecasts of generating capability three years into future are taken from Edison Electric Institute *Semi-Annual Power Surveys,* 1951–1969.

Peak loads forecasts three years into future are taken from the same source.

Backlogs data for steam turbine generators for United States utility service are provided by Edison Electric Institute and private sources.

74 observations.

Description of Variables:

FCSTDCAP(T) = forecasted increase in generating capability for United States utilities, three years into the future, in thousands of kilowatts, as of period T.

FCSTDPEAK(T) = forecasted increase in peak loads for United States utilities, three years into the future, in thousands of kilowatts, as of period T.

TOTKWBL(T) = total kilowatts backlog of unfilled utility orders in the turbine generator industry in the United States, as of period T (thousands of kilowatts).

Regression Results:

(a) As a function of peak loads:

$$FCSTDCAP(T) = 1.214 \ FCSTDPEAK(T) \qquad R^2 = .79 \quad D\text{-}W = 0.3*$$
$$(t = 29)$$

(b) As a function of backlogs:

OLS: $FCSTDCAP(T) = 16820 + 0.606 \ TOTKWBL(T)$
$(t = 15) \quad (t = 29)$

$R^2 = .92 \quad D\text{-}W = 0.6*$

2SLS: $FCSTDCAP(T) = 14213 + 0.638 \ TOTKWBL(T)$
$(t = 8.9) \quad (t = 19)$

$R^2 = .89 \quad D\text{-}W = 0.6*$

*H-L: $FCSTDCAP(T) = 16100 + 0.599 \ TOTKWBL(T)$
$(t = 2.0) \quad (t = 3.0)$

$R^2 = .14 \quad D\text{-}W = 2.0$

NOTE: This is equation defining Variable VAR 11 in the simulation.

APPENDIX 8.
Utility Retirements of Generating Capacity.

Data:

Information on retirement and additions of steam turbine generator capacity, United States utility service, from Edison Electric Institute, *Historical Statistics of the Electric Utility Industry*, and various Edison Electric Institute *Statistical Yearbooks*. Data on current year margin of reserves from Edison Electric Institute *Power Survey* publications.

Annual data, 1950–1968.

Description of Variables:

KWRETIRE(T) = steam turbine generator capacity retired from service, in period T, in thousands of kilowatts annual rate.

KWADD(T) = steam turbine generator capacity added to service in period T, in thousands of kilowatts annual rate.

PCMARGIN(T) = percent margin of generating reserve, United States utility industry.

OLS Regression Results: $R^2 = .70$ Durbin-Watson $= 0.4^*$

KWRETIRE(T) = 139   +   23.4 PCMARGIN(T)   +   .016 KWADD(T)
                (t = 2.8)   (t = 9.5)   (t = 3.8)

2SLS Regression Results: $R^2 = .65$ Durbin-Watson $= 0.4^*$

KWRETIRE(T) = 271   +   25.6 PCMARGIN(T)   +   .0247 KWADD(T)
                (t = 3.7)   (t = 4.7)   (t = 3.3)

*Hildreth-Lu Regression Estimates: $R^2 = .14$ Durbin-Watson $= 1.9$

KWRETIRE(T) = 57.9   +   2.51 PCMARGIN(T)   +   .022 KWADD(T)
                (t = 1.4)   (t = 0.2)   (t = 3.9)

Note: This is equation defining Variable VAR 61 in the simulation.

APPENDIX 9.
The Average Order Price.

Data:

Price index (1961 book price = 10,000) for steam turbine generators ordered from United States manufacturers, constructed as the average of prices of individual turbine generators ordered from all three firms. Quarterly data, 1951–1963.

Wholesale price index for all industrial commodities from U.S. Bureau of Labor Statistics, 1957–1959 = 100.

Kilowatts backlogs, orders, and manufacturing capacities, quarterly data for all three manufacturers.

Total of 45 observations.

Description of Variables:

PRICE(T)   = average order price index as of period T.

WPI(T)   = wholesale price index as of period T.

UTILIZ(T)   = industry utilization rate in period T.

$$= \frac{\text{TOTSHIP(T)}}{\text{TOTCAP(T)}}$$

where TOTSHIP(T) equals quarterly kilowatts shipments by all three firms in period T, and TOTCAP(T) equals total industry capacity in quarterly kilowatts in period T.

MINYRSBL(T)   = minimum years of backlog, across all three firms.

$$= \text{minimum of} \left\{ \begin{array}{l} \text{GEYRSBL(T)} \\ \text{WEYRSBL(T)} \\ \text{ACYRSBL(T)} \end{array} \right\}$$

where GEYRSBL(T), WEYRSBL(T) and ACYRSBL(T) are the General Electric, Westinghouse, and Allis-Chalmers backlogs, in years, as computed by dividing their kilowatts backlogs by their kilowatts manufacturing capacities in period T.

DUMMY(T)   = dummy variable for conspiracy period, equal to 1.0 for quarters up through second quarter of 1959, and equals zero thereafter.

TOTKWORD(T)   = moving 4-quarter average of total industry kilowatts orders in period T, in thousands.

PCTFOR(T)   = percentage of industry orders in current year going to foreign competitors, as of period T.

OPS(T)   = dummy variable for OPS price control period, equal to 1.0 for quarters from first quarter of 1951 through first quarter of 1953, inclusive, and equals zero in all other periods.

Statistical Results:

(a)   Price Level Without Dummy Variable for Conspiracy

(i) ordinary least squares:

$$\text{PRICE(T)} = \begin{array}{l} -276 \\ (t = 11) \end{array} + \begin{array}{l} 3.17 \text{ WPI(T)} \\ (t = 14) \end{array}$$

$$+ \begin{array}{l} 44.87 \text{ UTILIZ(T)} \\ (t = 7.2) \end{array}$$

$$+ \begin{array}{l} 10.63 \text{ MINYRSBL(T)} \\ (t = 6.4) \end{array}$$

$R^2 = .87$ Durbin-Watson $= 1.51$

(ii) two-stage least squares:

$$\text{PRICE(T)} = \begin{array}{l} -354 \\ (t = 3) \end{array} + \begin{array}{l} 3.72 \text{ WPI(T)} \\ (t = 5.2) \end{array}$$

$$+ \begin{array}{l} 73.3 \text{ UTILIZ(T)} \\ (t = 1.9) \end{array}$$

$$+ \begin{array}{l} 10.20 \text{ MINYRSBL(T)} \\ (t = 1.9) \end{array}$$

$R^2 = .79$ Durbin-Watson $= 1.2$

(iii) Hildreth-Lu regression estimates:

$$\text{PRICE(T)} = \begin{array}{l} -155 \\ (t = 7.9) \end{array} + \begin{array}{l} 2.67 \text{ WPI(T)} \\ (t = 10.0) \end{array}$$

$$+ \begin{array}{l} 36.3 \text{ UTILIZ(T)} \\ (t = 5.0) \end{array}$$

$$+ \begin{array}{l} 10.65 \text{ MINYRSBL(T)} \\ (t = 4.7) \end{array}$$

$R^2 = .78$ Durbin-Watson $= 1.9$

The following are ordinary least squares estimates:

(b)   Price Level With Dummy Variable for Conspiracy for Full 1951–1959

$$\text{PRICE(T)} = \begin{array}{l} -279 \\ (t = 9.2) \end{array} + \begin{array}{l} 3.19 \text{ WPI(T)} \\ (t = 10) \end{array}$$

$$+ \begin{array}{l} 44.29 \text{ UTILIZ(T)} \\ (t = 5.8) \end{array}$$

$$+ \begin{array}{l} 10.43 \text{ MINYRSBL(T)} \\ (t = 4.7) \end{array}$$

$$+ \begin{array}{l} .62 \text{ DUMMY(T)} \\ (t = 0.13) \end{array}$$

$R^2 = .87$ Durbin-Watson $= 1.51$

(c)   Price Level with Orders Rate Added as Explanatory Variable

$$\text{PRICE(T)} = \begin{array}{l} -279 \\ (t = 11) \end{array} + \begin{array}{l} 3.17 \text{ WPI(T)} \\ (t = 14) \end{array}$$

$$+ \begin{array}{l} 45.92 \text{ UTILIZ(T)} \\ (t = 7) \end{array}$$

$$+ \quad 10.61 \text{ MINYRSBL(T)}$$
$$(t = 6.3)$$

$$+ \quad .00000046 \text{ TOTKWORD(T)}$$
$$(t = .57)$$

$R^2 = .87$ Durbin-Watson $= 1.53$

(d) Price Level with Foreign Competition Added as Explanatory Variable

---

$$\text{PRICE(T)} \quad = \quad -264 \quad + \quad 3.04 \text{ WPI(T)}$$
$$(t = 9.7) \quad (t = 12)$$

$$+ \quad 42.57 \text{ UTILIZ(T)}$$
$$(t = 6.4)$$

$$+ \quad 11.12 \text{ MINYRSBL(T)}$$
$$(t = 6.4)$$

$$+ \quad 1.9 \times 10^5 \text{ PCTFOR(T)}$$
$$(t = 1.0)$$

$R^2 = .87$ Durbin-Watson $= 1.48$

(e) Price Level with OPS Government Price Controls Added as an Explanatory
Variable

$$\text{PRICE(T)} \quad = \quad -275 \quad + \quad 3.18 \text{ WPI(T)}$$
$$(t = 9.8) \quad (t = 10.0)$$

$$+ \quad 44.2 \text{ UTILIZ(T)}$$
$$(t = 5.6)$$

$$+ \quad 10.6 \text{ MINYRSBL(T)}$$
$$(t = 6.1)$$

$$- \quad 0.38 \text{ OPS(T)}$$
$$(t = 0.80)$$

$R^2 = .87$ Durbin-Watson $= 1.50$

(f) Price Level with Two Dummy Variables to Allow for a Differential Conspiratorial
Impact in 1951–1955 and in 1955–1959

$$\text{PRICE(T)} \quad = \quad -280 \quad + \quad 3.10 \text{ WPI(T)}$$
$$(t = 4.7) \quad (t = 6.0)$$

$$+ \quad 44.4 \text{ UTILIZ(T)}$$
$$(t = 4.0)$$

$$+ \quad 10.36 \text{ MINYRSBL(T)}$$
$$(t = 3.2)$$

$$+ \quad 0.80 \text{ DUMMY:1951–1955(T)}$$
$$(t = 1.0)$$

$$+ \quad 0.78 \text{ DUMMY:1955–1959(T)}$$
$$(t = 1.5)$$

$R^2 = .87$ Durbin-Watson $= 1.50$

NOTE: This is equation defining Variable VAR 27 in the simulation.

APPENDIX 10.
Long-Term Trend in Average Value Per Kilowatt of Steam Turbine Generators Shipped.

Data:

Four firms: General Electric Lynn, General Electric Schenectady, Westinghouse Philadelphia, and Allis-Chalmers.
Selected years between 1904 and 1970.

Description of Variables:

VALUE(I,T) = average value in constant 1957–1959 dollars per kilowatt of steam turbine generators shipped by the Ith firm in year.T.

GECUMKW(T) = cumulative kilowatts of steam turbine generators shipped by the General Electric Company since 1900, as of year T.

T = year, with range of values from 04 to 70.

SIZE(I,T) = average size, in kilowatts per unit, of steam turbine generators shipped by the Ith firm, in year T. (Product technology.)

ALLIS = dummy variable which equals 1.0 if observation pertains to Allis-Chalmers, and zero otherwise.

WESTING = dummy variable which equals 1.0 if observation pertains to Westinghouse, and zero otherwise.

Regression Results:

(1) Simple Trend: (Total no. of observations = 72.)
  (a) Log-log learning: $R^2 = .35$ Durbin-Watson = 1.38

$$\log(\text{VALUE}(I,T)) = \underset{(t=2.6)}{0.889} - \underset{(t=6.1)}{0.190} \log(\text{GECUMKW}(T)$$

  (b) Semi-log learning: $R^2 = .42$ Durbin-Watson = 1.71

$$\text{VALUE}(I,T) = \underset{(t=10.)}{1.063} - \underset{(t=7.2)}{0.0677} \log(\text{GECUMKW}(T))$$

  (c) Linear: $R^2 = 0.35$ Durbin-Watson = 1.56

$$\text{VALUE}(I,T) = \underset{(t=20.)}{0.42} - \underset{(t=6.1)}{0.136 \times 10^{-5}} \text{GECUMKW}(T)$$

  (d) Time Trend: $R^2 = 0.42$ Durbin-Watson = 1.72

$$\text{VALUE}(I,T) = \underset{(t=14.)}{0.63} - \underset{(t=7.2)}{0.0060} T$$

(2) Adding the Product Technology Proxy Variable (total observations = 57):

(a) Without dummy variables for firms: $R^2 = 0.60$ Durbin-Watson $= 1.7$

$$\log(\text{VALUE}(I,T)) = 0.22 - 0.11 \log(\text{SIZE})I,T))$$
$$(t = 0.6) \quad (t = 3.2)$$

$$- 0.093 \log(\text{GECUMKW}(I,T))$$
$$(t = 2.4)$$

(b) With dummy variables for firms: $R^2 = 0.65$ Durbin-Watson $= 1.7$

$$\log(\text{VALUE}(I,T)) = 0.11 - 0.08 \log(\text{SIZE}(I,T))$$
$$(t = 2.3)$$

$$- 0.10 \log(\text{GECUMKW}(I,T))$$
$$(t = 2.7)$$

$$+ 0.09 \text{ WESTING} + 0.17 \text{ ALLIS}$$
$$(t = 1.3) \quad\quad\quad (t = 2.8)$$

APPENDIX 11.

Data:

(a) Power Capacitors: Total industry data, for years 1921 to 1968.
Total of 48 observations.

(b) Power Transformers: Total industry data, for years 1933–1941, 1945–1968.
Total of 33 observations.

Description of Variables:

CVALUE(T) = average dollars per kilovar selling price of the largest-selling-volume model of power capacitors, in constant 1957–1959 dollars, as of year T.

CUMKVAR(T) = cumulative kilovars of power capacitors shipped by the total United States industry since 1918, as of year T.

TVALUE(T) = average value in constant 1957–1959 dollars per MVA of power transformers shipped by the total United States industry in year T.

CUMMVA(T) = cumulative megavolt-amp of power transformers shipped by the total United States industry since 1900, as of year T.

Regression Results:

(a) Power Capacitors:

Log-log learning curve: $R^2 = .95$ Durbin-Watson $= 0.29$

$$\log(\text{CVALUE}(T)) = 6.76 \ - \ 0.55 \ \log(\text{CUMKVAR}(T))$$
$$(t = 41.) \ \ (t = 29.)$$

Semi-log learning curve: $R^2 = .68$ Durbin-Watson $= 0.15$

$$\text{CVALUE}(T) = 108. \ - \ 10.4 \ \log(\text{CUMKVAR}(T))$$
$$(t = 12.) \ \ (t = 10.)$$

Linear: $R^2 = .20$ Durbin-Watson $= 0.07$

$$\text{CVALUE}(T) = 32.0 \ - \ 0.36 \times 10^{-3} \ \text{CUMKVAR}(T)$$
$$(t = 6.6) \ \ (t = 3.4)$$

Time trend: $R^2 = .65$ Durbin-Watson $= 0.14$

$$\text{CVALUE}(T) = 101. \ - \ 1.77 \ T$$
$$(t = 11.) \ \ (t = 9.3)$$

(b) Power Transformers

Log-log-learning curve: $R^2 = .49$ Durbin-Watson $= 2.1$

$$\log(\text{TVALUE}(T) = 0.60 \ - \ 0.42 \ \log(\text{CUMMVA}(T))$$
$$(t = 1.3) \ \ (t = 5.5)$$

Semi-log learning curve: $R^2 = .16$ Durbin-Watson $= 2.1$

$$\text{TVALUE(T)} = 0.25 \quad - \quad 0.032 \ \log(\text{CUMMVA(T)}$$
$$(t = 3.2) \quad (t = 2.5)$$

Linear: $R^2 = .18$ Durbin-Watson $= 2.1$

$$\text{TVALUE(T)} = 0.087 \quad - \quad 0.55 \times 10^{-4} \ \text{CUMMVA(T)}$$
$$(t = 4.8) \quad (t = 2.0)$$

Time trend: $R^2 = .18$ Durbin-Watson $= 2.1$

$$\text{TVALUE(T)} = 0.20 \quad - \quad 0.0027 \ \text{T}$$
$$(t = 3.7) \quad (t = 2.6)$$

NOTE: The extreme autocorrelation present in the regressions on capacitor data does not preclude choice of trend on the basis of the rather large differences in goodness of fit.

DIRECT COSTS PER KILOWATT OF STEAM TURBINE GENERATORS SHIPPED.

Data:

Three firms: General Electric Schenectady, Westinghouse Philadelphia and Allis-Chalmers.

Selected years between 1937 and 1963.

Total of 47 observations.

Description of Variables:

COST(I,T)   = estimate of average direct cost, in constant 1957–1959 dollars per kilowatt, of steam turbine generators shipped by the Ith firm in year T.

CUMKW(I,T) = cumulative kilowatts shipped by the Ith firm since 1900, as of year T.

SIZE(T)   = an index of the average physical size of steam turbine generators shipped in year T.

PRICE(T)   = price index for steam turbine generator orders received in year T.

The variable COST(I,T) is the direct cost in constant 1957–1959 dollars per kilowatt, of the Ith firm in year T, under the assumption that the Ith firm had General Electric's product mix.

Regression Results:

(a)   Simple learning curve: $R^2 = 0.31$

$$\log \text{COST(I,T)} = 4.00 \; - \; 0.102 \log \text{CUMKW(I,T)}$$
$$(t = 17.) \quad (t = 4.5)$$

(b)   Adding size of unit, and price level variables: $R^2 = 0.44$

$$\log \text{COST(I,T)} = 0.18 \; - \; 0.106 \log \text{CUMKW(I,T)}$$
$$(t = 0.2) \quad (t = 4.7)$$
$$- \; 0.70 \log \text{SIZE(T)}$$
$$(t = 3.1)$$
$$+ \; 0.32 \log \text{PRICE(T)}$$
$$(t = 2.4)$$

(c)   Previous model, estimated in two-stage least squares: $R^2 = .16$

$$\log \text{COST(I,T)} = 1.53 \; - \; .006 \text{ CUMKW(I,T)}$$
$$(t = 0.8) \quad (t = .05)$$
$$- \; 0.42 \text{ SIZE(T)}$$
$$(t = 1.2)$$
$$+ \; 0.0002 \text{ PRICE(T)}$$
$$(t = .0005)$$

NOTE: These are equations for Variables VAR 67, VAR 70, VAR 83 in the simulation.

APPENDIX 13.
MODELS OF OVERHEAD COSTS.

Data:

Three firms: General Electric Schenectady, Westinghouse Philadelphia, and Allis-Chalmers (turbine generator operations only).

Annual data: 1946 to 1963 for General Electric and Westinghouse;
1946 to 1962 for Allis-Chalmers.
As taken from divisional profit and loss statements, and after reconciliation of differing accounting conventions within the limits feasible.

Description of Variables:

OVERHEAD(T) = total dollars "overhead" expenditures in year T, in millions of current dollars.

SALES(T) = total dollars net sales billed in year T, in millions of current dollars.

STRIKE = dummy variable which equals 1 for year 1956 and 0.33 for year 1957, and zero otherwise, to compensate for impact of Westinghouse strike.

(a) Regression Results (Simple Ratio Rule):

General Electric: $R^2 = .71$ Durbin-Watson = 0.3

OVERHEAD(T) = 3.28 + 0.118 SALES(T)
              (t = 1.2) (t = 6.1)

Westinghouse: $R^2 = .88$ Durbin-Watson = 1.6

OVERHEAD(T) = 0.71 + 0.218 SALES(T) − 8.29 STRIKE
              (t = .5)   (t = 9.4)   (t = 3.3)

Allis-Chalmers: $R^2 = .55$ Durbin-Watson = 0.7

OVERHEAD(T) = 2.13 + 0.114 Sales(T)
              (t = 3.3) (t = 4.3)

(b) Regression Results (Targeted Expenditures (Lintner, etc.) Model):

General Electric:

OLS: $R^2 = .31$ Durbin-Watson = 1.3
[OVERHEAD(T) − OVERHEAD(T − 1)] = 1.72 + 0.0353 SALES(T)
                                    (t = 0.9) (t = 1.7)

                        − 0.300 OVERHEAD(T − 1)
                            (T = 2.4)

2SLS: $R^2 = .30$ Durbin-Watson = 1.3

$$[\text{OVERHEAD}(T) - \text{OVERHEAD}(T-1)] = 2.03 + 0.0298\ \text{SALES}(T)$$
$$(t = 0.9)\ (t = 1.1)$$

$$-\ 0.27\ \text{OVERHEAD}(T-1)$$
$$(t = 1.9)$$

Westinghouse:

OLS: $R^2 = .56$ Durbin-Watson = 1.8

$$[\text{OVERHEAD}(T) - \text{OVERHEAD}(T-1)] = 0.51 + 0.214\ \text{SALES}(T)$$
$$(t = 0.2)\ (t = 3.2)$$

$$-\ 1.09\ \text{OVERHEAD}(T-1)$$
$$(t = 4.0)$$

2SLS: $R^2 = .55$ Durbin-Watson = 1.9

$$[\text{OVERHEAD}(T) - \text{OVERHEAD}(T-1)] = -0.19 + 0.25\ \text{SALES}(T)$$
$$(t = .06)\ (t = 1.9)$$

$$-\ 1.21\ \text{OVERHEAD}(T-1)$$
$$(t = 2.7)$$

Allis-Chalmers:

OLS: $R^2 = .51$ Durbin-Watson = 2.0

$$[\text{OVERHEAD}(T) - \text{OVERHEAD}(T-1)] = 0.82 + 0.082\ \text{SALES}(T)$$
$$(t = 1.1)\ (t = 3.2)$$

$$-\ 0.52\ \text{OVERHEAD}(T-1)$$
$$(t = 3.1)$$

2SLS: $R^2 = .19$ Durbin-Watson = 1.0

$$[\text{OVERHEAD}(T) - \text{OVERHEAD}(T-1)] = 0.25 + .157\ \text{SALES}(T)$$
$$(t = 0.2)\ (t = 3.0)$$

$$-\ 0.74\ \text{OVERHEAD}(T-1)$$
$$(t = 3.0)$$

(c) Regression Results (Competing Explanatory Variables):

R^2(Percentage of Variance Explained)

	Overhead Expenditures Per Year as a Linear Function of:			
	Net Sales Billed	Contribution Dollars	Profits Before Tax	Orders Received
General Electric	.71	.73	.54	.005
Westinghouse	.88	.81	.09	.30
Allis-Chalmers	.55	.68	.10	.19

NOTE: The models outlined in (b) above defined VAR 103, VAR 104, VAR 105 in the simulations. In this model, estimated coefficient "a" equals the built-in annual inflation in overhead spending, "b1/b2" equals the target overhead spending ratio, and "b2" equals the speed of adjustment coefficient.

APPENDIX 14.
Manufacturing Capacity.

Data:

Estimated annual manufacturing capacity, five days per week, three shifts per day, in kilowatts, at the product mix which prevailed during the year for that manufacturer, converted into equivalent quarterly series, 1951–1962.

Total kilowatts backlog for General Electric, Allis-Chalmers, and Westinghouse, quarterly data, 1951–1963.

Total of 48 observations.

Description of Variables:

GECAP(T) = manufacturing capacity of General Electric, as of period T, in kilowatts per year.

WECAP(T) = manufacturing capacity of Westinghouse as of period T, in kilowatts per year.

ACCAP(T) = Allis-Chalmers kilowatts manufacturing capacity, in kilowatts per year, as of period T, where T refers to quarterly time.

ACUTILIZ(T) = Allis-Chalmers utilization rate, as of period T, as fraction of manufacturing throughput capacity.

$$= \frac{ACSHIP(T)}{ACCAP(T)}$$

where ACSHIP(T) equals Allis-Chalmers 4-quarter moving average shipments as of period T, and ACCAP(T) equals Allis-Chalmers manufacturing capacity in kilowatts as of period T, annual rates.

ACKWBL(T) = Allis-Chalmers kilowatts backlog as of period T.

GEKWBL(T) = General Electric kilowatts backlog, as of period T.

WEKWBL(T) = Westinghouse kilowatts backlog, as of period T.

STRIKE = dummy variable for 1955–1956 Westinghouse strike.

TREND = time trend variable, equal to 60, 61, 62, etc., year.

Statistical Results:

(a) *General Electric:*

OLS: $R^2 = .71$ Durbin-Watson = 0.6*

$$GECAP(T) = 340{,}009 + 1.22\ WECAP(T-4)$$
$$(t = 0.3)\quad (t = 10)$$
$$+ 0.156\ GEKWBL(T-4)$$
$$(t = 3.3)$$

*H-L: $R^2 = .03$ Durbin-Watson = 1.6

$$\text{GECAP} = 858{,}000 + 0.16 \text{ WECAP}(T - 4)$$
$$(t = 7.1) \qquad (t = 1.2)$$
$$+ .002 \text{ GEKWBL}(T - 4)$$
$$(t = .07)$$

(b) *Westinghouse:*

OLS: $R^2 = .91$ Durbin-Watson = 1.5*

$$\text{WECAP}(T) \; 1{,}751{,}000 + 0.74 \text{ GECAP}(T - 4)$$
$$(t = 2.9) \qquad (t = 17)$$
$$+ 0.078 \text{ WEKWBL}(T - 4)$$
$$(t = 2.1)$$
$$- 1{,}951{,}000 \text{ STRIKE}$$
$$(t = 5.5)$$

*H-L: $R^2 = .09$ Durbin-Watson = 1.8

$$\text{WECAP}(T) = 1{,}343{,}000 + 0.14 \text{ GECAP}(T - 4)$$
$$(t = 1.9) \qquad (t = 1.8)$$
$$+ 0.11 \text{ WEKWBL}(T - 4)$$
$$(t = 1.5)$$
$$- 1{,}870{,}000 \text{ STRIKE}$$
$$(t = 1.9)$$

(c) *Allis-Chalmers:*

OLS: $R^2 = .92$ Durbin-Watson = 0.74*

$$\text{ACCAP}(T) = -8{,}063{,}000 + 310{,}500 \text{ ACUTILIZ}(T - 4)$$
$$(t = 13) \qquad (t = 3.2)$$
$$+ .0928 \text{ ACKWBL}(T)$$
$$(t = 3.7)$$
$$+ 162{,}000 \text{ TREND}$$
$$(t = 14)$$

*H-L: $R^2 = .32$ Durbin-Watson = 2.0

$$\text{ACCAP}(T) = -701{,}000 + 27{,}500 \text{ ACUTILIZ}(T - 4)$$
$$(t = 2.6) \qquad (t = 4.0)$$
$$+ .010 \text{ ACKWBL}(T)$$
$$(t = 0.2)$$
$$+ 203{,}500 \text{ TREND}$$
$$(t = 0.16)$$

NOTE: These are equations defining Variables VAR 38, VAR 39, and VAR 40 in the simulation. H-L refers to Hildreth-Lu regression results.

APPENDIX 15.
Market Share Determinants.

Data:

Quarterly data on share of total industry kilowatts orders for steam turbine generators, for domestic service, for period 1951–1962 inclusive.

Total of 48 observations.

Description of Variables:

DGESHARE(T) = change in General Electric fractional share of industry orders, in period T.

= GESHARE(T) − GESHARE(T − 1)

where GESHARE(T) is General Electric's share in period T of industry kilowatts orders (moving 4-quarter average of share in each quarter).

GEYRSBL(T) = General Electric years of backlog, as of period T, computed as the ratio of total General Electric kilowatts backlog of unshipped orders, divided by total General Electric manufacturing capacity, in kilowatts per year, as of period T.

DGESHCAP(T) = change in General Electric fractional share of industry manufacturing capacity as of period T.

$$= \frac{\text{GECAP(T)}}{\text{TOTCAP(T)}} - \frac{\text{GECAP(T} - 1)}{\text{TOTCAP(T} - 1)}$$

where GECAP(T) is General Electric manufacturing capacity, in kilowatts in period T, and TOTCAP(T) is total industry manufacturing capacity in kilowatts.

ACSHARE(T) = Allis-Chalmers fractional share of industry kilowatts orders, in period T (moving 4-quarter average of share in each quarter).

ACYRSBL(T) = Allis-Chalmers years of backlog as of period T, computed as ratio of total Allis-Chalmers kilowatts backlog of unshipped orders, divided by total Allis-Chalmers manufacturing capacity, in kilowatts per year, as of period T.

DACSHCAP(T) = change in Allis-Chalmers fractional share of total industry manufacturing capacity, as of period T.

$$= \frac{\text{ACCAP(T)}}{\text{TOTCAP(T)}} - \frac{\text{ACCAP(T} - 1)}{\text{TOTCAP(T} - 1)}$$

where ACCAP(T) is Allis-Chalmers manufacturing capacity, in kilowatts per year, as of period T, and TOTCAP(T) is total industry manufacturing capacity, in kilowatts per year.

PRICE(T) = index of 4-quarter moving average industry price level as of period T, for turbine generator orders, where 1961 book price level = 1.00.

RELGEPRICE(T) = index of relative General Electric price, as of period T, computed by dividing average General Electric multiplier on book price, by average industry multiplier on book price, on quarterly basis.

Regression Results:

(a) *General Electric:*

OLS: $R^2 = .14$ Durbin-Watson = 2.2

DGESHARE(T) = 2.05 − 1.98 RELGEPRICE(T)
            (t = 2.2)   (t = 2.1)
                 − .025 GEYRSBL(T)
                    (t = 1.9)
                 + 0.972 DGESHCAP(T)
                    (t = 1.4)

2SLS: $R^2 = .06$ Durbin-Watson = 1.8

DGESHARE(T) = 1.71 − 1.68 RELGEPRICE(T)
            (t = 1.4)   (t = 1.4)
                 − .014 GEYRSBL(T)
                    (t = 0.6)
                 + 2.86 DGESHCAP(T)
                    (t =1 .7)

(b) *Allis-Chalmers:*

OLS: $R^2 = .54$ Durbin-Watson = 1.0*

ACSHARE(T) = −3.17 + 3.00 RELGEPRICE(T)
            (t = 3.2)   (t = 3.0)
                 + .245 PRICE(T)
                    (t = 4.6)
                 + .038 ACYRSBL(T)
                    (t = 2.0)
                 + 3.34 DACSHCAP(T)
                    (t = 2.6)

2SLS: $R^2 = .54$ Durbin-Watson = 1.0*

ACSHARE(T) = −2.84 + 2.67 RELGEPRICE(T)
            (t = 2.1)   (t = 2.0)
                 + .255 PRICE(T)
                    (t = 3.3)
                 + .031 ACRYSBL(T)
                    (t = 1.0)
                 + 4.02 DACSHCAP(T)
                    (t = 1.8)

*H-L: $R^2 = .19$ Durbin-Watson $= 1.8$

$$ASCHARE(T) = -4.95 + 4.34 \ RELGEPRICE(T)$$
$$(t = 1.9) \quad (t = 1.8)$$
$$+ \quad .130 \ PRICE(T)$$
$$(t = 0.9)$$
$$+ \quad .085 \ ACYRSBL(T)$$
$$(t = 1.8)$$
$$+ \quad 0.66 \ DACSHCAP(T)$$
$$(t = 0.7)$$

NOTE: The General Electric equation defines VAR 96 in the simulation; the Allis-Chalmers equation defines VAR 89. H-L refers to Hildreth-Lu technique for autocorrelation.

APPENDIX 16.
GENERAL ELECTRIC'S STRATEGY: SHARE V. EARNINGS.

Data:

Information on relative prices of General Electric, Westinghouse, and Allis-Chalmers obtained from electrical litigation proceedings, quarterly data, 1948–1963.

Sales, profit data are annual series converted into equivalent quarterly series, 1951–1963.

Average price index is moving 4-quarter average of index of order prices, 1951–1963 (1961 book price = 1.00).

Total of 41 observations.

Description of Variables:

RELGEPRICE(T) = index of relative General Electric price, computed by dividing average General Electric multiplier on book price by the average industry (Allis-Chalmers, Westinghouse, and General Electric) multiplier on book price, on quarterly basis.

DELTAPRICE(T) = change in order price index over four periods (one year).

= AVGPRICE(T) − AVGPRICE(T − 4) where AVGPRICE (T) is the 4-quarter moving average price level in period T, for the total industry.

GEPRATE(T) = General Electric profit rate on turbine generators, in period T, expressed as fraction.

$$= \frac{GEPRFT(T)}{GESALES(T)}$$

where GEPRFT(T) is total dollars General Electric profit and GESALES(T) is total dollars General Electric sales revenue, in period T.

GESHARE(T) = General Electric's fractional share of total kilowatts industry orders in period T, moving 4-quarter average.

OLS Regression Results: $R^2 = .48$ Durbin-Watson = 1.9

RELGEPRICE(T) = 0.95 + 0.25 GEPRATE(T)
(t = 49) (t = 2.8)

+ .039 GESHARE(T − 4)
(t = 1.9)

− .024 DELTRPRICE(T)
(t = 1.3)

2SLS Regression Results: $R^2 = .41$ Durbin-Watson = 1.8

RELGEPRICE(T) =	0.98	+	.08 GEPRATE(T)
	(t = 60)		(t = 0.2)
		+	.048 GESHARE(T − 4)
			(t = 2.2)
		−	0.007 DELTAPRICE(T)
			(t = 2.9)

NOTE: This is equation defining Variable VAR 23 in the simulation.

APPENDIX 17.
A Note on Cost Accounting Practices and Pricing Strategy

Strategic behavior is determined in part by the reported operating results of the business. But each firm collects and reports (to its own management) its operating results—in particular, the *costs* of the business—in a unique manner, in accordance with the arbitrary accounting practices of that firm. Thus, strategic behavior will be influenced by accounting convention. From litigation testimony, the following is apparent:[1]

The Westinghouse Cost System for Turbines

Westinghouse managers in this marketplace employed a profit and loss statement which was based only upon the *turbine* (Lester, Pa.) portion of the business. Generators, the other half of a turbine generator set, were built, and subjected to pricing and cost control, in East Pittsburgh. Turbines accounted for about three quarters of the total value of a typical turbine generator contract. At General Electric, on the other hand, both the turbines and the generators appear to have been costed, and priced, within the same cost center, the same manufacturing facility, and the same management organization and profit center. One suspects that this gave General Electric managers better cost information, and greater strategic coordination, as befits a market leader.

The Westinghouse cost system distinguished between two major types of total cost: the so-called *direct* costs (which were put into "inventory" during the production of the machines), and other costs, representing *overheads* and other costs which were expensed directly at the time they were incurred. Direct costs at Westinghouse encompassed three major items: direct material, direct labor, and other factory expense, all at standard rates. Differences between *standard* direct costs, and *actual* direct costs, were expensed monthly.

Overhead costs at Westinghouse were likewise subdivided into finer categories: "committed" costs which were committed on a program basis, and "managing" costs such as marketing, product development, and other administration. These were expensed as incurred.

Since Westinghouse managers made an important distinction in their books between direct and overhead costs, our own analysis of manufacturer costs proceeded accordingly.

The General Electric Cost System

Unlike Westinghouse, General Electric accumulated direct costs on a job-by-job basis, and eschewed any standard cost system for direct labor and material. Thus,

---

[1] These data are collected from the deposition testimony of Carl Buehler, L. M. Eikner, and Howard T. Duff, stenographer's minutes, Ohio Valley Electric v. General Electric et al., 62 Civ. 695, S.D.N.Y.

there were no direct cost variances to be expensed in the current operating statement; all actual direct costs were put into inventory until time of shipment.

General Electric also treated its overhead costs differently from Westinghouse; here, General Electric employed a standard cost system. General Electric defined two major categories of overhead expenditures: "indirect manufacturing expense" (IME) and "applied apparatus expense" (AAE), both of which were applied to individual turbine jobs in proportion to actual direct labor expenditures, according to a standard rate. In periods of slack throughput, there was generally an *under* liquidation of actual IME costs. When the factory was very busy, however, there tended to be an *over* liquidation of IME. Subsequent changes in the definition of these overhead costs (in particular, the transition to a category of engineering expenditures termed PECE, for "product engineering costs and expenses") did not change the basic principle.

In addition to indirect manufacturing expense, and engineering expenditures, General Electric also categorized a substantial proportion of its overheads as "commercial and administrative" expense. This category of overheads appears to have been expensed on a current basis.

In analyzing prices, and in preparing bids on individual jobs, General Electric pricers appeared to lean most heavily upon *actual direct* costs and *standard overhead* costs, with cost data spanning both the turbine and the generator portion of operations.

In summary, both General Electric and Westinghouse accumulated direct costs in work-in-process inventory, until date of shipment. However, Westinghouse accumulated *standard* direct costs, and expensed the variances, whereas General Electric accumulated *actual* direct costs.

Impact on Timing of Reported Earnings

The difference in *direct cost* reporting methods would affect the timing of reported earnings. Under conditions of accelerating throughput, the Westinghouse cost system would probably yield negative direct cost variances, and would tend to inflate current earnings, relative to those under the General Electric system. In a downturn, on the other hand, General Electric reported earnings would tend for a time to be inflated relative to those of Westinghouse.

For *overhead* costs, we may draw just the opposite conclusion. Since General Electric employed a standard overhead cost system, while Westinghouse expensed its overhead in the current period, General Electric's reported earnings would tend to be smoothed, with *higher* reported earnings than those of Westinghouse during periods of minimum business activity, and with *lower* reported earnings than those of Westinghouse during periods of maximum business activity.

On balance, these two contrasting accounting systems may have provided an optimal strategic "fit" for the respective competitors, and their leader-follower roles. The reason: if one wishes to encourage operating managers to resist slashing prices during a business downturn, one will design an accounting system which tends to even out the profit flows, thereby shielding managers from the full fury of profit-performance pressures. This would probably be the pricing behavior appropriate to a market leader. The General Electric cost accounting system, which both *smoothed* profit flows overall (through the workings of the standard overhead system), and also *retarded* the profit flows over the business cycle (through the absence of a standard direct cost system), worked to reduce the short-run profit pressures on the General Electric operating managers, and encouraged its managers to buffer market shocks in the conjectured price-leader mode.

The Westinghouse system, relative to General Electric's worked in the contrary direction, and one would therefore expect to see Westinghouse managers more prone to lead the way with price reductions during a business downturn, and also to be the first to raise prices when demand strengthened once again. As the analysis of market-share strategy indicates, this is precisely the behavior which one observes in the turbine generator industry over the 1948–1963 period.

APPENDIX 18.
The Integrated Model.

Chart A18.1 is a flow chart of that portion of the system concerned with utility operations. Chart A18.2 shows that portion of the system concerned with the physical production of turbine generators by the three manufacturers. Chart A18.3 depicts the links within the manufacturer, financial, and strategic sectors of the model.

The final integrated manufacturer-customer system is represented by a 94-equation model. The full set of relationships can be used to simulate the contemporaneous behavior of all of the variables in the system. Table A18.1 is a glossary of the variables which are employed in the final integrated model. Table A18.2 defines the final model in mathematical terms.

THE UTILITY SUBSYSTEM

CHART A18.1. The Utility Subsystem.

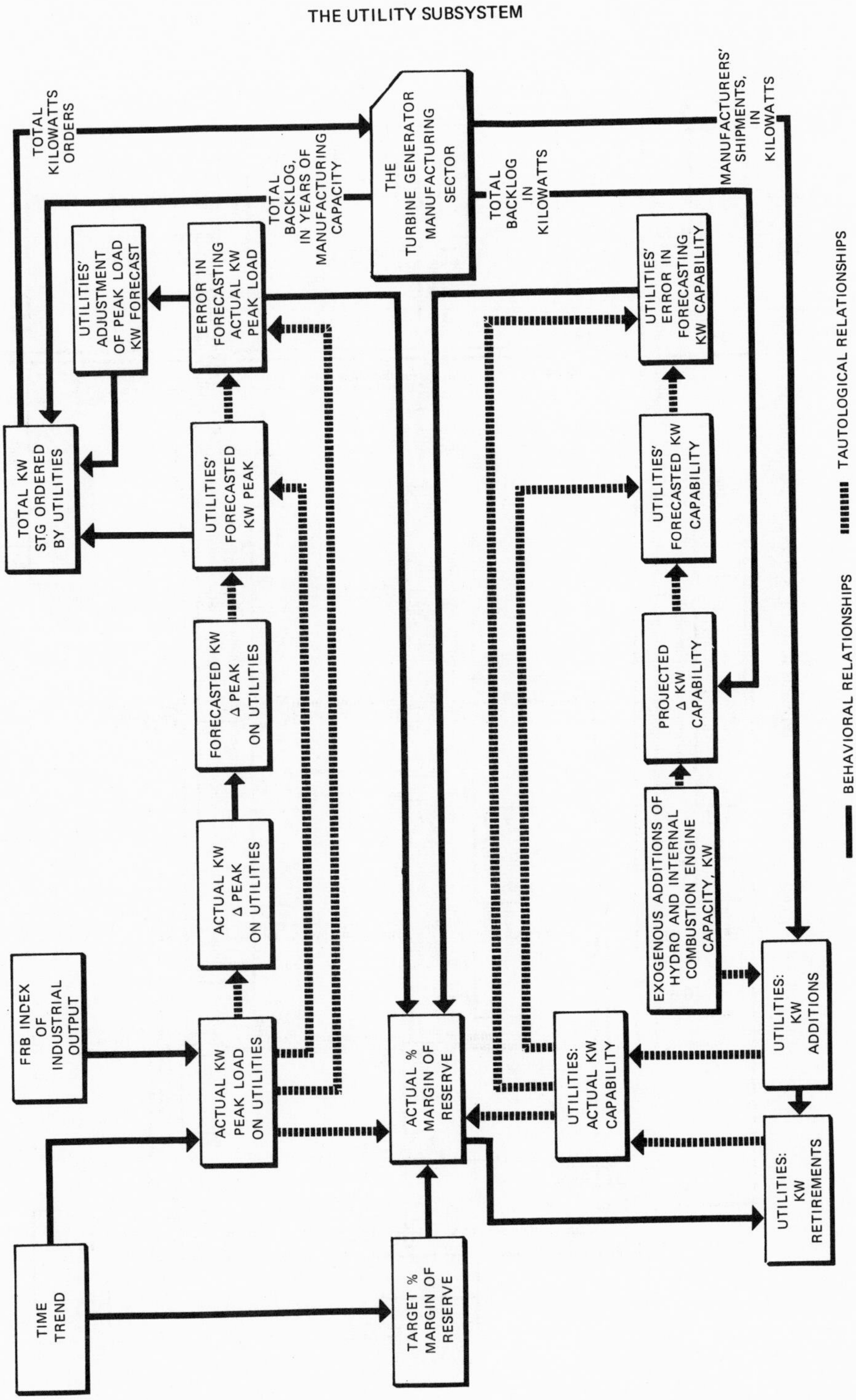

BEHAVIORAL RELATIONSHIPS

TAUTOLOGICAL RELATIONSHIPS

TIME TREND

FRB INDEX OF INDUSTRIAL OUTPUT

TARGET % MARGIN OF RESERVE

ACTUAL KW PEAK LOAD ON UTILITIES

ACTUAL KW Δ PEAK ON UTILITIES

FORECASTED KW Δ PEAK ON UTILITIES

UTILITIES' FORECASTED KW PEAK

ERROR IN FORECASTING ACTUAL KW PEAK LOAD

UTILITIES' ADJUSTMENT OF PEAK LOAD KW FORECAST

TOTAL KW STG ORDERED BY UTILITIES

TOTAL KILOWATTS ORDERS

THE TURBINE GENERATOR MANUFACTURING SECTOR

TOTAL BACKLOG, IN YEARS OF MANUFACTURING CAPACITY

TOTAL BACKLOG IN KILOWATTS

MANUFACTURERS' SHIPMENTS, IN KILOWATTS

ACTUAL % MARGIN OF RESERVE

UTILITIES: ACTUAL KW CAPABILITY

EXOGENOUS ADDITIONS OF HYDRO AND INTERNAL COMBUSTION ENGINE CAPACITY, KW

PROJECTED Δ KW CAPABILITY

UTILITIES' FORECASTED KW CAPABILITY

UTILITIES' ERROR IN FORECASTING KW CAPABILITY

UTILITIES: KW ADDITIONS

UTILITIES: KW RETIREMENTS

THE MANUFACTURER OPERATIONS SUBSYSTEM

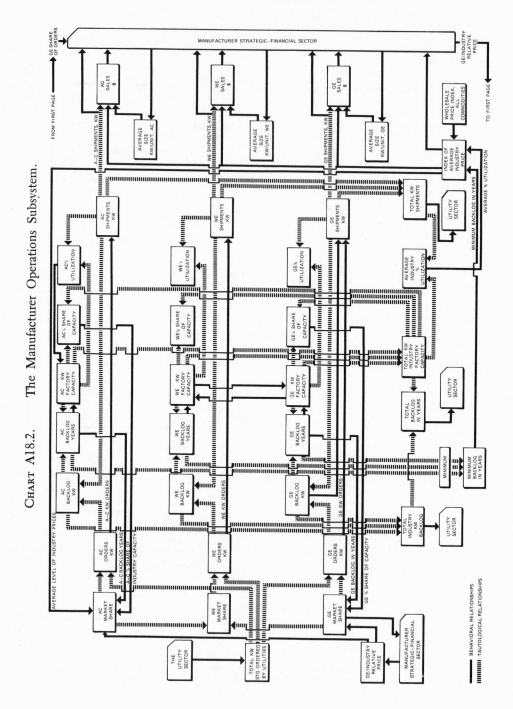

CHART A18.2.   The Manufacturer Operations Subsystem.

CHART A18.3.   The Manufacturers' Strategic-Financial Subsystem.

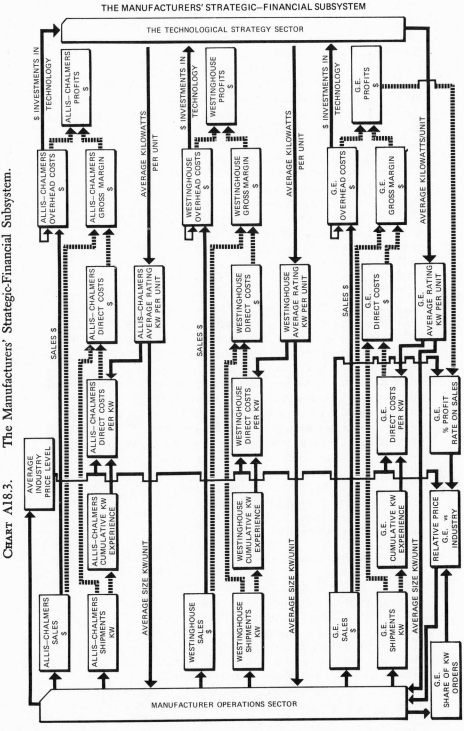

TABLE A18.1.
LIST OF VARIABLES.

ENDOGENOUS

VAR3 = peak load, kilowatts
VAR4 = 3-year-out forecast of peak load, kilowatts
VAR5 = 3-year-out forecast of increase in peak load, kilowatts
VAR6 = historical 5-year increase in peak, kilowatts
VAR7 = error in forecasting peak, 3-years-out, kilowatts
VAR8 = error in forecasting peak, 3-years-out, as fraction of load
VAR9 = forecast 3-years-out, of capability, kilowatts
VAR10 = generating capability, kilowatts
VAR11 = forecast 3-years-out, increase in capability, kilowatts
VAR12 = total industry backlog, kilowatts
VAR13 = error in forecasting capability, kilowatts
VAR14 = error in forecasting capability, as fraction of capability
VAR15 = utility reserve margin, kilowatts
VAR16 = utility reserve margin, as percent of capability
VAR17 = forecast of peak 2-years-out, kilowatts
VAR18 = change in peak load forecasts, kilowatts
VAR19 = total kilowatts ordered by utilities
VAR20 = total industry backlog, in years of capacity
VAR21 = General Electric share of order, percent
VAR22 = change in General Electric share of orders, percentage points
VAR23 = General Electric 4-quarter-average price relative to industry, ratio
VAR24 = General Electric backlog, in years of capacity
VAR25 = annual General Electric change in 4-quarter-average share of capacity
VAR26 = Allis-Chalmers share of orders, fraction
VAR27 = industry price level, index number (1961 book = 10,000)
VAR28 = Allis-Chalmers backlog, in years of capacity
VAR29 = Allis-Chalmers annual change in 4-quarter-average share of capacity
VAR30 = Allis-Chalmers change in share of orders, fraction
VAR31 = Westinghouse change in share of orders, fraction
VAR32 = Westinghouse, share of orders, fraction
VAR33 = General Electric kilowatts orders
VAR34 = Westinghouse kilowatts orders
VAR35 = Allis-Chalmers kilowatts orders

VAR36 = total industry utilization ratio: $\dfrac{\text{shipments quarterly}}{\text{capacity annual}}$

VAR38 = General Electric capacity in kilowatts per year, rate
VAR39 = Westinghouse capacity in kilowatts per year, rate
VAR40 = Allis-Chalmers capacity in kilowatts per year, rate
VAR41 = total industry capacity in kilowatts per year, rate
VAR42 = General Electric share of capacity, fraction
VAR43 = Westinghouse share of capacity, fraction
VAR44 = Allis-Chalmers share of capacity, fraction
VAR45 = General Electric shipments, kilowatts per quarter
VAR46 = 3-quarter-average of historical orders, kilowatts, centered on 10 periods ago
VAR47 = Westinghouse shipments, kilowatts per quarter
VAR48 = Westinghouse 3-quarter-average of historical orders, kilowatts

TABLE A18.1. (*Continued*)

VAR49 = Allis-Chalmers shipments, kilowatts per quarter

VAR50 = Allis-Chalmers factory utilization rate, ratio: $\dfrac{\text{quarterly shipments}}{\text{annual capacity}}$

VAR51 = total industry shipments, kilowatts per quarter

VAR52 = General Electric kilowatts backlog

VAR54 = Westinghouse kilowatts backlog

VAR56 = Westinghouse backlog, in years of capacity

VAR57 = Allis-Chalmers kilowatts backlog

VAR58 = minimum backlog, in years, among the three competitors, lagged one quarter

VAR60 = additions to generating capability, steam kilowatts per quarter

VAR61 = retirements from generating capability, steam kilowatts per quarter

VAR62 = General Electric sales revenue, dollars per quarter

VAR63 = Allis-Chalmers sales revenue, dollars per quarter

VAR64 = General Electric cumulative shipments, kilowatts to date

VAR65 = Westinghouse shipments, kilowatts to date

VAR66 = Allis-Chalmers shipments, kilowatts to date

VAR67 = General Electric direct cost, dollars per kilowatt

VAR70 = Allis-Chalmers direct cost, dollars per kilowatt

VAR76 = Westinghouse sales revenue, dollars per quarter

VAR78 = Westinghouse overhead or period costs, dollars per quarter

VAR80 = Allis-Chalmers overhead or period costs, dollars per quarter

VAR81 = General Electric profits, dollars per quarter

VAR82 = Westinghouse profits, dollars per quarter

VAR83 = Westinghouse direct costs, dollars per kilowatt

VAR84 = Allis-Chalmers profits, dollars per quarter

VAR85 = General Electric profit ratio; profits to sales, before tax

VAR86 = 4-quarter-average price, index number basis (1961 book = 10,000)

VAR87 = change in 4-quarter-average price, index number basis

VAR88 = General Electric overhead costs, dollar per quarter

VAR89 = Allis-Chalmers 4-quarter-average share of orders, fraction

VAR90 = 4-quarter-average of orders by utilities, kilowatts

VAR91 = General Electric 4-quarter-average share of order, fraction

VAR92 = General Electric 4-quarter-average share of capacity, fraction

VAR93 = 4-quarter-average industry ratio of capacity utilized = $\dfrac{\text{quarterly shipments}}{\text{capacity at annual rate}}$

VAR94 = Allis-Chalmers 4-quarter-average share of capacity

VAR95 = Allis-Chalmers 4-quarter-average ratio utilized = $\dfrac{\text{quarterly shipments}}{\text{capacity annual}}$

VAR96 = General Electric change in average share of orders

VAR97 = General Electric sales revenue, dollars per year

VAR98 = Westinghouse sales revenue, dollars per year

VAR99 = Allis-Chalmers sales revenue, dollars per year

VAR100 = General Electric overhead costs, dollars per year

VAR101 = Westinghouse overhead costs, dollars per year

VAR102 = Allis-Chalmers overhead costs, dollars per year

VAR103 = yearly change in General Electric overhead, dollars

TABLE A18.1. (Continued)

VAR104	=	yearly change in Westinghouse overhead, dollars
VAR105	=	yearly change in Allis-Chalmers overhead, dollars
VAR106	=	General Electric cost, dollars per quarter
VAR107	=	Westinghouse direct costs, dollars per quarter
VAR108	=	Allis-Chalmers direct costs, dollars per quarter
VAR109	=	Lagged-2-year price index (1961 book = 100)

EXOGENOUS

X5	=	time trend (60.0, 60.25, 60.50, etc.)
X6	=	FRB index of industrial production (base 100 = 1957–1959)
X14	=	wholesale price index (base 100 = 1957–1959)
X45	=	index of industry size of unit, kilowatts (1965 = 100)
X50	=	Westinghouse strike, 1955–1956
X51	=	exogenous additions to utility capacity, internal combustion and hydro, in kilowatts per quarter

SUMMARY:
Total number of endogenous variables: 94.
Total number of exogenous variables: 6.

Version I

The first specification of the model (call it Version I) is shown in Table A18.2, in completely simultaneous form. Twenty-three of the 27 behavioral equations in the system involved current endogenous variables on the right-hand side. Under these circumstances, ordinary least squares (OLS) regression procedures will lead to inconsistent estimates of the parameters. Therefore, these 23 equations were re-estimated using two-stage least squares (2SLS). The remaining four behavioral equations in the system were estimated by ordinary least squares.

In summary, Version I consisted of 94 equations (27 behavioral and 67 tautological); 94 endogenous variables (40 lagged and 94 current); and 6 exogenous variables: (1) time trend, (2) Federal Reserve Board production index, (3) wholesale price index, (4) dummy for Westinghouse strike of 1955–1956, (5) average size of turbine generator, (6) exogenous additions to generating capacity (hydro, diesel, etc.); and one "minimum" operator. There were sufficient exogenous variables to use as instruments in 2SLS estimation, and the system of equations was mathematically complete.

TABLE A18.2.
A MODEL OF THE UTILITY-MANUFACTURER SYSTEM.
(VERSION I)

$$V3 = A1 \cdot e^{B1 \cdot X5} \, X6^{B2}$$
$$V4 = V3 + V5$$
$$V5 = A2 + B3 \cdot V6$$
$$V6 = V3 - V3(t - 20)$$
$$V7 = V4(t - 12) - V3$$
$$V8 = V7/V3$$

TABLE A18.2. (Continued)

$$V9 = V10 + V11$$
$$V11 = A3 + B4 \cdot V12$$
$$V13 = V9(t - 12) - V10$$
$$V14 = V13/V10$$
$$V15 = V10 - V3$$
$$V16 = 100.0(V15/V10)$$
$$V16 = A4 + B5 \cdot X5 + B6 \cdot V8 + B7 \cdot V14$$
$$V17 = V4(t - 4) + V18$$
$$V18 = A5 + B8 \cdot V7$$
$$V90 = A6 + B9 \cdot V4 + B10 \cdot V20 + B11 \cdot V18$$
$$V22 = V21 - V21(t - 1)$$
$$V96 = A7 + B12 \cdot V23 + B13 \cdot V24 + B14 \cdot V25$$
$$V89 = A8 + B15 \cdot V23 + B16 \cdot V86 + B17 \cdot V28 + B18 \cdot V29$$
$$V30 = V26 - V26(t - 1)$$
$$V31 = -(V22 + V30)$$
$$V32 = V32(t - 1) + V31$$
$$V33 = V19 \cdot V21$$
$$V34 = V19 \cdot V32$$
$$V35 = V19 \cdot V26$$
$$V27 = A9 + B19 \cdot X14 + B20 \cdot V93 + B21 \cdot V58$$
$$V38 = A10 + B22 \cdot V39(t - 4) + B23 \cdot V52(t - 4)$$
$$V39 = A11 + B24 \cdot V38(t - 4) + B25 \cdot V54(t - 4) + 1{,}950{,}000 \cdot X50$$
$$V40 = A12 + B26 \cdot V95(t - 4) + B27 \cdot X5 + B28 \cdot V57(t - 4)$$
$$V41 = V38 + V39 + V40$$
$$V42 = V38/V41$$
$$V43 = V39/V41$$
$$V44 = V40/V41$$
$$V25 = V92 - V92(t - 4)$$
$$V29 = V94 - V94(t - 4)$$
$$V45 = A13 + B29 \cdot V46 + B30 \cdot V47$$
$$V46 = (V33(t - 9) + V33(t - 10) + V33(t - 11))/3.0$$
$$V47 = AA1 + BB1 \cdot V48$$
$$V48 = (V34(t - 10) + V34(t - 11) + V34(t - 12))/3.0$$
$$V49 = AA2 + BB2 \cdot V35(t - 10)$$
$$V50 = V49/V40$$
$$V51 = V45 + V47 + V49$$
$$V36 = V51/V41$$
$$V52 = V52(t - 1) + V33 - V45$$
$$V24 = V52/V38$$
$$V54 = V54(t - 1) + V34 + V47$$
$$V56 = V54/V39$$
$$V57 = V57(t - 1) + V35 + V49$$
$$V28 = V57/V40$$
$$V12 = V52 + V54 + V57$$
$$V20 = V12/V41$$
$$V60 = AA3 + BB3 \cdot V51(t - 2)$$
$$V61 = A14 + B31 \cdot V16 + B32 \cdot V60$$
$$V10 = V10(t - 1) + V60 \cdot V61 + 1000.0 \cdot X51$$
$$V62 = A15 + B33 \cdot V45 \cdot V27$$

TABLE A18.2. (Continued)

$$V76 = A16 + B34 \cdot V47 \cdot V27(t - 8)$$
$$V63 = A17 + B35 \cdot V49 \cdot V27(t - 4)$$
$$V64 = V64(t - 1) + V45$$
$$V65 = V65(t - 1) + V47$$
$$V66 = V66(t - 1) + V49$$
$$V67 = A18 \cdot V64 \, e^{B36} \cdot X42 \, e^{B37} \cdot V109 \, e^{B38}$$
$$V83 = A18 \cdot V65 \, e^{B36} \cdot X43 \, e^{B37} \cdot V109 \, e^{B38}$$
$$V70 = A18 \cdot V66 \, e^{B36} \cdot X44 \, e^{B37} \cdot V109 \, e^{B38}$$
$$V103 = A19 + B39 \cdot V100(t - 4) + B40 \cdot V97$$
$$V104 = A20 + B41 \cdot V101(t - 4) + B42 \cdot V98$$
$$V105 = A21 + B43 \cdot V102(t - 4) + B44 \cdot V99$$
$$V81 = V62 - V88 - V106$$
$$V82 = V76 - V78 - V107$$
$$V84 = V63 - V80 - V108$$
$$V85 = (V81 + V81(t - 1) + V81(t - 2) + V81(t - 3))/V97$$
$$V86 = (V27 + V27(t - 1) + V27(t - 2) + V27(t - 3))/4.0$$
$$V23 = A22 + B45 \cdot V85 + B46 \cdot V91(t - 4) + B47 \cdot V87$$
$$V87 = V86 - V86(t - 4)$$
$$V26 = 4.0 \, V89 - V26 - V26(t - 1) - V26(t - 2) - V26(t - 3)$$
$$V19 = 4.0 \, V90 - V19 - V19(t - 1) - V19(t - 2) - V19(t - 3)$$
$$V21 = 4.0 \, V91 - V21 - V21(t - 1) - V21(t - 2) - V21(t - 3)$$
$$V92 = (V42 + V42(t - 1) + V42(t - 2) + V42(t - 3))/4.0$$
$$V94 = (V44 + V44(t - 1) + V44(t - 2) + V44(t - 3))/4.0$$
$$V93 = (V36 + V36(t - 1) + V36(t - 2) + V36(t - 3))/4.0$$
$$V95 = (V50 + V50(t - 1) + V50(t - 2) + V50(t - 3))/4.0$$
$$V91 = V96 + V91(t - 1)$$
$$V97 = V62 + V62(t - 1) + V62(t - 2) + V62(t - 3)$$
$$V98 = V76 + V76(t - 1) + V76(t - 2) + V76(t - 3)$$
$$V99 = V63 + V63(t - 1) + V63(t - 2) + V63(t - 3)$$
$$V88 = V100 - V88(t - 1) - V88(t - 2) - V88(t - 3)$$
$$V78 = V101 - V78(t - 1) - V78(t - 2) - V78(t - 3)$$
$$V80 = V102 - V80(t - 1) - V80(t - 2) - V80(t - 3)$$
$$V100 = V103 + V100(t - 4)$$
$$V101 = V104 + V101(t - 4)$$
$$V102 = V105 + V102(t - 4)$$
$$V106 = V67 \cdot V45 \cdot X14/100.0$$
$$V107 = V83 \cdot V47 \cdot X14/100.0$$
$$V108 = V70 \cdot V49 \cdot X14/100.0$$
$$V109 = V27(t - 8)/100$$
$$V58 = \text{minimum of} \left\{ \begin{array}{l} V24(t - 1) \\ V28(t - 1) \\ V56(t - 1) \end{array} \right\}$$

NOTE: See table A18.1 for a definition of all of the variables. The Vs refer to endogenous variables. The Xs refer to exogenous variables. The As and Bs are parameters in the behavioral equations.

Driving the Model: Utility Load Growth

Utility peak loads "drive" our model of the total industry. For this purpose we employed a simple-two-variable model of kilowatts peak load for the utility industry, incorporating an underlying exponential growth trend, modulated by fluctuations in economic activity. The annual rate of increase in peak electric power loads is assumed to be independent of manufacturer strategies in the short time span encompassed by this model. This ignores the fact that, in the long run, there *is* a feedback due to the demand for electric power being price- and technology-sensitive.

Simulations with Version I

Version I of the model was programmed, solved, and used to extrapolate quarterly solutions for each of the variables, through the relatively brief period 1963–1965. The year 1962 was the last year for which values for the complete set of endogenous variables were available.

Clearly, the individual elements of the model had been based upon a mixed bag of data. Some of the behavioral equations were based upon 1951–1969 data; others upon a shorter time period. The earliest date at which any actual historical data terminated was the fourth quarter of 1962. Thus, for simultaneous equations forecasting purposes, to check the reasonableness of the model, 1963–1965 was only *partly* virgin territory. Nevertheless, as a validation check, values for the six exogenous variables were fed into the system for the period 1963–1965, as well as actual values of the lagged endogenous variables prior to the first quarter of 1963. Thereafter, all variables were computed in a strictly endogenous manner, and the model solved for 1963–1965.

Needless to say, given a modest input of exogenous data to an industry system which may have biased estimates on the endogenous variables, and a model which is almost totally "closed," there is a maximum opportunity for errors to accumulate. This is particularly the case in a multi-period simulation, wherein the errors of one period become built into the starting solution of the next period. We eschewed the alternative, more cautious approach of validation via *one period* extrapolations, since such a conservative approach would tell us little about the long-run dynamics of the system when it was used under alternative behavioral rules—the purpose for which the model had been built.

Values of exogenous variables were entered for the period *after* 1962 and the system was used to predict values of endogenous variables for the post-1962 period. Each quarter employed the computer solution of the previous quarter as a starting point.

Due to the presence of the "minimum" operator working upon backlogs in the key price equation, it was necessary to proceed one period at a time, and the minimum backlog was made a lagged endogenous variable, selected by inspection in each period, then fed into the next quarter's solution. This made for tedious computer work.

One test of validity is the ability of the model to predict actual behavior post-1962. In this context it is awkward that the competitive structure of the industry actually changed after 1962. The simulation is based on the premise that all three domestic manufacturers continued to serve the market, despite the fact that Allis-Chalmers temporarily dropped out of the turbine generator market after 1962. The simulation simply ignores this fact.

Three statistics are useful for evaluation of the Version I model: average industry price, the utilities' orders of turbine generators, and utility generating reserves. Actual post-1962 data are available for comparison purposes on these three variables. Both actual and predicted prices showed an upward trend from the low price level which prevailed at the end of 1962. The predicted price was some five percentage points higher than the actual price was in early 1964 (due to the presence in the simulation runs, and the absence in real life of high-cost Allis-Chalmers?).

When it came to predicted orders, Model I did not forecast very well what actually happened. The forecasted volume of orders was significantly lower than the known actual volume of orders for this time period—by about 30 percent. One reason the model was underforecasting orders for 1963–1965 was because of the unprecedented activity of utilities in ordering nuclear generating capacity at that time. Furthermore, the model was underforecasting utility revisions of their peak load forecasts— such upward revisions were truly large in 1963–1965—and this further depressed the predicted volume of orders.

The third evaluating statistic was percentage reserves of utility generating capacity. Version I of the model underpredicted reserves for 1963, and then overpredicted them for 1964 and 1965, with an error on the order of two or three percentage points.

Not only was the short-term forecasting performance of the Version I model only "fair," but we were also troubled by four additional problems:

(1) We wanted to use the model to test alternative, complex, strategic decision rules by management. For these purposes, the simultaneous equations (Version I) model had serious limitations. Without reverting to burdensome and costly constrained solutions on the computer, only the most simple decision rules could be tested. This was a mechanical problem, relating to how a system of equations is solved mathematically, but it was a crippling feature of the simultaneous equation approach.

(2) While we could obtain consistent estimates by using 2SLS procedures, this did not permit attention to another serious problem in our estimates: serial correlation. Here, Hildreth-Lu adjustments were called for, but it did not seem feasible to correct for both serial correlation and inconsistent estimates at the same time.[1]

(3) We were not satisfied with the linkage between orders and shipments for each firm in the model. The Version I model was naive in this respect: kilowatts shipments were merely lagged kilowatt orders. We wanted to use, instead, a more realistic model: that the kilowatts orders obtained in each quarter would be shipped in future quarters according to a Poisson distribution, the parameter of which was the average weighted ratio of backlog to manufacturing capacity (backlogs "pressure") for the relevant time span of manufacture (see Chapter Five). This simultaneous equations Model I was intractable in terms of solving the complex relationships which were involved.

---

[1] C. Hildreth and J. Y. Lu, *Demand Relations with Autocorrelated Disturbances*, Technical Bulletin No 276 (Michigan State University, 1960).

(4) Finally, our validation criteria were inappropriate, since they stressed the ability of the model to track quarter-to-quarter variations in price, orders, and generating reserves over 1963–1965; that is, in the *short*-run. Much of the short-term variation in price, orders, and reserves, over 1963–1965, could be random noise in the data, and very difficult to forecast. Moreover, we had not built this model for use as a short-term quarterly forcasting device. The model might help us understand the long-term consequences of manufacturer strategy. In order to assess what would happen in the industry, under alternative manufacturer strategies, it would be necessary to run the simulation over a much longer time period.

We see here an interesting parallel between our own evaluation problem in the simulation, and that of corporate management. Because the results of a strategic decision could only be perceived after the lapse of five or ten years, it was not sufficient to appraise a management decision on the basis of two- or three-year operating results.

Version II (Fully Recursive)

To deal with these various problems, an alternative model was built and designated "Version II." This was a fully recursive specification of virtually the identical model. The simultaneous equations problem was (nominally) avoided by lagging the current endogenous explanatory variables when necessary, by one quarter. All parameters were then reestimated. The model could now be solved as a simple computer program, and alternative management decision rules could be entered, even if they were complex condition statements, or constraints. Finally, we could now deal with the serial correlation problem in our estimates.

The system was made fully recursive through changing the specification of 10 of the behavioral equations, to incorporate lagged versions of the respective endogenous variables, rather than current endogenous variables. This approach was adopted with some temerity. Fully recursive simultaneous systems are particularly vulnerable to specification error and to serial correlation in the error terms, and both were surely present. Furthermore, as Franklin Fisher has emphasized, ordinary least squares estimates do not become consistent by the mere act of changing a current endogenous variable to a recent past value of the same variable, even if triangularity of the system is thereby achieved.[2]

Other benefits, however, influenced the adoption of the fully recursive format. It seemed better to have usable—if second-best—estimates of the long-range results of a strategy decision, rather than no estimate at all. An unexpected fringe benefit in practice was the fact that the fully recursive model appeared to deliver more reliable forecasts of utility orders, utility reserves, and the average industry price level—at least as measured by their long-term average values.

We commenced our forecast of 1972 operating results from a launching pad in 1956 and accumulated our quarterly errors from that point on.

To help dampen any "explosions," one precaution was added; namely, market shares were constrained to lie within the following limits:

[2] Franklin M. Fisher, "Dynamic Structure and Estimation in Economy-Wide Econometric Models," in J. S. Duesenberry, G. Fromm, L. R. Klein, and E. Kuh (editors), *The Brookings Quarterly Econometric Model of the United States* (Chicago: Rand McNally, 1965), Chapter 15.

	Upper Constraint on Market Shares	Lower Constraint on Market Shares
General Electric	75%	20%
Westinghouse	75%	20%
Allis-Chalmers	20%	0.5%

These constraints were loose, in terms of the actual historical experience of these three firms. The resulting model was well-behaved.

Charts Al8.4, Al8.5 and Al8.6 show actual versus predicted orders, prices, and utility reserves, for the 17-year prediction period, using the fully recursive (Version II) model. The mean values and standard deviations of three evaluating statistics are shown in Table Al8.3. We judge the results quite good.

This Version II model therefore became the basis for the 1956–1972 simulations of results under alternative General Electric strategies, as described in Chapter Fourteen.

TABLE A18.3.
ROOT MEAN SQUARE ERROR OF ACTUAL VERSUS PREDICTED
VALUES FOR ORDERS, PRICES, AND UTILITY RESERVES, 1956–1972
(VERSION II)

	Average Value: 1956–1972		Root Mean Square Error
	Actual	Predicted	
Orders (Millions of Kilowatts Per Quarter)	6.49	7.19	4.76
Price Index (1961 Book = 100)	86.4	97.9	31.0
Utility Generating Reserves (Percent)	22.0	23.1	3.4

Price Conspiracy Revisited

This book throughout has pointed to the dearth of convincing evidence as to any impact of the price-fixing conspiracy in the electrical industry, upon actual order prices for turbine generators. We can now use the Version II model to test for the impact of the meetings upon price—both directly *and indirectly.* We add dummy variables to our price *and* market share relationships to measure any differential effects which may be attributed to conspiracy. The statistical results of adding a dummy variable to the market share equations were as before: the dummy variables were not significant; there is no discernible impact according to these measures.[3]

But whether statistically significant or not in the *individual price* and market share relationships, conspiracy might have a discernible cumulative impact upon the be-

---

[3] In the Allis-Chalmers market share equation, the dummy variable for conspiracy had an estimated coefficient of .039, a standard error of .077, and a t-statistic of 0.51. In the General Electric market share equation (actually, change in market share), the dummy variable for the conspiracy period had an estimated coefficient of .0434, a standard error of .0975, and a t-statistic of 0.45. We conclude that there is no statistical evidence of "factory load-sharing" through conspiracy.

CHART A18.4.   Turbine Generator Orders, 1956–1972.

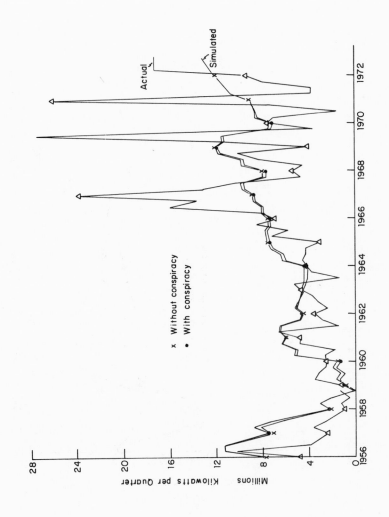

CHART A18.5.   Order Price Index: 1956–1972.

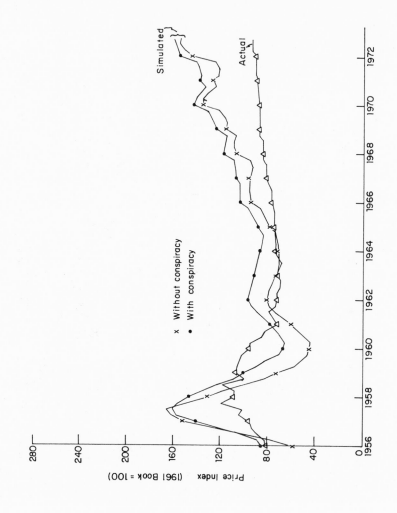

CHART A18.6.   Utility Generating Reserves, 1956–1972.

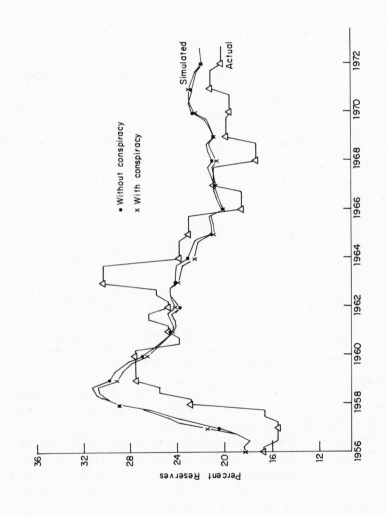

havior of the total integrated model, particularly through the interaction of price and market share. The revised equations for price and market share, incorporating the estimated (but nonsignificant) conspiracy effects, were inserted into the Version II model, and the full 1956–1972 simulations were run again, for purposes of comparison with the benchmark. The results of this "conspiracy simulation" for prices, orders, and utility reserves, are shown in Charts A18.4, A18.5 and A18.6, and Table A18.4.

TABLE A18.4.

COMPARISON OF ACTUAL VERSUS SIMULATED RESULTS: ORDERS,
PRICES, AND UTILITY GENERATING RESERVES, 1956–1972
(VERSION II)

	Physical Orders (Millions of Kw/Qtr.)		Order Price Index (1961 Book = 100)		Utility Generating Reserves (Percent)	
	Mean	Standard Deviation	Mean	Standard Deviation	Mean	Standard Deviation
Actual 1956–1972	6.487	5.819	86.4	12.08	21.99	4.01
Simulation Without Conspiracy[a]	7.185	3.229	97.9	31.76	23.10	2.94
Simulation With Conspiracy[b]	7.113	3.232	110.9	26.43	23.02	3.01

[a] Data for 1948–1963 were used for estimating purposes, overlapping part of the simulation period.

[b] Conspiratorial impact is measured by dummy variables which are operative during the 1955–1959 period of maximum conspiracy. Dummy variables were employed in the estimation of equations for the order price index and the market share of each of the competitors.

The "conspiracy" rate of orders is almost identical with the "nonconspiracy" rate of orders. Predicted utility reserves under the "conspiracy" model, are virtually identical to those under the "nonconspiracy" model.

The simulation predicted the price climb of the middle 1950s, and the subsequent price collapse commencing in 1958, but the amplitude of the predicted price movement is exaggerated. Commencing in the middle 1960s, the model predicts industry selling prices to commence a steady year-by-year climb, but in fact industry order prices did not increase so rapidly. Furthermore, we can now discern significant differences between the prices under "conspiracy," by comparison with "nonconspiracy." Conspiracy prices tend to be higher—by about 8 or 9 percent. We can therefore grant this one final estimate to the conspiracy impact estimators.

What conclusions may we draw from these results? First, there is here some evidence of interacting effects between price levels and market-sharing agreements, as a result of conspiracy. Second, the price collapse of 1958–1959 was *not* due to the removal of a conspiratorial prop—it occurs in our simulation even without conspiracy.

This tends to weaken the fanciful damage theories paraded before the courts during the electrical litigation. Finally, it is clear that the behavior of the actors in the turbine generator industry has changed, so that behavioral rules developed from the 1950s apply no longer in the 1970s. The most obvious ground rule which has changed is the lack of one competitor holding approximately 10 percent share: Allis-Chalmers.

Our own theory is that Allis-Chalmers, with its high costs, tended to place a floor under the industry price level during the 1950s. When this floor was removed, industry prices sagged to a new, lower long-term level, particularly when combined with new "pressure pricing" tactics post-1963. As a result, prices in 1972 were actually much lower than they would have been had a more "competitive" industry structure been maintained.

Index

Acceleration, order, defined, 50–51
Adelman, M. A., 150
AEP (American Electric Power), 196, 223
Allis-Chalmers, 3, 4, 8, 133, 214, 244, 287; percentage of market share of, 1, 295; and average manufacturing delay, 87, 89–90; backlogs of, 92, 93, 185–186; order prices of, 106, 108, 110, 112, 114–115; escalation practices of, 125–128; and product mix factor, 128–129; long-term trends in value at, 133, 137; direct costs of, 139, 147, 148–149, 150; overhead costs of, 154, 155–156, 160–161; manufacturing capacity expansion at, 166, 181–182, 184, 188; and leadership-followership roles, 204–206; price-size relationships at, 211; funding of technological change by, 217–219; alternative technological strategies used by, 223; and market share, 226–228, 232, 233, 234, 235; and judgmental simulations, 249, 252–254, 257, 264–277 passim; and optimizing simulations, 259, 261, 279, 281; best strategy for, 282; variations in profit results for, 282–285
American Gas & Electric, 193
American Power Conference, 178
Arrow, Kenneth J., 13
Association of Edison Illuminating Companies (AEIC), 41
Averch-Johnson theory of public utility behavior, 198

Backlog(s), 113–114, 185–186; unfilled order, 81–83; and throughput, manufacturers', 92–93; data, and order prices, 108; meetings to balance, 111–112; relative to capacity, 186; and market share, 233
Backman, Jules, 60
Baumol, William J., 5, 10, 36, 246, 260, 286, 288; on maximizing sales, 255, 276–277
Bertrand, Joseph, 246, 254–255, 275–276, 286, 288
Book prices, 119–120; impact of escalation terms on, 122
Boston Consulting Group, 14
Brown Boveri, 165
Buehler, C. F., 140
Buffering, 234–235, 237, 241
"Building block program," 223–224

Capability, generating, 103–104; misestimating future, 95–96; utility forecasts of, 97–99; changes in, 101–103
Capacity, rate of utilization of factory, 108; and direct costs, 144, 146, 149–150, 152–153
Carlson, John R., 197
Chamberlin, Edward Hastings, 36
Clayton Act, 292
Coddington, Alan, 36
Commonwealth Edison, 200
Concentration, 24–25; strategies which increase, 288; public policy thinking on, 292–295
Conflict and cooperation, in oligopoly, 281–282
Conjectural interdependence, 36–39
Connecticut Light and Power, 77, 78
Consolidated Edison, 77, 78, 96, 214, 219
Conspiracy, impact on price levels of, 111, 124; alternative test of, 112–113

Cordiner, Ralph J., 240
Cost structures, utility, 198–199; and long-term trend in fuel-consumption efficiency, 199–200; and long-term trend in investment costs, 200; and impact of plant scale, 201–203
Costs, learning, and technology, in oligopoly, 12–15. *See also* Direct cost(s); Overhead costs
Cournot, Augustin, 5, 246, 253–254, 275–276, 286, 288
Cox, George, 83, 84, 88
Cyert, Richard M., 7, 291

Decision rules, 247–248, 249, 258
Deconcentration, 286–287; strategies tending toward, 288, 290; public policy thinking on, 292–295
DELTA-PRICE, 259
Demand, 27–28
Differential prices, 105
Dillard, J. K., 99–100
Direct cost(s), 22, 139, 152–153, 161–162; management testimony on variation in, 139–144; model of, 144–148; statistical results of model of, 148–149; and factory utilization, 149–150; and technology transfer, 150–151; elasticities, 151–152; impact of demand euphoria, 152. *See also* Overhead costs
Du Pont, 14, 15

Ebasco Services, Inc., 52
Edison, Thomas, 20, 168
Edison Electric Institute (EEI), 41, 67, 98–99, 165–166, 181, 220; *Power Survey* of, 95, 97, 99, 165; on utility funding of research and development, 222
Eikner, L. M., 166–168
Equilibrium growth path, reaching, 29–34
Escalation: types of, 117–118; history of, 118–119; limits on, 119–123; impact of, on prices, 123–124; practice among manufacturers, variations in, 124–128

Federal Power Commission, 50, 67, 97,

202, 222; *National Power Survey* of, 71; underforecasting long-term demand by, 71–72
Federal Reserve Board index of industrial production, 263
Federal Trade Commission, Concentrated Industries Project of, 293–294, 295
Fellner, William, 5, 36–37, 246; on maximizing sales, 260, 278; on maximizing total industry profits and present value, 261, 280
Final prices, 105, 122–123
Firm price contracts, 117–118, 119
Fisher, Franklin, 256, 277, 286, 288
Fisher, Irving, 5, 260, 261, 279
Ford, Bacon & Davis (consulting engineers), 149
Forrester, Jay W., 63–64
Funding of technological change, 215–216, 296–297; by Westinghouse, 216–217; by Allis-Chalmers, 217–219; by General Electric, 219–222; role of utilities in, 222

Galbraith, John Kenneth, 7, 190
Game plans, alternative, 247–249
General Electric, 3, 4, 8, 223, 287, 291, 296; percentage of market share of, 1; profitability of, 5; relationship between managers and chief executive at, 10; trend extrapolation models of, 55; and manufacturing lead time, 83–84; and average manufacturing delay, 87, 88–89; backlogs of, 92–93, 185–186; order prices of, 106, 108, 109, 110, 112, 114; escalation practices of, 119, 120, 121, 125–127; bidding on TVA Paradise power station by, 119, 121–122; and product mix factor, 128–129; long-term trends in value at, 132, 137–138; direct costs of, 139–142, 147, 148–149, 150; overhead costs of, 154–155, 156, 160, 161–162; manufacturing capacity expansion at, 166, 168–173, 178–184, 188, 189; pressure unit built by, 193; size of turbine generator units at, 194–

195, 196–197; and leadership-followership roles, 204–206; price-size relationships at, 210–211; funding of technological change by, 219–222; and market share, 226–268, 231, 232–233, 235; integration of strategy with corporate goals at, 235–240; statistical analysis of strategy at, 240–245; and judgmental simulations, 249–258, 264–277 *passim*; and optimizing simulations, 259, 261, 278–281; best strategy for, 282; variations in profit results for, 282–285

General Electric Lynn, 133, 168, 170–171, 173

General Electric Schenectady, 133, 148, 168, 170–173

General Motors, 297

Ginn, William S., 166, 238, 239–240

Goals, 247–248; setting of, and feedback of results, 235–236; corporate, 236; profit, 236–237; market share, 237; long-term market share, 241

Growth: uncertainty of, in long run, 68–72; short-run fluctuations in, 72; maximizing, 256–258, 276, 278

Guyol, N. B., 59

Harlan, Neil E., 14

Hart, Philip, 294–295

Harvest market share strategy, 252–253, 273–275, 282, 288

Hedrick, Charles L., 7

Henderson, Bruce D., 14–15

Herfindahl index (HERF), 259, 280, 281

Hill, Herman, 141, 171, 179

Historical behavior, 249, 264–271, 288

Hydroelectric power, 103

IBM, 297

Indices escalation, 117, 119, 120–121

Industrial Reorganization Act, 295

Inflation, general factor price, and direct costs, 144, 145, 152

Installation delay, 81, 90–91

Johnson, Lyndon, 292

Johnston, J., 35

Joshua Hendy Iron Works, 173–174

Kefauver, Estes, 295

Kilbourne, Charles, 42–44, 62–63, 73–74, 91

Kilovar, defined, 133 and n

Kisselgoff, Arram, 59

Koyck, L. M., 157

Kraftwerk Union (Germany), 296

Kuyper, William, 139–140

Leadership-followership roles in technology, 204–206, 211–213, 223–225

Learning, and technology, and costs, in oligopoly, 12–15

Lindseth, Elmer L., 99–100

Lintner, John, 157, 255

Loads, forecasting of peak, 68, 95; and uncertainty of growth in long run, 68–72; and short-run fluctuations in growth, 72; short-term, by utilities, 72–74; case histories of, 74–78; statistical evidence of, by utilities, 78–79; statistical results of updating, by utilities, 79

MacAvoy, Paul W., 60, 61, 62

Machlup, Fritz, 8

Mack, Donald R., 65–66

McLane, Daniel, 84

Management organization and objectives, in oligopoly, 9–12

Mann, Michael, 293–294, 295

Manufacturing capacity strategy, 163–164; historical record of, 164–166; of individual competitors, 166–168; history of General Electric's, 168–173, 178–180, 182–184; history of Westinghouse's, 173–178, 178–180, 182–184; explanation of, 180–184; and backlogs, 185–186; and shipments smoothing, 187; utilization of, 187–188; and costs and benefits, 188–189; and market share, 234

Manufacturing delay, 81; and unfilled order backlogs, 81–83; and manufacturing lead time, 83–85; average, 85–88; and statistical estimation of factory throughput (individual competitors), 88–90; and simulation model, 90. *See also* Installation delay

March, J. G., 291

Market share strategy, 226, 237; of orders, 226–228; and consumer preference, 228–230; and manufacturer preference, 231; relative prices and, 231–233; backlogs and, 233; manufacturing capacity and, 234; buffering of, 234–235, 241; "norms" in, 237; and "managed" operating results, 237–239; and "balance" in reported operating results, 239–240; profit rate v., 240–241; analysis of General Electric's profit rate–market share relationship, 240–245; goals, long-term, 241; hold long-term, and buffer, 249–252, 271–272, 288; hold long-term, 252, 272–273, 288; harvest, 252–253, 273–275, 282, 288; and profit results, cause of variations in, 282–286; strategies which maintain status quo in, 288

Marris, Robin, 256–257, 278, 288

Marshall, Alfred, 13, 34

Marx, Karl, 34

Microeconomic theory, 292

Modigliani, Franco, 59

Morehouse, Edward W., 59

Morgenstern, Oskar, 7–8, 36, 246–247

MVA, defined, 134 and n

National Science Foundation, 220

Neal, Philip C., report of, 292–293, 295

Neumann, John von, 246–247

New England Electric System, 47–48

Nordhaus, William D., 15

North American Rockwell, 8

Northern States Power, 74–75, 78

Obsolescent generating capacity, retirement of, 101–103

Oligopoly theory, 7–8; setting for model of, 8–19; long-run model of (duopoly assumed), 19–36; short-run model of (conjectural independence), 36–39

Operating results: "managed," 237–239; "balance" in reported, 239–240; actual, 248

OPS, 109, 110

Order prices, 105, 117, 120, 149; "value" philosophy of, 105–107; data on, 107–109; results of model of turbine generator, 109–113; strategic implications for, 113–116; feedback of, upon costs, 144, 146–147

Order(s), for turbine generators: statistical record of, 40–42; factors influencing demand for (manufacturer view), 42–46; factors influencing demand for (utility view), 47–54; acceleration, 50–51; demand for, and planning models employed by industry, 54–56; simple model of, 56–58; short-term, statistical results of, 58–59; studies of long-run demand for, 59–63; studies of short-run and interactive demand for, 63–66; inflow data, 107–108

Outages, reserves for scheduled and unscheduled, 95

OVEC (Ohio Valley Electric Corporation), 150, 217

Overhead costs, 22, 139, 153, 161–162; level of, 153–156; and relationship to long-run theory, 156; short-run fluctuations in, 156–161. *See also* Direct cost(s)

Parkinson, C. Northcote, 11, 143

Patinkin, Don, 34

Performance standards, need for, 297–298

Peters, John, 84

PETS (price in effect at time of shipment), 117, 118–122

Power capacitors, long-term trends in value of, 131, 133–135

Power transformers, long-term trends in value of, 131, 134–135

Present value: maximizing (GE), 260–

261, 279–280, 288; maximizing total industry, 261–262, 280–281, 288

Price change, feasible annual, 25–27

Price controls, 110–111

Price-size relationships, 206–207; in turbine generators, 208; and "tipping the price curve," 208–211; and motivations for leadership in curve tipping, 211; and motivations of follower firms, 212–213

Pricing response, to inflation, sensitivity of, 113

Product-line pricing strategy, 136–137, 137–138, 207

Product mix, 151, 168; differences in, 128–129; adjusting long-term values for, 135–137

Production experience of firms, cumulative, and direct costs, 144–145, 148–149, 152

Profit(s): and discretionary overhead, 22–25; maximizing (output), 253–254, 275–276; maximizing (price), 254–255, 275–276; maximizing, subject to share constraint, 256, 276, 277; maximizing total industry, 261, 280–281; and market share results, cause of variations in, 282–286; versus risk, 286

Public Service Gas & Electric Company, 55–56

Pugh, Alexander L., III, 63, 64–65, 66

Relative prices, 105, 247; and market share, 231–233

Reps, David, 55

Research and development expenditures, see Funding of technological change

Reserves, utility, 103–104; necessity of generating, 94–96; targeted, and forecasting error, 96–97; and forecasts of generating capability, 97–99; impact upon margins of, 99–101

Risk: technological, 213–215; profit versus, 286

Roos, C. F., 59

Sales: maximizing, 255–256, 276–277;

maximizing (GE), 260, 278–279, 282, 288

Scale economies, 295–296

Schabtach, Carl, 197

Scherer, F. M., 8

Schumpeter, Joseph A., 2, 5–6, 190, 225; empirical test of hypothesis of, 17–19

Shepherd, William G., 8

Sherman Antitrust Act, 35, 297

Shipments smoothing, 187

Shubik, Martin, 7, 36

Simulations: judgmental, 249–258, 263–278; optimizing, 258–262, 278–281

Smithies, A., 35

Solow, Robert M., 13–14

Southern California Edison, 77–78

Southern Company, The, 48

Sporn, Philip, 60, 71, 223

Stability, of the system, 34–36

"Standardization" strategy, 223–224

Stigler, George, 293

Stone & Webster, 75

Strategy, integration of, with corporate goals, 235–240. See also Manufacturing capacity strategy; Market share strategy; Technological strategy

Suits, C. Guy, 60

Swidler, Joseph, 222

Sylos-Labini, Paolo, 8, 12–13, 36

Task Force on Antitrust Policy, 292

Technological strategy, 190–191; and technological change in turbine generators, 191–198; and utility cost structures, 198–203; leadership-followership roles in, 204–206; and price-size relationship, 206–213; and technological risks, 213–215; and funding of technological change, 215–222, 296–297; for follower firms, 223–225

Technology: costs, learning, and, in oligopoly, 12–15; production of, 15–17; production function, 28–29; product versus manufacturing, 135–136, 150; product, impact on direct costs of, 144, 145–146, 148, 152; transfer among competitors, and direct costs, 144, 146, 150–151, 152–153

Tennessee Valley Authority (TVA), 119, 121–122, 196

Thomson-Houston works, 168

Throughput: statistical estimation of factory, 88–90; manufacturers' backlog and, 92–93

"Tipping the price curve" strategy, 138, 208–211; motivations for leadership in, 211

Turbine generators: long-term trends in value of, 131–133, 134–135; and steam conditions (temperature and pressure), 191–194; and heat rates, 194; and unit size (kilowatts), 194–197; path of technological change in, 197–198

Turvey, Ralph, 60

U.S. Bureau of Labor Statistics, Wholesale Price Index of, 107, 117

Utilities, funding of research and development by, 222

Value, long-term trends in, 130–135; adjustment of, for product mix, 135–137; differences in, among firms, 137–138. *See also* Present value

Vennard, Edwin, 59

Vernon, John M., 8, 60, 62–63

Von Szelikski, Victor S., 59

Welfare: effects, 262–263; implications, 286–290

Westinghouse, 4, 8, 245, 287, 296; percentage of market share of, 1; and fac- tors influencing demand for turbine generators, 46; planning models employed by, 55–56; and average manufacturing delay, 87, 89; backlogs of, 92, 93, 185–186; order prices of, 106, 108, 110, 112, 114; escalation practices of, 121, 124–127; and product mix factor, 128–129; long-term trends in value at, 137; direct costs of, 139, 147, 148–149, 150; overhead costs of, 154–155, 156, 158–160, 161, 162; manufacturing capacity expansion at, 166–168, 173–182, 188, 189; pressure unit built by, 193; size of turbine generator units at, 195–196; and leadership-followership roles, 204–206; price-size relationships at, 210–211; funding of technological change by, 216–217; alternative technological strategies used by, 223–224; and market share, 226–228, 232, 235; and judgmental simulations, 249, 252–254, 257, 264–277 *passim*; and optimizing simulations, 259, 261, 279–281; variations in profit results for, 282–285

Westinghouse Philadelphia, 133, 148, 173, 176, 178

Westinghouse Pittsburgh, 173

Westinghouse Sunnyvale (California), 173–174, 175, 178

White Sale (1955), 52, 59, 106, 119, 120, 245

Williamson, Oliver E., 10, 256, 257, 278

Wilson, Charles ("Electric Charlie"), 119, 169

Wright, T. P., 14

Yates, John P., 91